George Brown Millett

The First Book of the Parish Registers of Madron, in the County of Cornwall

George Brown Millett

The First Book of the Parish Registers of Madron, in the County of Cornwall

ISBN/EAN: 9783337019679

Printed in Europe, USA, Canada, Australia, Japan

Cover: Foto ©Lupo / pixelio.de

More available books at **www.hansebooks.com**

THE FIRST BOOK

OF THE

Parish Registers of Madron,

IN THE

County of Cornwall:

EDITED,

WITH AN APPENDIX AND NOTES,

BY

GEORGE BOWN MILLETT,

MEMBER OF THE ROYAL COLLEGE OF SURGEONS,
HONORARY SECRETARY OF THE ROYAL GEOLOGICAL SOCIETY OF CORNWALL,
ETC.

PENZANCE:
BEARE AND SON, 21, MARKET PLACE.
1877.

1333888

TO

THE PEOPLE OF CORNWALL,

"ONE AND ALL,"

AND ESPECIALLY TO THOSE WHO BY BIRTH OR DESCENT ARE
CONNECTED WITH THE

PARISH OF MADRON,

THESE PAGES ARE AFFECTIONATELY DEDICATED BY

THE EDITOR.

Preface.

THE first book of the Parish Registers of Madron is a small folio volume of two hundred and eighteen pages; of these just two hundred are well filled with entries, ten are more or less written upon, and eight are blank. The leaves are of parchment, many of them being in a very dilapidated condition. A few of the entries are altogether illegible, others have been in part or entirely torn away, and some even ruthlessly cut off by the trimming knife of the bookbinder.

The early part of the Register of Baptisms is unfortunately lost—that is to say from the year 1577, at which date the Registers of Marriages and Burials commence, to the year 1592—and at various places throughout the book a leaf or more is wanting. The earliest entry is that of the burial of John, son of Richard Fynnie, dated 20th May, 1577. From this time to the year 1607 the entries that remain are neatly and clearly written in the same hand, and are evidently transcribed from older manuscript, according to Canon 70, of 1603, though damp has made sad havoc with the first four pages. The fact that they are transcribed must be borne in mind, and will suggest the possibility of clerical errors, as well as account for certain minor inconsistencies. Judging from the manuscript and from the varying colour of the ink, it appears to have been the custom not to make the entries in the book one by one as they occurred, but to write in a large batch of a year or more at a time; and it is noticeable that when a new handwriting appears it is usually at the commencement of the year, old style. The date at which a certain handwriting ends, and the known date of the death of an incumbent, do not coincide. It is plain then that in those days the incumbent did not himself write the entries in the book in which they are now preserved, but he probably kept a rough register of Baptisms, Marriages, and Burials, which was periodically copied into the volume destined for its reception.

The following pages contain virtually a complete copy of the record that has been handed down to us,—the oft-recurring "was baptized," "was married," with similar repetitions, being the only words omitted, and these are here replaced by the heading lines. Wherever an entry or a page is missing, its absence is indicated by a line of dots or asterisks. All names of persons and places have been scrupulously copied letter by letter from the original, and the eccentricities and variations in spelling (which it seemed to me very desirable to preserve) will form not the least interesting feature in the book. Erasures, interlineations, or peculiarities, are for the most part noticed at the foot of each page on which they occur, but additional scraps of information will in some cases be found under the date of the entries, in the notes which follow the Appendix.

A person accustomed only to nineteenth century writing would probably not find it an easy matter to decipher the antiquated caligraphy of a past age, but it is the partial obliteration which has taken place that makes the interpretation so difficult in the present case. Those only who have been engaged upon a similar undertaking can form any estimate of the time and trouble involved in such a task. In reading the black-letter portion of the manuscript, there is the common difficulty in distinguishing *n*'s from *u*'s, between which there is absolutely no difference in appearance. Two *m*'s are equally perplexing, for when

PREFACE.

these letters occur together it is impossible to determine, except by the surroundings, whether they are *m*'s, *n*'s, or *u*'s. Since three strokes stand for *m*, and two for *n* or *u*, so six strokes might represent two *m*'s or *nnu*, as well as the interchanges that can be produced with these three letters; but each of these combinations would be written thus *unu*, and as *u* also frequently stands for *v* the complication may be carried further. With regard therefore to such names as Saundry, Launder, Frauncis, etc., it is quite a matter for consideration whether they should be read Sanndry, Launder, and Franncis, or as above; but having spelt these and like names as appears to me to be most probably correct, I here call attention to the subject so that others may form their own opinion. No great stress however need be laid on this difficulty as a source of error in the present instance, for after the black letter (which includes the transcribed portion) ceases, with the year 1607, the names mentioned will be found clearly written in both ways.

Among male Christian names there are few that are very strange or unusual, though there are many that to modern ears sound quaint and old-fashioned. Perhaps the most curious are Emmett (p. 7 :), Halenight (which has its antithesis Loveday among the names of women, p. 12 :), Madern (in every possible variety of spelling) and Morva (p. 44 :) from the parishes so named, Rowan (p. 3.), and Udyo (p. 45:). With regard to Christian names of women, free scope has been given to the imagination, and, besides being quite as quaint as those of the opposite sex, they are far more varied and fanciful. We find :— Addama (p. 24.), Anquito (p. 22:), Armanell (p. 28.), Duens (p. 10.), Earth (p. 16.), Ebbott (p. 8:), Eppow (p. 54:), Fortune (p. 44:), Gratiana (p. 22:), Jaquelinah (p. 24:), Jaquite (p. 22:), Jollyan (p. 33.), Jonefred (p. 37.) and Jenyfret (p. 35:), Lovedyo (p. 27.) and Lowdy (p. 33.), Kay (p. 58:) and Key (p. 51:), Mellioner (p. 43.), Mildren (p. 19.), Milson (p. 32.), Norowe (p. 43.), Olsett (p. 29.), Pascus (p. 8.) and Pasques (p. 55.), Porthesia (p. 24 :), Redigon (p. 8.), Richo (p. 5:), Syve (p. 48.), Tamer (p. 19.), Tammeris (p. 23 :), Temperance (p. 31.), Tiberia (p. 7 :), Wany (p. 5 :), and many others. Sometimes too the names of men are used for those of women; thus—Nicholl (p. 13 :) and Pascow (p. 31.) are frequently so used, though probably the latter was intended for Pascha, the feminine of Pascoe (which by the way is vulgarly pronounced Paska in this neighbourhood), signifying Easter child; and throughout, Philip is as frequently written for a woman's name as for a man's,—there is absolutely no means of distinguishing between the two except by the context; but where it is evident that the feminine name is intended, Philippa has been used in the Index. Certain names, now understood to be entirely distinct from each other, were formerly—as we find by these Registers—often written indiscriminately the one for the other. Such are Nicholas and Nicholls, Reginald and Reynold, Gerard and Garret, Pearce and Peres, Maurice and Morish, &c., with several different ways of spelling the same names.

Surnames too it appears were used in a vague and uncertain manner, and were sometimes assumed or given with an utter disregard to all hereditary nomenclature, which at the present day would be most inconvenient and unjustifiable. "The son of Nicholas, the joyner" (p. 43 :), "one Richard, a poore man" (p. 45 :), "Margarett, an Irishe woman" (p. 42 :), and numerous others, have little for which to thank the scribe who enrolled their names in the Parish Record. The unsettled state of surnames is further proved and exemplified by the following rather long list of aliases which occur in this book :—

Amcare *alias* James 5.
Ames *alias* Ash 51.
Angovo *alias* Thomas 7 :
Aukow *alias* Harries 57 :
Argall *alias* Carpenter 45 :
Ash *alias* Ames 51.
Bougoo *alias* Pears 56.
Begoo *alias* George 48 :
Bennet *alias* Harrie 4 :
Bodenar *alias* Noy 30 :

Boos *alias* Gymbalo 48.
Bond *alias* Synkow 58 :
Cally *alias* Howes 58 :
Carpenter *alias* Argall 45 :
Chopy *alias* Row 97.
Clearo *alias* Harryo 44 :
Cock *alias* Hoilo 69.
Cornish *alias* Pnynn 73.
Cossen *alias* Maddern 98.
Cotha *alias* Sakarin 50 :

Crankan *alias* Symon 31 :
Daddow *alias* Thomas 70 :
Davyo *alias* Rowan 7.
Dreanegles *alias* James 13.
Edwardes *alias* Portere 4 :
Gardenge *alias* Michell 45 :
Geeno *alias* Sudgiow 44 :
George *alias* Begoo 48 :
Gover *alias* Skinner 55 :
Gymbalo *alias* Boes 48.

PREFACE.   vii

Harrie *alias* Bennet 4:   Maddern *alias* Cossen 98.   Rowe *alias* Stephens 13.
Harries *alias* Martin 62:   Madren *alias* Richard 6:   Sakaria *alias* Cotha 50:
Harries *alias* Ankow 57:   Martyn *alias* Harries 62:   Sennen *alias* James 58:
Harry *alias* Penreeth 96,   Michell *alias* Gardenge 45;   Skinner *alias* Gover 55:
Harrye *alias* Cleare 44:   Mulfra *alias* James 17.   Stephens *alias* Rowe 13.
Hoile *alias* Cock 69.   Nicholl *alias* Porteer 48:   Stephens *alias* Stinion 13.
Hoskin *alias* Kigwin 50.   Nicholls *alias* Trereif 31.   Stephens *alias* Trevawin 57.
Hoskyn *alias* Trembath 51:   Nicholls *alias* Trovello 72:   Stiniou *alias* Stephens 13.
Hoskyn *alias* Trombah 6.   Nighten *alias* Jeffrio 5.   Sudgiow *alias* Goene 41:
Howes *alias* Cally 58:   Noy *alias* Bodenar 30:   Symon *alias* Crankan 31:
James *alias* Amearo 5.   Noy *alias* Lawrie 48:   Synkow *alias* Boud 58:
James *alias* Mulfra 17.   Payan *alias* Cornish 73.   Teage *alias* Laudy 58:
James *alias* Rosemorran 63.   Pears *alias* Beagoo 56.   Thomas *alias* Angove 7:
James *alias* Sennen 58:   Penreeth *alias* Harry 96.   Thomas *alias* Daddow 70:
James *alias* Tremothack 2. 93.   Polgoone *alias* Thomas 48.   Thomas *alias* Roberts 7.
James *alias* Treneglos 57:   Porteer *alias* Nicholl 48:   Thomas *alias* Polgoone 48.
James *alias* Rosemorran 63.   Portere *alias* Edwardes 4:   Trembah *alias* Hoskyn 6.
Jeffrie *alias* Nighten 5.   Richard *alias* Lewer 31.   Trombath *alias* Hoskyn 51:
Kigwin *alias* Hoskin 50.   Richard *alias* Madren 6:   Tremothack *alias* James 2. 93.
Lake *alias* Lane 50,   Richard *alias* Whitowell 4:   Treneglos *alias* James 57:
Lane *alias* Lake 50.   Roberts *alias* Thomas 7.   Trereif *alias* Nicholls 31,
Lawrie *alias* Noy 48:   Rosemorran *alias* James 63.   Trevawin *alias* Stephens 57.
Lewer *alias* Richard 31.   Row *alias* Chepy 97.   Trovello *alias* Nicholls 72:
Laudy *alias* Teage 58:   Rowan *alias* Davyo 7.   Whitewell *alias* Richard 4:

Thanks to the imperfect but phonetic spelling of the period, it is easy to determine how the names of persons and places were then pronounced; and, since there is a tendency to disguise the sound of our Cornish names in such a manner that we do not know them with their foreign ring, it is well that we have some means of refreshing our memories with the original pronunciation. As a rule in all Cornish names the accent is laid on the second syllable in words of two syllables, and on the next to the last in words of more than two. There are some exceptions, but, for the most part, names, differently accentuated by the inhabitants of the more remote districts, are not essentially Cornish. Surely Lord *Penzance* does not take his title from the name of this little borough any more than Marazion is to be found on the shores of Mount's Bay; and can it be possible that young Tom *Tresider* (of the Guards) and Nugent *N*ankivell (of the Civil Service) are any relation to the true Cornish families of Tresider and Nankivell? The saints who have given their names to the parishes in this neighbourhood—St. Madern or Madron among them—were not of Cornish extraction. France sent holy men and women to the south coast, and Ireland supplied the west with prodigies of goodness and of prowess. A mere eccentricity of spelling would not be likely to mislead an expert, nor need a novice be disappointed if he fails at first to recognise the name he seeks. We know that it is possible to spell some words, correctly as to sound, without a single letter that rightly belongs to them, and, judging from what I have seen of Parish Registers, it would not be advisable to give up search until extremes have been reached.

From an historical point of view something may be indirectly learnt from these pages, though they are particularly barren in those quaint notes and pithy bits of information, which often add so much to the value and interest of such old books; still even here we can read the signs of the times and draw our inferences. That the custom of not solemnizing Marriages during Lent was, for the most part, strictly observed in this parish, is very evident. It is noteworthy too that there are no registers either of Baptisms, Marriages, or Burials for the year 1595, the year of the attack of a party of Spaniards upon Paul, Newlyn, and Penzance; but there is no allusion to the marauders, as in the Registers of Paul. The Commonwealth and Puritanical times have left their mark on these Registers, though happily they then escaped with less disturbance than those of many other parishes. Whether we must attribute the unsatisfactory state of the record towards the end of the 17th century to the general laxity of post-restoration days, or to the troubled times of the greater revolution, is uncertain: more probably a non-resident vicar was to blame, for notwithstanding that Master Reginald Trenhayle may have busied himself about affairs of state—and his bones found a resting-place in Westminster Abbey—still the confused entries, written by many hands during the later years of his incumbency, tend to prove that he neglected his parochial duties. Immorality leaves but comparatively slight traces of its existence: there are in all about sixty entries of Baptism and Burial of illegitimate children, and previously to 1630 such entries are most frequently marked by the addition of the word *spur*, a contraction of *spurius* (p. 46.); sometimes, and more rarely, by a harder name. Nor have we any reason for supposing that there was any suppression of the truth, since it is plain that our predecessors did not hesitate to call a spade a spade. During the reign of the Merry Monarch the Register is peculiarly free from entries of this nature.

Probably the sanitary arrangements of the inhabitants of the parish, three and even two centuries ago, were not as complete as they might have been. There are indications that infectious diseases were somewhat prevalent at certain periods; the entry of burial of one member of a family being not unfrequently followed by other such entries of the same. Upon two occasions the locality was visited by a very fatal sickness or plague: it appeared first in 1578, and again in 1647, lasting about six months (from June to November) at each outbreak. The first visitation was the more fatal,—whole families seem to have been swept away; and at one time the number of burials reached as many as five a day. Not less than one hundred and fifty persons were buried within the time mentioned, whilst the average death-rate previously, and for some time after, did not exceed three per month. In the previous year the celebrated Black Assizes took place at Oxford—the gaol fever having broken out on the seventh of July, 1577—though there could scarcely have been any connexion between the two, and it most probably was but a local epidemic of a very serious nature. The second visitation is mentioned more than once by "Alexander Daniel, of Larcgan," to whose manuscript I have so often referred in the notes. Besides speaking of the vicar of Madron, John Keat, who died at Nanceglos as was "supposed of ye plague," he says in the smaller volume of his manuscript, under July, 1647, "My daughter, Jaquelina, sick of a feaver nere to death. She doubted lest if she had died then (the plague being at Pensance and in Maddren Parish) they would report that she died of e pest, but I willd her to joine in prayer to God," etc. From this it appears that a certain amount of reproach was attached to the disease.

Some four hundred times do we find the badge of gentility in one form or another in these pages. Just eighty-two names have "Mr." prefixed, whilst the greater part of the remainder are distinguished by having the word "gent" appended. There are but five esquires (the title occurring seven times only), and since they are so few it may be well to mention them. They are—Richard Lanyon (p. 7.), Richard Trevaunyon (p. 30.), William Harris, of Kenegy (p. 38:), John Lanyon (pp. 45. 50: 51.), and Francis Jones (p. 56.). Twice, and twice only, do we find a higher title, and that in Sir John H .... (p. 37.), and Sir Thomas Fanshowe (p. 56:). The decaying page hinders our learning more of the former: the latter is not unknown in the chronicles of his country. He held the office of Remembrancer in the Court of Exchequer, and upon the death of his father, in 1665, inherited his title of Lord Viscount Fanshawe, of Donamore, in Ireland. His eldest half-sister married Sir Christopher Hatton, heir to the Lord Chancellor of that name. He was twice married: first to Catherine, daughter and heiress of Knighton Ferrers, Esq., of Bedford-bury, in Hertfordshire, and secondly to Sarah, daughter of John Evelyn, Esq., of West Deno, in Surrey, and widow of Sir John Wray, of Glentworth, in Lincolnshire. That he is the person referred to in the Register is evident from the *Memoirs of Lady Fanshawe*. She writes (at p. 57):—
"I was at Penzance with my father, and in the same town was my brother Fanshawe and his lady and children. My father and that family embarked for Morlaix, in Brittany, with my father's now wife, which

PREFACE.   ix

he had married out of that family. My cousin Fanshawe, of Jenkins, and his eldest son being with them went also over, but being in a small vessel of that port and surprised with a great storm, they had all like to have been cast away, which forced them to land in a little creek, two leagues from Morlaix, upon the 28th of March, 1646; and five days after the Prince* and all his council embarked themselves in a ship called the Phœnix, for the Isles of Scilly. They went from the Lands-end, and so did we; being accompanied with many gentlemen of that country, among whom was Sir Francis Basset, Governor of the Mount, an honest gentleman, and so were all his family; and in particular we received great civility from them."

With regard to the state of trade in this locality during the period comprised within this first book of the Registers, we have but slight particulars upon which to base an opinion. The terms merchant and smith occur just twenty and ten times respectively, but they refer more than once to the same individual; and it is hardly possible during all this time that there could have been but one cutler, one glover, one joiner, one shoemaker, or one coffin maker, yet no more are mentioned.

The old mode of registration ended with the year 1812. Books of a different character were then required by law, and it so happened that at Madron, when the change was made, a new book had lately been commenced, and was but little written in. Possibly, the numerous blank leaves of parchment suggested to the then incumbent a design, which he carried into effect. He prefaced his labour of love with the following note:—" March 13, 1815. Finding the ancient Parish Register much decayed, worm-eaten, and perishing, I have this day begun to copy it herein. Wm. Tremenheere, A.B., Vicar." Whilst the work was in progress the old book seems to have been re-bound. (See note, p. 46). At this time probably occurred that shameful clipping of edges (already alluded to) and loss of leaves, besides a very considerable derangement of chronological order and pagination, not only by misplacing leaves, but, making the confusion greater, by binding several of them wrongside out. Mr. Tremenheere endeavoured to rectify these blunders as far as possible, and it is not uncommon to find such marginal notes as—" for page 143 turn over five leaves," "this leaf bound the wrong way," "for page 131 v. next page but three," and so on; but one or two of the reversed leaves escaped his notice, and the entries on such as copied by him are consequently wrongly dated. He concluded thus:—" Finished by intervals and at leisure, after many intermissions, interruptions, and delays, this Fourth Day of June, 1817. (*Nulla dies sine linea*. Evenings at home)." So commendable was his attempt to make a duplicate of this valuable record, thus threatened with destruction, that it is with regret I allude to the marring effect of his inaccuracy and omissions in copying it. It is necessary however, in self-defence, for me to mention the fact, since upon comparing the present work with Mr. Tremenheere's copy (which is kept in the parish chest, in the church at Madron, and being more easily read is perhaps more often referred to than the Register itself) many differences will be found. Reference to the original must decide between us. And here let me say, what many persons already well know, though there is oftentimes some misapprehension upon the subject, that in point of law certified extracts from the original Parish Register only are evidence. Of the six thousand entries set forth in the following pages not one would be received as proof of a Baptism, Marriage, or Burial in a court of law; but having by this means found a required entry we need have no difficulty in procuring a certified copy of the original from the proper authority—the vicar of the parish. The "Ancient Register" is still the real source of legal certificates, and its state of preservation and continued safe keeping become matters of paramount importance.

"*Decayed, worm-eaten, and perishing*," such are the words of the vicar with regard to the Parish Register of Madron upwards of half a century ago. Add but the fair wear and tear—not to mention damp or neglect—of more than fifty years, and judge of its probable condition at the present time. Such a whole-

* Afterwards Charles II.

PREFACE.

some horror have I of the word *restoration* in its conventional meaning, that I refrain from using it in connexion with my self-imposed task; but, with the consent of the vicar, it has been my endeavour to do something towards the preservation of the original manuscript, by carefully strengthening the broken leaves, re-uniting the tattered fragments, and re-arranging the pages in chronological order. It is almost unnecessary for me to say that no entry has been re-written or re-touched,—so unjustifiable and objectionable a practice serves, in my opinion at least, to throw more or less suspicion upon the genuineness of the entry. I have however ventured to re-number the pages in red, since the old numbering was but partial and imperfect.

Time, damp, and the bookbinder have each done something towards the destruction of the volume, yet the greater part remains—dating from three hundred years ago; and it is in the hope of adding permanency to so valuable a local record, and of facilitating reference to it, that the present work has been undertaken. With regard to the value of Parish Registers in general, of the best mode of directing attention to their wealth, and of the most effectual means of preserving them, it is useless for me to speak. So much has been already said upon the subject, and so little has been done for their protection, that one more protest from this westernmost corner of Cornwall will not avail. The administration of the law is lax; the destroyer in varied guise is for the most part ceaselessly at work; "everybody's business is nobody's business;" and the "title deeds of the people" are in danger.

In conclusion, I gladly take this opportunity of expressing my indebtedness to the clergymen of this neighbourhood, who, from time to time during the last ten years, have courteously allowed me free access to their Parish Registers, and to documents relating to their churches: especially to the Rev. MICHAEL NOWELL PETERS, of Madron; the Rev. JOHN MARTYN COLLYNS, of Sancreed; the late Rev. JOHN RAMSAY MC DOWELL, formerly of St. Just-in-Penwith, and his successor, the Rev. HENRY STUART FAGAN; the late Rev. ROBERT FRANCIS BUTE RICKARDS, formerly of Constantine; the late Rev. THOMAS PASCOE, formerly of St. Hilary; the Rev. JOSEPH SYDNEY TYACKE, of Helston; the Rev. RICHARD MALONE, formerly of Paul, now of Potton, Bedfordshire; the Rev. DAVID JOHN HARRISON, of Ludgvan; the Rev. THOMAS BORLASE COULSON, of Buryan; the Rev. EDWARD MORRIS PRIDMORE, of Brenge; the Rev. GEORGE LEY WOOLLCOMBE, formerly of Sennen, now of St. Mewan; the Rev. WILLIAM WRIOTHESLEY WINGFIELD, of Gulval; and the Rev. PREBENDARY HEDGELAND, of Penzance. I should be sadly remiss too did I fail to acknowledge the ready assistance I have received from the Rev. CHARLES WILLIAM BOASE, of Exeter College, Oxford; as well as, and particularly, from Dr. WILLAN, of Penzance.

And now it only remains for me to refer the reader to the Registers themselves, in the hope that hidden fact may be brought to light, or interest aroused—

> "Go, search it there, where, to be born and die,
> Of Rich and Poor make all the History."

GEORGE BOWN MILLETT.

PENZANCE, 24th *September*, 1877.

List of Subscribers.

John Amphlett, Clent, Stourbridge.
John Eglington Bailey, F.S.A., Stretford, Manchester.
Henry Howard Batten, Charity Commission Office.
Joseph Childs Batten, 93, Fleet Street, London, E.C.
Charles Batts, Flynone House, Swansea.
The Rev. Aubrey Brisbane Berry, M.A., Penzance.
The Rev. Charles William Boase, M.A., Exeter College, Oxford. *Two copies.*
Francis Boase, M.R.C.S., Mayor of Penzance.
George Clement Boase, 15, Queen Anne's Gate, Westminster.
Henry Boase, Wellfield Works, Dundee.
John Josias Arthur Boase, Exmouth.
Thomas Hacker Bodilly, Alverton Cottage, Penzance.
Ralph Hacker Bodilly, 23, North Parade, Penzance.
Thomas Robins Bolitho, Pendrea, Penzance.
William Bolitho, Jun., D.L., Ponsandane, Penzance. *Two copies.*
The Rev. William Borlase, M.A., Vicar of Zennor.
William Copeland Borlase, M.A., F.S.A., Laregan, Penzance. *Two copies.*
Edmund M. Boyle, 14, Hill St., Berkeley Square, London.
Charles Bridger, F.R.H.S., 17, Selwood Terrace, South Kensington.
Captain W. E. G. Bulwer, Quebec House, East Dereham, Norfolk.
Colonel Joseph Lemuel Chester, F.R.H.S., &c., Linden Villas, Blue Anchor Road, Bermondsey, London, S.E.
George Edward Cokayne, M.A., F.S.A., Lancaster Herald, College of Arms, London.
Henry Roberts Cornish, Market Place, Penzance.
The Rev. Thos. Borlase Coulson, M.A., Rector of Duryan
James Sampson Courtney, Alverton House, Penzance.
William Prideaux Courtney, 15, Queen Anne's Gate, Westminster, S.W. *Two copies.*
The Devon and Exeter Institution.
The Rev. John Ingle Dredge, Vicar of Buckland Brewer, Bideford.
Edwin Dunkin, F.R.S., 14, Kidbrooke Park Road, Blackheath, London, S.E.
Robert Dymond, F.S.A., Bampfylde House, Exeter.
Edward Fisher, Fairfield, Dawlish.
Alfred Scott Gatty, Ecclesfield, Sheffield.
Charles Henry Gatty, Felbridge Park, East Grinstead.
W. Garnett, Quernmore Park, Lancaster.
The Rev. Prebendary Hedgeland, M.A., Vicar of St. Mary's, Penzance.
The late William Jory Henwood, F.R.S., F.G.S., &c.
Miss Frances Margery Hext, Lostwithiel.
Richard Hosking, M.R.C.S., Penzance. *Two copies.*
R. Hovenden, Heathcote, Park Hill Road, Croydon.

Joseph Jackson Howard, LL.D., F.S.A., Honorary Editor of the *Miscellanea Genealogica et Heraldica*.
Henry Julian Hunter, M.D., Penzance.
The Rev. William Iago, B.A., Sec. S.A. for Cornwall, Westheath, Bodmin.
The Rev. John Jane, Rector of SS. John and George, Exeter.
The Rev. Wladislaw Somerville Lach-Szyrma, M.A., Vicar of St. Peter's, Newlyn, Penzance.
Northmore Hearle Pearce Lawrence, Launceston.
Captain William Stephen Luke, R.N., 21, Cromwell Crescent, South Kensington.
Sir John Maclean, F.S.A., &c., Bicknor Court, Colefield.
Thomas Maddern, Penzance.
George W. Marshall, LL.D., F.S.A., 60, Onslow Gardens, London.
Towers Trevorian Millett, Madras Police.
James Barclay Montgomery, M.D., F.R.C.P., Penzance. *Two copies.*
William Noye, 38, Sutherland Square, London, S.E.
Richard Oliver, Dunedin, New Zealand.
Daniel Parsons, Stuart's Lodge, Malvern Wells.
Hodgson Pascoe, Penzance.
Thomas William Pengelly, Madron.
Richard Pentreath, 11, Albert Street, Newington Butts, London, S.E.
The Penzance Library.
The Rev. Michael Nowell Peters, M.A., Vicar of Madron.
S. G. Pike, Devonport.
Jonathan Rashleigh, High Sheriff of Cornwall, Menabilly.
Evelyn W. Rashleigh, Menabilly.
Joshua Brooking Rowe, F.S.A., 16, Lockyer Street, Plymouth.
St. Mary's Church, Penzance.
Sir John St. Aubyn, Bart., M.P., St. Michael's Mount, and Trevethoe, Lelant. *Two copies.*
Captain W. J. St. Aubyn, Chatham.
The late John Symons, Sennen. *Two copies.*
Lewis Charles Thomson, 14, Seaton Terrace, Plymouth.
Hugh Seymour Tremenheere, C.B., M.A., F.G.S., 43, Thurloe Square, Brompton, London, S.W.
Charles Reynolds Trenwith, Hayle.
S. Vosper-Thomas, Lamorna Cottage, Wimborne Minster.
The late William Wallis, Penzance.
Edward Arthur White, F.S.A., Elvet, Durham.
Albert Charles Wildman, Penzance.
Leonard Richard Willan, M.D. *Cantab.*, Penzance.
Michael Williams, Tregullow, Scorrier.
W. W. Willink, 3, Hyde Park Street, London, W.
Thomas Alexander Wise, M.D., Upper Norwood, Surrey.
Sir Albert William Woods, F.S.A., Garter King of Arms, College of Arms.

Signs, &c.

[ ]   Words and dates within brackets are not to be found in the original.
 Ditto   in Italics within brackets are upon the authority of the late Vicar's copy.
———   Where a blank space has been left in the original.
. . . .   Illegible or missing.
* * * *   Gap,—loss of a page or more.
[+]   Denotes the commencement of another handwriting.
The year *old style* is given on the left of each column, and *new style* in the centre.
In the Index a full stop following the figure denotes the first column, and a colon the second.

Addenda et Corrigenda.

The following will be found in Bishop STAFFORD's Register, at Exeter:—

"Universis Sancte matris ecclesie filiis ad quorum noticiam presentes litere pervenerint Edmundus miseracione divina Exoniensis episcopus salutem cum benedictione et graciam Salvatoris. Cupientes ea que devocionis et cultus divini augmentum respiciunt sinceris affectibus promovere, Ut in capella beate Mario in Villa de Pensansz, in Cornubia nostro Exoniensis dioceseos situata, divina per quoscunque presbiteros ydoneos, absque preiudicio matricis ecclesie, valeant celebrari, dum tamen eorum quorum interest accedat assensus, tenore presencium licenciam concedimus specialem, presentibus ad nostrum beneplacitum duraturis. Datum in hospicio nostro London XV die mensis Junii, Anno D. supradicto (*i.e.* 1397) et nostro consecrationis anno secundo.

"XVI die mensis predicti ibidem consimilis litera emanavit pro capella beati Ermeti apud Marghasyow in parochia S. Illarii."

"1400. Sep. 22, dominus concessit licenciam ut capella S. Brigide, in parochia S. Materni Exoniensis dioceseos situata, divina, absque preiudicio matricis ecclesie loci huiusmodi, valeant celebrari, ad beneplacitum," &c.

Page 4.   The date 1603, old style, is accidentally placed after instead of before the 25th March.
,,   19.   The new hand [+] commences with the last entry in July, 1666, not with April 11.
,,   20.   Before 16th October, 1668, add [+] as well as the date 1668, old style, in brackets to the left; "June 2, Jacob, son of Tonken Boase," evidently belongs to the year 1668.
,,   30.   1587, Nov. 19, for *Olere* read *Clere*, and dele note.
,,   37.   Line 2, second column, dele [Alice].
,,   38.   "1653, Sept. 26, John, son of John Usticke, of Botallack, and Margarett, daughter of Robert Shearme, were married at Maddren, 26th Sept., Anno Dom. 1653."—See St. Just Registers.
,,   72.   1713, Nov. 25, for *Deogry Nichols* read *William Boase;* and insert next before this entry, "1712-13, Feb. 10, Deogry Nichols, of Penzance, and Blanch Leha, of Paul, at Paul."
,,   75.   Line 14, after "the second bears" insert "Trevanion."
,,   78.   ,,   17.   The Rev. Duke Pearse is stated by his representatives to have died at the age of 27 years, but the age given on his monument is distinctly 34.
,,   79.   ,,   9, "viventis," *Sic.*—Query viventi.
,,   84.   ,,   25, for *Mousehole* read *Madron.* The Chapel at Mousehole (p.88) was dedicated to S. Mary.
,,   84.   Robert [Paschow or] Paslew was probably Vicar 1476—98.   He resided at Exeter College 1457—76, and was Principal of Plomer Hall, 1458.—*Anstey's Monumenta Academica*, 675—77.
,,   85.   Reginald Trenhayle matriculated at Exeter College, Oxford, 11th Oct., 1653.   A Reginald Trenhayle, of Madron, matriculated at the same College 23rd December, 1684, and was B.A., 12th Oct., 1688.—Query his son.
,,   95.   Line 18, for *Larigan* read *Larregan*.
,,   98.   ,,   12 from bottom, for *Ceeley* read *Ceely*.

N.B.—It has only been thought necessary to notice errors which, if left uncorrected, would be misleading.

No. 2. Madron Church.

The Register of Baptisms.

Parish of Madron, Cornwall.

* * * * * * * * * * * * * * *

[1592.*]
.... of James Bossaverne.
[Sept.] 24, was baptized Joane, the daughter of John Cornish.
  ,,   24, was baptized John, the base sonne of Joan Raw, spur.†
October [8], was baptized Elizabeth, the daughter of Edward Luddra.
  ,,   8, was baptized Elizabeth, the daughter of Thomas Luke.
  ,,   18, was baptized Thomas, the sonne of Peter Bowes.
  ,,   20, was baptized Raphe, the sonne of Richard Broach.
  ,,   22, was baptized John, the sonne of William Estligh.
  ,,   28, was baptized Sampson, the sonne of John Richard.
Novemb. 5, was baptized Joane, the daughter of John Martyn.
  ,,   12, was baptized John, the sonne of William Joffry.
  ,,   26, was baptized Mary, the daughter of James Dawbyn
  ,,   30, was baptized Jermyn, the sonne of Robert Luke.
Decemb. 10, was baptized Joane, the daughter of Richard James.
  ,,   17, was baptized Robert, the sonne of Agnes Barber, spur.†
  ,,   17, was baptized Elizabeth, the daughter of Rawe Davye.
  ,,   28, was baptized Joane, the daughter of William Lawrenc.
  ,,   31, was baptized Margaret, the daughter of Morishe Roch.
January 1, was baptized John, the sonne of Robert Dunkyn.
  ,,   3, was baptized Phillip, the daughter of Thomas Barnard.
  ,,   21, was baptized John, the sonne of William Maderne.
February 11, was baptized Ann, the daughter of Emanuell Bell.
  ,,   16, was baptized William, the sonne of John Brockhurst.
  ,,   17, was baptized Arthur, the sonne of John Hext, Gent.
  ,,   .. was baptized Bennet, the sonne of Maderne Anbone.
  ,,   .. was baptized Jane, the daughter of Peter Porteor.
Marche 4, was baptized Elizabeth, the daughter of [John] William.
  ,,   4, was baptized Agnes, the daughter of John Nowell.
  ,,   4, was baptized Margery, the daughter of William Richard.
  ,,   11, was baptized William, sonne of John Holla.
  ,,   15, were baptized Nicholas and Jone, children of William Rawlyn.

1593.
Aprill 22, was baptized Mathew, the sonne of John Buskeyning, Jun.
  ,,   22, was baptized Ann, the daughter of John Jermyn.

---

* The earlier portion of this Register is missing. It doubtless—like the Register of Marriages and Burials—originally commenced in the year 1577.
† *Spurius.*

N.B. This page is a full copy of the original—the punctuation being additional. It will serve to show the style of entry which is continued throughout the book.

A

REGISTER OF BAPTISMS.

April 27, Ann, daughter of John Tonkyng.
May 3, Stephen, son of William Trewryn.
,, 13, Elizabeth, daughter of Raphe Bykham.
June 1, Mawd, daughter of Richard Noye.
,, 3, Jane, daughter of John James Tromethack.
,, 23, Mary, daughter of Nighteu Jeffry.
July 1, Agnes, daughter of John Honywell.
,, 8, Elizabeth, daughter of Raph William.
,, 15, John and Edward, sons of John Rodda.
,, 15, Richard, base son of Pacyeus, spur.
Aug. 12, Elizabeth, daughter of ——
,, 26, Ann, daughter of William Legow.
Sept. 2, Honour, daughter of William Treve.
,, 2, Robert, son of John, the roper.
,, 16, Ann daughter of Richard Hawes.
,, 30, Mary, daughter of James Champion.
,, 30, Margaret, daughter of William Pedenbussath.
Oct. 10, Jone, daughter of William Escott.
,, 28, Sampson, son of Thomas Lake.
Nov. 1, Mary, daughter of Henry Stephens.
,, 18, ...
,, 18, ...
,, 25, Ann, daughter of John Tremethack.
Dec. 2, John, son of Thomas Rawe.
,, 2, Elizabeth, daughter of Sampson Noye.
,, 7, Elizabeth, daughter of William Blighe.
,, 16, Thomas, son of William Argall, Jun.

[1594.]
Jan. 2, Clarene, daughter of William Maderne.
,, 27, ... son of John Shillinge.
,, 27, ... daughter of William Champyon.
Feb. 2, John, son of Thomas Bodye.
,, 10, Elizabeth, daughter of Edward Jenckyn.
,, .. Nicholas, son of Morish Roch.
,, .. [John], son of Henry Trythall.
,, 17, Ann, daughter of George, the miller.
,, .. Thomas, son of Richard Bennet.
March 3, Joane, daughter of Richard Dounall.
,, 15, Elizabeth, daughter of Richard Georg.
,, 17, Richard and Thomas, sons of John Richard.
,, 17, Mary, daughter of William Lewer.
,, 17, Henry and Elizabeth, children of James Melyauneck.
,, 20, Thomas, son of Jerman Morish.

1594.
,, 30, Robert, son of William Foster.
April 3, Samuell, son of James Michell.
,, 3, Robert, son of Richard Trythall.
,, 7, Richard, son of Raphe Lanyon.
,, 7, Andrew, son of Robert Noy.
,, 14, Katherin, daughter of John Giles.
May 9, ... of John Brockhurst.
,, [21], Richard, son of John Davye.
June [22], Madern, son of John Legow.
July 1, Alexander, son of Richard Bennet.
,, 8, Ann, daughter of Raph . . . .
,, 14, Elizabeth, daughter of John Buskening, Jun.

July 28, John, son of Richard . . . .
Aug. 4, Nicholas, son of Henry Hooper.
,, 11, John, son of . . . .
,, .. Katherin, daughter of Phillip Sampson.
,, 27, Richard, son of John Michell.
,, 27, ... daughter of Agath Bla..ch.
,, 31, Robert, son of Sampson Noy.
,, 31, Joane, daughter of Thomas Robert.
Nov. 10, Elizabeth, daughter of Launcelot Garland.

1596.*
July 14, Thomas, son of Raphe Lanyon, gent.
,, 17, Mary, daughter of William Maderne.
Aug. 1, Son of Richarde Beunett.
,, 20, Raphe, son of William Cardewe.
,, 22, Marye, daughter of John Davye.
Sept. 10, Joane, base daughter of Emet Rodda.
,, 12, Thomas, son of Rychard Benuett.
,, 21, Sampson, son of John Tregenhoe.
,, 26, The son of William Sacarya.
,, 29, William, son of Rawe Thomas.
,, .. 6, Alls, daughter of William Lawrenc.
,, .. Alls, daughter of James Hoskyns.
,, .. The daughter of Thomas Boskenninge.
,, 7, Elizabeth, daughter of Henry Hooper.
,, 30, William, son of John James.
Dec. 5, Joane, daughter of John Noale.
,, 6, Nicholas, son of John Maderne, of Peneans.
,, 31, Georg and Sampson, sons of Elizabeth Buswarthen.

[1597.]
Jan. 1, The son of Bennet Tremethacke.
,, 1, Rebecca, daughter of Thomas Bodye.
,, 23, Symon, son of John Brockehurste.
,, 30, Susan, daughter of Thomas Drewe.
Feb. 13, Mary, daughter of John Olyver.
,, 14, Roger, son of Reynold Cosen.
,, 16, Rebecca, daughter of Thomas Burnowe.
,, 20, Clarene, daughter of John Legowe.
,, 23, Thomas, son of John Thomas.
,, 24, Elizabeth, daughter of German Geifo.
March 2, Jane and Elizabeth, daughters of James Champion.
,, 13, Florenc. daughter of John Swaffield.
,, 20, Elizabeth, daughter of ——
,, 23, Thomas, son of Sampson Noye.

1597.
July 31, Henry, son of Teage Dillen.
Aug. 6, John, son of William Lewer.
,, 7, Robert, son of Mr. John Hixt.
,, 7, Josepthe, son of Phillip Sampson.
Sept. 1, Allie, daughter of John Cowliuge, gent.
,, 18, Edward, son of James Trevalles.
,, 25, Joane, daughter of John Tregirthen.
,, 28, Allie, daughter of Robert Luke.
Oct. 1, Roberte, son of William Tereife.

---
* No entries from November 10, 1594, to July 14, 1596.

PARISH OF MADRON.

Nov. 9, Marke, base son of Marke Carthewe.
„ 31, Elizabeth, daughter of William Legowe.

[1598.]

Jan. 18, Katherin, daughter of John Game.
Jan. 28, Joane, daughter of Thomas Argall.
Feb. 12, William, son of Richard Harrye.
„ 12, John, son of Pascowe Pendyne.
„ 25, Alexander, son of Raphe Byckham.
Mar. 11, Elizabeth, daughter of James Angove.
„ 14, Christian, daughter of Mathew Penmenith.
„ 17, Elizabeth, daughter of Carlyon, gent.
„ 18, Elizabeth, daughter of Jerman Morishe.
„ 19, Richard, son of Thomas Fenyo.
„ 21, Richard, son of Sampson Noye.
„ 21, Ann, daughter of Thomas Tremethack.

1598.

April 12, Katheren, daughter of Morish Roche.
„ 23, Mary, daughter of Richard Edward.
May 28, Christoper, son of John Thomas.
June 26, Richard, son of William Noye.
„ 28, William, base son of Jeny Anhaye.
July 7, William, son of William Launder.
„ 16, Grace, daughter of John James, Jun.
„ 17, Mary, daughter of Henrie Buskeninge.
„ 19, Thomas, son of Thomas Anbone.
„ 23, John, son of John Richard.
„ 23, Agnes, daughter of Richard Hawes.
„ 23, Jane, daughter of James Mycholl.
Aug. 13, Peter, son of John Trelill.
„ 13, Joane, daughter of Saundry Maderne.
„ 20, John, son of Richard Trythall.
„ 20, Jane, daughter of John Barnycote.
Sept. 3, Robert, son of John Cotha Mitchell.
„ 9, Richard, base son of John Crankan.
„ 24, Joane, daughter of Richard Bennett.
Oct. 7, John, son of Thomas Crudge.
„ 29, Thomas, son of Launcelot Garland.
Dec. 3, Thomas, son of Anthony Polkinghorne.
„ 31, Thomas, base son of Margerie Michell.

[1599.]

Jan. 28, William, son of ——
Feb. 12, Maderen and William, sons of William Champion.
„ 12, Elizabeth, daughter of Edward Jenkyn.
„ 19, Katherin, daughter of William Rowlynn.
March 7, Mary, daughter of John Coyle.
„ 11, Thomas, son of Richard Andryllier.
„ 11, Susan, daughter of John Tremethack.
„ 18, Robert, son of Robert Dunkyn.
„ 18, Raphe, son of Rowan Marke.
„ 21, Clarene, daughter of James Trevallis.

1599.

„ 28, John, son of John Swaffen.
April 11, John, son of Raphe Lanyon, gent.
„ 15, Elizabeth, daughter of James Trembah.
„ 19, Petherick, son of Thomas Robert.
May 3, Symon, son of Jermen Give.

May 9, Ann, daughter of Thomas Michell.
„ 9, Maryo, daughter of Degorie Duke.
„ 17, Joane, daughter of John Trembah.
June 1, Alexander, son of Richard Georg.
„ 3, William, son of John Brockhurst.
„ 12, Margerie, daughter of Pascaw Pendene.
„ 24, James, son of Robert Hamett.
July 22, John, son of Charles Sudgiow.
„ 22, Agnes, daughter of Robert Tomne.
„ 26, Blauch, daughter of James Dawbyn.
Aug. 5, Richard, son of Nicholas Connock.
„ 12, Edward, son of Rowan Davye.
Sept. 2, Ann, daughter of Edward Luddra.
„ 9, Abraham, son of William Richard.
„ 16, Henry, son of Bennet Champion.
„ 16, William, son of Henrie Hooper.
„ 27, Henry, son of Nicholas Game.
„ 29, Susan, daughter of John Bone.
Oct. 18, Jane, daughter of Sampson Noye.
„ 20, Clarene, daughter of John James, Jun.
Nov. 10, William, son of Robert Trencyre, gent.
„ 10, Joane, daughter of William Mulfra.
„ 11, Margerie, daughter of William ....
„ 27, Prudene, daughter of John Jenkin.
„ 30, Jane, daughter of John Game.
Dec. 2, Joane, daughter of William Legowe.
„ 9, Katherin, daughter of John Champion.
„ 21, William, son of Richard Ammeare.
„ 23, Ellynor, daughter of Edward Peeter.
„ 25, Elizabeth, daughter of John Michell.

[1600.]

Jan. 5, Ann, daughter of John Slade.
„ 20, Richard, son of Martin Mayne.
„ 26, John, son of Richard Donnall.
„ 27, William, son of John Clymmowe.
„ 27, Elizabeth, daughter of Rawe ——
Feb. 6, Walter, son of Raphe ——
„ 10, William, son of William Argall.
„ 13, Katherin, daughter of Thomas Carne.
„ 21, Thomas, son of Hew ——
„ 22, Ann, base daughter of Margerie ....
„ 24, Katherin, daughter of John Oliver.
March 8, Richard, son of Richard Harrie.
„ 22, Agnes, daughter of Robert Luke.
„ 22, Christian, daughter of John Nole.

1600.

„ 30, Mary, daughter of John William.
April 8, Ruth, daughter of John Richard.
„ 20, Honor, daughter of Thomas William.
„ 2.. Chesten, daughter of Thomas Sugiow.
May 1, Christian, daughter of James Michell.
„ 4, Ann, daughter of William Launder.
„ 15, John, son of Thomas Fennye.
June 8, Elizabeth, daughter of Peter Gymball.
„ 8, Katherin, daughter of ——
„ 15, William, son of William Tereve.
„ 16, Bennet, son of Richard Tremethack.
„ 22, Ann, daughter of William Noye.

REGISTER OF BAPTISMS.

June 24, John, son of Raphe Byckham.
July 15, Alexander, base son of Jedna Peres.
Aug. 3, Thomas, son of Thomas Bodye.
Sept. 12, Honour, daughter of Morishe Roche.
Oct. 5, William, son of Nicholas Maderne.
,, 5, Sampson, son of John Portere.
,, 19, Elizabeth, daughter of John Tremethack.
Nov. 2, William, son of William Lewer.
,, 2, Joan, daughter of William Lower.
,, 18, Ellinor, daughter of Jane Clies, spur.
,, 20, Raph, son of Jermen Morishe.
,, 23, Ann, daughter of Abraham Lecke.
,, 29, Elizabeth, daughter of John Morishe.
,, 30, Thomas, son of John James, Jun.
Dec. 3, Agnes, daughter of Joseph Lympany.
,, 10, Richard, son of William Tonkyn.
,, 10, John, son of Thomas Michell.
,, 14, Katheren, daughter of John Trembah.
,, 24, Chesten, daughter of Sampson Noye.
,, 26, Stephen, son of Richard Rowlande.

[1601.]

Jan. 20, Grace, daughter of Edward Lawrene.
,, 27, Katherin, daughter of John Barnycote.
Mar. 16, Joane, base child of William Hewe.
,, 22, Orpheus, son of Robert Dunkynne.

1601.

,, 29, William, son of Phillip Sampsonn.
April 28, The base child of Prudene Anthonye.
July 4, The son of William Nenys.
,, 12, William, son of Thomas Jeffrye.
,, 30, Ann, daughter of William Mulfra.
Aug. 30, William, son of John Synkoe.
Sept. 3, Nicholas, son of Thomas Fleming, gent.
,, 3, Elizabeth, daughter of Roan Davy.
,, 6, Sampson, son of John Howe,
,, 15, Awdry, daughter of Thomas Crudg, gent.
,, 20, Joune, daughter of John Game.
,, 21, Thomas, son of John Trelill.
,, 27, John, son of Robert Jenkyune.
Oct. 4, Elynor, daughter of John Jenkynne.

[1602.]

Jan. 22, Richard, son of Robert Hamett.
Feb. 2, William, son of Thomas William.
,, 2, Joane, daughter of Thomas Bawden.
,, 2, Elizabeth, daughter of James Michell.
,, 4, Elizabeth, daughter of Thomas Lake.
,, 14, English, daughter of Robert Thomas.
,, 16, Elizabeth, daughter of Rychard Michell.
,, 21, John, son of John Sacaria.
,, 21, Elizabeth, base child of Ann Baude.
March 7, John, son of Roan Davye.

1602.

,, 28, William, son of John Slader.
April 1, Ann, daughter of Richard Edward.
,, 5, Pascaw, daughter of John Luke.
,, 5, Margaret, daughter of Charells Sudgiow.
,, 15, Grace, daughter of Morish Roche.

April 18, Thomas, son of John James.
,, 18, Allice, daughter of William Launder.
May 30, William, son of William Watkins.
June 3, Robert, son of William Edmondes.
,, 3, John, son of Peter Russell.
July 4, Jane, daughter of Reynold James.
,, 11, John, son of Robert Dunkyn.
,, 11, Aves, daughter of Richard Bennet.
,, 23, Elizabeth, daughter of Thomas Ambone, Sen.
Aug. 30, Thomas, son of John Swaffen.
Sept. 5, John, son of Thomas Fynnic.
,, 26, Thomas, son of John Gregor.
Oct. 3, John, son of John Draper.
,, 7, William, son of William Tonckyn.
,, 7, William, son of William Rawlyn.
,, 10, Elizabeth, daughter of Thomas Carne.
,, 11, Jane, daughter of William Jeffric.
,, 28, Henrie, son of Richard Bennet, alias Harrie.
,, 31, Thomas, son of John Trogirthen.
Nov. 7, Phillip, son of William Noye.
,, 14, John, son of John Trembahe.
,, 21, Thomas, son of Raph William.
,, 25, Maderne, son of John Hew.
,, 25, Richard, son of John Chamberlen.
Dec. 7, Grace, daughter of Thomas Fleming, gent.
,, 12, Elizabeth, daughter of John Ambrose.
,, 19, Grace, daughter of John Oliver.
,, 24, Georgo, son of Sampson Noye.
,, 24, Elizabeth, daughter of John Tremethack.
,, 26, Sara, daughter of John Whitewell, alias Richard.

[1603.]

Jan. 6, John, son of John Edwardes, alias Portere.
,, 6, Allice, daughter of James Dawbin.
,, 16, Susan, daughter of Thomas Bodie.
Feb. 12, Sampson, son of William Hew.
,, 20, Elizabeth, daughter of Richard Stephen.
,, 27, Georgo, son of Nicholas ——
March 6, Raphe, son of John Rodda.
,, 20, Raphe, son of Raphe Bickam.
,, 20, Allice, daughter of William Legow.
,, 25, Peter, base son of William Anbone.

1603.

April 3, Katherin, daughter of John Sinkoe.
May 23, Mathew, son of John Boskyn.*
,, 22, Peter, son of Peter Russell.
,, 24, Edward, son of Edward Jenkin.
June 12, William, son of Justinian Stephen.
,, 24, Marie, daughter of John Cowlen, gent.
Aug. 28, Marie, daughter of William Tref, gent.
Sept. 11, Dorothie, daughter of Thomas Michell.
,, 21, Mathew, son of Richard Clies.
Oct. 9, Katherin, daughter of Robert Duukyn.
,, 30, Allie, daughter of Joseph Lympanie.
,, 30, Elizabeth, daughter of John Draper.
,, 30, Phillip, daughter of John Morish.

* Query a clerical error for Hoskins.

PARISH OF MADRON.

Nov. 24, Roger, son of John Game.
Dec. 18, John, son of William Mulfra.

[1604.]

Jan. 1, John, son of John Thomas.
 ,, 19, William, son of Baldwyn Williams.
 ,, 24, Symon, son of Rapho Lanyon, gent.
Feb. 12, Thomas, son of William Howes.
 ,, 26, Margaret, daughter of William Edmonde.
 ,, 26, Thomas, son of Thomas Fleming, gent.
 ,, 26, Richard, son of John Jenkin, of Peusans.

1604.

April 1, —— son of Phillip Sampson.
 ,, 1, Clarence, daughter of John Gregor.
May 27, William, son of Peter Ileforde.
 ,, 27, Joane, daughter of Thomas William.
June 10, Gartered, daughter of Jerman Morisho.
July 8, —— daughter of John Luke.
 ,, 9, Marie, daughter of John Harbert.
 ,, 9, Anne, daughter of Richard Michell.
 ,, 22, John, son of Thomas Bodye.
 ,, 29, Walter, son of John Broker.
Aug. 12, Frances, son of William Bennet.
 ,, 12, Elizabeth, daughter of Richard Tromethack.
 ,, 26, James, son of Thomas Jeffrie, *alias* Nighten.
Sept. 2, John, son of Richard James, *alias* Ameare.*
 ,, 2, Jane, daughter of Thomas Bowden.
 ,, 9, Jane, daughter of John Stoane.
Oct. 7, Frances, daughter of John Slader.
 ,, 11, Katheren, daughter of Roger Wills.
 ,, 28, Richard, son of Degorie Duke.
 ,, 28, William, son of Richard Geles.
Nov. 1, Grace, daughter of William Nenes.
 ,, 2, Thomas, son of Edward Trithall.
 ,, 6, Marie, daughter of William Watkyns.
 ,, 11, William, son of Thomas Vellye.
 ,, 25, Ann, daughter of John Merefelde.
 ,, 25, Margaret, daughter of Reginald James.
 ,, 30, John, son of William Sommer.
Dec. 9, Thamazin, daughter of Richard Stephen.
 ,, 12, John, son of John Edwarde.

[1605.]

Jan. 13, Prudence, daughter of Richard Hawes.
 ,, 20, Thomas, son of William Mote.
March 8, Anna,† daughter of Joseph Lympany.
 ,, 16, William, son of William Legow.
 ,, 19, William, son of John Hoskyn.

1605.

 ,, 30, John, son of John Hew.
April 4, Richard, son of Thomas Fyunye.
May 9, Clarence, daughter of John Tregirthen.
 ,, 19, Margaret, daughter of William Sacaria.
 ,, 20, Margaret, daughter of Charles Sudgiow.
 ,, 20, Aunys, daughter of John Jenkyn.

May 29, Alexander, son of William Alger.
June 2, Sampson, son of William Noye.
 ,, 9, Thomas, son of Justinian Stephens.
 ,, 24, Richard, son of Henrie Hooper.
 ,, 29, —— daughter of Edmond Clies.
 ,, 30, Margaret, daughter of John Draper.
 ,, 30, Charitie, daughter of William Trelill.
July 6, —— son of John Bosvine, of Penzanc.
 ,, 21, Grace,* daughter of John Sampson, smithe.
 ,, 28, James, son of John Rodda.
 ,, 31, Susan, daughter of John Hicks.
Aug. 4, Elizabeth, daughter of Robert Thomas.
 ,, 11, Elizabeth, daughter of John Richards.
 ,, 11, John, son of Thomas Cowlyn, gent.
 ,, 11, Ann, daughter of David Poulease.
Sept. 1, Joane, daughter of John James, Jun.
 ,, 8, John, son of Emanuel Bluet.
Oct. 11, Richard, son of Garret Lauder.
 ,, 13, Elizabeth, daughter of William Tonckyn.
 ,, 20, John, son of Peter Cloke.
Nov. 10, Robert, son of Richard Harrie.
 ,, 28, Jane, daughter of Barthelmew Edie.
 ,, 28, John son of John Cosen.
Dec. 2, Ann, daughter of Richard Trott.
 ,, 15, William, son of John Thomas.
 ,, 18, Elizabeth, daughter of John Oliver.

[1606.]

Jan. 12, Richard, son of Sampson Noye.
 ,, 12, Wany, daughter of Martin Champion.
 ,, 19, James, son of William Bone.
 ,, 22, Samuell, son of John Willy.
 ,, 28, Annyce, daughter of Richard Lawrence.
Feb. 3, John, son of Rapho Noye.
 ,, 9, John, son of John Hoskin.
 ,, 9, William, base child of Marie Phillip, s.
 ,, 14, Margaret, daughter of William Jeffrie.
 ,, 17, Jeny, daughter of John Sacaria.
 ,, 23, John, son of John Dodo.
 ,, 23, Wallter, son of John Stoane.
Mar. 13, Honor, daughter of Edward Trithall.
 ,, 16, Katheren, daughter of John Trenhaile.
 ,, 19, Joane daughter of John Chamberlaine.

1606.

 ,, 30, Mary, daughter of Robert Dnukyn.
April 6, Katheren, daughter of Degorie Duke.
 ,, 6, Ann, daughter of John Morish.
 ,, 19, —— daughter of John Ambrose.
 ,, 21, Annice, daughter of William Luer.
June 1, William, son of William Mote.
 ,, 1, Margaret, daughter of John Champion.
 ,, 8, Aune, daughter of Nowell Argall.
 ,, 9, Anne, daughter of Thomas Fleming, gent.
July 27, John, son of Richard Nickles.
 ,, 28, Anne, daughter of Mr. John Game.
 ,, 28, Richo, daughter of Leonard Rosvcue.
Aug. 18, Prudence, daughter of Georg Lanyon, gent.

---

* James, *alias* Ameare, has been erased, and Stephens written over in a later hand.
† Altered from Amye.

* Added in a later hand.

B

REGISTER OF BAPTISMS.

Aug 20, Richard, son of William Mulfra.
 ,, 31, Maderne, son of William Legow.
Sept. 19, Frances, son of John James.
 ,, 21, Alce, daughter of John William.
Oct. 5, William, son of John Valentyne.
 ,, 10, Susan, daughter of John Midlamo.
 ,, 13, Richard, son of William Watkins.
 ,, 28, Sampson, son of Richard Hiden.
Nov. 23, William, son of Thomas Bowden.
Dec. 7, Gavrigan, son of William Bocs.
 ,, 7, Joane, base child of Jeles Bartlot.
 ,, 7, —— base child of John Baragwanath.
 ,, 14, —— daughter of William Edmonds.
 ,, 14, Luce, daughter of John Draper.
 ,, 16, Honor, daughter of Thomas Cowlen, gent.
 ,, 16, Hary, son of John Whitwell.

[1607.]

Jan. 11, James, son of William Argall.
 ,, 25, Silvester, son of John Hoskyn, *alias* Trembah
 ,, 25, Pawle, son of Richard Jecles.
 ,, 25, Richard, son of William Marten.
 ,, 28, Elizabeth, daughter of Thomas Michell.
[+] 1607.
April 4, Clarene, daughter of Jermau Morishe.
 ,, 22, Richard, son of Lawrene Michell.
 ,, 24, June, daughter of Mr. Joseph Limpenyo.
 ,, 30, Alse, daughter of John Champion.
May 31, Hughe, son of William Lawnder.
June 21, Marye, daughter of Morishe Roche.
 ,, 24, Henry, son of Mr. Thomas Vellye.
 ,, 28, Anne, daughter of John Sawndrye.
July 12, Grace, daughter of John Harberte.
 ,, 12, Elner, daughter of Thomas William.
 ,, 19, Blanche, daughter of Mr. William Touken.
Oct. 4, Haniball, son of Bartholomew Edye
Nov. 15, Grace, daughter of Mr. John Game.
 ,, 29, John, son of John James, the younger.
Dec. 23, Blanche, the daughter of Richard Tratt.
 ,, 25, Alse, daughter of John Stone.

[1608.]

Feb. 7, Hughe, son of Charles Ellis.
 ,, 7, Elizabeth, daughter of Mr. William Trereife.
 ,, 14, Elizabeth, daughter of John Mathew.
1608.
Mar. 26, Prudene, daughter of Thomas Bowden.
July 31, Elizabeth, daughter of Richard Lawrence.
Ang. 5, Methusela, son of John Rodda.
 ,, 5, Alse, daughter of Richard Michell.
 ,, 10, Sebell,* daughter of William Legoe.
 ,, 14, Grace, daughter of Lawrene Willoe.
 ,, 28, —— daughter of Henry Hooper.
Sept. 11, John, son of Mr. Joseph Lympenyo.
 ,, 11, Phillip, son of William Thomas.
 ,, 13, Elizabeth, daughter of Thomas Fleming, gent.

* Added in a different hand.

Sept. 25, Joane, daughter of John Buswathack.
Oct. 12, Thomasin, daughter of Thomas Bodye.
 ,, 30, Elizabeth, daughter of Gilbert Harris.
Nov. 5, William, son of John Sampson, smithe.
 ,, 6, Roberte, son of John Tricke.
 ,, 13, Raphe, son of John Harberte.
 ,, 13, Bartholomew, son of Robert James.
 ,, 13, Jane, daughter of John Oliver.
 ,, 20, Margaret, daughter of Richard Bennett.
 ,, 28, Roger, son of Richard Game.

[1609.]

Jan. 6, Jane, daughter of William Robbins.
 ,, 13, Annis, daughter of Mr. John Clies.
 ,, 15, Elizabeth, daughter of Sampson Noye.
 ,, 25, Haniball, son of John Hughe.
 ,, 29, Anne, daughter of Thomas Cowlen, gent.
 ,, 29, Henrye, son of Garratt Lawnder.
March 5, William, son of John Gregor.
 ,, 5, Gillian, daughter of John James, Jun.
1609.
 ,, 30, Elizabeth, daughter of William Bocs.
April 2, William, son of German Geiffe.
 ,, 14, William, son of John Edwardes.
 ,, 30, Marye, daughter of Mr. James Dingley.
May 8, Henry, son of Mr. Roger Polkinhorue.
 ,, 14, William, son of George Lanyon, gent.
 ,, 25, John, son of William Anbone.
 ,, 25, Blanche, daughter of Thomas Leathe.
 ,, 28, Emanuell, son of Richard Hichen.
June 18, Agnes, daughter of John Hoskin, Jun.
 ,, 30, Elizabeth, daughter of Degorye Duke.
July 2, John, son of Edward Seese.
 ,, 9, George, son of John Uprighte.
 ,, 9, Ellen, daughter of Thomas Nighten.
 ,, 28, Grace, daughter of Mr. William Madren, Sen.
 ,, 30, Jane, daughter of William Edmondes.
Aug. 2, Paskus, daughter of John Mathew.
 ,, 27, Nicholas, son of Thomas Bowden.
Sept. 3, Alexander, son of Edmond Clies.
 ,, 3, The daughter of Edmond Clies.
 ,, 3, Elizabeth, daughter of Arthur Carter.
Oct. 1, —— —— of John Jenkin.
 ,, 5, Richard, son of William Madren, *alias* Richarde.
 ,, 8, John, son of William Bennett.
 ,, 15, Hugh, son of Mr. Joseph Limpanye.
 ,, 23, Adam, son of Adam Rawlin.
Nov. 8, Jane, daughter of William Lanyon, gent.
 ,, 12, Alse, daughter of Harry Foster.
Dec. 10, Thomas, son of John Luke.
 ,, 10, Agnes, daughter Andrew Bale.
 ,, 14, John, son Mr. John Game.

[1610.]

Jan. 7, Jane, base child of Nan Baude.
 ,, 17, Anthony, son of Mr. Robert Dunkin.
 ,, 19, William, son of Edward Lawrye.
 ,, 28, Agnes, daughter of John Talmenith.

PARISH OF MADRON.

Feb. 9, Gavrigau, son of Richard Game.
,, 18, Ellen, daughter of Robert Connell.*
,, 18, Alse, daughter of Nicholas Rider.
,, 21, John, son of Marten Champion.
,, 21, Sampson, son of Gilbert Harris.
,, 21, Thomas, son of John Hoskin.
,, 25, Elizabeth, daughter of John Stone.
1610.
Mar. 25, Henrye, son of John Rowan, *alias* Davye.
April 9, —— —— of John Luke, of Penzauc, smithe.
,, 15, Edward, son of Thomas William.
,, 22, Sibill, daughter of Wm. Legow, Jun.
May 13, Elizabeth, daughter of John Trick.
,, 13, Alse, daughter of German Morishe.
June 10, Elizabeth, daughter of Willm. Mulfra.
,, 17, Henry, son of John Roberte, *alias* Thomas.
July 1, Margaret, daughter of Thomas Bossoliack.
,, 8, John, son of John Duke.
,, 8, John, son of John Collins.
,, 13, John, son of Richard Lanyon, Esq.
,, 31, Sara, daughter of William Legow, the elder.
Aug. 5, John, son of Justinian Stephins.
,, 5, Tamzine,† daughter of John Sampson.
,, 19, Jane, daughter of Richard Tratt.
Sept. 2, —— son of Henry Clies.
,, 9, Elizabeth, daughter of Emannell Bluett.
Oct. 1, Margery, daughter of John Mathew, of St. Justo.
,, 8, Henry, son of William Watkins.
,, 14, Blanche, daughter of John Michell.
Nov. 1, William, son of Richard Michell.
,, 1, Amy, daughter of Richard Stephins.
,, 6, Mary, daughter of Thomas Fleming, gent.
,, 11, Mary, daughter of John Midlam.
,, 18, John, son of William Trefill.
,, 25, Peeter, son of John Trenhaile.
Dec. 3, Joane, daughter of John Ambell.
,, 9, William, son of John Howe.

[1611.]

Jan. 1, Emanuell, son of Hanibal Lavelis, gent.
,, 1, Nicholas, son of John Phillips.
,, 13, Joane, daughter of Robert James.
,, 14, Jane and Alse, daughters of John Webber, *alias* Vellye.
,, 20, Jane, daughter of Bartholomew Edye.
,, 20, Ann, daughter of Otes.
,, 23, Joane, daughter of Degory Duke.
,, 25, Nicholas, son of John Champion.
Feb. 8, Katherin, daughter of Teage Loddye.
,, 10, Thomas, son of Humphry Hutchins.
,, 20, Thomas, son of Thomas Harbert.
March 3, Richard, son of Richard Geeles.
,, 8, Frances, daughter of John Chinge.
,, 17, John, son of John Luke.

* One stroke of the last n has evidently been accidentally omitted in the original, so that the name might be read Connell. See Baptisms, 1615, April 8, &c.
† Written above Katherine erased.

Mar. 21, Ann, daughter of Mr. William Madren, Jun.
,, 21, Mary, daughter of Richard Game.
,, 21, Joane, daughter of John Slader.
1611.
April 7, Hercules, son of John Willye.
,, 7, Edward, son of Richard Hitchens.
,, 10, John, son of John Harbert.
,, 10, Amy, daughter of John Lawrenc.
,, 11, Alse, daughter of Mr. John Clies.
,, 14, —— —— of Peeter Cloke.
,, 14, Nicholas, son of —— Thomas, *alias* Angove.
,, 18, Elizabeth, daughter of Mr. Joseph Limpenye
,, 21, Humprye, son of Peeter Elfford.
,, 21, Katherin, daughter of John Honichurch, gent.
May 11, Mawde, daughter of John Sawndrie.
,, 16, Harrie, son of William Robins.
June 2, Kathern, daughter of John Edwardes.
,, 6, Thomas, son of Charles Ellis.
,, 22, Marie, daughter of Thomas Chinalls, gent.
,, 23, Sacharias, son of John Gregor.
July 7, Walter, son of William Lower, gent.
,, 7, Katherin, daughter of Edward Seese.
Sept. 9, Anne, daughter of Mathew Edes.
Oct. 13, William, son of Sampson Noie.
,, 13, Orpheus aud Ann, son and daughter of Thomas Booden.
Nov. 28, Phillip, daughter of Thomas Fleming, gent.
Dec. 8, William, son of Thomas Cowling, gent.
,, 17, Ellin, daughter of John Game, gent.

[1612.]

Feb. 6, Marten, son of Walther Bosaverne.
,, 10, Tonken, son of William Younge, gent.
,, 17, Frances, daughter of Pascoe Barne.
[+] 1612.
April 5, William, son of Richard Game.
,, 11, Thomas, son of Edward Bone.
June 14, Henery, son of William Edmonds.
July 12, Blanch, daughter of William Waters.
,, 20, Ursula, daughter of Will. Maddren, Jun.
,, 29, John, son of John Ambell.
,, 29, Elizabeth, daughter of Steven Barber.
,, 31, Tiberia, daughter of James Dingle, gent.
Sept. 19, Phillipp, son of Thomas Carne.
Oct. 16, John, son of Walter Tresies.
Nov. 6, Richard, son of William Ambone.
,, 8, Ann, daughter of Wm. Lego, Sen.
Dec. 15, Blanch, daughter of Richard Tratt.
,, 29, John, son of George Hutchens, Cler.

[1613.]

Jan. 20, Hugh, son of Thos. Chinals, gent.
March 9, Arthure, son of Ralph Noye.
,, 24, William, son of David Penleas.
1613.
April 5, Nicholas, son of Henery Hooper.
,, 7, Emmett, son of Willm. Robbins.
May 1, John, son of Adam Rawlyn.

REGISTER OF BAPTISMS.

May 4, Richard, son of Jo. Trick.
„ 5, Richard, son of Joseph Lympanie.
July 9, John, son of Robert Trencere, gent.
„ 11, Marye, daughter of Willm. Lego, Jun.
„ 24, John, son of Rodger Polkinghorne, gent.
Aug. 1, Ann, daughter of John Duncken.
Sept. 5, Blanch, daughter of Mathew Hawes.
„ 29, John, son of Edward Penhall.
Oct. 4, Blanch, daughter of Emanewell Blewett.
„ 24, John, son of John Harbert.
Nov. 1, Jane, daughter of John Saundrye.
„ 7, James, son of Nicholas Roberts.
„ 14, Nicholas, son of John Boswathack.
„ 17, Jane, daughter of John Phillipps.
„ 18, Sara, daughter of John Game.
„ 22, Thomas, son of John Clies, gent.
„ 22, Grace, daughter of Willm. Maddren, Jun.
„ 25, Nicholas, son of Richard Harrye.

[1614.]
Jan. 12, William, son of Willm. Tristram.
Feb. 15, Margery, daughter of Degorye Duke.
„ 16, Elizabeth, daughter of Arthure Edye.
„ 23, Ann, daughter of John Jeffrye.
Mar. 16, Margarett, daughter of Sampson Noye.
„ 16, Jane, daughter of Richard Hutchens.

1614.
May 26, Rodger, son of John Ellis.
June 10, Jane, daughter of Thomas Buttemore.
„ 13, Judeth, daughter of Tho. Mulford.
„ 19, Peeter, son of Richard Tratt.
July 17, Jane, daughter of Henery Fosse.
Aug. 24, William, son of Henery Penticost.
Sept. 1, Clarience, daughter of Walter Bosaverne.
„ 1, Thomas, base son of Jane Calensowe.
„ 7, John, son of Pascowe Barne.
„ 7, Christover, son of William Harrye.
„ 18, Barnard and William, sons of Rich. Giles.
Oct. 9, William, son of Anthony Tresies.
Dec. 25, Kathren, daughter of Willm. Symon.
„ 17*, Ann, daughter of Jo. Toncken.
„ 28, Mary, daughter of Edward Bone.

[1615.]
Jan. 1, Ann, daughter of John Champen.
„ 16, Bennett, son of Francis Lanyon.
Feb. 5, William, son of John Howe.
„ 5, Redigon, daughter of Edward Sandrye.
„ 26, William, son of Bartholomew Edye.
„ 28, Marye, daughter of John Harbert.
March 4, Walter, son of Walter Tresyse.
„ 4, Richard, son of Robart Fynnye.
„ 4, Grace, daughter of Thomas Leigh.

1615.
April 1, Richard, son of Wm. Lego, Sen.
„ 1, Sampson, son of Nowell Argoll.
„ 8, Pascus, daughter of Tho. Jeffrye.

April 23, John, son of James Pendeene.
„ 25, Edward, son of Joseph Lympanye.
May 5, Ebbott, daughter of Tho. Chinalls, gent.
„ 24, Margarett, daughter of Wm. Mulfra.
„ 28, Kathren, daughter of Willm. Edmonds.
„ 30, Ann, daughter of James Rawe.
June 14, William, son of Wm. Maddren, Jun.
„ 20, Richard, son of Tho. Argoll.
„ 25, Richard, son of Tho. Chesheere.
Sept. 10, John, son of James Fynnie.
„ 12, John, son of Richard, ye smith.
„ 15, Robert, son of John Sampson.
„ 17, Kathren, daughter of Rich. Nicklis.
Nov. 19, Elizabeth, daughter of Mr. John Clies.
Dec. 17, Thomas, son of William Boes.
„ 24, Mary, daughter of John Trick.

[1616.]
Jan. 3, Thomas, son of John Game, gent.
Feb. 16, Ann, daughter of Alexander Lanyon.
„ 22, Mathew, son of Degorye Duke.
„ 22, Elizabeth, daughter of Nicholas Roch.
„ 25, Richard, son of Richard Hutchens.
„ 25, Robert, son of John Boswathack.

1616.
April 8, Maurie, son of Robert Connell.
„ 13, English, daughter of Ralph Noye.
„ 18, John, son of Jermain Luke.
„ 28, Jane, daughter of Thomas Fleminge, gent.
May 7, John, son of John Taylor.
„ 19, James, son of William Umfry.
June 23, Sampson, son of Francis Lanyon.
July 14, Ann, daughter of Thomas Holla.
„ 14, Alice, daughter of Wm. Bennett.
Sept. 14, Kathren, daughter of Thomas William.
„ 15, Margarett, daughter of Arthur Edye.
Oct. 19, Mary, daughter of Nowell Argoll.
„ 27, John, son of John Luke.
„ 31, Walter,* son of Sampson Noye.
Nov. 24, Grace and Ann, daughters of Rich. Rosemorau.
Dec. 14, Emanewell, son of Jo. Hoskyn.
„ 22, Mary, daughter of John Mathewe.

[1617.]
Jan. 5, Francis, daughter of Emanewell Bluett.
Feb. 14, Noy, son of Thomas Chessheere.
Mar. 24, John, son of Richard Harrye.

1617.
April 6, John, son of John Hoskyn.
„ 20, Andrew, son of John Stone.
June 8, William, son of John Harbert.
„ 15, William, son of Rich. Bennett.
„ 19, Joane, daughter of Willm. Maddren, gent.
July 20, Francis, son of William Noseworthye, gent.
„ 27, Maude, daughter of Alexander Lanyon.

* Written in different hand and ink upon erasure of what appears to have been William.

* Sic.

PARISH OF MADRON.

Aug 24, John, son of William Lego, Jun.
„ 30, George, son of Willm. Mulfra.
Sept. 17, Elizabeth, daughter of Thomas Holla.
Oct. 8, Margarett, daughter of John Trick.
Nov. 30, Mary, daughter of Willm. Chirgwin.
Dec. 7, Symon, base child of Wm. Launder.

[1618.]

Jan. 2, Emanewell, son of Degory Duke.
March 4, Jane, daughter of Tho. Chinalls, gent.
„ 5, Nowell, son of Thomas Argoll.
„ 20, Joseph, son of James Wannell.
„ 20, Nowell, son of John Taylor.
1618.
April 7, William, son of Richard, the smith.
„ 14, Mary, daughter of John Taylor.
„ 28, Thomas, son of Emanewell Bluett.
May 10, Robert, son of Thomas Cowlinge, gent.
Aug. 24, Susan, daughter of John Clies, gent.
Sept. 15, Thomas, son of Thomas Jeffrye.
„ 22, Margarett, daughter of Wm. Bocs.
Oct. 10, Thomas, son of Thomas Bagg, gent.
Nov. 11, Jone, daughter of Peeter Nickles, Jun.

[1619.]

Jan. 2, William, son of John Stone.
„ 2, Symon, son of Alexander Bennett.
Feb. 10, John, son of Bennett Harrye.
„ 17, Dennys, son of Robert Connell.
„ 24, John, son of Thomas Releigh.
„ 28, John, son of Richard Jenckyn.
„ 28, Marye, daughter of John Sandry.
Mar. 10, Christover and Samewell, sons of Bartholomew Edye.
„ 10, John, son of William Umfrye.
„ 17, Ann, daughter of Rodger Polkinghorne, gent.
1619.
„ 27, Ann, daughter of William Noseworthye.
April 13, William, son of Thomas Becalegg.
June 20, Jane, daughter of Richard Bennett.
„ 26, William, son of Richard Champen.
July 4, John, son of John Rawe.
„ 11, Thomas, son of Henery Foster.
„ 15, Richard, son of John Sampson.
„ 27, Elizabeth, daughter of Richard Hutchens.
1620.
May 13, Jane, daughter of Mr. Edward Mundaye.
„ 13, Kathren, daughter of Pascowe Barne.
June 6, Marye, daughter of Umfrie Hutchens.
Sept. 14, Alice, daughter of John Trick.
Nov. 5, Margarett, daughter of John Clyes, gent.
„ 10, Bridgett, daughter of James Fynnye.

[1621.]

Jan. 12, Jane, daughter of Richard John.
Feb. 19, Marye, daughter of John Mathew.
„ 26, Nathaniell, son of Lewes Hocken.
Mar. 11, John, son of Alexander Bennett.

Mar. 22, John, son of Arthure Edye.
„ 24, John, son of William Bone.
1621.
April 8, Thomas and Joane, son and daughter of John Stone.*
„ 18, Margarett, daughter of Arthure Edye.
May 13, William, son of John Duke.
June 24, Jane. daughter of William Mulfra.
July 3, John, son of John Champen.
Sept. 9, John, son of John Hoskyn.
„ 17, James, son of John Bodye.
Nov. 18, Margarett, daughter of Tho. Baggs, gent.
„ 30, Margarett, daughter of Thomas Chinalls, gent.
Dec. 8, Marye, daughter of William Harrye.
„ 14, Jane, daughter of Nowell Argoll.

[1622.]

Jan. 6, Joane, daughter of Robert Connell.
„ 13, William, son of Richard Bennett.
Feb. 10, Sampson, son of Walter Pender.
Mar. 13, Thomas, son of William Chirgwine.
„ 24, Richard, son of Will. Maddern, gent.
1622.
May 12, Alice, daughter of Thomas Cowlinge, gent.
„ 26, Joane, daughter of John Dunckin, gent.
July 6, John, son of Thomas Fleminge, gent.
Sept. 29, Peter, son of Alexander Lanyon.
Oct. 6, Joane, daughter of Davy Lanyon.
„ 13, Ann, daughter of Richard Jenkyn.
„ 18, Susan, daughter of Thomas Hosken.
„ 21, Bridgett, daughter of Bennett Harrye.
Nov. 9, John, son of Reignauld John.
„ 19, Ann, daughter of John Sampson, gent.
Dec. 8, John, son of Alexander Bennett.
„ 24, Maurish, son of Maddren Lego.

[1623.]

Jan. 13, William, son of Richard West.
Feb. 20, Marye, daughter of William Launder.
„ 26, Constance, daughter of Richard Lanyon.
Mar. 12, William, son of James Hearle.
1623.
April 24,† Alice, daughter of Robert Trewren.
May 10, John, son of Walter Mitchell.
„ 17, John, son of Samewell Edye.
June 12, William, son of John Duke.
„ 29, John, son of Mathew Weary.
July 16, Ann, daughter of Rich. Champen.
Aug. 11, Margarett, daughter of Robert Duncken, Cler.
Sept. 8, Kathren, daughter of John Clies, gent.
„ 8, Elizabeth, daughter of John Duncken, gent.
„ 8, John, son of Henery Lutye.
„ 14, Thomas, son of Thomas Holla.

---

* This entry has been erased, and "Richard and Sarah, son and daughter of John Stone," written above it in a different hand and ink.
† The 4 is an addition in a different ink.

REGISTER OF BAPTISMS.

Oct. 28, Thomas, son of William Kostell.
Nov. 9, John, son of John Polkinghorne.

[1624.]

Jan. 7, Marye, daughter of Richard John.
,, 11, Ralfo, son of Thomas Mathew.
,, 23, Robert, son of John Harbert.
,, 28, Reynauld, son of John Boswathack.
Feb. 10, Marye, daughter of William Anthonye.
Mar. 30,* Clarence, daughter of Rich. West.

1624.

Mar. 25, William, son of Richard West.
May 11, Duens, daughter of Thomas Nighten.
July 20, William, son of Thomas Sudgeo.
Aug. 15, William, son of William Mulfra.
Sept. 17, William, son of Robert Trewren.
,, 21, Christaboll, daughter of Symon Francis.
Oct. 5, Grace, daughter of James Bonithon, gent.
Nov. 26, Thomas, son of Thomas George.
Dec. 29, Ann, daughter of John Reignald.
,, 21,† Margarett, daughter of William Maddren, gent.

[1625.]

Jan. 9, Mary,‡ daughter of Robert Fynnyo.
,, 23, Elizabeth, daughter of Ralph Noye.
Feb. 6, Ann, daughter of Robert Carne.
,, 21, John, son of Nicholas Genver.
,, 13, Mary, daughter of Samewoll Edye.
Mar. 12, Ann, daughter of Nowell Argoll.
,, 13, Marye, daughter of Alexander Bennett.

1625.

April 6, John, son of Bennett Bone.
,, 30, Ann, daughter of Bennett Cotha.
June 30, John, son of Paskowe Barne.
July 13, William, son of Richard West.
Aug. 10, John, son of Annanias Horsford.
Sept. 4, William, son of William Mulfra.
,, 11, Marerye, daughter of Thomas Jencken.
,, 18, Roger, son of John Tompkyn.
Oct. 9, Chesten, daughter of William Kestell.
Nov. 3, John, son of Will. Boskoninge.
,, 6, Thomas, son of John Benver.
Dec. 16, William, son of Edward Lego.
,, 30, Anthonye, son of Anthony Gubbs.

[1626.]

Feb. 27, William, son of William Robbyns.
March 6, Susanna, daughter of William Jenckyn.
,, 9, Margery, daughter of John Bosaverne.
,, 19, Mary, daughter of Richard Penrose.

1626.

April 20, Ann, daughter of William Rawlyn.
May 7, Ann, daughter of Tho. Glover.
June 10, Richard, son of John Hoskyn.
,, 11, Thomas, son of John Harbert.

June 21, Noye, son of Maddren Champen.
July 16, Mary, daughter of Thomas Beccalogge.
Sept. 3, Elizabeth, daughter of Thomas Newton.
,, 10, Avis, daughter of Robert Trewren.
Oct. 20, Robert, son of Jermaine Luke.
Nov. 9, John, son of William Anthonye.
Dec. 6, Thomas, son of William Harrye.

[1627.]

Jan. 1, Grace, daughter of Nicholas Maddren, gent.
,, 14, Cornelius, son of Cornelius Cross.
Feb. 7, Kathren, daughter of Thomas Sudgeo.
,, 14, Annys, daughter of Thomas Treganhorne.
,, 22, Henery, son of William Davye.
March.. Dyna, daughter of Emanuell Bluett.

1627.

April 20, Margery, daughter of —— Gaaye, gent.
May 20, Marye, daughter of Samewell Edye.
,, 28, John, son of Martyn Thomas.
June 15, Susan, daughter of Thomas Jencken.
July 1, John, son of Gabriell Somer.
,, 8, Thomas, son of James Dingle.
Aug. 14, Nicholas, son of Richard Tom.
Sept. 15, Thomas, son of William Jeffrye.
Oct. 20, Alice, daughter of Thomas Holla.
Dec. 9, Thomas, son of Richard Penrose.
,, 20, John, son of John Polzewe.

[1628.]

Jan. 12, Mary, daughter of Richard Lamyn.
,, 24, John, son of William Buryan.
,, 30, William, son of Symon Synckowe.
Feb. 4, George, base child of George Bluett.
,, 12, Robert, son of William Rodda.
,, 14, Ann, daughter of Nowell Argoll.
,, 23, Mary, daughter of John Holla.
March 2, William, son of Robert Trowren.
,, 8, Margarett, daughter of Riugnald John.
,, 14, Ann, base child of Edward Bennett.
,, 20, Elizabeth, base child of —— Syer.

1628.

April 10, Ann, daughter of David Lanyon.
,, 30, Joane, daughter of Alexander Lanyon.
May 18, John, son of Samewell Sissell.
June 15, William, son of William Nicholls, gent.
Aug. 1, William, son of William Hatherley, gent.
,, 10, William, son of Will. Chirgwyn.
,, 18, Bennett and Pascowe, sons of Erasmus Pascowe.
Feb.* 10, Elizabeth, daughter of Will. Jencken.
Oct. 4, William, son of John Stephens.
Nov. 10, Elizabeth, daughter of Ralph Morish.
,, 12, Phillipp, daughter of Nicholas Maddren, gent.
,, 16, John, son of Honerye Tremenheere.
Dec. 28, Joane, daughter of Anthonye Gubbs, gent.

---

* Sic. † Sic.
‡ Written in a different hand and ink above Bridgett erased.

• Sic.

PARISH OF MADRON.

[1629.]

Jan. 1, William, son of Gabriell Somer.
Feb. 14, John, son of Richard Cunnacke.
 ,, 20, Susan, daughter of Prudence Jencken, spur.
 ,, 26, Honor, daughter of John Tremellyn.
Mar. 14, Annis, daughter of Tho. Roberts.
[+] 1629.
April 12, John, son of Edward Paskoe.
May 3, Katherin, daughter of John Cowlinge, gent.
June 14, Ann, daughter of Reignald John.
July 10, Richard, son of Richard Raw.
Aug. 20, John, son of Samewell Edye.
Sept. 5, Ann, daughter of Henry Pencast.
Oct. 16, Richard, son of Thomas Cock.
Nov. 20, John, son of Maddern Robbyn.
Dec. 14, William, son of William Anthonye.

[1630.]

Jan. 6, Mary, daughter of Gabriell Somer, gent.
Feb. 4, James and Joane, children of Nicholas Mitchell.
 ,, 16, John, son of Simon Sinckowe.
 ,, 23, Henry, son of Henry Paskowe.
Mar. 10, Ann, daughter of William Rawlin.
 ,, 20, Mary, daughter of Richard Connack.
 ,, 24, William, son of William Harry.
1630.
 ,, 29, Mary, daughter of John Harbert.
April 23, Roger, son of Roger Polkinghorne, gent.
May 5, John, son of William Davy.
 ,, 7, Elizabeth, daughter of John Keat, gent.
June 10, Elizabeth, daughter of Paskoe Barne.
Aug. 5, John, son of John Randall.
[Sept.] .. Ann, daughter of Robert Carne.
[Oct.] .. William, son of William Launder.
[Nov.] 8, Robert, son of William Trencere.

[1631.]

Jan. 20, John, son of John Polzew.
 ,, 27, Mary, daughter of John James.
 ,, 28, Sampson, son of William Battyn.
Feb. 6, Francis, son of Willim Roskymmer, gent.
 ,, 6, Alice, daughter of Thomas Holla.
 ,, 13, Thomas, son of James Troloweth.
 ,, 27, Sara, daughter of John Cowling, gent.
March 4, Ann, daughter of William Hockyn.
 ,, 11, Katheren, daughter of Mr.Thomas Jenckyn.
1631.
April 17, John, son of William Harry.
 ,, 22, Alice, daughter of John Umfry.
May 19, John, son of John Keat, gent.
June 12, Mary, daughter of William Rawlyn.
 ,, 19, Katheren, daughter of Ananyas Hosford.
July 16, Elizabeth, daughter of Reignald John.
Aug. 10, William, son of John Hoskyn.
 ,, 14, John, son of William Nicholls, gent.
Sept. 24, Grace, daughter of Nicholas Maddern, gent.
 ,, 29, Thomas, son of Nicholas Flemynge, gent.

Nov. 13, John, son of Martyne Sampson.
Dec. 7, Jicholas,* son of John Thomas.

[1632.]

Jan. 16, John, son of Madderne Hugh.
Feb. 4, Ann, daughter of William Jonckyn.
 ,, 6, Robert,† son of Sampson Hollier.
 ,, 14, Gillian, daughter of William Hockyn.
 ,, 20, Salomon, son of John Bonner.
 ,, 28, Thomas, son of Gabriell Somer, gent.
Mar. 10, Richard, son of Nowell Argall.
 ,, 13, Thomas, base son of Alice Launder.
 ,, 23, Henry, son of Henry Frosso.
1632.
April 16, Blanch, daughter of John Lamerton.
 ,, 30, Henry, son of Samewell Sissoll.
May 20, Thomas, son of John Cowlinge, [gent.]
 ,, 20, John, son of John Cowlinge, the elder.
July 10, William, son of William Jeoffrye.
 ,, 16, Ann, daughter of Thomas Noye.
Aug. 3, Nicholas,‡ son of Edward Edwards.
Oct. 14, Katheren, daughter of Robert Carne.
Nov. 8, John, son of William Anthonye.

[1633.]

Jan. 22, Eliassaph, son of Alexander Daniell.
 ,, 30, William, base son of William Williams, of Waymoth.
Feb. 9, Nicholas, son of Nicholas Flemynge, gent.
 ,, 12, Penticost, son of John Hoskyn.
 ,, 22, David, base son of Robert Watkins.
Mar. 17, Elizabeth, daughter of Mr.Thomas Jonckyn.
 ,, 17, Susan, daughter of Thomas Roberts, the glover.
 ,, 24, Mary, the daughter of William Trenecre.
 ,, 24, Ann, daughter of Richard Connack.
1633.
April 4, Jane, daughter of Maddern Longoe.
 ,, 6, Francis, son of John Keat, gent.
May 1, Grace, daughter of Thomas George.
June 2, Roger, son of Anthony Gubbs, gent.
Aug. 11, Elizabeth, daughter of Richard Luddra.
 ,, 18, Nicholas, son of William Nicholls, gent.
Sept. 1, William, son of John Champion.
 ,, 8, Mary, daughter of Thomas Noye.
Oct. 6, John, son of William Teage.
Nov. 12, Richard, son of John Umfrye.
 ,, 16, Elizabeth, daughter of John Cowlinge,gent.
Dec. 10, Ann, daughter of Mychaell Skynner.

[1634.]

Jan. 1, Thomas, son of William Jenckyn.
Feb. 9, Elizabeth, daughter of William Keylie.
 ,, 16, Nicholas, son of John Benner.
 ,, 20, William, son of William Tresvenack.
March 9, William, son of David Lanyon.

---

* Sic.   † Written in a different hand and ink upon erasure.
‡ "Nicholas, the son," is written in different hand and ink upon erasure of " .... the daughter."

REGISTER OF BAPTISMS.

March 9, Elizabeth, daughter of Umphrye Martyn.
,, 16, Margarett, daughter of John Nooall.
,, 19, Houer, daughter of George Noye.
1634.
April 13, Peeter, son of William Chergwine.
May 13, John, son of William Lander.
,, 20, Richard, son of William Antonye.
July 7, Elizabeth, daughter of John Cowlinge, the elder.
,, 11, John, son of Nicholas Fleminge, gent.
Aug. 6, Mary, daughter of John Mulfra.
Sept. 7, Phillipp,* daughter of William Nicholls, gent.
,, 12, John, son of Alexander Daniell, gent.
Oct. 13, Richard, son of William Treneere.
Dec. 16, Roger,* son of John Lamerton.
[1635.]
Jan. 1, Margarett,* daughter* of Samewell Sissell.
,, 10, Thomas, base son of Thomas Martyn and Margarett Trelill.
,, 16, Phillipp, base son of Will. Clyes and Alice Lander.
Feb. 15, David, son of Thomas Grosse, gent.
,, 20, John, son of Ralph Morish.
,, 24, Richard, base son of Alexander Clyes and Eliz. Lawrence.
March 1, Sampson, son of Authonye Gubbs, gent.
,, 10, Alice, daughter of Bennett Angwine.
,, 17, Henory, base son of John Stinian and Alice Michell.
1635.
April 4, Martyne, son of Martyne Bosaverno.
,, 26, Francis, son of John Cowlinge, gent.
May 2, Margarett, daughter of John Kete, Clerke.
June 6, John, son of William Harrye.
July 10, Grace, daughter of Pawle Nicholls.
Aug. 13, Annanias, son of Annanias Horsford.
Nov. 10, Roger, son of Nicholas Fleming, gent.
Dec. 28, Elizabeth, daughter of John Oliver.
[1636.]
Jan. 20, Jane, daughter of John Newman, gent.
Feb. 2, Mary, daughter of Francis Logg.
,, 2, Mary, daughter of John Batten.
,, 20, William and John, sons of Willm. Jenckyn.
,, 26, John, son of Thomas Jenckyn.
Mar. 20, Joseph, son of John Beuver.
1636.
May 2, Thomas, son of Thomas Morish.
,, 10, Thamsyn, base child of Alexander Clyes.
June 5, Kathren, daughter of John Polsewo.
,, 6, Thomas, son of Ralph Morish.
July 6, John, son of George Phillipps.
Aug. 9, John, son of John Mulfra.
,, 9, Thomas, base son of Thos. Stevens and Kathren Williams.

Sept. 7, Nicholas, son of James Loose.
,, 7, Nicholas, son of Thomas Burch.
,, 11, Richard, base son of Richard Buckler and Eliz. Bar[bor.?]
Oct. 9, Robart, son of Robart Coleman, gent.
Nov. 6, Elizabeth, daughter of John Pendone.
,, 13, Ann, daughter of Mathew Hosken.
,, 20, Elizabeth, daughter of Richard Trick.
Dec. 4, John, son of John Stevens.
[1637.]
Jan. 1, Elizabeth, daughter of Nicholas Fleming, gent.
,, 1, Grace, daughter of William Sudgeow.
,, 28, George, son of Michell Sparnan.
Feb. 4, Ann, daughter of William Lemyn.
,, 11, John, son of Digorye Nicholas.
,, 18, Grace, daughter of Luke Tollar.
,, 25, Henory and Ann, son and daughter of Nich. [Rawlyn.]
Mar. 13, Ann, daughter of Samewell Sissell.
,, 21, Robert, son of Robert Toncken.
[+] 1637.
,, 29, Thomas, son of John Lamerton.
April 23, Jane, daughter of Nicholas Boswnthack.
May 24, Grace, daughter of Ralph Morish.
,, 28, Jane, daughter of Thomas Morish.
June 3, Thomas, son of John Cowlinge, ye elder, and Agnis, his wife.
,, 4, Agnes, daughter of John Kete, gent.
,, 7, Blanch, daughter of Halenight Stephens.
,, 18, Elizabeth, daughter of Richard Duke.
July 9, George, son of John Umphrye.
,, 9, Margaret, daughter of John Batten.
,, 16, Peeter, son of Thomas Jenckyn
,, 16, Martine, ye base son of Martine Rodda, begoten upon ye body of Margaret Lawrence.
,, 21, Joseph, son of William Bellamye.
,, 21, Ralph, base son of Alice Williams, servant to Ralph Harry.
,, 23, Margery, daughter of Reignald John.
,, 28, Kathren, daughter of John Hugh.
,, 30, Margaret, daughter of Thomas Bond.
Aug. 6, George, son of Allexander Daniell, gent.
,, 6, Thomas, son of William Jeofery.
,, 28, Margaret, daughter of Martine Bosaverne.
Sept. 3, Ann and Katheren, daughters of William Rawlyn.
,, 3, Peter, son of Zacharias George.
,, 10, Richard, son of Maderne Leagoe.
,, 10, Blanch, daughter of Henry Tremynheere.
,, 10, Elizabeth, daughter of Thomas Roberts.
,, 21, Redygon, daughter of William Younge.
Oct. 18, Ruth, daughter of William Treneere.
Nov. 5, Dorothye, daughter of Mr. William Nicholls.
,, 5, Mary, daughter of Mr.* Thomas Lanyon.
,, 5, Charitye, daughter of William Micchaell.

---

* Written in different hand and ink upon erasure.   * Superadded.

PARISH OF MADRON.

Nov. 5, Gilbert, base son of Gilbert Bishopp, begoten on the body of Elizabeth Taylor.
„ 17, John, son of Mr. Richard Keygwin.
„ 19, Thomas, son of Arthur Noye.

[1638.]

Feb. 7, Richard, son of Nicholas John, gent.*
„ 13, Ruth, daughter of Robert Meldren.
„ 21, David, son of David Penlease.
March 5, Blanch, daughter of Mr. Nicholas Flemynge
„ 18, Robert, son of Robert Kerrowe.
„ 24, Elizabeth, base child of Elizabeth Amye; Richard Duke, reputed father.
1638.
„ 31, Alice, daughter of Thomas Cock.
April 1, Lancelot, son of John Benallack, ye younger.
May 6, Sampson, son of William Rodda.
„ 27, Constance, daughter of Mr. John Cowlinge.
June 10, Barnard, son of David Lanyon.
„ 10, Kathern, daughter of John Jacka.
„ 10, Nicholas, son of Henry Tregerthen.
July 22, Mary, daughter of John Rodda, ye younger.
„ 29, Sampson, son of Thomas Noye.
Aug. 5, William, son of Phillip Paskoe.
„ 19, Richard, son of John Stephens, *alias* Stinion.
Sept. 10, Susanna, daughter of John Stephens, *alias* Rowe.
„ 16, Jermyn, son of John George.
„ 16, Elizabeth, daughter of John Battyn.
Oct. 21, Joseph, son of Richard Bose.
Nov. 18, Dyna, base child of Blanch Holla; John Nicholls, reputed father.

[1639.]

Jan. 1, John, son of John Benver.
„ 13, Robert, son of Mr. William Nicholls.
Feb. 16, Agnis, daughter of Richard Trick.
„ .. Mary, daughter of Mr. John Kete.
„ 24, Richard, son of Richard Rosemorran.
March 3, Thomas, son of Thomas Hacker.
„ 10, John, son of Thomas Pryor.
„ 10, Joseph, son of William Jenckynge.
1639.
„ 25, William, son of Thomas Calenzoe.
April 5, Ann, daughter of Nicholas Flemynge.
„ 13, Sara, daughter of Tho. Rawline.
„ 21, Phillip, daughter of Mr. Richard Keygwin.
May 1, Joane, daughter of Nicholas Rawlyne.
„ 12, Beniamyn, son of Phillip Poryman.
June 9, Prudence, daughter of Grigorye Nicholls.
„ 16, Honor, daughter of John James, *alias* Dreanegles.
„ 21, William, son of David Penlease.
„ 25, William, son of George Noye.
Aug. 4, Tobyas, son of Gabriell Summer.
„ 11, Richard, son of John Polscive.
July 28, Walter, son of Martyn Bosavern.*

Sept. 15, Grace, daughter of Mr. Henry Polkinghorne
Oct. 6, John, son of John Stinian.
Dec. 2, Honor, daughter of John Lamerton.
„ 7, John, son of Thomas Sampson.
„ 22, Tiberia, daughter of Thomas Jenkyn.
„ 23, Steeven, son of Thomas, the potter.
„ 26, Steeven, son of William Prust.

[1640.]

Jan. 12, Thomas, son of George Blewet.
„ 22, Thomas, son of Arthur Noye.
Feb. 3, Alice, daughter of John Stephens, *alias* Roe.
Mar. 13, Thomas, base son of Edward Burroes, begoten on the body of Mary Stone.
„ 21, William, son of Mr. John Cowlinge.
1640.
May 20, John, son of Nicholas Boswathack.
June 6, John, son of Thomas Kerrowe.
„ 28, John, son of Othonell Wale.
July 12, Mary,* daughter of Mr. Richard Keygwin.
„ 19, Elizabeth, daughter of Mr. William Nicholls
Aug. 9, Grace, daughter of Mr. Henry Polkinghorn
„ 16, William, son of Henrye Tremenh[ecre.]
„ 24, Robart,‡ son of William Roskorlath.
„ 31, John, son of James Trenwith.
Sept. 2, Thomas, son of Cathrin .... †
.... 2, Thomas, son of Thomas Hubbord.

[1641.]

Jan. 8, William, son of Thomas Noye.
Feb. 2, Grace, daughter of Mr. John Kete.
„ 20, Sackfeild, son of Thomas Roberts.
[+] 1641.
April 23, John, son of John Barnes, and Ann, his wife.
May 21, John, son of Richard Trick, and English.
June 9, Jane, daughter of Samewell Sissell, and Margarett.
July 25, John, son of Richard Rosemoran. and Elizabeth.
Aug. 1, John, son of Robert Bennett, and Christian.
„ 8, John, son of John Lanyon, and Ann.
Sept. 12, Ann, daughter of William Prust, and Elizabeth.
„ 26, Kathrein, daughter of Thomas Sampson, and Jane.
Oct. 28, Otts, base son of Joane Lawrence.
„ 21, Isabolla,§ daughter of Richard Keigwin. and Margery.
Nov. 4, Blanch, daughter of Hen. Polkenhorne, and Thomazin.
„ 14, Ann, daughter of Robert Mildren, and Aunys.
„ 21, Jone, daughter of John Holla, and Alice.
Dec. 5, William, son of William Lawrenc, and Nicholl.

---

* This entry is an interlineation in a different hand and ink.

* Written in a different hand over Phillip erased. ‡ — over John.
§ — over Constance.
† Added in a different hand and ink on margin at foot of page.

REGISTER OF BAPTISMS.

[1642.]

Jan. 1, Thomas, son of Thomas Jenckyn, and Ann.
„ 30, John, son of Thomas Fenny, and Margarett.
Feb. 10, Ralph, son of John Udye, and Avis.
„ 27, Jermyn, son of Will. Michell, and Joane.
March 5, Thomas, son of Richard Luddrah, and Elizabeth.*
„ 13, Thomas, son of John Bodye, Jun., and Jane.
„ 13, Anthony, son of Phillip Lanyon, and Agnes.
1642.
July 2, Sicely, daughter of Gilbert Bishopp.*
Aug. 1, Richard, son of John Stephens, and Luce.

[1643.]

Jan. 10, Oner, daughter of William Nicholl, and Jone.
1643.
April 18, Thomas, son of Thomas Lanyon, gent.†
„ 24, Oner, daughter of Thomas Lego, and Alice.
Dec. 24, Ann, daughter of William Toncken.

1644. **[1645.]**
Feb. 7, Was borne Edward, son of Edward Primerose.‡
[1645.]
.... 16, Sara, daughter of Thomas Lego.
.... 7, Mary, daughter of Maddren Lego.
.... 18, James and Ursula, son and daughter of Thomas C[allenzeow.?]
„ 22, Blanch, daughter of John Hugh.
„ 28,§ Richard, son of Martine Rodda.
Nov. 1, Grace, daughter of William Toncken.
„ 2, Mary, daughter of Ralph Thompson.
Oct.|| 12, Debora, daughter of John George.
„ 13, Margarett, daughter of William Lodye.

[1646.]

Jan. 24, John, son of William Diggens.
[+] 1646.
April 12, Jane, daughter of James Trenwith.
„ 17, Joane, daughter of Henry Edmonds.
May 31, Bennatt, son of Arundell Sakerley.
June 21, Marrian, daughter of Thomas Hacker.
„ 21, Anne, daughter of Lewes Roberts.
„ 23, Thomas, son of James Tregerthen.
„ 28, William, son of William Penticost.
„ 28, Margarett, daughter of John Battyn.
„ 28, John, son of John Mathew.
July 24, Robert, son of John Kete, gent.
Aug. 4, Dyna, daughter of Reynold Bose.
„ 4, Mary, daughter of Grace Foster, spur.
„ 6, Henry, son of Nicholas Hoskyn.
„ 14, Elizabeth, daughter of Richard Keygwin.

* This entry is an interlineation in a different hand and ink.
* Written in a different hand on blank space after Aug. 1, 1642. Dated 1643.
† There are no entries for the year 1644 with the exception of this, which is an addition in a different hand.
‡ Altered from 21. || Sic.

Aug. 16, John, son of John Pollard.
„ 24, Mary, daughter of William Mulfra.
„ 27, Peter, son of Abraham G[r]egar.
„ 30, John, son of Thomas Jenken.
Sept. 5, William, son of Walter Noye.
„ 6, Jone, daughter of William Lawrey.
„ .. William, son of Jo....
„ .. Jone, daughter of ....
„ 16, Mary, daughter of ....
„ 20, John, son of John ....
„ 25, James and John, sons of William Williams.
Oct. 4, Richard, son of John Saundry.
„ 11, Jone, daughter of John Boddy, Jun.
„ 25, Avis, daughter of Walter Reede.
„ 30, Richard, son of Thomas Polkenhorne.
Nov. 8, Thomas, son of James Nicholl.
„ 22, John, son of Thomas Morrish.
„ 22, Elizabeth, daughter of Thomas Pike, gent.
„ 29, Thomasine, daughter of William Sampson.
Dec. 26, Tobias, son of William Cowlinge.
„ 27, Alice, daughter of Nicholas Rawlings.

[1647.]

Jan. 3, Richard Lamyn, son of Will. Lamyn.
„ 10, Jane, daughter of Robert Harry.
„ 24, Henry, son of Joseph Wannell.
„ 24, Anthony and William, sons of John Tirroll.
„ 24, Jone, daughter of John Trenecre.
„ 24, Jane, daughter of William Hall.
Feb. 21, Nicholas, son of Richard Trick.
„ 28, Margarett, daughter of Tho. Callenzeow.
March 7, Jone, daughter of Thomas Bonithon.
„ 14, Thomas, son of William Noye.
„ 14, John, son of Robert James.
„ 21, Margery, daughter of Henry Tregerthen.

[+] 1647.
„ 28, Thomas, son of William John.
„ 28, Sara, base child of William Manly.
„ 31, Anne, daughter of Bennatt Gennens.
April 25, Alice, daughter of Joseph Gubbs, gent.
„ 25, Mildren, daughter of Edward Box.
„ 25, Michell, daughter of Richard Rosemorran.
May 2, Mary, daughter of William Diggens.
„ 2, Alice, daughter of John Harrie.
„ 16, Elizabeth, daughter of John Robarts.
„ 16, Mary, daughter of Giles Trebehar.
„ 30, Robart, son of Henry Edmonds.
June 13, Mary, daughter of Richard Noye.
July 4, Jane, daughter of Thomas Symons.
Aug. 14, Francis, son of Robart Colman.
„ 29, Martha, daughter of John Blazeris.
„ .. Thom ....
„ .. Elizabeth, daughter of Jo. ....
Oct. 10, John, son of James Newham.
„ 16, William, son of John Legowe.
„ 16, Jane, daughter of John Kete, gent.
Nov. 28, Rebecca, daughter of John Tremenheare.
Dec. 12, Blanch, daughter of Thomas Bond.
„ 26, Anne, daughter of Emett Robins.

PARISH OF MADRON.

[1648.]

Jan. 23, Alice, daughter of Nicholas Bosewarrack.
Feb. 12, Arthur, son of Walter Saundry.
,, 12, Grace, daughter of John Hitchens.
,, 13, Emanuell, son of William Jenken.
,, 13, Jone, daughter of John Meaior.
,, 27, Katherine, daughter of Morish Carne.
March 5, Robecca, daughter of William Ponticost.
,, 11, Margarett, daughter of John Cock.
,, 18, Robart, son of John Finny.
,, 18, William, son of William Battyn.
,, 18, Margaret, daughter of Arundell Shackerly.

1648.

April 25, Agnes, daughter of Martyn Rodda.
,, 29, Margarett, daughter of John Barnes.
May 13, Nicholas, son of William Michell.
,, 13, Mary, base child of John Prust.
,, 28, —— child of Thomas Callensow.
June 8, John, son of John Stephens.
July 1, Walter, son of Oliver Wolcock.
,, 15, John, son of Nicholas Phillipp.
,, 15, Thomas, son of Thomas Thomas.
,, 30, John, son of Thomas Jeffry.
Aug. 6, Mary, daughter of Maddern Legawe.
,, 13, Honor, daughter of Nicholas Hoskyn.
,, 20, John, son of Henry Dunkin.
,, 27, William, son of William Mulfra, of Gulvall.
,, 27, Alice, daughter of William Gies.
Sept. 3, John, son of William Couchie.
,, 3, Bernard, son of Jasper James.
,, 10, Agnes, daughter of Sampson Lanion.
,, 30, John, son of Thomas Polkenhorne.
Nov. 5, Stephen, son of William Luke.
,, 11, John, son of George Richard.
,, 13, Hugh, son of William Lanion, of Gulvall.
,, 13, Margarett, daughter of Henry Chinalls.
,, 17, ... of John Sampson, the younger.
,, 20, Anne, daughter of Methusala Rodda.
Dec. 3, Paschow, son of Paschow Tincombe.
,, 3, Margarett, daughter of Thomas Foster.
,, 31, Agnes, daughter of Bennatt Lanion.

[1649.]

Jan. 14, Francis, son of Stephen Cock.
,, 14, Phillipp, the daughter of Degory, the cooper.
,, 20, Mary, daughter of William Noye.
Feb. 4, Jane, daughter of William James.
,, 11, Margaret, daughter of John Batyn.
,, 24, Charles,* son of Robert Colman.
,, 25, Charles, son of John Luke.
,, 26, John, son of John Tonken.
,, 26, Willmet, daughter of Richard Martyn.
March 5, Jane, daughter of Nicholas Jasper.
,, 18, Humphry,* son of Thomas Lamone.
,, 19, Jane,* daughter of Peter Boase.
,, 19, John, son of Walter Noye.

Mar. 20, Mary, daughter of Gilbert Ficks.

1649.

,, 25, Thomas, son of Marten Sampson.
April .. .... daughter of John Mulfra.
,, 11, Mary, daughter of John Richards.*
,, ... son of Morish Connell.
,, ... of William Honichurch, gent.
,, 20, Peter, son of Thomas Hacker.
,, .. Edward, son of John George.
,, .. Alice, daughter of William Lawrey.
,, .. Elizabeth, daughter of John Stephens.
May .. John, son of Richard Newhall.
,, .. Robart, son of Marke Lanion.
,, .. Honor, daughter of James Nicholl.
,, .. Henry, son of John Tremenheare.
June .. Elizabeth, daughter of Nich. Rawlen.
,, .. Anne, daughter of John ——
,, .. Susan, daughter of William Christopher.
July .. Charles, son of John Legawe.
,, .. Anne, daughter of John Stephens, alias Rowe.
,, .. Jone, daughter of Thomas Rawling.
,, .. Alexander, son of John John, of Gulvall.
,, 29, Richard, son of Richard Legawe.
Aug. 26, Tho., son of Arthur Noye.
,, 26, Alice, daughter of Peter John.
Sept. 1, Jone, daughter of Francis Lanion.
,, 2, Ellouer, daughter of Richard Banfield.
,, 9, John, son of John Seese.
,, 9, Roger, son of Joell Garratt.
,, 16, Margarett, daughter of John Lanion.
,, .. Ann, daughter of Francis Lawrey.
Oct. 7, Mary, daughter of John Trencere.
Nov. 11, Thomas, son of John Meager.
Dec. 9, Roger, son of John Sampson, the younger.
,, 23, Anne, daughter of John Cossens.
,, 25, George, son of George Cloake.
,, 26, Margory, daughter of Henry Dunking.
,, 27, Stephen, son of William Jenken.

[1650.]

Jan. 5, Hugh, son of William Fosse.
,, 5, Anne, daughter of John Ellis.
,, 6, Thomas, son of Thomas Robarts.
,, 6, Anne, daughter of James Pike.
,, 19, John, son of John Tregunnow.
Feb. 2, Margarett, daughter of John Maddern.
,, 16, Bennatt, son of Richard Trick.
,, 25, Mary, daughter of Martyn Gwonnapp.
,, 25, Was borne Thomasine, daughter of John Hitchens.†
March 2, Grace, daughter of Henry Edmonds.

1650.

April 7, Thomas, son of Richard Rosemorran.
,, 7, Elizabeth, daughter of Nathanaell Trenerry

---

* Re-written.
* This entry is an addition in different hand and ink.
† This entry is an interlineation in a different hand and ink.

REGISTER OF BAPTISMS.

April 22, Was borne Somer, son of William Honichurch, gent.*
May 5, Earth, daughter of Martyn Sampson.
,, 5, Issabell, daughter of John Barnes.
,, 5, Phillipp, daughter of Thomas Callensow.
,, 12, Elizabeth, daughter of John Hugh.
June 9, Jane, daughter of George Blewatt.
,, 9, Ruth, daughter of Degory Nicholls.
,, 16, William, son of Giles Thomas.
,, 16, Martyn and Jane, children of James Newham.
July 25, Arundell, son of John Ellary.*
Aug 31, Margarett, daughter of John Harrie.
Sept. 1, Mary, daughter of Thomas Morish.
,, 8, Grace, daughter of William Michell.
,, 19, Thomas, son of Walter Fynney.
,, 21, Elizabeth, daughter of William Cowling.
Nov. 9, David, son of John Lanion.
,, 9, The daughter of Samuell Nicholas.

[1651.]
Jan. 11, Nicholas, son of Nicholas Jasper.
,, 11, Thomas, son of Henry Eva, of Gulvall.
,, 18, Martyn, son of Martyn Rodda.
Feb. 8, Jane, daughter of Thomas Fleming.
1651.
Mar. 27, Francis, son of Bennatt Lanion.
,, 27, Edward, son of Christopher Boddy.
April 26, Thomas, son of Thomas Eshame.
May 10, John, son of John Maddern.
,, 10, Anne, daughter of Thomas Pike.
,, 10, Jane, daughter of Robart Gooble.
,, 19, John, son of Phillipp Michell.
,, 14, Eunice, daughter of Richard Stone.*
,, 19, Jane, daughter of Robart Luty.
June 1, Richard, son of William John.
,, 1, Alexander, son of Mathew Reede.
,, 1, Blanch, daughter of John Battyn.
,, 8, Thomas, son of Richard Trick.
,, 15, Joue, daughter of Maddern Legawe.
,, 21, Mary, daughter of William Boase.
,, 22, John, son of John Ellis.
July 1, Honor, daughter of Salamon Cocke.
,, 27, David, son of Francis Lanion.
Sept. 11, John, son of William Noye.
,, 20, Mary, daughter of Walter Noye.
Nov. 22, Edward, son of James Noye.
Dec. 14, Eunice, daughter of Richard Stone.
,, 20, Katherine, daughter of Peter Degory.

[1652.]
Jan. 3, Mary, daughter of William Penticost.
1652.
April 3, John, son of William Michell.
,, 10, Thomas, son of William Lanion, of Gulvall.
May 15, Jane, daughter of John Sampson, Jun.
June 29, William, son of John Mathew.*

June 31, Mary, daughter of Robart Colman.
,, 24, Was borne Henry, son of John Hitchens.*
July 15, Thomas, son of Richard Legawe.
Sept. 3, Honor, daughter of Samuell Edy.
,, 30, Honor, daughter of Gilber[t] Thick.
Nov. 27, Anne, daughter of Christopher Boddy.

[1653.]
Feb. 2, Mary, daughter of John Barnes.
,, 5, Elizabeth, daughter of Walter Saundry.
,, 5, Phillis, daughter of Nicholas Jasper.
,, 7, Was borne Elizabeth, daughter of William Honichurch, gent.*
March 5, Grace, daughter of Rich. Trick.
1653.
,, 25, Mary, daughter of Sampson Lanion.
,, 30, Henry, son of William Mulfra.
,, 30, Richard, son of Thomas George.
April 11, Walter, son of Walter Noye.
,, 30, Thomasine, daughter of Nicholas Hoskyn.
May 21, Ascott, son of John Treneere.
,, 21, John, son of John Tonken.
,, 30, Ralph, son of Thomas Rowe.
,, 30, Phillipp, daughter of Richard Martyn.
June 3, William, son of William Fosse.
,, 3, Mary, daughter of William Anthony.
,, 29, Peter, son of John Williams.
July 2, James, son of Samuell Nicholas.
,, 2, Elizabeth, daughter of Thomas Fleming.
,, 16, William, son of John Hugh.
,, 29, Margarett, daughter of Edward Rawling.
Aug. 21, Margery, daughter of Phillipp Michell.

Was borne—
Nov. 16,† Anne, daughter of John Bosekennen.
,, 21, Anne, daughter of Hugh Edwards.
Dec. 13, Henry, son of Henry Saundry.
,, 26, John, son of Richard Stone.*
,, 13, Harris, son of Martyn Maddern, gent.
,, 27, John, son of John Legawe.

[1654.]
Jan. 4, Alice, daughter of Methusalah Rodda.
,, 14, John, son of John Bennatt.
Mar. 17, Mary, daughter of John Michell.
1654.
April 10, John, son of Martyn Rodda.
,, 14, Elizabeth, daughter of Bennatt Lanion.
May 29, Constance, daughter of James Noye.
June 20, George and Sampson, sons of Walter Noye
July 13, John, son of John Ellis, geut.
Aug. 1, Jane, daughter of John Barnes.
Sept. 6, Edward, son of John Richards.
Oct. 18, John, son of John Sampson, the younger.
,, 21, Elizabeth, daughter of Michaell Nicholas.
Nov. 10, Sciprian, son of Peter Degory.

---
* This entry is an interlineation in a different hand and ink.

* This entry is an interlineation.
† From this time until the end of the year 1660, O.S., the date of birth, not baptism, is entered.

PARISH OF MADRON. 17

Dec. 15, Stephen, son of William Brathorie.
,, 28, Degory, son of John Hutchens.

[1655.]

Jan. 15, Elizabeth, daughter of John Buskennen.
,, 20, Constance, daughter of Thomas Lanion, gent.
Feb. 9, Jane, daughter of Richard Legawe.
,, 15, Prudence, daughter of Thomas Fleming, gent.
,, 26, Catherine, daughter of William Lawrey.
March 1, Martha, daughter of Richard Noye.
,, 2, George, son of Richard Trick.
,, 24, Emanuel, son of Mathew Drew.

1655.
,, 30, William, son of Gilbert Thick.
April 3, John, son of Thomas Morish, the younger.
,, 27, William, son of William Nicholls, gent.
May 15, Peter, son of James John.
June 15, Edward, son of Edward Nickles.
,, 22, Elizabeth, daughter of Samuell Edye.
July 1, Arthur, son of John Tonken.
,, 9, Jone, daughter of Hugh Edwards.
,, 12, Margery, daughter of William James, *alias* Mulfra.
Aug. 6, Thomas, son of Nicholas Cock.
,, 12, Sicely, daughter of John Luke.
Nov. 4, Grace, daughter of Thomas Baynard.
,, 8, William, son of William Trewren, gent.
,, 10, Elizabeth, daughter of Bennat Lanion.
Dec. 21, John, son of Richard Martyn.

[1656.]

Jan. 16, Zacharias, son of Thomas George.
,, 25, An, daughter of John Leagow.*
March 1, ... daughter of William Fosse.

1656.
,, 29, George, son of Christopher Boddy.
June .. John, son of William Honichurch, gent.
,, 6, Richard, son of Sampson Thomas.
Aug. 14, John, son of Bennat Davye.
Sept. 1, Was baptized Agnes, daughter of Lewes Bennett, and Jone, his wife.*
,, 2, Anne, daughter of Phillipp Argoll.
,, 4, Dorithie, daughter of William Nicholls, gent.
,, 15, Elizabeth, daughter of Richard Lanion, the youngest.
,, 18, Thomas, son of Richard Osbern.
Oct. 6, Anne, daughter of Sampson Lanion.
,, 19, Phillipp, daughter of John Bennatt.
Nov. 11, Mary, daughter of Henry Saundry.

[1657.]

Jan. 24, Ralph, son of Thomas Morish, the younger.
,, 29, William, son of James Noye.
Feb. 4, Thomas, son of Humfry Stone.

Feb. 27, Richard, son of Samuell Edye.
March 4, Roger, son of John Ellis.

1657.
,, 29, Joane, daughter of Thomas Hugh.
April 15, Ralph, son of John Richards.
,, 15, Anne, daughter of Walter Noye.
[May] 7, ... daughter of ....
,, 17, Anne, daughter of John Barnes.
,, 27, Mary, daughter of Thomas Fleming, gent.
June 23, Peter, son of John Anbone.
July 26, Chesten, daughter of Phillipp Argall.
Sept. 7, Anne, daughter of William James, otherwise Mulfra.
,, 17, Grace, daughter of John Williams.
Oct. 26, Elizabeth, daughter of Robart Sampson.

[1658.]

Jan. 13, Elizabeth, daughter of James Noye.
,, 27, James, son of Peter Williams.
Feb. 1, Mary, daughter of Nicholas Cock.
,, 3, John, son of John Edwards, otherwise Porteere, the younger.
,, 7, James, son of Nicholas Osbern.
,, 8, Duke, son of John Hitchens.
,, 17, Ralph, son of John Pollard, the younger.
Mar. 10, Joane, daughter of John Bosekennen.
,, 19, Thomas, son of Richard Stone.*
,, 20, Mary, daughter of Edward Nickles.

1658.
,, 28, Hugh, son of William Lawrey.
April 20, English, daughter of Richard Trick.
May 18, Anne, daughter of Thomas Hew.
June 4, Margarett, daughter of William Edye.
,, 5, Bridgett, daughter of Michaell Nicholas.
,, 8, Anne, daughter of Thomas Morish, Jun.
,, 12, Siceley, daughter of Hugh Edwards.
,, 17, Thomas, son of John Sampson,† Jun.
,, 26, Elizabeth, daughter of James Gilbert.
July 28, William, son of William Nicholls, gent.
Aug. 19, Jane, daughter of Thomas Rodda.
,, 21, Katherine, daughter of John Williams.
Oct. 28, Mary, daughter of Thomas George.
Dec. 11, Joane, daughter of Richard Martyn.

[1659.]

Feb. 15, Elizabeth, daughter of Peter Williams.
March 9, Jane, daughter of Thomas Baynard.

1659.
,, 29, Japhett, son of Richard Noye.
April 1, Thomas, son of Thomas Fleming, gent.
,, 30, Elizabeth, daughter of Samuell Edye.
May 16, Thomas, son of William Fosse.
June 16, William, son of William Honichurch.
,, 19, Richard, son of Henry Saundry.
Aug. 1, Dorothie, daughter of John Lanion.
,, 6, Anne, daughter of Richard Lanion, Jun.

---

* This entry is an interlineation in a different hand and ink.

* This entry is an interlineation in a different hand and ink.
† Re-written.

E

REGISTER OF BAPTISMS.

.... 22, Grace, daughter of William R[odda], Jun.
,, 26, Phillipp, daughter of James Gilbart.

[1660.]

Jan. 26, Thomas, son of John Richards.
Feb. 18, Mathias, son of Robart Sampson.
,, 21, Margarett, daughter of John Gilbart, Jun.
1660.
April 8, George, son of John Edwards, *alias* Portcero.
,, 11, William, son of Edward Nickles.
June 11, James, son of Walter Legawe.
July 10, Bennat, son of John Williams.
,, 25, Elizabeth, daughter of Nicholas Fleming, gent.
,, 31, Mary, daughter of James Bennatts.
Aug. 13, Richard, son of Robart Gobble.*
Oct. 11, Phillipp, daughter of Will. Nicholls, gent.
,, 30, Faithe, daughter of Bennatt Champion.
Nov. 24, Blanch, daughter of Bennatt Davye.
,, 26, Michaell, son of Michaell Noye.
Dec. 16, Richard, son of Sampson Rodda.

[1661.]

Jan. 2, Hugh, son of John Harrie.
,, 23, Avis, daughter of Tristram Phillipps.*
Feb. 4, William, base child of Grace Williams.*
,, 18, Hugh, son of Will. Mulfra, otherwise James
,, 18, Richard, son of Roger John.
,, 19, John, son of John Gilbart, Jun.
,, 20, Joane, daughter of William Edye.
March 1, Frances, daughter of John Bosekennen.
,, 23, Thomas, son of Thomas Hugh.
1661.
Was baptized
April 4,† Ann, daughter of Richard Symons.
,, 7, Was borne Sicely, daughter of Richard Stone. Baptised 19th April.‡
,, 14, John, son of Thomas Fleming, gent.
,, 21, Elizabeth, daughter of Tho. Morish, Jun.
,, 21, John, son of Thomas Rodda.
May 26, Nicholas, son of John Thomas.
,, 26, Honor, daughter of James Gilbart.
June 16, Elizabeth, daughter of Phillipp Argall.
,, 23, Thomas, son of Christopher Bodennar.
,, 23, Robart, son of John Tonken.
July 14, Jane, daughter of Ralph Hacker.
,, 14, Christian, daughter of Nicholas Skinner.
Aug. 4, Samuell, son of Hugh Hall.
,, 10, Mary, daughter of John Pollard.
Sept. 15, Grace, daughter of Jo. Bromwell.
,, 22, Nicholas, son of William G....
,, 22, Joane, daughter of Richard John.
,, 29, Charles, son of John Luke.
Oct. 6, Margery, daughter of Jacob Penhallow.

* This entry is an interlineation in a different hand and ink.
† From this time the date of baptism is again entered, with a few exceptions.
‡ This entry is an interlineation.

Oct. 19, Rebecca, daughter of John Lanion.
,, 20, Anne, daughter of Tonken Boase.
,, 21, Richard, son of John Kote, gent.
,, 27, John, son of Richard Maddern.
Nov. 24, Joane, daughter of Tho. George.
Dec. 22, Margery, daughter of Tho. Edwards.

[1662.]

Jan. 5, Elizabeth, daughter of Jo. Sampson, Jun.
,, 6, Agnes, daughter of Joseph Gubbs, gent.
,, 9, Mary, daughter of John Williams.*
Feb. 9, Will., son of Martyn Maddern, gent.
,, 9, Charles, son of Thomas Goffrey.
March 2, William, son of John Trevethan, marchant.
1662.
April 27, Martyn, son of Sampson Thomas.
May 7, Sieprian, son of Sampson Rodda.*
,, 4, Joane, daughter of Tho. Richards.
June 8, John, son of Richard Osbern.
,, 15, Alexander, son of Richard Symons.
,, 21, Thomas, son of Thomas Chirgwin.
July 3, Was borne Morrett, son of Thomas Tyag.
,, 4, Was baptised Jo., son of William Honichurch, gent.
,, 6, Peter, son of Thomas Gregar.
,, 20, Susan, daughter of Richard Saundry.
,, 28, Katherine, daughter of George Crowell.
Aug. 3, William, son of Humfry Nicholas.
,, 10, Emanuell, son of Nicholas Cock.
,, 14, Martyn, son of Martyn Gwennapp.
Sept. 19, Was borne John, son of Thomas Cowling, gent., and baptised the 27th of the same moneth.
Oct. 4, Was baptised Margarett, daughter of Lewis Gennens.
,, 26, Elizabeth, daughter of James Roger.
Nov. 1, Hester, daughter of Robert Lutye.
,, .. Thomas, son of Nich. Fleming, gent.
,, ... daughter of Thomas James.

[1663.]

Jan. 2, Mary, daughter of Thomas Hugh.
,, 3, Charles, son of John Richards.
,, 18, Elizabeth, daughter of John Rundell.
,, 18, Grace, daughter of Walter Rodda.
,, 25, Joane, daughter of Will. Sampson.
Feb. 2, Benjamin, son of Richard Paull.
,, 7, Anne, daughter of James Gilbart.
,, 7, Robart, son of Robart Sampson.
,, 7, James, son of Bennatt Maddern.
,, 7, Rebecca, daughter of Thomas Benmor.
,, 24, Mathew, son of John Thomas.
March 2, John, son of Jacob Penhallow.
,, 5, Henry, son of Henry Siscoll.
1663.
,, 25, Sara, daughter of Jo. Edwards, *alias* Portcere
,, 29, Thomas, son of Thomas Baynard.

* This entry is an interlineation in a different hand and ink.

PARISH OF MADRON.

April 5, Honor, daughter of Martyn Davye.
,, 20, John, son of John Badcock.
,, 20, Will., son of Grace Williams, the reputed father . . . .
,, 21, Nicholas, son of Thomas Fleminge, of Landithy, gent.†
May 17, William, son of Martyn Rodda, Jun.
,, 24, Mary, daughter of William Anthony.
,, 31, William, son of William Michell.
June 6, Mary and Dorothie, children of Lawrence Gea[re.]
,, 14, Robart, son of Thomas Morish.
,, 29, Katherine, daughter of Tho. Hall.
July 19, Daniell, son of John Trevithan.
,, 19, William, son of William Rodda.
,, 19, Elizabeth, daughter of Mathew Skinner.
Aug. 13, Ellener, daughter of William Pearse.
,, 14, Phillipp, son of Phillipp Arthur.
Sept. 13, Jane, daughter of Henry Saundry.
,, 27, Scisely, daughter of Nich. Launder.
Oct. 18, Susan, daughter of Rob. Tonken, Jun.
,, 25, Peter, son of William Boase.
Nov. 21, Mary, daughter of Roger John.
,, 21, Joane, daughter of Nath. Trewren.
,, 22, Tamer, daughter of Edward Nicholas.
,, 30, Mildren, daughter of Robert Cowling, gent.

[1664.]
Mar. 20, William, son of John Boskenen.*
1664.
,, 25, Mary, daughter of Emanuell Hoskyn.
April 24, Edward,‡ son of William John.
,, 24, Nich., son of Tho. Edwards.
. . . . 1, John, son of Alexander Reede.
,, 1, Maddern, son of Thomas Hugh.
,, 31, Richard, son of Richard Paull.
,, 31, Phillipp, daughter of Richard Symons.
July 10, Diana, daughter of Hugh Hall.
Aug. 9, Margarett, daughter of William Trewren.
,, 14, Martyn, son of John Bromwell.
,, 22, Hanna, daughter of Thomas Hoskyn.
,, 26, Sampson, son of John Keato, gent.*
,, 28, Thomas, son of Thomas George.
Sept. 11, Anne, daughter of William Edye.
Nov. 13, James, son of James Thomas.
,, 21, James, son of James Jenken, gent.
Dec. 10, John, son of Jo. Trevethan, marchant.§
,, 31, Christopher, son of Thomas Fleming, gent.

[1665.]
Jan. 15, Hugh, son of William William Michell.
,, 17, Frances, daughter of Tho. Cowling, gent.
,, 22, Joane, daughter of James Gilbart.

† This entry is an addition in a different hand and ink, obliterating the latter portion of the preceding entry, which had been already imperfectly erased.
* This entry is an interlineation in a different hand and ink.
‡ Inserted in a different hand and ink on blank space.
§ An interlineation.

Feb. 5, James, son of John Gilbart.
,, 5, Martyn, son of Richard Maddarn.
,, 5, Margarett, daughter of Jo. Pollard.
1665.
April 7, Mary, daughter of Henry Seysell.
,, 16, Marrett, son of John Rundell.
,, 22, Was borne Nich., son of Nich. Richards.*
May 21, Anne, daughter of Martyn Richard.*
,, 28, John, son of Walter Lanion, gent.
,, 28, William, son of William Genver.
June 4, Arthur, son of Edward Jones.
,, 4, William, son of Walter Harrie.
,, 25, Joseph, son of Rob. Tonken, Jun.
,, 25, Arthur, son of Bennatt Maddern.
July 13, Was borne Nicholas, son of William Honichurch, gent.
,, 24, Charles, son of Rob. Roskorla.
,, 30, James, son of James Perrow.
,, 30, Nicholas, son of Robart Lutye.
Aug. 6, John, son of Robart Sampson.
,, 20, Tho., son of Thomas Martyn.
,, 20, George, son of John Chirgwin.
,, 20, Grace, daughter of Thomas Treloweth.
Sept. 5, Beniamyn, son of Humfry Jacka.
,, 14, Stephen, son of Thomas Edye.
,, 17, Leonard, son of William Pearse.
,, — Thomas, son of Humfry Pearse.
Oct. 8, William, son of William Jeffry,
,, 9, Richard, son of Thomas Hall.*
,, 12, Ralph, son of Ralph Beard.
,, 13, Joane, daughter of Thomas Chirgwin.
,, 13, Richard, son of Walter Rodda.
,, 21, Christopher, son of John Williams.
,, 22, Richard, son of Ralph Hacker.
Nov. 25, Martyn, son of Martyn Davye.
Dec. 26, Stephen, son of Roger Kneebone.

[1666.]
Jan. 14, Mary, daughter of Martyn Rodda, Jun.
,, 28, John, son of Zacharias Gregar.
March 6, Phillipp, son of John Harris, gent.
,, 7, Nicholas, son of Nicholas Fleming, gent.
[+] 1666.
April 11, Mary, daughter of Thomas Edwards.
May 27, Elizabeth, daughter of William Boase.
June 2, Jacobb, son of Tonken Boase.
,, 3, Mary, daughter of Nicholas Tregertheu.
,, 29, Mary, daughter of Othniell Benmor.
July 1, John, son of Thomas James.
,, 13, Liden, daughter of James Bennett.
,, 22, Phillipp, daughter of John Lanion.
,, 29, Haniball, son of William Lawrey.
,, 29, Elizabeth, daughter of John Richards.
,, 30, Mary, daughter of Tho. Rodda.
,, . . , Jane, daughter of Humfry Jack[a.]
Aug. 19, Anne, daughter of Bennet Maddern.

* This entry is an interlineation.

REGISTER OF BAPTISMS.

Aug. 24, Phillipp, daughter of John Keate, gent.
„ 27, Mary, daughter of James Jenken, gent.
Sept. 2, Gartherod, daughter of William Michell.
„ 4, Joane, daughter of William Callensow.
„ 16, Constance, daughter of William Lanion.
„ 16, Sara, daughter of John Chirgwin.
Oct. 7, Grace, daughter of Emanuell Hoskyn,
„ 20, Dorithey, daughter of James Gewell.
„ 26, Honor, daughter of John Bennett.
Nov. 1, John, son of John Barnes, Jun.
„ 20, Richard, son of John Cock.
[+] Dec. 7, Richard, son of Richard Treviler.
„ 24, Thomas, son of William Sloop.*
„ 25, John, son of Nicholas Keygwin.
„ 26, John, son of John Jaspar.
„ 26, John, son of Tho. Bennatt.

[1667.]

Jan. 13, Lidea, daughter of James Gilbart.
„ 27, Tho., son of Henry Saundry.
„ 27, Eliz., daughter of William Pearse.
Feb. 3, Sampson, son of Tho. Morish.
Mar. 24, Peter, son of William Rawling.

1667.

„ 30, Joane, daughter of Ralph Beard, marchant.
April 3, John, son of James Perrow.
„ 9, Tho., son of Will. Nicholls, gent.
„ 14, Peter, son of Tho. Goorge.
„ 14, Alice, daughter of Martyn Richards.
„ 14, Winifred, daughter of Tho. Burch.
* * * * * * * * * * * * * * *†

[1668.]

Oct. 16, John, son of George Humfreys.
„ 28, William, son of Thomas Edwards.
Nov. 1, Francis, daughter of Zacharias Gr[egar.]
„ 15, Job, son of Thomas Morish.
„ 22, Elizabeth, daughter of William Lanion.
„ 25, Anne, daughter of Edward Spriddle.
Dec. 6, Margarett, daughter of John Chirgwin.
„ 6, Thomas, son of Thomas John.
„ 13, Jane, daughter of Nicholas Michell.
„ 14, Elizabeth, daughter of William Penleaso.
„ 20, Thomasine, daughter of Nicholas Phillipps.

[1669.]

Jan. 17, Martyn, son of Marten Richards.
„ 24, Margarett, daughter of Richard Daniell.
„ 30, Richard, son of Marten Rodda, Jun.
Feb. 12, Walter, son of William Gewell.*
„ 20, Elizabeth, daughter of John Gilbart.
„ 23, William, son of William Trewren, gent.
March 7, John, son of Thomas Stephens.
„ 14, John, son of Ralph Battyn.*
„ 23, James, son of James Bennett.
June 2, Jacob, son of Tonken Bosso.*

* This entry is an interlineation in a different hand.
† One leaf missing.

1669.

April 17, Margarett, daughter of James Perrow.
„ 18, William, son of William Rawling.
„ 18, Thomas, son of Thomas Burch.*
May 16, Honor, daughter of Will. Donithorn, of Gulvall.
„ 17, Was borne Mary, daughter of Francis Newman, gent.*
June 20, Elizabeth, daughter of Ralph Beard, marchant.
„ 28, William, son of Mr. Reginald Trenhaile, vic.
July 2, John, son of James Jenken, gent.
„ 24, Helen, daughter of John Keate, gent.*
„ 5, Mary, daughter of Robart White, marinor.
„ 18, Bernard, son of George Guy.
Aug. 15, Robart, son of Robart Scuddan.
„ 15, Mare, daughter of Nicholas Michell.*
„ 22, Phillipp, son of Phillipp Eddye.
Sept. 5, Avos, daughter of John Stephens.
„ 19, Anne, daughter of Humfrey Jacka.
Oct. 2, Priscilla, daughter of Walter Kenshem.
„ 16, William, son of Henry Sandry.
„ 30, Ellonore, daughter of Ralph Eddye.
„ 30, Joane, daughter of Bennett Champion.
Nov. 5, Ursula, daughter of Thomas Lanion, Jun.
„ 14, Trestrem, son of William Sleope.

[1670.]

Feb. 15, Martha, daughter of Henry Siscell.
„ 27, Elizabeth, daughter of Thomas Hall.
Jan. 7, Mary, daughter of Peter Jenken, marchant*

1670.

April 4, Bernard, son of Eleana Lanion.
„ 4, Elizabeth, daughter of John Trevethan.
„ 17, John, son of William Argall.
May 2, John, son of John Pryar.
„ 21, William, son of William Pearce.
June 5,† Thomas, son of Thomas Touken.
Nov. 29, Ursula, daughter of William Sampson.*
[June?] 20, Salamon, son of Othniell Beumer.
Sept. 4, Jane, daughter of James Semmeus.

1671.

Sept. 28, Was borne Francis, son of Francis Newman, of Penzance, gont., and Dorothy, his wife.
April 22, Mary, daughter of John Phillips.
Sept. 20, Christian, daughter of Tho. Edwards.
Nov. 6, Lewis, son of Zacharias Gregar.
„ 28, Thomas, son of Thomas Champion.
Dec. 18, Katheron, daughter of Peter Jenken, merch.
„ 1, William, son of William Gewell.
May 5, Was borne Mary, daughter of Charles Pike, gent.

* This entry is an interlineation in a different hand.
† From this date until April 19th, 1673, the entries are very irregularly written, and in different hands. They occur in the order in which they are here placed.

PARISH OF MADRON.

1673.*
April 19, John, son of Bennet Lanion.
„ 20, William, son of Stephen Luke.
„ 20, William, son of John Gift.
„ 22, William, son of Will. Michell.
May 10, An, daughter of Roger Robins.
„ 24, Kathrayne, daughter of Sampson Rodda.
June 22, Kathrayne, daughter of Richard Prouse.
July 12, Ebbott, daughter of Homphry Lanyon.
Aug. 3, Margary, daughter of Richard Maddarn.
„ 24, Margary, daughter of Marten Hall.
Sept. 12, Richard, son of Richard Konnack.
„ 14, Jane, daughter of Richard Leagow.
Oct. 25, Margarett, daughter of William Michell.
„ 26, Elizabeth, daughter of Ralph Eddye.
Nov. 1, Alice, daughter of Sampson Harrie.
„ 12, Ralph, son of William Rodda.
„ 16, Susana, daughter of Nicholas Michell.
„ 29, Alice, daughter of Thomas George.

[1674.]
Jan. 18, Jone, daughter of Richard Dawes.
Feb. 14, Robart, son of William Trewren, gent.
„ 15, Jane, daughter of Nicholas Cock.
„ 16, Marten, son of John Bromwell.
Mar. 15, John, son of Thomas Gregar.
„ 22, William, son of John Thomas.

1674.   [vicar.
April 10, An, daughter of Mr. Rignald Trenhayle,
„ 11, Cordelliah, daughter of Thomas Fleming,
„ 12, Samwell, son of William Nicholas. [gent.
May 3, William, son of John Barnes.
„ 9, Was born Thomas, son of Charles Pike, gent.
„ 31, Was baptised Au, daughter of John Gilbart.
June 7, Robart, son of Thomas Loddra.
July 5, An, daughter of Abraham Callaway.
„ 5, William, son of William Toocker.
„ 19, Nicholas, son of Roger Sampson.
Sept. 13, Edward, son of William Garland.
Oct. 10, William, son of Thomas Champian.
Nov. 15, John, son of William Cowling.
Dec. 6, Elizabeth, daughter of Thomas John.

[1675.]
Jan. 1, John, son of Sampson Harrey.
„ 17, Thomas, son of John Daniell.
„ 17, John, son of John Boddy.
Feb. 3, Elizabeth, daughter of Henry ——
„ 28, Jemmima, daughter of Robart Harry.
March 5, Thomas, son of Ralph Lanyon, gent.

1675.
„ 28, Richard, son of William Nicholas.

---

* There are no entries for the year 1672 in this place, but some will be found among the irregular entries which are collected and chronologically arranged further on. The Registers were evidently very imperfectly kept about this time, but there is no reason to suppose that any portion is wanting, as there are corresponding irregularities amongst the entries of Marriages and Burials. The writing is the same as before June 5th, 1670. This hand begins in 1666—gives place to the previous hand at the end of the same year—and recommences where the leaf is missing.

April 11, Mary, daughter of Benett Lanion.
„ 17, Was born An, daughter of Charles Pike, gent.
May 8, Amey, daughter of James Oliver.
June 12, James, son of John Barnes.
„ 16, William, son of Nicholas Cock.
„ 27, John, son of John Dawe.
July 25, Mark, son of William Knebon.
Sept. 19, Jeremyah, son of Thomas Gift.
Oct. 16, Tabytha, daughter of Marten Hall.
„ 16, Elizabeth, daughter of Thomas Thomas.
Nov. 14, John, son of Roger Robins.
„ 14, Jane, daughter of Robart Bennett.
Dec. 11, Richard, son of Richard Leagow.
„ 11, Grace, daughter of John Bremble.
„ 12, Grace, daughter of John Richards.

[1676.]
Feb. 2, Tobias, son of Thomas Loddra.
„ 6, Elizabeth, daughter of Nicholas Phillipps.
„ 24, Nicholas, son of Sampson Harry.
„ 27, Ann. daughter of John Parsons.
Mar. 18, Richard, son of Thomas Leagow.
„ 19, Jane, daughter of Ralph Eddye.

1676.
„ 26, John. son of Jacopp Cock.
April 7, James, son of James Bennetts.
May 9, Petar, son of Richard Leagow.
„ 6, James, son of James Nicholas.
„ 13, Thomas, son of Marten Rodda.
„ 14, Margarett, daughter of Hugh Sampson.
„ 28, Marcy, daughter of Enock Jenken.
June 22, Gurthrod, daughter of George Blewett.
„ 26, Luke, son of George Stephens.
July 2, Richard, son of John Cock.
„ 26, Noll, daughter of Arthur Tonken.
Aug. 6, Sampson, son of John Thomas.
„ 6, Ann, daughter of William Leagow.
Sept. 14, Jerremiah, son of Thomas Gift.*
„ 28, Was borne Jane, daughter of David Hall.
„ 30, Ann, daughter of John Tregonow.
Oct. 1, Margarey, daughter of Burnard Ustick.
Nov. 1, Thomas, son of Thomas Calensow.
„ 1, Arthur, son of William Dease.
„ 1, Edward, son of Thomas Calensow.
„ 19, Elizabeth, daughter of John Eddye.
Dec. 16, George, son of George Sampson.
„ 17, Elizabeth, daughter of John Davies.
„ 22, Alexandar, son of Alexandar Staden.

[1677.]
Feb. 10, Mary, daughter of Ralph Lanyon, gent.
„ 10, Lidgia, daughter of Edward Nicholas.
„ 11, James, son of Nicholas Michell.
March 3, Humphry, son of Humphry Lanyon.
„ 9, Francis, son of William Michell.
„ 18, John, son of John Clearke.

---

* This entry is an interlineation in a different hand.

REGISTER OF BAPTISMS.

1677.
April 22, Nicholas, son of Sampson Harrey.
,, 29, Margery, daughter of Richard Maddarn.
May 6, Marten, son of Nicholas Sampson.
,, 13, Daniell, son of John Daniell.
,, 26, Ralph, son of Thomas Richards.
June 10, George, son of George Blewett.
June 17, William, son of John Gilbart.
,, 23, Edmond, son of Richard Evah.
July 22, Ann, daughter of Bennett Lanyon.
,, 29, Rubin, son of Richard Sandars.
Aug. 5, Jane, daughter of John Barns.
,, 12, John, son of William Mechell.
Sept. 10, Charles, son of Charles Williams.
,, 16, Elizabeth, daughter of Thomas Luddra.
Oct. 1, John, son of Emaniwell Jenken.
Dec. 16, Mary, daughter of Marten Hall.
,, 30, Thomas, son of William Leagow.

[1678.]
Jan. 21, James, son of John Parsons.
Feb. 10, Avies, daughter of Davied Hall.
,, 19, Marc, daughter of Humphry Lanyon.
,, 25, Grace, daughter of Thomas Gregar.
Mar. 24, Ann, daughter of Jacobb Cocke.
1678.
,, 29, Honor, daughter of John Yeale.*
April 6, Kathraino, daughter of John Cowling, gent.
,, 7, Aun, daughter of Nicholas Rodda.
,, 13, Sebella, daughter of John Cleark.
May 12, Edward, son of James Cocke.
,, 29, Elizabeth, daughter of William Michell.†
June 2, John, son of John Rodda.
,, 2, Richard, son of John Kneebon.
,, 2, Elizabeth, daughter of William Knebone.
,, 20, Florance, daughter of Thomas Gift.†
July 7, Nicholas, son of John Boddye.
,, 16, Was born Honor, daughter of Charles Pike, gent.
Aug. 4, —— daughter of William Nicholas.
,, 18, William, son of William Boase, Jun.
Sept. 8, An, daughter of Burnard Ustick.
,, 29, John, son of Richard Leagow, Jun.
Nov. 30, Eave, daughter of Richard Leagow, smith.
Dec. 6, Aun, daughter of Phillipp Lanyon.
,, 29, Mary, daughter of Richard Paule.

[1679.]
Jan. 12, John, son of Hugh Sampson.
,, 12, Mary, daughter of Rogar Robins.
Feb. 15, Joane, daughter of Nicholas Phillipps.
,, 23, John, son of John James.
,, 23, Blauch, daughter of Bennett Lanyon.
March 1, Mary, daughter of Ralph Eddye.
1679.
April 4, Was born Alexander, son of Alexander Roed

April 6, Jone, daughter of James Oliver.
,, 26, Gratiana, daughter of Mr. Christopher Pendar.
May 5, Cardelia, daughter of Robart Garland.
,, 9, Dorcas, daughter of Mr. William Pearce.
,, 18, Phillipp, son of John Collings.
June 27, Grace, daughter of Hercules Pedwell.
,, 28, John, son of John Batten.
July 11, John, son of Oliver Tresteane, gent.
,, 13, Richard, son of John Chirgwin.
,, 21, James, son of Mr. Reginald Trenhayle, vicar
Aug. 15, Avies, daughter of Arundell Ellary
,, 21, Nicholas, son of Thomas Calensow.†
,, 17, Hugh, son of Thomas Lanyon.
,, 24, Margary, daughter of George Christophars
,, 24, Cathrayne, daughter of John Cock.
,, 30, Mary, daughter of William Thomas.
,, 31, John, son of John Stephens.
,, 31, Margarett, daughter of Stephen Eddye.
,, 31, Alice, daughter of Edward Richards.
Sept. 21, Digory, son of Thomas Burch.
Oct. 5, Davied, son of Davied Hall.
,, 26, Mary, daughter of George Stephens.
,, 26, Petter, son of Peter James.
Dec. 15. James, son of Degory Marshall.
,, 20, Wilmott, daughter of William Anthony.
,, 26, James, son of Walter Wolcock.
,, 26, Mary, daughter of Thomas Grose, gent.

[1680.]
Jan. 5, Nicholl, daughter of William Lawrey.
,, 18, Marten, son of Marten Hall.
,, 18, Elizabeth, daughter of Thomas Noye, Sen.
,, 18, Jaquite, daughter of Richard Evah.
March 6, Murgarett Yeale, daughter of John Yeale.*
[+] Feb. 1, Anquite, daughter of John Barns.
,, 13, Alice, daughter of Richard Connack.
,, 14, John, son of James Nicholas.
1680.
,, 28, Margarett, daughter of Homphry Lanyon.
,, 28, Au, daughter of William Bennetts.
April 4, William, son of Richard Prouse.
,, 11, Charles, son of John Parsons.
,, 12, An, daughter of Richard Paule.
May 2, An, daughter of Thomas Leddra.
,, 23, Alice, daughter of Sampson Harry.
June 13, Charles, son of Thomas Noye, Jun.

* * * * * * * * * * * * * * *‡

July 4, Jane, daughter of Richard Legow.
,, 25, Jane, daughter of Nicholas Michell.†
Sept. 12, Bathsheba, daughter of Peter Eddye.
Oct. 24, John, son of Arthur Tonken.
,, 31, Thomas, son of Thomas Brush.

---

* This entry is an interlineation in a different hand.
† This entry is an interlineation.
* This entry is an interlineation in a different hand.
‡ A page of irregular entries occurs here, for which see further on.

PARISH OF MADRON.

[1681.]

March 6, Richard, son of Richard Legow.
,, 18, John, son of Ralph Lanyon, gent.

1681.
,, 27, Mary, daughter of John Trevethan, marchant.
,, 27, Elizabeth, daughter of George Blewett.
,, 27, Jone, daughter of the covn maker.‡
April 24, An, daughter of John Stephens.
May 7, Sara, daughter of William Edwards.†
,, 25, Walter, son of Bennett Lanyon.
June 5, Charity, daughter of William Bennetts.
,, 5, William, son of John Boddye.
,, 13, Marten, son of John Dun.
July 3, Nicholas, son of Nicholas Simons.
,, 24, William, son of John Cocke.
Aug. 21, William, son of Hugh Lawry.
Sept. 18, Honor, daughter of Richard Legow.
Oct. 16, Ralph, son of John James.
,, 23, Margarett, daughter of Thomas Fosse.
,, 30, Thomas, son of Nicholas Rodda.
,, 30, Aves, daughter of Stephen Eddye.
,, 30, John, son of Charles Legow.
Nov. 5, —— daughter of William Trewren, gent.
,, 13, Jane, daughter of William Fosse.
Dec. 18, Mary, daughter of John Chirgwin.

[1682.]

Jan. 14, Margaret, daughter of Thomas Richards.
,, 22, Ralph, son of Ralph Eddye.
Feb. 5, Thomas, son of Thomas Noye.
,, 12, Margary, daughter of Robart Bennett.

1682.
May 8, —— daughter of John Clearke.
June 18, Richard, son of Richard Maddarn.
,, 24, Kathren, daughter of John Sampson.
July 20, Jone, daughter of Willm. Osbarn.
Aug. 27, An, daughter of Michaell Nicholas.
Sept. 24, Phillipp, son of George Sampson.
,, 24, William, son of John Toman.
Nov. 12, Phillipp, daughter of Willm. Cowling.
,, 12, An, daughter of William Rodda.
Dec. 9, Henary, son of James Oliver.
,, 17, Thomas, son of Thomas Noye, Sen.

[1683.]

Jan. 21, Jonathan, son of John James.
,, 21, John, son of Warner Biggs.
Feb. 16, Elizabeth, daughter of Ralph Lanyon, gent.
,, 17, Edward, son of Edward Nicholas.†
,, 18, Margarett, daughter of Sciprian Rodda.
,, 18, Sampson, son of John Thomas.
,, 18, Amy, daughter of John Barns.

1683.
Mar. 25, Pacience, daughter of Tho. Calensow.

Mar. 29, Mary, daughter of George Blewett.†
April 22, William, son of George Pearce.
,, 22, Grace, daughter of James Trick.
May 20, Jane, daughter of Sampson Harrye.
,, 27, Henary, son of John Stephens.
,, 27, Grace, daughter of Peter John.
June 3, Elizabeth, daughter of Thomas Noye, Jun.
,, 12, Mary, daughter of George Stephens.
,, 24, —— daughter of Absolom Row.
July 22, Mary, daughter of Richard Legow.
Aug. 5, Jone, daughter of James Nicholas.
Sept. 9, Mary, daughter of Thomas Sampson.
Nov. 9, James, son of John Davye.
Dec. 1, Elizabeth, daughter of Richard Pearce.
,, 9, William, son of John Hand.

[1684.]

Jan. 13, Phillepp, daughter of Peter Eddye.
Feb. 10, Sciprian, son of Sciprian Rodda.

1684.
June 8, Alice, daughter of John Rodda.
July 13, John and Jone, son and daughter of Will. Tooker.
,, 20, John, son of Arthur Touken.
Aug. 10, Elizabeth, daughter of Robart Nankollas.
,, 24, Margarett, daughter of Thomas Fosse.
Sept. 4, Willmott, daughter of William Brown.
,, 14, John, son of David Richards.†
Dec. 7, John, son of Ralph Osbarn.

[1685.]

Mar. 20, An, daughter of Charles Williams.
,, 23, Mary, daughter of Thomas Sampson.

1685.
April 11, Richard, son of Richard Leagoe, Jun.*
,, 26, Elizabeth, daughter of Sciprian Rodda.
May 24, Elizabeth, daughter of Abraham Chirgwin.
,, 31, Dorothie, daughter of John Mathew.
June 7, Hugh, son of Hugh Lawry.
,, 28, William, son of George Edwards.
July 26, Elisha, son of Charles Beckerlegg.
Sept. 12, Elizabeth, daughter of Edward Edwards.
,, 27, Tammeris, daughter of John Sampson.
Nov. 8, Henry, son of John Boddye.
,, 12, Jone, daughter of William Bennetts.
Dec. 20, William, son of Thomas Noye, Jun.

[1686.]

Jan. 3, Robart, son of William Holla.
,, 27, Samwell, son of William Nicholas.
,, 30, Elizabeth, daughter of James Oliver.
Feb. 14, English, daughter of Richard Pearce.
,, 21, Thomas, son of Thomas Kimpe.
,, 28, Mary and Martha, daughters of William Edwards.

---

‡ Query coffin maker.
† This entry is an interlineation.

† This entry is an interlineation.
* This entry, dated 1685, is written in a different hand and ink on the margin at the foot of a page, and follows the entry dated June 12, 1685.

REGISTER OF BAPTISMS.

1686.
June 20, Robart, son of Robartt Bennett.
Aug. 27, Thomas, son of Peter John.
Sept. 19, Samwell, son of Robart Nankollas.
  „   25, Elizabeth, daughter of Mr. Christopher Veale.
Oct. 31, David, son of David Richards.
Dec. 5, Hugh, son of Edward Nicholas.
  ,. 12, Addama, daughter of Solomon Cock, of Golval.
  „   26, An, daughter of William Pearce.
  „   27, Elizabeth, daughter of Richard Legow, smith.

[1687.]
Jan. 1, Abraham, son of Abraham Chirgwin.
  „ 8, Ralph, son of Ralph Richards.
  „ 9, Ralph, son of Ralph Osbarn.

Feb. 6, John, son of George Blowett.
  „   6, James, son of James Nicholas.
  „ 13, Charles, son of Thomas George.
1687.
April 17, —— daughter of John Mathew.
  „   23, Roger, son of John Ellis, gent.
June 4, Anthony, son of Arthur Tannar.
July 17, Grace, daughter of William Rodda, Jun.
  „   17, Phebe, daughter of John Daniell.
Aug. 7, Jane, daughter of William Nicholas.
  „   21, John, son of Siprian Rodda.
  „   28, Sampson, son of Thomas Noye, Sen.
Sept. 4, Elizabeth, daughter of George Cocke.
  „   11, Margaret, daughter of Peter Gregor.
Oct. 22, Jone, daughter of James Chirgwin.
Nov. 6, Thomas, son of James Hoskon.
  „   6, —— daughter of Nich. Harry.
Dec. 6, Richard, son of John Gilbart.‡

[Irregular Entries.*]

1663.   [22
Dec. 21, Was born Jane, daughter of Ralph Hacker
1667.   [27
Nov. 20, Was born Mary, daughter of Ralph Hacker
1668.
Oct. 3, William, son of William Sampson.   15
1669.
May 14, An, daughter of John Davey.   329
1670.
Dec. 5, Ursillah, daughter of William Sampson. 16
[1671.]
Jan. 31, Jane, daughter of Nicholas Phillipps. 19
1671.
Aug. 10, John, son of Humphry La[nyon.]   21
[1672.]
Mar. 16, George, son of William Noye.   20
1672.
Sept. 19, Ann, daughter of James Semmens.   24
Oct. 6, Cathraine, daughter of Charles Pike, gent.
                                               [25
[1673.]
Jan. 27, Elizabeth, daughter of Thomas Lanyon. 13

March 2, Elizabeth, daughter of William Sampson. 23
1673.
April 13, John, son of Benet Lanyon.   32
May 29, Grace, daughter of Thomas Burch.   26
 . . . . . Vernan, son of Michaell Browne.†   30
June 20, Margery, daughter of John and Mary Keigwin. 31
Nov. 1, Benjamin, son of James Bennett.   33
  „   24, Grace, daughter of Thomas Lanyon.   14
[1674.]
Feb. 10, Joseph, son of Sampson Gubbes, marchant.
                                               [34
March 2, Elizabeth, daughter of William Sampson. 13
  „   4, John, son of Nicholas Phillipps.   35
1674.
Aug. 24, Mary, daughter of James Semmens.   40
Oct. 21, Thomas, son of Peter Jenken, marchant. 36
Nov. 2, Elizabeth, daughter of Will. Gewell.   46
  „   3, Jone, daughter of Christopher Pender, gent.
        and Jaquelinah, his wife.   45
  „ 24, Joseph, son of William Noye.   28
[1675.]
Jan. 12, An, daughter of Nicholas Symons.   37
Feb. 14, Porthosia, daughter of John and Mary Keigwin. 38
  „ 22, John, son of John Davey.   39

---

* The following entries of Baptisms are written indiscriminately with but little attention to arrangement or order, on 16 pages (which immediately follow the regular entries), and one page which occurs, as already noticed, under the date of 1687. Since it would be a matter of the utmost difficulty to find any particular entry, in consequence of the confused state of this portion of the Register, these entries are here arranged in chronological order; but the figures to the extreme right will serve to show the order in which they occur in the original. These 17 pages are for convenience here lettered a, b, c, &c., and the last entry in a page has the letter of the page to which it belongs affixed to the number, so that reference to the original is thus facilitated. Some of these pages have but one entry—some but a few—others are well filled; and there is much variety in the style of writing.

‡ Here the regular entries of Baptisms end in this first book.
† This entry is at the upper edge of a page, and has been in great part cut off by the bookbinder. The date is entirely gone, but that of the entry which precedes it is 14th May, 1669. It is here placed before the entry which follows it in the original. N.B. Vernan, son of Michaell Browne, was buried 13th December, 1673.

PARISH OF MADRON.

1675.
April 10, Marey, daughter of Benet Lanyon. 41
June 12, Mary, daughter of John Clearke. a18
Aug. 9, Stephen, son of William Thomas, of Penzance. 42
Oct. 28, Was born William, son of John Pedwell. 43
Nov. 27, Joseph, son of Othuell Benmer. 44
,, 29, Was born Frances, son of Richard John. 68
,, 30, Was born Henery, son of Henry Ustick, gentelman, and he was baptized ye 12 of Decemb. 69

[1676.] [70
Jan. 19, Was born Mathew, son of Alexander* Reed.
1676.
April 25, Robart, son of John Callensow. 71
May 16, Nicholas, son of Thomas Edwards. 73
,, 30, Mathew, son of Mathew Skinner. 72
Oct. 20, Mary, daughter of Somer Honichurch, gent. [74
Dec. 20, Was borne Eliz., daughter of John and Mary Keigwin, of Penz., and baptized ye 5th of January, 1676-7. 75

[1677.]
Jan. 13, Christopher, son of Christopher Pender, gent., and Jaqulynah, his wife. 76
Feb. 6, Was born Thomas, son of Mr. Thomas Eastlack. 77
1677.
Mar. 28, Richard, son of Richard Giles. 78
June 6, Was born Constance, daughter of John Pedwell. 79
Aug. 15, Christian, daughter of Nicholas Symons. 80
Oct. 8, Was borne Mathew, son of Alexander Reede. 81
Nov. 29, Was born An, daughter of Henry Usticke, and baptised the 12th of Decembar. 82
Dec.† 4, Edward, son of James Collet. 1
1678.
Sept. 30, Was borne Elloner, daughter of William Calensow. 83
Nov. 22, Edward, son of James Collett. 84
1679.
April 4, Was borne Alexander, son of Alexander Reede. 85
,, 4, Was born Sebbella, daughter of Henary Usticke, gent., and baptised the 14th day of yo sam month. 86
Aug. 21, Was born Rebeka, daughter of John Hancock, gent. d89
Oct. 11, Margarett, daughter of Petar Carpentar. 88
Nov. 15, Abraham, son of Charles Williams. 87
1680.
July 1, John, son of John Michell. 103
,, 17, Was born William, son of William Noye. 98

Sept. 20, Elizabeth, daughter of Thomas Gift. 99
Dec. 26, Was born John, son of William Bose, Jun.

[1681.] [100
Jan. 1, Was born Martha, daughter of John Pedwell. 101
,, 20, Was born Mary, daughter of Mr. Thomas Eastlack. 102
1681. [1682.]
March 1, Was born Tristram, son of Richard Rawlings. 104
1682.
May 19, Mary, daughter of John Pedwell. 106
Aug. 2, Elizabeth, daughter of Somer Honichurch, gent. 107
Dec. 14, Was born Elizabeth, daughter of John Hancock, gent. e108

[1683.]
Jan. 22, William, son of Thomas Gift. 112
Mar. 11, Mary, daughter of Brian Fenne. 111
,, 22, William, son of William Michell. 105
1683.
Aug. 30, Was born Julian, daughter of Bathrem Boson, gent. 109
Nov. 10, Was born Willmott, daughter of John Hancock, gent. 117
,, 27, Was born Elizabeth, daughter of John Bonettow. 114
Dec. 10, Was born Edward, son of Richard Rawlings [115
,, 24, Was born John, son of Henary Usticke, gent., and baptised ye 7th of Janiwary after. 110
,, 25, Mary, daughter of James Collett. 116

[1684.]
Mar. 18, Was born Margarett, daughter of Vincent John. 113
1684.
July 5, Margret, daughter of John Pidwell. 121
,, 25, Richard, son of Richard Walko. 122
Aug. 2, Richard, son of William Michell. 123
,, 17, Margary, daughter of Petar Carpenter. 124

[1685.]
Jan. 30, Was born Martha, daughter of Mr. Thomas Eastlack. 119
,, 31, Joue, daughter of John Veale. 118
Mar. 10, Was born Henary, son of Henary Mulfra. [120
1685.
,, 29, Waltar, son of Brian Fenne. 125
April 11, Robt., son of R. Lgge.* 131
June 11, Was born Elizabeth, daughter of Thomas Pedwell. 186

* Written in a different hand upon erasure.   † Query month and year.   * Query Legg, or Leggo.

REGISTER OF BAPTISMS.

June 16, Alice, daughter of Somor Honichurch, gent. [132
Sept. 24, Was born Jonathan, son of Barthram Boson, gent. 134
,, 30, Was born Mary, daughter of John Hancock, gent. 130
Oct. 20, Was born William, son of John Bouetto. [135
Dec. 3, Was born Mary, daughter of Alexander Read. 127
,, 15, Was born Richard, son of Richard Rawlings [128
,, 15, Was born Mary, daughter of Henary Usticke gent., and baptised ye 30th of the sam month. 129

[1686.]

Mar. 12, John, son of John Jane. 126
1686.
May 1, Was borne Allis, daughter of John Stone. [133
Sept. 30, Elizabeth, daughter of Petar Carpentar. 138
1687.
Mar. 31, Elizabeth, daughter of Robart Mines. 198
May 14, Mary, daughter of John Jane. 139
June 1, Was born Deborah, daughter of John Hancock, gent. 140
,, 15, Mary, daughter of William Calensow. 141
Nov. 9, Was born Barthram, son of Barthram Boson, and Amy, his wife. 142
,, 27, Was born Thomas, son of Thomas Pedwell, [188

[1688.]

Feb. 2, Henary, son of Charles Beckerlegg. 201
1688.
April 9, James, son of James Collett. 144
May 4, William, son of Somer Honichurch, gent. [145
,, 18, William, son of Richard Walke. 146
Sept. 13, Charles, son of Richard Usticke, gent. 147

[1689.]

Feb. 10, Peter, son of Thomas Thomas. 148
March 4, William, son of William John. 143
1689. [149
May 17, Was born Jone, daughter of John Gregar.
,, 26, Was born John, son of John Hancock, gent. [150
June 29, Was born Elizabeth, daughter of Waltar Bromwell. 151
July 4, Was born Kathren, daughter of John Bonettow. 152
,, 17, Was born Susanna, daughter of Alexander Read. 154
Sept. 29, Elizabeth, daughter of Samwell Bayle. 155
Oct. 1, Was born Kathren, daughter of Edward Primrose. 48
,, 19, Was born Elizabeth, daughter of Mr. Will. Tonken. 57

Nov. 1, Was born Hugh, son of Honiball Sandry. 4
,, 10, Jone, daughter of John Jane. 153
,, 16, Charles, son of Charles Beckerlegg. 202
Dec. 20, Was born John, son of Solomon Evah, and Elizabeth, his wife. 156

1690.
April 27, Was born Kathron, daughter of Richard Gwennapp. 160
June 21, An, daughter of Thomas James. 55
,, 24, Marten, son of William Bose, Sen. 158
,, 26, Was borne John, son of Thomas Chirgwin. [95
July 14, Elizabeth, daughter of Richard Walke. 50
Aug. 7, Mary, daughter of John Toman. 51
Sept. 14, Was born John, son of John Bonettow. 161
,, 29, Jemmima, daughter of William Calensow. [61
Dec. 12, An, daughter of Mr. William Whitte. 62
,, 26, Was born Mary, daughter of Edward Primrose. 49

[1691.]

Feb. 5, Was born Jone, daughter of Mr. Thomas Eastlack. 159
,, 7, Arise, daughter of Japeth Nuye. 162
,, 7, Was borne John, son of John Bollock, gent. [96
,, 14, Richard, son of John Pearce. 97
,, 23, John, son of Peter Carpentar. 157
1691.
June 3, Robart, son of Robart Mines. 199
,, 29, Peter, son of Thomas Pedwell. 194
July 4, Was born Mary, daughter of Mr. John Hotsun. 59
,, 17, Was born Jone, daughter of Alexander Read. 168
Aug. 14, Was born John, son of Richard Gwenapp. [165
Sept. 11, Was born Sarah, daughter of Stephen Perdew. 136
Oct. 5, Jone, daughter of William John. 65
,, 12, Pettar, son of John Jane. 64
,, 19, Henry Sandry, son of Thomas Sandry. 3
,, 20, Aann, daughter of Henry Gondry. 47
,, 24, Jaquite, daughter of Richard Anderton. 60
Nov. 8, Was born Liddiah, daughter of Somer Honichurch, gent. 2
Dec. 9, Was born Elizabeth, daughter of John Gregar. g169

[1692.]

Jan. 5, Mary, daughter of Charles Beckerlegg. 203
,, 14, Marten, son of Nicholas Gwenapp. 167
,, 19, Charles, son of Thomas James. m200
Feb. 6, Jane, daughter of William Whitte. 63
,, 6, An, daughter of Walter Bro[mwell.] 163
March 1, Was born William, son of Mr. Thomas Eastlack. 52
,, 3, Was born Uriah, son of Mr. William Tonken. 58

PARISH OF MADRON. 27

Mar. 17, Was born Thomas, son of Vincent John. 166
1692.
April 17, Roger, son of Thomas James. 56
,, 29, Was born Grace, daughter of John Hancock, gent. 53
May 10, Richard, son of Sampson Keate, gent. *n*212
June 23, John, son of William Edwards, [*alias* Porteare.] 196
July 2, John, son of Samwell Bayle. 54
Aug. 24, John, son of John Laniou, of Lauyon, gent. [187
,, 28, Phinchas, son of Brian Fenuye. 66
Nov. 30, Sarah, daughter of Honiball Sandry. 5
,, 30, Was born William, son of William Edwards, [*alias* Porteare.] 197

[1693.]
Jan. 7, An, daughter of David Richards, and Christian, his wife. 7
,, 29, Was born Marten, son of Robart Mathies, marinor. 11
Feb. 2, John, son of Georg Jenken. *l*193
1693.
Mar. 30, Avise, daughter of John Honichurch, of Loudon, gouldsmith. 9
,, 31, An, daughter of Thomas James. 10
April 15, Ambrose, son of Sampson Keate, gent. 213
The said Ambrose was buried May 22nd, 1781, in the 89th year of his age, by me,
Wm. Borlase, Vicar of Madron.
July 6, Was born Thamson, daughter of Thomas Robarts. 170

1694.
April 15, William, son of Charles Beckerlegg. 204
,, 24, Thomas, son of Thomas James. *c*67
,, 28, Thomas, son of John Calenso. 189
May 26, Peter, son of William Row. 190
Aug. 20, Grace, daughter of Walter Bromwell. 164
Sept. 24, Was born Thomas, son of Thomas Robarts. [171
Oct. 12, Jane, daughter of Henary Usticke, gent. 12
Dec. 27, Ann, daughter of Honiball Sandry. 6

[1695.]
Feb. 5, Was born Bridgett, daughter of Stephen Perdew. 137
March 3, Samwell, son of Thomas Eastlack, marchand [214
1695.
June 8, Emanuel, son of James Nicholls. 176
Oct. 19, Was borne John, son of Richard Giles. 93
Nov. 16, Lovedye, daughter of Thomas Pedwell. 92

[1696].
March 1, Honor, daughter of Thomas Sampson. 174
,, 10, Was born Elizabeth, daughter of Thomas Robarts. 172
1696.
,, 27, Honor, daughter of Charles Beckerlegg. 205

June 3, Richard, son of Thomas Eastlack, marchand. [217
,, 26, Robecka, daughter of Thomas James. 94
Dec. 27, Robert, son of Robert Mathews, marrinnor. [216

[1697.]
Jan. 20, Was born William, son of Walter Jewell. [185
,, 12, Joh., son of Arthur Rogers, of Penzance. [243
March 9, Was born An, daughter of John Long, gent. [215

1697.
April 8, Was born Walter, son of Walter Bromwell [173
,, 30, Jno., son of Tho. Robert. 175
,, 30, Honiball, son of Honiball Sandry. 8
May 17, Was born Trestrain, son of Trestram Lutey, of ye Town of Penzance. *h*177
June 29, Peter, son of Thomas Pedwell. 91
Oct. 2, Was born Richard, son of Richard Connack. [90

[1698.]
Feb. 2, William, son of Sampson Mathews, of this Parish. 181
1698.
April 17, Was born Thomas, son of Duke Robarts. [*j*180
Oct. 9, Oliver, son of Charles Beckerlegg. 206
Nov. 29, Mary, daughter of William Edwards, *alias* Porteare. 195
Dec. 13, Julyan, daughter of James Nicholls. 178
,, 25, Robert, son of Arthur Rogers, of Penzance. [*q*244
1699.
April 16, Honnor, daughter of William Row. 191
,, 30, Mathias, son of John Daniell. 218
June 10, Was born Phillipp, son of Mr. John Longe. [219
Oct. 4, Was born Abraham, son of Abraham Callaway. 208
Nov. 6, Was born Robartt, son of Henry Edmonds. [220

[1700.]
Mar. 11, Ann, daughter of James Harry, of ye Town of Penzance. 182
1700.
Sept. 19, An, daughter of John Davye. 228

[1701.]
Feb. 26, Was born Kathren, daughter of Richard James. 222
1701.
April 7, Was born Elizabeth, daughter of Mr. John Longe. 221
June 7, John, son of John Daniell. 224
Aug. 1, Mary, daughter of Edward Collett. 210

REGISTER OF BAPTISMS.

Oct. 17, Was born Sarah, daughter of Marten Write, of ye Town of Penzance. 226
,, 24, William, son of James Fox, and Armanell, his wife. 227
Nov. 20, Alexander, son of Alexander Gendall. 230

1702.

April 21, Elizabeth, daughter of James Hamond, gent. 231
July 24, Elizabeth, daughter of Henry Row. 207
Aug. 10, Elizabeth, daughter of John Davye. 229
Nov. 28, William, son of Robart Harry, Jun., and Mary, his wife. 232

1703.

May 24, Was born Grace, daughter of Mr. John Longe. 223
,, 24, Ann, daughter of Medlen* Freinde. 234
June 17, Was born Elizabeth, daughter of Christopher Williams. 235
Aug. 21, Richard, son of Thomas James. p236
Sept. 13, Edward, son of James Hamond, gent. 238
Nov. 25, William, son of William Thomas. 239
,, 30, William, son of John Legow, and Ann, his wife. 237

* Query Medlen for Magdalen.

[1704]

Jan. 16, An, daughter of Richard Wallish. 211
Feb. 14, Was born Jane, daughter of Abraham Callaway. 209

1704.

Aug. 8, Jane, daughter of Phillipp Sampson. i179

[1705.]

Feb. 2, Thomas, son of Robart Harrye, Jun., and Mary, his wife. 233

1705.

July 7, James, son of William Row. 192
Aug. 28, Was born Tristrem, son of Tristram Rawlings. 240
Nov. 5, Susanna, daughter of Mr. John Long. o225

[1706.]

Feb. 10, Thomas, son of Ralph Richards, of Bosollow [241

1707.

Dec. 28, Mathew, son of Mathew Hall. 242

1724. [1725.]

Jan. 20, Was born Hannah, daughter of Joseph Beard, of Penzance. 183

1726.

July 18, Was born Susannah, daughter of Joseph Beard, of Penzance. k184

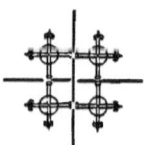

The Register of Marriages.

G E O R G I V S H V C H I N S I N A R T I B V S M A GISTER	**Mariages beginninge in anno 1577.**	P R E D I C A T O R V E R B I D E I E T V I C A R I V S S A N C T I P A T E R N I

1577.
September 20, Were maryed Hughe Cooke, of Pawle, and Agnes, the daughter of John Legowe.
January 19, were maried Richard, the sonne of Sampson John Richard, and Grace Harvy.
„ 19, were maried Thomas Sudgiow and Elizabethe, the daughter of John Manewell, of Lytell Collan.
„ 19, were maried Peter Rawlyn and Hellynor Boshober, of Gwynnep.
Aprill 21, were maried Peter and Hellynor, servauntes to Wallter Lanyon, gentellman.
1578.
August 4, were maryed William Dennyce and Margaret Dove.
„ 10, were maried Thomas, the sonne of William Argall, and Joan, the daughter of Valentynn Weymuowthe.
November 24, were maried John Lanyon and Margaret, the daughter of Sampson John Richard.
January 16, were maryed Peeter Polteere and Jane Holla, vidua.
October 18, were maried Maderen Tremethacke and Mawde, the daughter of John Robert, of St. Martyns.
1580.
„ 24, were maried Lawrence Perue and Jane Blacke.
November 6, were maried John Thomas and Agnis, the daughter of Jeffrye Sudgiowe.
„ 20, were maried William Lawrence and Annys Leha.
„ 20, were maryed John Christopher and Olsett, the daughter of Hew Argall.
January 15, were maried John Davie and Elizabethe, the daughter of John Maderne.
„ 15, were maried Vyvian Nickles and Elizabeth James.

N.B. The Register of Marriages has a Title page, from which the above heading within lines is taken. The Royal Arms—France and England quartered—appear at the top, surrounded by that scroll-like style of ornamentation peculiar to the reigns of Elizabeth and James I. There is also a male figure to the left, and some attempt at outline embellishment, but the design is evidently very incomplete. GEORGE LITTCHINS, M.A., was Vicar of Madron from 1601 to 1627, and therefore at the time this transcript was made, for these Registers of Baptisms, Marriages, and Burials were transcribed from older Registers in the year 1607. The entries on this page are verbatim copies of the original, and it will be seen that there are none for the year 1579.

REGISTER OF MARRIAGES.

1581.
April 10, John Neale and Joan Cuntyes.
„ 13, Peter Sympson and Elizabeth Rawlynge.
„ 14, William Sorell and Margaret Lcha.
Oct. 8, James Varwell and Jeny Hake.
Nov. 5, Rowan and Phillip.
„ 12, John Tremethack and Elizabeth, his wife.*
„ 19, John James and Jenet.
„ 19, Richard Donnall and Joane.
„ 27, Samuell Belpit and Katherin Fleming.

[1582.]
Jan. 30, William Jciles and Elizabeth.
1582.
June 24, John Atkyns and Elizabeth Clyes.
July 29, Sampson Bell and Allice.
„ 31, John Tonekynge and Elynor.
Aug. 5, William Nicholas and Joane Penmenyt.
„ 20, David Thomas and Margaret Carvanell.
Sept. 5, John Tayler and John† Richard.

[1583.]
Jan. 21, John Tregirthen and Elizabethe, the servant of John Lower.
„ 24, Nicholas Harrye and Allyce, the servant of Thomas Clyes.
Feb. 3, Richard Kerowe and Elizabethe, the daughter of Michell Skadon.
„ 4, John Edye and Hellen, the late wief of John Penmenytt.

1583.
April 20, John Anthony and Jane Amys.
June 17, Jefrie Movera and Joane.
„ 17, Richard George and Joane.
July 30, Thomas Guye and Elizabeth.
Aug. 22, Edward Black and Joane, the daughter of James Angove.
Oct. 1, William Caunter and Florence Foskue.‡
„ 4, Symon Davides and ——
„ 20, Henrie Thomas and Charity, the daughter of John George.
Nov. 10, Peter Gymboll and Elizabeth Toneking.

[1584.]
Jan. 26, John Marke and Joane Goodale.
1584.
Aug. 16, John Maderen, the younger, and Ann, the daughter of Richard Trevannyon, Esquior
Sept. 27, Teage Billen and Agnes.
„ 27, Raph Champion and Margerie.
Oct. 4, John Roddu and Joane.
„ 4, John —— and Elizabeth.
„ 11, Thomas Davye and Sisolie.
„ 11, John Swayer and Joane.

Oct. 18, Nicholas Jenkinge and Margaret.
„ 18, William Roger and Redigon.
„ 18, John William and Elizabeth.
„ 20, Morgan Flynn and Hellen.
Nov. 26, Humfrie Polwigen and Elizabeth.
„ 26, Richard Perse and Elizabeth.

[1585.]
Jan. 24, John Thomas and Willmet.
„ 24, John Richard and Joane.
1585.
May 9, William Vicker and Joane.
„ 25, Edward Lerebye and Elizabeth.
Sept. 23, William Drake and Amy.
„ 26, George Weymond and Agnes.
Oct. 3, Pascawe Pendene and Joane.
„ 10, John Argall and Jonne.
Nov. 2, Peter William and Joane.
„ 14, John Pennalerick, of Helston, and Elizabeth

[1586.]
Jan. 17, Stephen Thomas and Joane.
1586.
April 25, Robert Dunkinge and Joane.
May 14, Thomas Velly and Jane.
Oct. 2, Andrew Hambling and Joane.
Nov. 6, William Lower and Elizabeth.
„ 6, John Symon and Joane.

[1587.]
Jan. 16, Thomas Tregirthen and Elizabeth.
Feb. 13, John Nole and Agnes.
1587.
June 5, Richard Carew and Elizabeth.
„ 12, William Dudowe and Elizabeth.
„ 12, Barthelmew Poter and Elizabeth.
July 22, Sampson Noye and Jane.
Sept. 24, John William and Jane.
Oct. 1, John Shoh and Chesten.
Nov. 1, Petherick Boyer and Katherin.
„ 19, Richard Henry Olere* and Jane.

[1588.]
Jan. 28, Robert Noy, alias Bodenar, and Thomazin.
„ 28, Henrie Thomas and Joane.
1588.
May 12, William Rawlinge and Joane.
June 9, Edward Luddra and Katherin.
„ 22, Maderen Bone and Joane.
Oct. 13, German Morish and Allie.
„ 17, John Sudgiow and Ann.
„ 18, William Redwood and Jane.
„ 19, John Cowlinge and Allie.

[1589.]
Jan. 29, Thomas Lakes and Joane.
Feb. 3, William Cardew and Ellynor.

---

* From this date the entries in the original are usually, though not invariably, made in this form, but to avoid unnecessary repetition the words "his wife" are afterwards here omitted.
† Probably a clerical error for Joan.
‡ Query an abreviation of Fortescue.

* Query Cler. for Clericus.

PARISH OF MADRON.

1589.
May 10, Richard Penquitt and Allyce.
June 8, John Scaddan and Christian.
July 13, Richard Peres and Elizabeth.
Aug. 3, John Richard and Joane.
Sept. 21, James Tremethack and Margery.
Oct. 6, Thomas Drew and Elizabeth.
,, 6, Raphe John and Ursula.
,, 26, James Bossaverue and Joane.
,, 26, Richard Thomas and Agnes.
Nov. 9, Richard Hoskyn and Elizabeth.
,, 9, Richard Davy and Constanne.
,, 16, Barnard Pennallvean and Jane.
,, 23, William Foster and Katherin.

[1590.]
Feb. 8, Richard Thomas and Sybill Wemuoth, widow.
March 2, Thomas Hills and Katherin Dennye.
,, 3, William Maderne and Jane, daughter of Henrye Polkinhorne.

1590.
June 13, William Jefrie and Allice.
,, 28, John Buskeninge, the youngest, and Joane.
July 12, Ciprian Bennet and Elizabeth.
Sept. 27, Raphe Thomas and Joue.
Oct. 4, William Tereife* and Elizabeth, the daughter of Nicholas Flemynge.
,, 24, John, son of Henrie Game, and Mary, daughter of John Richard, *alias* Lewer.
,, 24, Henry Stephen and Elizabeth.
,, 25, Robert Jane† and Joane.
Nov. 15, Thomas Bodye and Charitie.
,, 22, Richard James and Katherin.
,, 22, William Palmer and Margaret.
,, 24, Robert Tippet and Temperance.
Dec. 20, Robert, son of Richard Treneyr, gentelman, and Mary, daughter of William Askot, gent.

1591.
June 6, Robert John and Elizabeth.
Sept. 6, James Trevalles and Elizabeth.
,, 27, Robert Pretor and Thomazin.
Oct. 3, Raph John and Agnes.
,, 11, William Hann and Jane.
Nov. 3, James Dawbyn and Allice, daughter of Richard Treneyre, gent.
,, 7, William Argall, the younger, and Agnes.
,, 21, William Legowe and Jane.

[1592.]
Jan. 22, Phillip Sampson and Pascow Mitchell.
1592.
Mar. 29, Henry Hooper and Ursula.
April 3, Thomas Penmenith and Elizabeth.

April 3, Mathew Penmenith and Marye, daughter of Richard Treneyre, gent.
May 1, Richard Bastian and Mary.
,, 7, John Brockhurst and Margaret.
,, 28, Emanuell Bell and Katherin.
Oct. 1, John Lewes and Joane.
,, 15, John Michell and Elizabeth.
,, 30, Henry Smyth and Margaret.
Nov. 25, Robert William and Katherin.

[1593.]
Jan. 21, John Symon, *alias* Crankan, and Joane.
☞ 1593.
June 10, Richard Breach and Mary.
,, 23, Richard Hawes and Jane.
Aug. 29, Thomas Rawe and Elizabeth.
Sept. 1, Richard Trythall and Margaret.
,, 16, Thomas Flemyng and Jane.
Oct. 28, John Alforde and Margaret.
Nov. 4, John Stone and Elizabeth.
,, 18, Thomas Carne and Katherin.
,, 19, John Bewforde and Mary.
,, 28, John Synckbock and Katherin.
Dec. 9, Richard Bennet and Jane.

[1594.]
Jan. 13, Drew James and Margaret.
,, 20, John Champion and Joane.
1594.
April 14, Thomas Robert and Grace.
,, 29, Richard Edwardes and Margaret.
July 1, Francis Michell and Thomazin.
,, 3, Henry Roberts and Elizabeth.
,, 3, Petherick Boyer and Katherin.
Aug. 18, John Chamberlen and Agnes.
Oct. 6, Richard Morris and Agnes.
,, 27, John Richard and Elizabeth.
Nov. 4, James Trevalles and Elizabeth.
1596.*
July 27, John James, the elder, and Wilmot.
,, 28, John James, the younger, and Jane.
Nov. 7, Charles Sudgiow and Elizabeth.
,, 8, John Trelill and Jane.
,, 15, Reynolde Cosen and Thomasyn.
,, 21, Richard Amnear and English.
,, 21, Richard Saundry and Jane.
,, 22, William Noye and Margaret.
,, 29, John Hugh and Katherin.
,, 30, Thomas Anbone and Susan.
,, 30, William Cally and Alice.
,, 30, John Tracy and ——

1597.
Oct. 2, John Tremethack and Elizabeth.
,, 28, Richard Bowes and Florence.
1598.
May 1, Thomas Stephens and Joane.

---

* *i.e.* William Nicholls, of Tereife.
† Altered from James.

* There are no entries from Nov. 4th, 1594, to July 27th, 1596.

REGISTER OF MARRIAGES.

June 11, Degorie Duke and Elizabeth.
,, 13, Thomas Burnow and Allie.
,, 26, William Mulfra and Mary.
July 25, Robert Nicolls and Barbara.
Sept. 11, William Tonking and Katherin.

[1599.]

Jan. 21, John Richard and Joane.
,, 22, Thomas Syse and Joane.
Feb. 12, John Jenkin and Allice.
,, 12, Nicholas Connock and Phillip.
,, 12, Edward Peter and Joane.

1599.
May 29, John William and Elizabeth.
June 11, Richard Tremethack and Joane.
,, 24, John Slader and Richoe.
,, 27, John Buskenning, the elder, and Jane.
Oct. 15, Thomas Forse and Allice.
,, 28, John Lethebye and Elizabeth.
,, 29, Josepth Lympany and Agnes.
Nov. 26, Rowan Marke and Elizabeth.
,, 27, John Anthony and Agnes.
,, 27, Launclot Garland and Trefyna.

[1600.]

Jan. 27, Thomas Jeffrie and Ann.
,, 30, Thomas Robert and Joane.

1600.
April 14, James Midlame and Joane.
,, 27, Edward Lawrene and Agnes.
Aug. 4, John Morish and Margaret.
,, 10, John Portere and Jane.
Sept. 25, Anthony Clies and Richoe.
Nov. 2, William Nenis and Milson.
,, 23, Geles Bartlet and Luce.

[1601.]

Jan. 25, John Luke and Jane.

1601.
June 7, Peter Russell and Margerie.
,, 11, John Nole and Sycely.
Sept. 12, John Richard and Marye.
,, 15, Edward Reynold and Joane.
,, 15, Christopher Game and Agnes.
,, 20, John Hoskynn and Margerie.
Oct. 19, John Gregor and Jane.
,, 24, Werne John and Ellynor.
,, 25, Thomas Velly and Ursula.
,, 27, Thomas Bowden and Florenc.

[1602.]

Jan. 21, William Hew and ——
,, 24, William Edmondes and Ann.
,, 24, Sampson Noye and Ann.
Feb. 1, Richard Michell and Alos.
,, 11, John Harbert and Jane.
,, 14, John Chamberlyn and Jane.
+,, 16, Roger Baboll and Jane.   +

1602.
May 25, John Anbrose and Margerie.
,, 27, John Draper and Wynifred.
July 12, William Trewren and Elizabeth.
,, 12, Richard Alexander and Jane.
,, 29, William London and Jellian.
Oct. 24, John Rodda and Jane.
,, 24, John Hikx and Allice.
Nov. 7, Nowell Argall and Charitie.
,, 7, Thomas Griffen and Margaret.
,, 24, Henry Cleve and Elizabeth.

[1603.]

Jan. 30, Bennet Cullan and Florene.
,, 31, John Pollard, gent., and Elizabeth.
Feb. 28, Justinian Stephens and Ursula.

1603.
June 5, William Blache and Jane.
,, 20, John Nicholl and Jane.
Oct. 16, Richard Jelles and Allic.
Nov. 14, John Cardow and Elizabeth.
,, 20, Edward Trithall and Margaret.
Dec. 11, William Bennet and Jane.

[1604]

Jan. 15, John Stone and Alic.
Feb. 19, Roger Wylls and Chesten.

1604.
May 1, Raphe Noye and Margaret.
,, 16, Thomas Cowlyn, gent., and Katherin Lavelis
,, 28, Edmond Clies and Margaret.
,, 29, Noye Anboue and Joane.
Sept. 24, Raphe —— and Margaret.
Nov. 11, John Vallentine and Margaret.

[1605.]

Jan 31, Barthelmew Edye and Jane.
Feb. 2, William Pryor and Annyee.

1605.
June 10, Emannell Blewet and Gartered.
,, 22, Richard Lawrene and Ursula.
,, 23, Adam Rawlyn and Phillip.
July 7, Richard Nickles and Elizabeth.
Aug. 3, James Mulfra and Jane.
,, 4, Richard Alexander and Jane.
Oct. 19, Thomas Holla and Mary.
Nov. 10, George Lanyon, gent., and Prudenc.

[1606.]

Jan. 21, William Lanyon, gent., and Mary Lavelis.
,, 22, Haniball Lavelis, gent., and Anne.
,, 29, John Willy and Grace.
Feb. 10, Robert Downing and Katheren.
,, 15, John Hingstone and Marye.

1606.
May 27, John Wobber and Jane.
,, 29, William Marten and Agnes.
Nov. 7, Thomas Chullwill and Mary.
,, 16, Edward Savhell and Elizabeth.

PARISH OF MADRON.

Nov. 23, John Hoskyn, the younger, and ....
[1607.]
Jan. 13, Lawrene Michell and Jane.
 ,, 15, Gilbert Harry and Lowdy.
 ,, 17, Richard Kelter and Margaret.
[+] 1607.
April 25, John Thomas and Amy.
July 5, Mr. Roger Polkinghorne and Grace.
 ,, 6, Mr. John Clies and Blanche, daughter of Hugh Trevanyou, Esquior.
 ,, 13, Mr. Robert Sampson and Jane.
Nov. 15, John Mathew and Elizabeth.
 ,, 26, John Noale and Mary.
1608.
Mar. 28, Edward Seese and Jane.
 ,, 29, German Goiffe and Jane.
April 10, Mr. George Lanyon and Blanch.
 ,, 17, Willm. Robbins and Willmett.
 ,, 21, John Trick and Jellyan.
June 19, Frances Lanyon and Elizabeth.
Aug. 28, John Upright and Elizabeth.
Sept. 25, Degorye Duke and Grace.
Oct. 2, Henry Foster and Prudenc.
Nov. 11, Paskew Michell and Alse.
 ,, 20, Thomas Leath and Elizabeth.
 ,, 22, Humfrie Hutchins and Elizabeth.
Dec. 15, Wm. Younge, gent., and Katherin.

[1609.]
Jan. 10, Peeter Flinge and Jane.
 ,, 15, John Amble and Ann.
 ,, 20, Thomas Velly and Elizabeth.
Feb. 8, William Legowe and Ann.
1609.
June 1, Peeter Nicholas and Alse.
July 23, Willm. Symons and Honor.
Oct. 21, Edmond Tuttlie and Jone.
 ,, 22, Mr. Robert Jagoe and Mary.

[1610.]
Jan. 21, John Marten and Agnes.
 ,, 23, William Michell and Mary.
1610.
April 16, John Chinge and Amy.
 ,, 17, John Rowse and Joane.
July 1, John Porteere and Margarett.
 ,, 22, Raphe Morishe and Mary.
 ,, 22, William Kerhis and Elizabeth.
 ,, 29, James Fonny and Mawde.
 ,, 31, Thomas Champion and Margaret.
Oct. 1, Henry Fosse and Ann.
 ,, 8, Thomas Chenalls, gent., and Margarett.
Nov. 24, Edward Legowe and Ann.
 ,, 25, Thomas Tregerthen and Christen.

[1611.]
Feb. 3, John Hoskin and Elizabeth.

1611.
July 28, John James Tremethack, Jun., and Jone.
Sept. 9, Bennat Cullan and Alse.
 ,, 16, Robert Bonne and Elizabeth.
 ,, 22, John Champion and Elizabeth.
Oct. 19, Paskoe Barno and Ursula.
 ,, 21, Walter Bosavarne and Margaret.
 ,, 28, Walter Treffe and Margaret.
Nov. 5, John Hoskin and Margaret.
 ,, 6, Richard Thomas and Bridget.
 ,, 29, Michell James and Jane.

[1612.]
Jan. 20, Edward Champion and Elizabeth.
 ,, 29, Thomas Buttamore and Jellian.
Feb. 11, Anthony Trezies and Elizabeth.
 ,, 18, John Weymouth and Jone.
[+] 1612.
May 22, Woolph Pawghe* and Wellmett.
Aug. 6, Edward Bone and Thamasin.
 ,, 24, John Ellis and Elizabeth.
Oct. 21, Richard Harry and Elizabeth.
Nov. 8, John Toncken and Ann.
 ,, 26, Phillip Randall, gent., and Ann.

[1613.]
Jan. 30, Thomas Will and Elizabeth.
 ,, 31, John Bone and Elizabeth.
 ,, 31, Nicholas Roborts and Joane.
Feb. 7, Mathew Howes and Marye.
1613.
June 5, James Barnell and Clarence.
 ,, 10, William Boskeninge and Ann.
Aug. 1, John Rawlyn and Honor.
Sept. 7, John Sudgiow and Ann.
Oct. 10, Emanowell Drowe and Grace.
 ,, 17, John Oliver and Joane.

[1614.]
Mar. 14, Arthur Edye and Alic.
 ,, 21, Nowell Argall and Ann.
1614.
Aug. 7, Thomas Argall and Elizabeth.
Sept. 4, Robert Fynnye and Marye.
 ,, 9, Thomas George and Marye.
 ,, 18, James Pendene and Margarett.
 ,, 25, Thomas Heox and Marye.
Oct. 9, Henery Tremenheere and Ann.

[1615.]
Jan. 23, Alexander Limpany and Phillipp.
 ,, 25, William Tresies† and Tirham.†
 ,, 26, Thomas Maddron and Ellenor.
1615.
July 2, Thomas Beeulogge and ——

---

* This name is almost totally obliterated: there is scarcely a vestige of ink remaining, but read by the depression which the ink has left, it certainly appears to be as above. In the Register of Burials, however, the same name occurs clearly written—"1614, June 8, Willmett Pawgye." † Doubtful.

July 10, Nicholas Roch and Ellen.
„ 24, John Taylor and ——
Aug. 14, Samuell Randall and Blanch.
Sept. 21, John Friggens and Kathren.
„ 25, John Cowlinge, gent., and Francis.*
Oct. 1, William Harris and Amy.
„ 7, Robert Roda and ——
„ 8, Nicholas Mitchell and ——
„ 22, Henery Newton and ——
[Dec.] 3, John Holla and ——

[1616.]

Jan. 14, Henery Cossan and ——
„ 27, Henery Wearne and ——
1616.
April 8, Germane Luke and Ann.
„ 18, Ralph Antony and Phillipp.
May 12, William Noseworthy and Kathren.
Aug. 7, Bennet John and Jane.
Sept. 3, Thomas, the glover, and Hanna.
„ 15, Richard Cocke and Jone.
Oct. 19, John Rowe and Elizabeth.

[1617.]

Feb. 9, Robert Silvestor and Mary.
„ 16, James Wannell and Ellen.
1617.
June 8, Thomas Argoll and Kathren.
Aug. 10, Richard Lanyon and Elizabeth.
Oct. 12, Hanyball Richard and Elizabeth.
Nov. 13, Peter Nickles and Ursula.
Dec. 9, John Tremellyn and Mary.

[1618.]

Jan. 26, Thomas Heex and Ann.
Feb. 16, Thomas Baggs and Elizabeth.
1618.
Sept. 20, John Tremethack and Jane.
„ 21, Richard Tomm and Margarett.
Nov. 8, John Pomery and Alice.
„ 8, John Hooper and Elizabeth.

[1619.]

Jan. 18, William Battyn and Elizabeth.
„ 30, Richard Bishopp and Thamsyn.
Feb. 4, Walter Pender and Ursula.
„ 8, John Jaylor and Joane.
1619.
June 9, Richard Jenkyn and Jane.
„ 15, John Trewryn and Margarett.
July 7, John Trevilor and Elnor.
Aug. 3, Richard Cocke and Grace.
„ 4, John Chergwin and Elizabeth.
1620.
Sept. 4, John Maddren, Jun., and Ann.
„ 17, John Fynny and Alice.
Nov. 13, Robert Lody and Garrett.

* Re-written upon erasure.

Nov. 20, Thomas Lake and Mary.

[1621.]

Jan. 14, Thomas Hutchens and Kathren.
„ 20, Sampson Lake and Kathren.
„ 27, Tho. George and Jane.
1621.
April 10, John Lethiby and Grace.
July 15, Thomas Sudgiowe and Elizabeth.
„ 22, Richard Hutchens and Joane.
Aug. 14, Pethrick Edward and Joane.
Sept. 8, Saundry Maddren and Tamsyn.
„ 17, John James and Hellen.

[1622.]

Jan. 15, Walter Mitchell and Kathren.
„ 18, Richard Cardewe and Annis.
1622.
May 5, James Earle and Amy.
„ 12, Tristrum Somery and Ann.
July 8, William Rodda and Elizabeth.
„ 13, Edward Lawrence and Margarett.
„ 14, Robert Trowren and Mary.
„ 21, John Hawes and Margarett.
1623.
June 15, John Beuver and Rebecka.
„ 21, John Polkinghorne and Ellen.
Sept. 7, William Sudgeo and Margarett.
Oct. 8, Thomas Lake and Elizabeth.

[1624.]

Feb. 1, Reynauld Boas and Mary.
1624.
April 14, Thomas Roberts and Jane.
„ 21, John Thomas and Ann.
„ 27, Michell Skinner and Ann.
May 6, Richard Boscenco and Clarence.
„ 17, James Marke and Gylian.
„ 24, Symon Francis and Ann.
July 18, James Hammott and Ellinor.
Aug. 9, Richard Hutchens and Elizabeth.
Sept. 25, Madron Champon and Chesten.

[1625.]

Jan. 4, John Bosaverne and Elizabeth.
„ 24, Ananias Horsford and Margarett.
Feb. 12, John Cocke and Francis.
1625.
June 5, John Lanyon and Jane.
„ 22, Gabriell Sommer and Margarett.
July 17, William Jencken and Joane.
„ 24, Rodger Gymboll and Joane.
Aug. 1, Ralph Morish and Elizabeth.
Nov. 6, Thomas Nowton and Kathren.

[1626.]

Jan. 10, Thomas, the tanner, and Ellen.
1626.
May 2, William Trencere and Elizabeth.

PARISH OF MADRON.

June 4, John Cloake and Margarett.
„ 10, Edward Edwards and Ann.
Sept. 3, William Hooper and Elizabeth.
Nov. 5, William Nighten and Elizabeth.
„ 10, James Troloweth and Grace.

[1627.]

Jan. 29, Roger Polkinghorne and Blanch.
Feb. 5, John Edward and Elizabeth.

1627.

April 9, Samuell Sycsell and Margarett.
„ 16, John Polzew and Kathren.
„ 20, Walter Bazaw and Kathren.
Sept. 9, Henery Jenckyn and Elizabeth.
Nov. 10, John Morish and Thamesyn.

[1628.]

Jan. 21, John Pawle and Sara.
Feb. 3, Henery Tremorne and Phillipp.
„ 4, Joseph Basslye and Grace.
„ 6, John Lamerton and Elizabeth.
„ 9, John Lamyn and Evelyn.

1628.

July 27, William Bennett and Ann.
Aug. 10, John Callye and Joane.
Nov. 9, William Williams and Jane.
„ 16, John Jeffrye and Alice.
„ 23, Pascowe Tyncombe and Margery.
„ 28, Richard Jacka and Maud.

[1629.]

Jan. 5, John Cowlinge and Francis.
„ 8, Thomas Hubbord and Elizabeth.
[+] 1629.
June 4, John Keat, gent., and Elizabeth, daughter of Thomas Flomynge, gent.
Oct. 11, George Noye and Elizabeth.
„ 25, William Teage and Kathren.
Nov. 7, Ralph Lawry and Elizabeth.

[1630.]

Jan. 18, James Trenwith and Elizabeth.
Feb. 3, John Cowlinge and Agnes, daughter of William Lowar, gent.

1630.

April 12, Bennet Angwyn and Jane.
„ 20, George Wolcock and Elizabeth.
Nov. 26, John Thomas and Grace.

[1631.]

Jan. 17, Richard Bennet and Joane.
„ 23, Martyne Sampson and Mary, daughter of William Lanyon.
Feb. 3, Thomas Legoe and Alice, the daughter of John Cowling, gent.
„ 21, Nicholas Flemynge, gent., and Ann, daughter of John Clise, gent.

1631.

Nov. 6, John Tonckyn and Alice.

Nov. 25, Robert Tompkyn and Catheren.

[1632.]

Feb. 6, Jespar James and Jane.

1632.

April 15, Diggory Glanfield and Jane, daughter of Will. Tampkyn.
„ 24, Pawle Nicholls and Agnis.
Aug. 4, Thomas Morish and Margaret.
„ 7, Roger Frost and Catheren.
Oct. 8, John Mulfra and Katheren.
Nov. 10, Richard Launder and Honor.

[1633.]

Feb. 4, Robert Meldern and Agnis.
„ 14, Maddarn Leagoe and Ann.
„ 16, Thomas Hutcheus and Christen, daughter of Martine Vibart.

1633.

April 28, William Tresvenack and Joane.
May 5, Umphrye Martyne and Jennyfret.
„ 12, Merret Furse and Christen.
„ 18, William Ballamye and Jane.
„ 25, Mathewe Hoskyn and Kathorin.
Nov. 9, Lewis Hockyn and Alice.
„ 16, Richard Duke and Elizabeth.

[1634.]

Jan. 19, James Loose and Elizabeth.
„ 25, John Nooall and Joane.

1634.

April 21, Thomas Lavelis, gent., and Margarett.
June 2, Thomas Bond and Jane, daughter of William L[anyon.]
„ 9, Martyne Bosaverne and Ann, daughter of Tho. Cowling.
„ 16, George Phillipps and Alice.
Oct. 13, John Manly and Margett.
Nov. 17, William Younge, gent., and Jone, daughter of Francis Glover.
„ 24, Henery Launder and Mary.

[1635.]

Jan. 24, Thomas Williams and Prudence.
„ 18,* Nicholas Hooper and Mary.

1635.

April 12, Francis Legg and Phillipp.
„ 19, John Oliver and Ann.
June 4, Nicholas John and Joane.
Oct. 11, James Fenny and Margarett.
„ 18, David Ponlease and Elizabeth.
Nov. 15, Richard Trick and English.
„ 24, Henery Avery and Ellen.
„ 28, Robert Colman and Mary, daughter of Tho. Fleming.
„ 28, William Williams and Margarett.

* Sic.

REGISTER OF MARRIAGES.

[1636.]
Jan. 17, John Stevens and Elizabeth, daughter of Jo. Stone.
 „ 24, Richard Lander and Alice.
 „ 31, Nicholas Buswathack and Alice.
Feb. 7, Robert Harry and Christen.
 „ 10, William Luke and Dorothy.
1636.
Aug. 14, Halnight Steven and Margarett.
Nov. 26, John Thomas and Joane.

[1637.]
Jan. 22, Zacharias Grogar and Joane.
 „ 28, Thomas Lanyon, gent., and Mary.
Feb. 10, John Mitchell and Ann.
1637.
April 23, Sampson Bossence and Earth.
July 16, John Edye and Avis.
Nov. 26, Thomas Pryer and Alice.
1638.
[May] 19, Phillip Peryam, Sen., and Elizabeth Champion.
[June] 10, William Jenckyn and Ann, daughter of John Hoskyn.
 „ 18, Morish Roch and Ann Vater, widow.
Aug. 29, Richard Treneero and Francis, daughter of John Ethaw.
Sept. 17, Thomas Culensoe and Katheren Trewheela.
 „ 23, William Sampson and Ann Parret.
Oct. 28, John Trebiver and Joane Champion, widow.
Nov. 4, Richard Seevins* and Jane, daughter of Richard Trott.
 „ 11, Thomas Finny and Alice Hoskyn, widow.
 „ 18, Thomas Beccalegg and Joane Hoskyn, widow.
 „ 25, Alexander Nicholas and Joane Glauvyle.
Dec. 1, Steevins† and Ann, daughter of Thomas Maddox.

[1639.]
Jan. 20, Thomas Sleepe and Jane, daughter of John Luke.
 „ 27, William Penticost and Elizabeth, daughter of Ellis Bonhet.
1639.
June 24, Phillip Carne and Blanch, daughter of Mathew Hawes.
Aug. 5, James Wannell, Sen., and Elizabeth Hancock
Sept. 21, William Trust and Elizabeth Thomas.
Oct. 6, John Finny and Margery, daughter of Digory Duke.
 „ 20, James Wannell, Jun., and Jone, daughter of Edward Sise.
 „ 28, John Cloke and Ann Penlease.
Nov. 3, Edward Kimpthorne and Mary Glover.

Nov. 30, Thomas Sampson and Jane Gross.
 „ 30, Nicholas Hoskyn and Sarah, daughter of Sampson Noye.
Dec. 21, Henry Kitt, gent., and Ann, daughter of Mr. Roger Polkinghorne.

[1640.]
Feb. 3, Walter Sanders and Jane, daughter of Digory Duke.
 „ 4, William Gross, gent., and Ann, daughter of Willm. Nosworthy.
1640.
April 20, William Tregeeo and Susan, daughter of Francis Lanyon.
 „ 25, Henry Paskoe and Julyan, daughter of John Luke.
May 1, Robert James and Margaret, daughter of Sampson Noye.
Aug. 5, William Restorlath and Alice Lander.
Oct. 16, Martine Rodda and Alice, daughter of Thomas Cock.
 „ 22, Phillip Perium, Jun., and Francis Barne.
Nov. 16, Henry Chinalls and Honor Trithall.
 „ 12,* Henry Edmonds and Jane Jenckyn.

[1641.]
Jan. 14, John Lanyon and Ann Thomas.
 „ 14, John Barne and Ann, daughter of Henry Newton.
 „ 14, Robert Carne and Ann, daughter of Oats Nickles.
Feb. 8, Theophilus Laugharne and Ann Madderne.
 „ 23, William Lawrence and Nicholl Marke.
 „ 20,* Francis John and Grace Betten, Sen.
* * * * * * * * * *
[+] 1644.
May 3, Phillipp Lanyon, gent., and Agnes, daughter of ....
 „ 10, Theophelus Laughorne and Ann, daughter of William ....
 „ 24, Richard Newton, Jun., and Ann Rosewarne, widow.
July 10, John Glasse and Jone.
Nov. 14, John Stephent and Luce Pellamonten.
 „ 22, John George‡ and Blanch, daughter of Jo. Perry.

[1645.]
Jan. 17, William Digens, merchant, and Ann, daughter of Jo. Gr[oss?]
 „ 24, William Werren and Elizabeth, daughter of Arthar§ Wolcock.
1645.
June 2, John Harrey and Barbra.
Oct. 8, Nicholas Hosken and Elizabeth Noye.

---

* Query a clerical error, " t " being omitted after the first letter.
† Sic. Query "Thomas Stephens, alias Trevawin." See Burials, 1647, April 30.

* Sic. † Re-written upon erasure.
‡ John George is written in a different hand and ink where a blank had been left.
§ Written in a different hand and ink over Will. erased.

PARISH OF MADRON.   37

Oct.   9, John Hodge and Ann.
 ,,   20, Arundell Sackerley and Bridgett.
Nov. 10, Walter Noye and Margarett.
*
[1646.]
Jan. .. Sir John H .... the ....
           levinge in the Bor ... of ...., and Marye,
           daughter of .... within the Pisho
           of Madderne.†
[+] 1646.
April 19, William Mulfra and Prudence.
May 28, John Trenoere and Priscilla.
June 13, John Batten and Mawd.
 ,,   20, William Noye and Ebbot.
July 4, John Roberts and Rachiel.
 ,,   6, Francis Tremenheere and Mary.
Aug. 12, John Legaw and Honor.
 ,,   24, Richard Champion and Ellenor.
 ,,   27, Jonathan Pilson and Anne.
Sept. 9, William Cowling, gent., and Phillipp.
 ,,   14, Thomas Thomas and Grace.
Oct.   3, Christopher Glasan and Prudence.
 ,,   12, Robert Fynney and Jone.
 ,,   26, John Tregunnow and Anne.
Nov. 21, Richard Nuhall and Margarett.
 ,,   30, Richard Angwin, gent., and Grace.
[1647.]
Feb. 13, John Fynney and Elizabeth.
 ,,   15, Arthur Fight and Priscilla.
1647.
April 24, John Hutchens and Margerie.
May 19, Peter John and Mawde.
June 22, John Giles and Anne.
 ,,   25, John Bowden and Elizabeth.
 ,,   29, Thomas Foster and Elizabeth.
July 1, John Rawling and Margarett.
 ,,   21, Henry Dunkin and Jenefred.
Aug. 8, Thomas Thomas and Earth.
Nov. 6, Sampson Lanion and Margarett.
 ,,   20, John Sampson, Jun., and Anne.
 ,,   20, Richard Sudgeow and Blanch.
 ,,   24, Richard Geare and Margarett.
 ,,   27, Christopher Champion and Susan.
 ,,   30, Paschow Tyncombe and Margery.
Dec. 11, Robart Edmonds and Blanch.
 ,,   18, Arthur Noye and Alice.
 ,,   27, John Williams and Susan.
[1648.]
Jan.   8, Thomas Stephens and Susan.

Jan. 22, Richard Marten and Chesten.
 ,,   .. George [Re]nowden and [Alice.]
 ,,   23, Gilbert Fix and Katharine.
Feb. 5, Bennatt Lanion and Martha.
1648.
April 29, George Blewett and Margarett.
 ,,   29, John Edy and Grace.
May 6, Salamon Cock and Grace.
July 1, Martyn Gwennapp and Sara.
 ,,   15, John Cossens and Elloner.
 ,,   29, Methuselah Rodda and Grace.
Oct. 16, John Richards and Alice.
 ,,   16, Richard Newhall and Anne.
 ,,   30, Nicholas Rawlings and Elloner.
Nov. 11, John Luke and Margarett.
 ,,   18, John Maddern and Jone.
Dec. 27, James Pike and Julian.
 ,,   30, Thomas Rawlyn and Jane.
 ,,   31, William Boase and Anne.
[1649.]
Jan. 4, John Holla and Elizabeth.
 ,,   20, Marke Lanion and Elizabeth.
 ,,   20, Richard Legoe and Blanch.
Feb. 5, Joell Garrow and Blauch.
 ,,   6, Nathaniell Trenerry and Grace.
 ,,   6, John Tonken and Grace.
 ,,   9, Thomas Hubbard and Winyfred.
1649.
Mar. 26, Bernard Laity and Anne.
April 2, William Fosse and Margarett.
 ,,   2, William Bosekennen and Anne.
June 23, Francis Lanion and Rosamon.
 ,,   30, John Tonken and Jone.
 ,,   30, Richard Bolithoo and Phillipp.
Aug. 4, Peter Degory and Alice.
Oct. 13, Thomas Dee and Jone.
 ,,   13, Samuell Nicholas and Thomasine.
 ,,   20, Henry Williams and Jane.
Nov. 3, Walter Finny and Julian.
 ,,   17, William Painter and Jaquilina.
 ,,   24, Hugh Hobbs and Jone.
Dec. 8, Mathew Reede and Jone.
 ,,   8, Luke Stephens and Ellouer.
 ,,   22, Thomas George and Anne.
[1650.]
Feb. 23, Edward Rawlings and Mary.
1650.
June 22, William Bratcherie and Blauch.
Aug. 4, James Noye and Jone.
[Sept.] .. Ja. . . . .
Oct.   5, James John, Jun., and Margarett.
Nov. 16, Richard Osbern and Katherine.
 ,,   16, Phillipp Michell and Constance.
[1651.]
Jan.   4, John Cripps and Anne.
 ,,   9, John Monallack and Jane.

---

* A blank occurs here, and also between 24th January, 1644-5, and 2nd June, 1645. The two blanks together extend over rather more than half the page, and that which follows is entirely blank.
† The Rev. WILLIAM TREMENHEERE in his copy reads this entry "Sir John Harcias, ... of the ...... hainge in the Borough of (Swansea ?) and Margery," &c. The writing is very indistinct, but what remains does not seem altogether to agree with this reading. In the present tattered and mutilated condition of this upper edge of the page the surname, beyond the first letter, bears little or no resemblance to Harciss, and the name of the town is very doubtful. That which Mr. Tremenheere reads " hainge" is certainly "levinge" (i.e. living), and the wife's name is Mary.

J

REGISTER OF MARRIAGES.

1651.
April 12, Robert Weare and Senobia.
July 29, Gabriell Cock and Elizabeth.
Oct. 18, John Aubone and Paschas.
 ,,   18, Samuell Edy and Jone.
1652.
July 31, William Noye and Margarett.
 ,,   31, Richard Edwards and Jone Lanion.
Sept. 10, Thomas Holbert and Alice.
Oct.   9, Henry Saundry and Christian.
 ,,   9, James John and Jone.
 ,,   30, Nicholas Cock and Elizabeth.
1653.
May 30, John Bennatt and Anne.
Aug. 4, George Marrack and Susanna.
Sept. 12, John Anbone and Ellonor.
 ,,   24, Thomas Pearse and Jone.
 ,,   24, John Champion and Jone.
 ,,   24, John Randall and Anne.
 ,,   26, John Ustick and Margarett.
Dec. 17, John Blunt and Jone.
[1654.]
Jan. 27, Nicholas Nicholas and Anne.
Feb. 13, William Angove and Jane.
 ,,   13, Stephen Pardew and Sara.
1654.
April 15, Thomas Allan and Elizabeth.
May   6, William Pearse and Ellonor.
June 5, William Nicholls, gent., and Phillip.
 ,,   15, William Walsh and Jone.
Sept. 30, Humphry Nicholas and Mary.
Oct. 13, Lewis Bennatt and Jone.
 ,,   14, Richard Wolcock and Alice.
Dec. 28, Walter Hodge and Mary.
[1655.]
Jan. 8, Tho. Morish, the younger, and Willmott.
 ,,   17, William Trewren, gent., and Elizabeth.
 ,,   19, Walter Rodda and Anne.
 ,,   21, John . . . .
 .... 7, [John James and J]ulian.
1655.
 .... 22, John James and Anne.
 ,,   29, George Davye and Penelope.
 ..r. 29, Richard Carpesack and Jane.
 ..or. 26, Nicholas Fleming, gent., and Elizabeth, daughter of George Veale, gent.
[1656.]
Jan. 15, Phillipp Argall and Alice.
 ,,   19, Richard Lanion and Margery.
Feb. 2, Michaell Nicholas and Anne.
1656.
 .... 13, Thomas Chirgwin and Jane, daughter of Thomas Fleming, gent.
June 27, Walter Harrie and Jane.
July 10, John Williams and Katheren.

July 10, William Edye and Jane.
Aug. 1, William Luke and Anne.
 ,,   8, Thomas Roberts and Honor.
 ,,   22, Francis Trewren and Elizabeth.
Sept. 17, William Legowe and Margarett.
Oct.   3, Henry Tredenneck and Elizabeth.
Nov.   2, John Pollard, the younger, and Jane.
 ,,   7, James Gilbert and Honor.
Dec.   5, Robart Rodda and Anne.
 ,,   28, Mathew Skinner and Phillipp.
[1657.]
..ry. 2, James Nolan and Alice.
 ,,   20, Robart Gooble and Duens.
Mar. 13, John Bromewell and Constance.
1658.*
April 12, Michaell Tredenneck and Margarett.
 ,,   12, Nicholas Hooper and Margarett.
 ,,   23, Thomas Sise, marchant, and Elizabeth, daughter of Nicholas Fleming, gent.
..y 25, Christopher Bodenner and Sara.
..r.   1, John Glover and Anne Tirroll, widow.
 ,,   8, Thomas Fleming, of Landithy, gent., and Mary Harris, daughter of William Harris, of Kenegy, Esq.
 ,,   11, William Michell and Margarett.
 ,,   .. [Thom?]as Martyn and Joane.
* * * * * * * * * * * * * * *†
[1659.]
..... John . . . .
[1660.]
..... Michaell Nicholas and ....
 ,,   16, William Rodda and ....
July 29, Thomas Stephens and [Thomasine.]
Nov. 20, John Gilbert and ....
[1661.]
Jan. 28, Benedict Champion and ....
March 5, John Hicks, gent., and Katherine, the daughter of John Cowling, of Trengwainton, gent.
1661.
April 15, Robart Luty and Hellen.
 ,,   30, John Michell and Julian, the daughter of Richard Scaddon, of Ludgvan.
Sept. 21, Thomas Gregar and Lois.
Oct.   5, Will. Michell and Mary.
Dec.   7, Walter Lanion and Mary.
1662.
July 12, Richard‡ Maddern and Mary.
 ,,   19, Richard Stephens and Thomasine.
Sept. 26, Martyn Rodda and Jane.
 ,,§ 27, Tho. Hall and Chesten.
Nov. 15, Noye Champion and Redigon.

---

* The year 1657 is unnoticed. Is it possible that the entries for this year were accidentally omitted, or that there were no Marriages?
† A leaf missing here probably. ‡ Written above Bennat erased.
§ Oct. has been erased and the figures altered.

PARISH OF MADRON.

[1663.]
Jan. 2, Robart Tonken, Jun., and Margarett.
1663.
April 25, George Christopher and Barbary.
June 27, James Thomas and Mary.
Aug. .. John Sudgeow and Sebella.
Nov. 6, William Pearse and Elizabeth.
 „ 13, William Trewren and Katheren.
Dec. 15, James Jenken and Mary.
1664.
Oct. 8, Thomas Edye and Elizabeth.

[1665.]
Jan. 14, Zacharias Gregar and Grace.
 „ 14, Humfry Jacka and Margarett.
 „ 31, James Carpenter and Joane.
1665.
April 12, Robart White and Katherine.
 „ 28, William Jeffry and Elizabeth.
June 5, Humfry Pearse and Mary.
 „ 17, Scipio Stephens and Anne.
 .... ke and Anne.
 „ ...... Micholl and Honor.
 „ .. William Gewell and Bridgett.
 „ ...... Logowe and Paschas.
 „ 25, Ralph Battyn and Elizabeth.

[1666.]
Jan.? 6, Nicholas Keygwin and Garthered.
 „ 13, John Bennatt and Dorothie.
[+] 1666.
April 21, William Rawling and Elizabeth.
July 7, Ananias Hosford and Mary.
Aug. 20, Andrew Angwin and Alice.
Sept. 8, John Hitchcocke and Blanch.
 „ 8, John Barnes and Thomasine.
 „ 22, Uriah Tonken and Elizabeth.
Oct. 6, Eleanor Lanion and Honor.
 „ 6, Thomas Bennatt and Mary.
 „ 19, John Mathew and Jane.
 „ 20, Robert Thomas and Elizabeth.

* * * * * * * * * * * * * * *†

* A blank occurs here extending over about one-third of the page.
† A leaf missing here.

[+] 1673.
April 15, John Richards, of Paule, and Ann.
May 26, Justinian Pedwell and Sarah.
June 7, Alexander Richards, of Gulvall, and Mary.
July 22, John Richards and Chesten.
Sept. 12, Jenken Bodennar, of Paule, and Betrice.
Nov. 29, William Knoben and Cathraine.

[1674.]
Jan. 28, David Gift and Katherne.
 „ 31, Richard Jenken and Mary.
Feb. 7, Richard Giles and Ann.
1674.
April 27, Henry Trenwith and Constance.
May 16, Ralph Lanion, gent., and Pacience.
 „ 30, Somar Honichurch, gent., and Margery.
Aug. 8, William Hosken and Blanch.
Oct. 3, Alexander Reed and Mary.
Nov. 3, Richard Hosken and Kathren.
 „ 6, George Nichols and Jane.
 „ 27, Thomas Gift and Margarett.

[1675.]
Jan. 16, Peter James and Jaell.
 „ 16, Arthur Tonken and ——
1675.
Aug. 13, George Stephens and Mary.
Dec. 11, William Lanyon and Susanna.
1676.
April 22, Nicholas Sampson and Jane.
 „ 28, Thomas John and Margery.
 „ 29, Thomas Fostar and Jane.
June 10, Nicholas Conack and Kathrayne.
July 1, Thomas Richards and Mary.
Aug. 19, John Trelevar and Elizabeth.
 „ 19, James Collerk and Mary.
Sept. 22, Arundell Ellary and Mary.
 „ 30, James Cock and Mary.
Nov. 20, Henry Hosken and Ann.
1677.
April 28, John Veale, gent., and Honor.
June 23, Nicholas Rodda and Alise.
Sept. 3, Oliver Trestean, gent., and Dorothy.

[1678.]
Jan. 26, John Stephens and Honor.
 „ 26, Richard Walke and Jane.

The Register of Burials.

Burialls beginninge in anno 1577.

1577.	
Mayo	20, Was buried John Fynny, the sonne of Richard Fynnie.
Julye	14, was buryed Nicholas Veale, the sonne of William Veale, gentelman.
August	21, was buryed Wylliam Trewren.
Septembr.	the xiiijth, was buryed Mawde Pnugiow.
Novem.	16, was buryed Jellian, the daughter of Nicholas Cordeg.
,,	18, was buryed William Holla.
,,	18, was buryed Henrye, the sonne of Christopher Game.
Decembr.	30, was buryed William, the sonne of John Thomas.
Janua.	14, was buryed Joane, the daughter of Valentyne Wemuoth.
,,	16, was buryed Marke, the sonne of meretricis.
,,	20, was buryed Jane, the daughter of Henry John.
,,	20, was buryed Elizabeth Saloma.
Febr.	29, was buryed John, the sonne of James Trembath.
March	1, was buryed Joane, the daughter of John Bossy.
,,	2, was buryed Maryan, the servaunte of John Luer.
,,	3, was buryed John, the sonne of Nicholas Kinge.
,,	4, was buryed James Tremesncke.
,,	5, was buryed Nicholas Seymer.
,,	12, was buryed Grace, the daughter of Edward James.
,,	12, was buryed Henrye Logan.
,,	15, was buryed Elizabeth, the daughter of Henrye Foster.
,,	15, was buryed Henrye, the sonne of Bennet Herry.
May	1, was buryed Amye, the daughter of Mellior Soloma.
1578.	10, was buryed Richard Cosen, the elder.
June	7, was buryed John, the sonne of John Skotte.
,,	9, was buryed Richard and William, sonnes of John Skott.
,,	10, was buried James, the servant of Henry Polkinghorne.
,,	13, was buried Christian, the wief of John Skott.
,,	16, was buryed John Skott.
,,	20, was buryed William, the sonne of Marke Olyver.
,,	26, was buryed William, the sonne of Bennet Vyau.
,,	27, was buryed John, the sonne of Thomas Robert.
Julye	6, was buried Margerie, the daughter of Roger Tule.
,,	7, was buried Elizabeth *quædam, morbo convitiali laborans* :*
,,	7, was buryed Marye, the daughter of Richard Harry.

* The words in italics are written in a different style of letter.
N.B. This page is a verbatim copy of the original.

K

REGISTER OF BURIALS.

July 8, Robert, son of Nicholas Thomas.
„ 8, Thomas, son of William Hawke.
„ 8, Richard Harrie.
„ 8, Thomas Davye.
„ 8, Radigonn, daughter of William Hawke.
„ 9, Jane, daughter of William Hawke.
„ 11, Maderne, son of Thomas Bodenar.
„ 12, Jane, daughter of John Jollye.
„ 13, Jenett, daughter of Thomas Noye.
„ 14, Margerie, daughter of Henry Foster.
„ 14, Raphe, son of Thomas Noye.
„ 19, Henrie, son of Richard Maderne.
„ 21, Thomas, son of Leonard Gillard.
„ 22, Michaell, son of John, an Irishe man.
„ 22, Thomas, son of William Clies.
„ 23, John, son of Thomas Bodynar.
„ 24, Margarett, an Irishe woman.
„ 24, Allie, daughter of John Robartt.
„ 24, John Maye.
„ 25, Nicholas, son of John Goodale.
„ 25, John, son of Nicholas Carpenter.
„ 25, William Hawke.
„ 26, Katherine, wife of John Keygwyne.
„ 26, Cutberd, servaunt of Nicholas Carpenter.
„ 26, John, son of James Angosse.
„ 26, John Thomas.
„ 26, Agnes, wife of the said John Thomas.
„ 27, Nicholas Carpenter.
„ 29, Mawde, wife of William Bathe.
„ 30, Elizabeth, daughter of William Logan.
Aug. 3, Elizabeth, wife of John Pannalvyan.
„ 3, Agnes, daughter of John Carne.
„ 3, William, son of William Barnicott.
„ 3, John, son of Thomas Gaye.
„ 4, Katherin, daughter of John Irishe.
„ 6, Margarett, daughter of John Panalvian.
„ 6, John, son of Henrie Miller.
„ 6, William, son of John Goodale.
„ 7, Nicholas, son of John Panalvian.
„ 7, John, son of John Pannalvian.
„ 8, Elizabeth Nicholas, widow.
„ 8, Katherin, daughter of John Penminow.
„ 9, Edward, son of William Dennys.
„ 9, Thomas, son of John Pannalvean.
„ 10, John, son of John Goodale.
„ 10, Joane, daughter of Symon Peres.
„ 10, Christian, wife of John Goodale.
„ 10, Jonathan, son of John Goodale.
„ 10, Edward, son of John Thomas.
„ 11, Stephen Peares.
„ 11, John Porria.
„ 11, Agnes, daughter of Richard Rabnett.
„ 11, Thomas Davie, servant of John Maderne.
„ 11, Marten Smythe.
„ 12, Richard, son of Richard Rabnett.
„ 12, Fraunces, daughter of John Thomas.
„ 12, Richard, son of Roger Smythe.
„ 12, Joane, daughter of Elizabeth Benet, spur.
„ 13, Lodovicke Bell.

Aug. 13, John, son of Joane Thomas, merctr.
„ 13, Maryan Solloman.
„ 13, William, son of Thomas* Gaye.
„ 16, Allice, daughter of Stephen Anthony.
„ 17, Allice Terrenacke.
„ 17, John Vian, servant to Roger Tule.
„ 18, Elizabeth, daughter of Richard Tonkyn.
„ 18, Amye, daughter of Maderne James.
„ 19, Stephen Anthonye.
„ 20, Margaret, daughter of Richard Peres.
„ 21, Henrie, son of William Taber.
„ 21, Elizabethe, daughter of John Tredynneck.
„ 22, Jane Glover.
„ 22, Margarett Jane.
„ 24, Jane, wife of Stephen Peares.
„ 24, Richard Crankann.
„ 25, Katherin, daughter of John Terrynnack.
„ 26, Christopher Asye.
„ 26, Margaret, daughter of Henrie Logan.
„ 27, Christian Carne.
„ 27, Fraunces, daughter of John Terrynnack.
„ 29, John Terrynnacke.
„ 29, John Martynne.
„ 30, Richard, son of Elizabeth Syse, spur.
„ 30, Henrie, son of Richard Logann.
Sept. 1, Elizabethe Marten.
„ 3, John, son of Symon Cokewell.
„ 4, Tyrracke Bell.
„ 5, Jane, wife of Symon Cockwell.
„ 5, Richard, son of Christopher Game.
„ 8, Joan Porria.
„ 12, William, son of John Martin.
„ 13, Allice Genkinge.
„ 13, Richard, son of John Webber.
„ 17, John Saundrye.
„ 21, Jane, daughter of Walter Tyllam.
„ 22, Elizabethe Champion.
„ 23, Hellinor Foster.
„ 26, John Frauncke.
„ 26, William Lethebye.
„ 26, John, son of Symon Cockwell.
„ 27, Agnes, daughter of Maderne Wolcoke.
„ 29, John Bossava.
„ 30, Joane, daughter of Dionie Teller.
Oct. 2, William, son of Maderne Wolcock.
„ 3, Agnes, daughter of William Champion.
„ 8, William, son of William Wolcoke.
„ 11, Dionie Tayler.
„ 12, Elizabeth, daughter of Maderne Wolcoke.
„ 14, John, son of Sampson Barber.
„ 14, Margaret, servante of John Penmynow.
„ 16, Elizabethe, wife of John Mathew.
„ 18, Katherin, wife of Sampson Barber.
„ 18, Penticoste, daughter of Robert Angove.
„ 18, Hellen, daughter of Sampson Barber.
„ 22, Sampson Barber.
„ 24, William, son of Maderne Wollcoke.

* Written above John erased.

PARISH OF MADRON.

Oct. 26, Sampson Buswodnan.
,, 26, Allyce Barleighe.
,, 26, Elizabeth, daughter of Sacharie Champion.
,, 27, Barnardo Barber.
,, 27, Rychardo Champyon.
,, 27, Allice, daughter of Sacharie Champion.
,, 30, William, son of John Barnes.
,, 30, Richard Bennett Rowe.
,, 30, John Thomas Michell.
,, 31, Richard, son of Richard Treneyre.
Nov. 1, John, son of John Sellowe.
,, 4, Elizabeth, daughter of John Penmynowe.
,, 8, Norowe Champion, widow.
,, 10, Allyce, daughter of William Nashe.
,, 12, Joane, daughter of Maderne James.
,, 15, Elizabethe, wife of John Sellowe.
,, 17, Joane, daughter of William Robertes.
,, 18, Anthony,* son of George Hase.
,, 28, Richoe, wife of William Robertes.
,, 28, John, son of Richard Treanere.
,, 30, John, son of Maderne James.
Dec. 10, Richard, son of James Tremethacke.
,, 12, Thomas, son of James Tremethacke.
,, 14, Thomas, son of James Tuckye.
,, 14, Ursula, daughter of William Bowes.
,, 21, Rychard Shevanne.
,, 23, Thomas, son of John Rowe.
,, 26, William, son of William Robert.

[1579.]
Jan. 7, Thomas, son of Bennet Holla.
,, 12, Agnes, daughter of John Wallter.
,, 14, Thomas, son of John Wallter.
,, 15, Agnes, daughter of Symon Hooper.
,, 16, Rowe, servant of Robert Lavollis.
,, 31, Henrie, son of Richard Feeny.
Feb. 4, Nicholl, son of John Milcomb.

1579.
July 3, Margaret, wife of Thomas Dewen.
,, 13, John, son of Thomas Sudgiow.
,, 20, John, son of John Bennett.
Aug. 24, Katherin Barber.
Oct. 3, Sampson, son of Edward James.
,, 7, Elizabethe Ageare.
,, 16, John Treneare.

1580.
Sept. 21, John Maderne, of Pawle.
Oct. 5, Mellioner Saundrye.
,, 7, Agnes, daughter of John Bassett.
,, 23, John Brushe.
Dec. 3, Jane, daughter of John Marten.
,, 11, Edward James.
,, 17, Agnes, wife of Nicholas Tonkyn.
,, 27, Amye, daughter of Christopher Asye.

[1581.]
Jan. 27, Ursula, daughter of John Rodda.

Jan. 31, Richoe Robertt.
Feb. 1, John, son of John Thomas.
,, 9, Margerie, daughter of John Trithall.

1581.
Mar. 28, —— daughter of John Michell.
,, 28, Amye, daughter of John Suttonn.
,, 29, John, son of John Coome.
,, 31, John, son of William Sommer.
April 22, Jane, daughter of George Peeter.
May 15, Christian, daughter of Peter Rawlyn.
Aug. 10, John, son of John Thomas.
,, 11, William, son of Maderne James.

1582.
April 3, Jane, wife of John Brittayne.
,, 10, Margerye, wife of Thomas Trembathe.
,, 11, John Saundrye, son of John Saundry.
,, 19, Geoffrie Gene.
,, 28, —— daughter of William Anthony.
,, 28, Hellen, wife of William Pawle.
May 13, John Geoffrie.
,, 20, Joane, daughter of John Norishe.*
,, 26, The wife of Sacharie Champion.
June 24, Joane, daughter of John Goine.
Aug. 23, John, son of John Tonkinge.
,, 26, Joane, daughter of Thomas Abbott.
,, 26, Pascowe Carne.
Sept. 5, John, son of Emanuell, the smithe.
,, 5, John, son of Thomas, the smithe.
,, 7, Margaret, servante of Thomas Anbone.
Nov. 20, Elizabeth, daughter of William Mulfra.
Dec. 3, John, son of John Rodda.
,, 9, Robert Cowlinge, gentelman.
,, 18, The son of Thomas† Fleming.
,, 20, Richo, wife of Richard Vicker.

[1583.]
Feb. 17, Wallter, son of John Noye.
,, 17, Elizabeth, wife of Richard Paskowe.
March 1, The daughter of John Holla.
,, 7, Thomas Barber.
,, 9, William Trembahe.
,, 9, Henrye, son of Henry Polkinhorne.

1583.
April 10, The son of Nicholas, the joyner.
,, 17, John, son of John Tremethack.
May 18, John Buttler.
,, 20, Henrie, son of William Anthony.
,, 22, William Luggon. The same daye
,, 22, was buried John, son of Richard Roper.
,, 23, John, son of Richard Sampson.
June 14, Joane, daughter of John Martyne.
July 16, John, son of John Davye.
,, 20, Joane, daughter of John Richatt.
,, 23, Joane, wife of John Martynne.
Oct. .. Elizabethe Rodda, widow.

* Written after Barnard erased.

* Query a clerical error for Morishe.
† Written after Robert erased.

REGISTER OF BURIALS.

Oct. 5, Margaret, late wife of John Bone.
Nov. 9, John, son of Richard Donnall.
Dec. 20, Margaret Maderne, wife of John Maderne.
„ 26, Rafe Davyde.
„ 27, Richard, son of Richard Noye.

[1584.]

Feb. 1, Christyane Blacke.
„ 11, Elizabeth, daughter of William Bone.
„ 11, Joane, daughter of Richard George.
1584.
Mar. 26, Roberte Lavelis, gentelman.
„ 27, Marye, wife of John Nicholas.
April 30, Margaret, daughter of William Cally.
May 4, Thomas, son of John Doodowe.
„ 15, Richard Vicker.
June 12, John Gene.
Aug. 4, Nicholas, son of James Pollerd.
„ 13, William Bathe.
„ 13, Christian Bennett, widow.
„ 26, Arthur Clyes.
Sept. 10, William, son of Mr. John Hext.
„ 20, Mathew, son of Bennet Champion.
Oct. 11, Richard, son of William Scroll.
„ 15, John, son of John Thomas.
„ 20, John, son of John Trythall.
„ 25, Lowdye, daughter of Robert Noye.
„ 28, Margaret, daughter of Richard Cosen.
Nov. 22, John, son of Launcelot Garland.
„ 27, Marke Olyver.
Dec. 30, Marye, daughter of John James.

[1585.]

Jan. 1, Martenn William.
„ 5, Joane Roberte.
„ 6, Jane, daughter of Henrye Game.
„ 9, Thomas, son of Raw Tereyve.
„ 10, Mitchell Skaddan.
„ 15, John, son of John Richerd.
„ 21, William, son of John Michell.
„ 23, William Syse.
Feb. 8, Paskaw, wife of Richard Mulfra.
„ 15, John Buswarthen.
„ 30,* Ellynor, daughter of John Webber.
March 6, Jane Gyve.
„ 16, Elizabeth, daughter of Richard George.
„ 18, James Angove.
„ 23, John, son of Richerd Noye.
„ 24, Richard, son of John Bussaverne.
1585.
April 4, James, son of John Christopher.
„ 6, John, son of Maderne Wolcotte.
„ 19, Marye Pascawe.
„ 26, Agnes, wife of John Champion.
May 5, Jane Lewes.
„ 6, Ellynor Richoe.
„ 17, John, son of John Peeter.

* So.

May 18, Stephen Roberte.
„ 20, Grace, daughter of Allice Collan, widow.
June 27, Katherin, daughter of John Christopher.
„ 28, Bennet Harrye, alias Cleare.
July 21, Elizabeth, daughter of James Pollarde.
„ 28, Ann, daughter of Launcelot Garland.
Aug. 5, Marye, daughter of Symon Cowlinge.
„ 6, —— daughter of Christian Eva.
„ 7, Margaret, daughter of John Lonime.
„ 9, Margaret, wife of Stephenn Hooper.
„ 23, Marye, daughter of John Tremethacke.
Sept. 9, Teage, the blynde man.
„ 24, Katherin, daughter of John James.
„ 26, Fortune, daughter of John Rodda.
Nov. 20, Richard, son of James Michell.
Dec. 1, Joane, daughter of Jane Jeles, widow.
„ 1, Dyonie, daughter of William Jane.
„ 3, Elizabethe, wife of Oliver, the Brittonn.
„ 4, Richard, son of Richard Otes.
„ 5, John Synner.
„ 8, John, son of Christopher Game.
„ 19, John, son of Thomas Peter.

[1586.]

Jan. 6, John Callynsowe.
„ 9, Mathew, son of Peter Mulfra.
„ 17, Bennet Roberte.
„ 17, Margaret Cowlinge, widow.
„ 18, Nicholas Rawlynge.
„ 27, Margaret Jerman.
„ 29, John, son of John William.
Feb. 6, Elizabeth, daughter of John Palmer.
„ 10, Grace, daughter of John Richard.
„ 11, John Legowe.
„ 11, Joan, daughter of Silvester William.
„ 15, Elizabeth, daughter of John Treganhoe.
„ 17, Honour, daughter of John Trelyver.
„ 24, James Letchfeilde.
March 1, Jane Buswarthen, widow.
„ 2, John Peeter.
„ 5, Richard, son of Morva Jerman.
„ 11, Walter, son of John Richarde.
1586.
April 11, Elizabeth, daughter of Roger ....
„ 14, Jane, daughter of William Aubone.
„ 17, —— son of John Tollvan.
May 3, John Sudgiow alias Gene.
„ 5, Jane Cornewall.
„ 29, Hughe, son of Edward Talskus.
June 27, Elizabeth, wife of John Holla.
July 1, Thomas Treve.
„ 19, Agnes, daughter of John Water.
„ 31, Allice, daughter of Arthur Clyes.
Aug. 17, Sampson John Richarde.
Sept. 14, Thomas Abbott.
„ 16, Bennet Angove.
„ 26, John, son of William Clyes.
„ 29, Margaret Clyes, widow.
Oct. 2, Marye, daughter of Richard Launder.

PARISH OF MADRON.

Oct. 3, John, son of Barnard Genkinge.
,, 4, Jane Richard.
,, 10, John Bussoore.
Nov. 1, Emett, wife of Maderne James.
,, 9, Margaret, wife of James Tremethacke.
,, 19, John, son of William Lynne.
,, 28, John, son of Richard Amys.
Dec. 1, John, son of John Roger.
,, 1, Henrie, son of Thomas Sedgar.
,, 12, Allice Logan.
,, 30, Elizabethe Trembahe, widow.

[1587.]

Jan. 3, Edward Blacke.
,, 7, Jennet Bennett.
,, 11, Marie, daughter of Thomas Russell.
,, 22, Agnes, wife of Henrie Polpere.
,, 30, Joane, daughter of Thomas Tremethack.
Feb. 1, Hunniball, son of ——
,, 3, Charrells Dadgiell.
,, 9, Prudence, daughter of Emanuell Northie.
,, 27, John Maddren.
March 1, Elizabethe, daughter of John Olyver.
,, 3, Barnard, son of Mawde John, spur.
,, 14, John, son of William Eslye.
,, 21, Jane, daughter of John Gregor.
,, 22, Margaret Pethericke, widow.
,, 23, Matilda Logan, widow.

1587.
,, 30, Thomas Baragwannathe.
,, 30, Joane, daughter of Thomas Peres.
April 9, Henrie Trelyll.
,, 12, John, son of Robert Preter.
,, 13, Wylmott, daughter of William Tonkyn.
,, 15, Maderne, son of John Tayler.
,, 18, John, son of Edward Talskus.
,, 18, Chestena Dynnice.
May 8, Joane, daughter of James Argall.
,, 16, William Cargeas.
,, 20, Hughe Argall.
June 3, Marie, daughter of James Trembahe.
,, 17, Margaret Cargease, widow.
,, 28, Rychard Cossen.
July 2, John Bennett.
,, 2, John, son of John Lanyon, Esquior.
,, 5, Paskes, daughter of Pascow Trelill.
,, 9, Phillip, daughter of James Michell.
,, 20, Saundrie Allexander.
,, 23, William, son of Thomas Vellye.
Aug. 23, Agnes William, widow.
,, 24, Elizabeth, daughter of John Tollvan.
,, 26, Margaret Olyver, widow.
Sept. 5, John Mathewe.
,, 16, Jeunett Mann.
Oct. 1, Thomazine Madderue.
,, 3, Agnes Teage, widow.
,, 5, Jane Dewen, widow.
,, 7, Jane, daughter of John Crankan.
,, 8, Christopher, son of Thomas Chinallee.

Oct. 14, Jennet, wife of Richard Dewen.
,, 14, Roger, son of Sampson Bell.
,, 20, Joane Thomas, widow.
,, 22, Christian Lock, widow.
,, 28, Joane, wife of John Britton.
Nov. 1, Rychard, son of Richard Fenye.
,, 3, Richard, son of Henrie Foster.
,, 3, John, son of Joane Jeffrie, widow.
,, 7, Agnes, daughter of Richard Wattye.
,, 12, Raphe, son of John Lannyon.
,, 15, Roberte Bell.
,, 19, Richard, son of Richard Webber.
,, 21, Agnes, daughter of Henrie Foster.
,, 27, Jennet, wife of William Noye.
,, 27, John Tonkinge, the elder.
Dec. 3, Elizabeth, wife of William Joiles.
,, 3, Paskes, daughter of John Rowe.
,, 6, John Arnolde.
,, 8, Owen Irishe.
,, 14, Katherin Vyvian.
,, 16, Thomas, son of Frances Thomas.
,, 17, William Dynnis.
,, 21, Allyce, daughter of Christopher Game.
,, 28, Elizabethe, daughter of John Dewen.
,, 30, Henrye Wavers.

[1588.]

Jan. 5, Beccawe James, widow.
,, 12, Ellynor, wife of Fraunces Thomas.
,, 18, Allice, daughter of Richard Dewen.
,, 23, Ellen, daughter of John Mathewe.
,, 27, Elizabethe, wife of Edward Peres.
,, 29, Allice, daughter of Henrie Wavers.
,, 30, Agnes, wife of Edward Bose.
Feb. 1, Henrie Foster.
,, 28, Katherin Ryden.
March 1, John Argall, alias Carpenter.
,, 9, Thomas Adams.
,, 15, John Michell, alias Gardeage.
,, 17, William, son of Thomas Dewen.

1588.
April 1, Grace, daughter of William Lawrenc.
,, 8, Stephen Hooper.
,, 19, Nicholas Pennye.
,, 23, Marie, wife of William Allger.
,, 29, John, son of John Dadowe.
May 9, Richard Wattye.
,, 7, Hellen, wife of Udye Penmenith.
,, 9, John Rodda.
,, 9, Margaret, wife of John Barber.
June 7, Symon Blagrowe.
,, 7, Agnes, daughter of John Barber.
,, 9, James, son of Thomas Chinalls.
,, 15, Agnes, wife of John Trelill.
,, 15, Elizabeth Rowe.
,, 16, Agnes, daughter of Richard Tyer.
,, 17, One Richard, a poore man.
,, 18, William, son of Pethericke Boyer.
,, 20, Margaret, wife of Thomas Penmenith.

REGISTER OF BURIALS.

June 21, Phillip Carvannell, widow.
,, 27, Roger, son of Robert Preter.
,, 27, Joane, daughter of John Symon.
July 1, Robart White, marchant.
,, 22, Richard, son of Alle Nowell, spurius.
,, 24, Christian, wife of John Cowling, gentelman.
,, 30, Elizabeth, daughter of William Bligh.
,, 30, William, son of Richard Peres.
Sept. 6, Nicholas, son of John Phillip.
Dec. 10, Joane, daughter of Rawe William.
,, 12, John Keigwyne.

[1589.]

Jan. 1, John Hockken.
,, 2, Thomas, son of Symon Shepard.
,, 3, Walter, son of Silvester William.
1589.
Mar. 25, Allico Cosen, widow.
,, 30, Elizabeth, daughter of Madern John James.
,, 31, Charells, son of William Osborne.
,, 6, Valentyn Wennowthe.
April 9, Maderne John James.
,, 10, Katherin Hearen.
,, 11, James Mitchell.
,, 11, John Richarde.
,, 14, Ellizabeth, daughter of John Tremethack.
,, 16, Charells, son of John Richarde.
,, 20, Henrie, son of Robert Bodenar.
May 6, Thomas, son of John Thomas.
,, 8, Jane Nashe, widow.
,, 21, Wylliam Lynne.
,, 27, John, son of Robert Luke.
,, 29, Edward Talskus.
,, 31, Andrewe Hamblye.
June 7, John, son of Thomas Penmenith.
,, 7, Jeane Hoore.
,, 12, Jane, daughter of John James.

* * * * * * * * * * * * * *†

[1596.]
[Sept.] 9, Jennett Marten.
,, 12, Richard, son of John Jeffrie.
,, 14, Emett Rodda.
,, 16, Jane, wife of William Callye.
,, 27, Ursula, base child of John Roswaren.
,, 28, Richard, son of Thomas Chinalls, gent.
Oct. 6, Sampson, son of John Richard Symon.*
,, 8, The son of Thomas Fennye.

† Several leaves are here missing, there being no entries from June 12th, 1589, to September 9th, 1596. The Rev. WILLIAM TREMENHEERE, in a memorandum at the foot of the preceding page, has written the following:—
"...between the years 1589 and 1597 some leaves appear to be missing. Query whether not owing to the negligence of the bookbinder in 1816. W. T., V." The loss, however, which may have occurred at this time, is probably not so great as at first it appears to be, for, seeing that there are no entries either of Baptisms or Marriages from Nov., 1594, to July, 1596, the chances are that the Burials during the same period were unregistered also, though the reason for such a serious omission is not evident. It is possible that the entries for these twenty months were lost before this transcript was made; but it is curious that they should be wanting at the same date in the several Registers of Baptisms, Marriages, and Burials, unless in the original Register the entries of all three for each year were classed together, as was sometimes customary.
* Written thus—Symon.

Nov. 4, Thomas Luke.
,, 15, Katherin Garbye.
,, 27, Jane, daughter of Sylvester William.
Dec. 1, Elizabeth Nowell.

[1597.]

Jan. 5, Sampson, base son of Elizabeth Boswarthen
,, 5, Jane, servant of Thomas Chinalls.
,, 7, Jane, base child of Emett Rodda.
,, 30, Jane, wife of William Rycharde.
Feb. 3, John Richard Symon.
,, 10, Jane, daughter of William Jeiles.
,, 11, William, son of William Jeiles.
,, 21, John, son of John Richard Symon.
March 2, James, son of John Richard Symon.
,, 15, John Crankan.
,, 16, David, son of Henrie Calvennyth.
,, 24, Katherin Flemynge.
1597.
April 4, Wallter Edward.
,, 6, The daughter of Richard Peres.
,, 6, Wilmet, daughter of Richard Harrye.
,, 13, Barnardo Jenkynnes.
,, 13, Joane Brockehurste.
,, 15, Barnarde Pennallvean.
,, 15, Drewe James.
July 30, John Holla.
Aug. 9, Raphe Burnowe.
,, 15, Pasces Nancothann.
,, 21, John Anys.
,, 24, Jane, wife of Thomas Burnowe.
,, 27, Jane, daughter of Richard Georg.
,, 28, Joane, daughter of James Michell.
Sept. 6, Thomas Richard.
,, 6, Jellian Porrya.
,, 15, John Thomas Touckyn.
Oct. 2, Florene, servant of John Maderne, gent.
,, 19, Elizabeth, daughter of John Jenckynnes.
,, 23, Joane, wife of Launclot Garlande.
Nov. 2, Symon, son of John Broker.
,, 4, Jane, wife of William Maderne.
,, 11, Elizabeth Skaddan.
,, 19, John Sudgiow and Ann, his wife.
,, 23, Elizabeth, daughter of John Sudgiow.
,, 23, A French man.
Dec. 24, William Gillerd.
,, 25, Richard, son of Richard Ames.
,, 25, John, servante of John Jenckynnes.
,, 28, The son of Robert Dunkynne.
,, 28, Edward, son of James Trevallis.

[1598.]

Jan. 14, John Crudge, gentelman.
,, 14, Elizabethe James.
,, 16, Thomas, son of Peter Gymball.
,, 18, Tobyas, one that was drowned.
,, 19, Henrye Preater.
,, 21, Rebecca, daughter of Richard Donnoll.
,, 22, Elizabeth Davye.
,, 26, Blaunche Jenkynns.

PARISH OF MADRON.

Jan. 27, Sampsonn, son of John Shillinges.
" 30, Thomas Chinalls, the elder, gent.
Feb. 2, William, son of John Ollyver.
" 5, John Shillinge.
" 6, Joane, wife of Maderne James.
" 19, Ellyn, wife of John Lawrence.
" 22, Jermen, son of William Vycker.
" 27, Eme, daughter of Jeny Anhey, spur.
March 6, Margarie, daughter of Richard Holla.
" 11, James Jermyne.
" 14, Chesten Maderne.

1598.

" 28, Katheren, daughter of John Jeiles.
" 29, Richard, son of Sampson Noye.
April 2, The daughter of George Bollenowe.
" 9, Richard, son of Thomas Fennye.
May 2, Robert Trereife.
" 3, Robert, son of Thomas Treife.
" 4, Ursula, wife of James Trembahe.
" 19, Peter the shoomaker's wiefe.*
June 1, Elizabeth, wife of John Stoane.
" 16, John, son of Pascaw Pendene.
" 29, Allye, daughter of Barnard Jenkynes.
July 6, Hellen Neroe, an Irish woman.
" 11, Raphe Champion.
" 21, Margaret, wife of Christopher Game.
" 30, Elizabeth, wife of John Richard.
Aug. 14, Edward Augove.
" 15, Grace, daughter of John James, the younger
Sept. 1, Dyouice, the sister of owld Mistris Lewer.
" 16, Jane Shane.
" 28, Elizabeth, wife of Walter Lannyon, gent.
Oct. 3, Nathanniell, son of Thomas Sudgiow.
" 5, Robert, son of John Polhormall.
" 6, Jane, daughter of Richard Donnoll.
" 17, Jane, wife of John Polgoone.
" 21, Christopher, son of Richard Donnall.
" 21, Ann, daughter of William Anthony.
" 22, Richard Peres.
" 23, Clarene, daughter of William Maderne.
" 24, David Billen.
" 26, Fraunces Teage.
" 27, Michell Dryver.
" 27, Margarie, wife of Thomas Peeter.
Dec. 1, John Write.
" 24, Richard Dewen.

[1599.]

Jan. 6, The son of Thomas Flemmyng, gent.
" 28, William Serell.
Feb. 3, William Clyes.
" 7, Elizabeth, daughter of Rawe Vean.
" 26, Jane, daughter of John Barber.
" 26, Jane, wife of John Rodda.
Mar. 11, Peres Brittayne.
" 11, Raph, son of William Cardewe.

* See 1603, January 11.

Mar. 11, Joane, daughter of Thomas William.
" 14, Constaune, syster of David Penlease.
" 19, Marke Merrynne.
" 21, Richard Kerrys.
" 22, Margaret, wife of Henrye Smythe.

1599.

April 1, Hellen Gillerde.
" 9, Agnes Lewer, widow.
" 20, Joane Cornishe.
" 22, John, son of John Richerde.
" 24, Elizabeth, daughter of Nicholas Edye.
May 4, Symon, son of Jerman Geve.
" 6, Henrie Game.
" 9, Margaret, wife of Jermen Gyve.
" 23, George Peeter.
" 23, Ann, daughter of Thomas Michell.
" 24, Margaret, wife of Launelot Garland.
June 12, William, son of James Dawbyn.
" 14, Roger Trencyre.
" 15, Thomas Tremathacke.
" 24, John, son of John Brockhurste.
" 26, Allie, wife of William Sommer.
Aug. 4, John Gregor, the elder.
" 12, Agnes Tayler.
" 19, John Richard.
Oct. 1, Aves, wife of Rowan Marke.
" 6, John Renowden.
Nov. 5, Elizabeth, wife of John William.
Dec. 3, Michel Thomas, a Warwickshcire man, a sowldier.
" 7, Georg, an Hardfordsheir man, an Irish souldier.
" 9, Margerie, daughter of Richard Bonnsye.
" 10, John and John: Peter: Peter and Peter, French men, shipwrakt.
" 13, Two daughters of Phillip Sampsonns.
" 18, Jane Cosen.
" 19, Amye Champion.
" 27, John Pender.
" 28, Elizabeth, daughter of John Michell.
" 28, Richard, son of Marten Mayne.
" 28, Ann, daughter of John Slade.
" 28, Joane, daughter of Saundry Maderne.
" 28, The son of John Maderne, gentelman.

[1600.]

Feb. 6, Raphe William.
" 20, William, son of William Argall.
" 29, Prudene, daughter of James Dawbyn.
Mar. 12, The daughter of Rowan Marke.
" 14, Margerie, daughter of Pascawe Pendene.
" 14, Joane, wife of John Tayler.
" 15, Elizabeth, wife of John Buskenninge, Jun.

1600.

April 6, Ann, wife of John Nole.
" 9, Ruth, daughter of John Richard.
" 15, Joane, wife of John Richard.
" 25, Elizabeth, wife of John Tydwale.
" 29, Agnes, wife of John George.

REGISTER OF BURIALS.

May 15, Thomas Tobma.
June 1, Chesten, daughter of Joane Sudgiow.
,, 3, Joane, wife of James Varwell.
,, 3, Alexander, son of Richard Georg.
,, 8, Thomas, son of John Howe.
,, 11, Madern James.
,, 13, Joane, daughter of Thomas Argall.
Aug. 2, Agnes, wife of Roberte Treve.
,, 3, The daughter of John Dodowe.
,, 18, James Trevullis.
,, 24, Thomas, son of Launclot Garland.
Sept. 28, John, son of Rapho Byckham.
Oct. 5, Henrie, son of Teage Billen.
,, 16, Emanuell Northie.
,, 18, William Harberte.
Nov.* 20, John Tonkynn.
Dec. 2, Syve, wife of John Jermyn.
,, 3, Annys, wife of Josepth Lympany.
,, 7, John, son of John Thomas, *alias* Polgoone.
,, 20, Elynor, base child of Jane Clyes.
,, 25, Nicholas Udye.
,, 27, Richard, son of William Tonkynn.

[1601.]

Jan. 2, Agnes Penrose.
,, 25, Elynor, daughter of Edward Peter.
,, 27, Joane, daughter of Richard Bennett.
Feb. 1, Raphe Harberte, Clerke, Vicker of Madern.
,, 6, Jane, wife of Sampson Noye.
,, 21, Ann, daughter of Josepth Lympany.
,, 23, Margaret Polhormall.
Mar. 23, Cicely, wife of Thomas Velly.

1601.

April 3, James Mydlame.
,, 26, John Anthonye.
,, 28, Henrye, the masonne.
May 1, Elizabeth, daughter of Robert Hamett.
,, 1, Elizabeth Callye.
,, 15, Mistris Awdrye Crudge.
June 8, John Holla.
,, 15, John Barnycotte.
,, 22, Thomas Clyes.
July 4, William, son of William Nenys.
,, 7, Agnes Pumbrye.†
,, 19, John Lewer.
,, 20, Agnes Blaunche.
Aug. 16, Peter Boos, *alias* Gymbale.
,, 30, Rebecca, daughter of Degorye Duke.
Sept. 3, Agnes, wife of John Chamberleyne.
,, 5, The base child of William Maderno.
,, 16, Allice Michell.
Oct. 8, Ann, daughter of Richard Edwarde.
,, 27, Jane Nole.
Nov. 3, Sampson, son of John Howe.
Dec. 9, Thomas Cox, late of Bodmyn.
,, 14, Margery, wife of John Draper.
,, 18, William Captenn.

[1602.]

Jan. 20, Katherin, daughter of William Rawlyn.
Feb. 7, Joan, servant of Leonard Gillerde.
,, 11, William, son of James Dawbynn.
,, 14, Richard Halgarracke.
Mar. 22, Jane Donnall.

1602.

April 4, Jenye my frinde.
,, 13, Gysbrecht Mychelsoon Hopeusack, of Amsterdam.
,, 24, The daughter of Richard Edward.
July 15, Sampson Donnall.
,, 18, Thomas, son of John James, Jun.
,, 21, Edward Nenys.
Aug. 1, Allice Noye, widow.
Oct. 1, Thomas, son of John Gregor.
,, 7, John Trelill.
,, 21, Agnes Jenkyn.
Nov. 3, Thomas, son of John Swaffen.
,, 3, Henry, son of Richard Bennet, *alias* Harri.
,, 7, Jane, daughter of James Michell.
Dec. 9, John Georg, *alias* Begoe.

[1603.]

Jan. 11, Peter Russell, shomaker.
Feb. 21, Elizabeth, servant to Mr. James Pollard.
,, 26, Anne, daughter of John Game.
Mar. 14, William Aubone, the elder.

1603.

,, 28, John Hew.
April 10, Henrie Robbyns.
,, 12, Agnes, daughter of John Buskening, the elder.
,, 13, Joane Gregor, the elder, widow.
,, 13, Richard Trenere, gent.
June 6, Elizabeth Rodda, widow.
,, 17, Marie, daughter of John Oliver.
July 1, The ould Elizabeth Peter.
Aug. 14, Peter Nicholl, *alias* Portere.
,, 31, Susan, wife of Thomas Aubone.
Sept. 1, John Tangie.
,, 11, Michell Clies, of Peusanns.
Nov. 10, Ellynor, wife of Thomas Peter.
,, 22, Elliuor Cowlyn.
,, 24, The ould Jodna Buskenninge.
Dec. 11, James, son of Thomas Forse.

[1604.]

Feb. 8, Honor, daughter of Morish Roche.
,, 12, Roger, son of John Game.
,, 12, Richard, son of Thomas Crudge.
,, 29, Jane Wattie.
March 4, James Trembahe.
,, 9, Allie Lawrie, *alias* Noye.
,, 23, Richard, son of Robert Hammet.

1604.

,, 29, Margery, wife of Raphe Hoskyne.
April 3, William, son of Baldwyn Williams.
,, 6, Thomas Crudg, gentelman.

---

* In a different hand and ink.   † Altered from Parrye.

PARISH OF MADRON.

April 9, John Cardew.
,, 13, Anne, daughter of William Noye.
,, 16, John Tydwell.
,, 20, Richard, son of Raph Hoskyn.
,, 22, Raphe Hoskyn.
May 21, Elizabeth Wynselet.
,, 27, Katheren Dennyco, of Pensans.
June 2, Willmet Hary Clere, of Pensans.
,, 13, The ould William Argall.
July 8, Katheren, daughter of William London.
,, 8, Elizabeth, daughter of Edward Jenkyn.
,, 9, John Thomas, *alias* Polgone.
,, 17, Sampson, son of William Hew.
Aug. 15, Thomas, son of Raph Lawry.
,, 26, Mary, daughter of John Cowlyn, gent.
Sept. 2, Joane, wife of Richard Boden.
,, 20, Elizabeth, daughter of James Peros.
,, 21, Jane Tempie.
,, 23, John Jenkyn.
,, 23, Teage Bellyn.
Nov. 6, Henrie, servant of Mr. John Game.
Dec. 24, Elizabeth Fleming, widow.
,, 26, John, son of William Sommer, gent.

[1605.]

Jan. 12, Richard Tremethack.
,, 13, Raph Lanyon, gent.
Feb. 8, Katheron Argall.
,, 13, William Gregor.
,, 22, Thomas, son of William Mote.
,, 24, John Polhormall, the elder.
Mar. 15, —— son of Richard Clies, of Pensanc.
,, 21, Richard Undersonne.
,, 21, Ales, wife of Richard Alexander.
,, 24, Agnes Nenes.
,, 24, A poore Irish woman of Pensanc, called ——
1605.
May 12, Walter Lanyon, gent.
,, 26, Margaret Cohone, of Pensanc.
July 19, —— son of John Bosvine.
Sept. 18, Symon, son of Raph Lanyon.
,, 26, Elizabeth James.
,, 26, Catheren, daughter of Teag Bellyn.
Oct. 8, Alexander, son of William Algar.
,, 18, John, son of Emanuell Blewet.
,, 18, Ellen, daughter of Peter Elforde.
,, 28, Rebecca, daughter of John Vallentine.
,, 30, William, son of William Legow.
,, 30, Allice, wife of James Dawbyn.
Nov. 13, Jane, daughter of Thomas Bowden.
,, 24, Thomas Loppier, servant to Mr. William Tonkyn.
Dec. 8, James Mulfra.
,, 10, John, son of John Cozen.

[1606.]

Jan. 9, Margerie Roper, of Pensans.
,, 14, John Legow, the elder.
,, 22, Thomazine Noye.
Feb. 14, John Tregirthen.

Feb. 15, Joane Jeffrie.
,, 19, John, son of Raphe Noy.
,, 22, Richard, son of Richard Heiden.
,, 28, Lawrenc Champion.
Mar. 19, Margaret Clies.
,, 19, William, base child of William Noy.
1606.
April 1, Jane Clies, a poore woman, of Pensans.
,, 4, Jellian Gromohall, of Pensanc.
,, 28, Honor, daughter of William Lewer.
May 4, Elizabeth Trannack.
,, 29, Joane, daughter of Joane Champion.
June 1, John, base child of John Draper.
,, 7, Mellyor, wife of Henry Bossava.
,, 29, Elizabeth, wife of Thomas Bartlot.
Aug. 4, Clarene, wife of Henry Stephens.
,, 6, Margaret Purshall, of Pensanc.
,, 7, John Barber, of Ponsance.
,, 17, Allie, wife of John Cowlinge, gent.
,, 18, Prudene, wife of Georg Lanyon, gent.
,, 28, William Cowlinge.
,, 30, —— daughter of John Morish.
Sept. 12, Richard Kerrowe.
,, 14, Reginald Luke.
Oct. 19, Joane Mulfra.
,, 20, Richard, son of William Watkins.
Dec. 6, William, son of Thomas Bowden.
,, 16, Joane, base child of Jeles Bartlet.
,, 18, James Pollarde, gontelman.
[+] 1607.
April 9; Clarene Goathe.
June 10, Jane Calensowe.
July 4, William Lawnder.
Nov. 29, William, son of Robert Luke.
Dec. 1, Grace, daughter of John Harberto.

[1608.]

Feb. 12, Elizabeth Legowe.
,, 19, Mr. William Trereife.
,, 26, Hugh, son of Charles Ellis.
March 2, Marye, wife of Charles Ellis.
,, 18, John Swaffin.
,, 24, Elizabeth, wife of Degory Duke.
1608.
,, 26, William Wolcock, the older.
,, 26, James Michell.
,, 27, William, son of William Thomas.
April 19, Mr. William Tompkin, of Pensance.
,, 21, Katherin Trongove.
May 4, Jone, wife of John Swaffin.
,, 5, John Ambrose.
,, 15, The wife of Thomas Vellye.
,, 25, John Edye.
June 19, Walther Stone.
July 1, John James, the younger.
,, 4, Roberte, son of Mr. William Tereifo.
,, 10, Henryo, son of Mr. Robert Dunkinge.
,, 11, Elizabeth, daughter of Mr. William Tereife
,, 16, Jane, wife of Mr. Richard Bennett.

M

REGISTER OF BURIALS.

July 25, Marye, daughter of Mr. William Tereife.
Aug. 1, Mistris Elizabeth Tereife's man.
,, 7, Thomas, son of Robert Luke.
,, 21, James, son of Thomas Jeoffrie.
,, 24, Marye, daughter of John Harberte.
,, 25, Grace, daughter of Mr. John Game.
,, 29, William, son of John Buswathack.
,, 30, John, son of Phillip Sampson.
Sept. 22, Marye, daughter of Morishe Roche.
,, 22, Alse, daughter of Thomas Lake.
Oct. 5, Frances, son of William Bennett.
,, 9, Mistris Anne Pender.
,, 17, William Palmer.
,, 26, John, son of Mr. Joseph Limpenye.
Nov. 1, John Rawe, of Buswarva.
,, 4, Charitye, wife of Nowell Algor.
,, 5, Elizabeth, daughter of Gilbert Harris.
,, 8, Henry Allen.
,, 13, Robert, son of John Trick.
Dec. 6, Edmonde Jenkin, of Pensanc.

[1609.]

Jan. 29, Haniball, son of John Hughe.
Feb. 8, Harry, son of Thomas Vellye.
,, 17, Roger, son of Richard Game.
Mar. 13, Jellian, daughter of John James, the younger.

1609.

April 8, William, son of William Thomas.
,, 13, Jane, wife of John Edwards, *alias* Portcere.
,, 23, William, son of John Portcere.
May 6, William Redwoode.
,, 11, Jone Trasye.
,, 23, Richard Treveean.
June 16, Alse, wife of John Honywell
July 30, William, son of Mr. George Lanyon.
Aug. 4, Anne, daughter of John Michell.
Sept. 11, Nicholas, son of Thomas Bowden.
Oct. 26, James Fell.
Nov. 7, Thomas Lane, *alias* Lake.
,, 14, John Mulfra.
,, 30, Paskus, the drywoman, of Pensance.
Dec. 11, Richard, son of William Madren, the younger.
,, 13, Thomas, son of John Luke.
,, 16, Jane, wife of John Buskening, the elder.

[1610.]

Jan. 18, John, son of Mr. John Game.
,, 19, Margaret, wife of Rawe Veenn.
,, 22, Thomas Sudgiowe, *alias* Gecue.
,, 23, Ennce Kigwin, *alias* Hoskin.
Feb. 6, Clarene Hoare, an olde woman.
,, 22, John, son of Marten Champion.
March 7, Agnes, wife of Richard Morishe.
,, 7, The daughter of Rapho Noye.
,, 15, Jane Nonnis.
,, 17, Edward Trithall.

1610.

April 23, Katherin, daughter of Madren James.
May 1, Leonard Gillarde, of Pensance.
,, 2, Katherin Nighten, *alias* Jeoffrie.
July 10, Agnes, wife of William Algar.
,, 13, Richard, son of John Chamberlen.
Sept. 11, Katherin, daughter of John Sampson.
,, 26, Marye, daughter of Edward Trithall.
Oct. 1, Margery, daughter of John Mathew, of St. Juste.
,, 2, Margery, daughter of the same John Mathew.*
,, 30, The daughter of John Ambrose.
Nov. 6, James Dawbin.
,, 18, The daughter of John Sakaria, *alias* Coathe.
,, 20, Florene, wife of Bennet Collan.
Dec. 14, Blanche Ryden.
,, 28, John Marten.

[1611.]

Jan. 1, Jowannat Eddye.
,, 3, One Baliffe, a seaman, wch dyed at Pensanc.
,, 5, Mistris Alse Cocke.
,, 19, —— daughter of Bartholomew Edye.
,, 20, Alexander, a base child to one of Breage.
,, 28, Sacharius Champion.
Feb. 4, Alse, daughter of John Webber.
,, 10, Anne, wife of Henry Allan.
,, 14, Joane Pears, of Penzanc.
,, 15, Joane, daughter of Bartholomew Edye.
,, 22, Elizabeth Geene, *alias* Sudgiow.
Mar. 10, Alse, daughter of Edmond Clies.
,, 20, Henry, son of black Thomas.
,, 21, Robert, son of John Jenkin.
,, 23, Jane, daughter of John Ambell.

1611.

April 7, Hugh, son of Mr. Joseph Limpeny.
,, 14, The daughter of Degorye Duke.
,, 15, John, son of John Harbert.
,, 21, —— daughter of Marten Champion.
June 11, Mistris Alse Sicklemoore.
,, 22, William Edmonds, the cuttler, of Pensanc.
July 8, A child to William Anboue, unchristned.
Sept. 14, Richard Morishe.
Nov. 3, William Tonken, the younger.
,, 9, Marye John.
,, 12, A child to Richard Lanion, Esquior, unchristned.
Dec. 22, One John Thomas, a stranger.
,, 24, Harrie, son of Thomas Williams.

[1612.]

Feb. 13, Alse, daughter of John Clies, gent.
,, 17, Tompkin, son of William Younge, gent.
March 9, Willmett, wife of John James, in Church towne.

---

* *Sic.* It is not likely that two daughters of the same person bore similar Christian names, as would appear by this and the preceding entry. Possibly one should have been registered as "wife" of John Mathew.

PARISH OF MADRON.

Mar. 14, John, son of John Trick.
*
[+] 1612.
June 11, A child to Richard Lanyon, Esq., unchristned
" 20, Ann, daughter of William Lego, Jun.
" 30, Edward Hoskyn.
Sept. 24, William, son of Edward Ludra.
Nov. 26, Elizabeth, daughter of John Morish.
Dec. 8, John Honiwell.
" 14, William Flinge.

[1613.]

Jan. 20, John Sampson, gent.
Feb. 8, John Polpeero.
" 14, John, son of George Hutchins, Cler.
March 8, Joane Argall.
1613.
" 27, Dorothye Lothibye.
April 7, Richard Ames, *alias* Ash.
" 9, John Boskening, Sen.
" 18, John Religgye.
May 11, Jane, wife of John Webber.
June 24, A child of John Religgye.
Sept. 7, James Pollard, gent.
Oct. 5, John, son of Rodger Polkinghorne, gent.
Dec. 26, John, son of John Harbert.

[1614.]

Feb. 24, Alice Eva, servant to John Cowlinge, gent.
" 27, Elizabeth, daughter of Arthure Edye.
March 2, Edward, son of Thomas William.
1614.
June 8, Willmott Pawgye.
" 12, John Thomas.
Aug. 12, William Luer, gent.
Sept. 19, Barnard, son of Rich. Geeles.
" 29, William, son of Rich. Geeles.
Oct. 6, Trefina, wife of Launce Garland.
Nov. 24, John Gyles.
" 29, Marye Jeffrye.
" 30, Annis Stone.
" 30, Mrs. Kathren Sampson.
Dec. 6, Elizabeth, wife of Robert Luke.

[1615.]

Jan. 7, Peeter, son of Richard Tratt.
" 9, Ann, wife of John Cowlinge, gent.
Feb. 10, William, son of John Hewe.
" 16, William Trolill.
" 19, Ellenor Holla.
Mar. 15, John Webber, Sen.
1615.
April 5, Thomas Poeter.
May 3, John Shogs.
" 17, Francis, the taylor.
" 19, Thomas, son of John Jeffrye.

* A blank of nearly half a page occurs here.

June 5, Nowell Treugotholl.
" 8, Elizabeth Millett.
" 12, Joane, wife of John James Tremethack.
Aug. 17, Margarett Duucken.
Sept. 16, Elizabeth Ludldra.
Nov. 12, Elizabeth Chinalls.

[1616.]

Jan. 20, Sampson, son of Nowell Argoll.
" 17,* Thomas Argoll.
" 29, Joane Argoll.
Feb. 4, John, son of John Hoskyn.
" 5, John Rowse.
" 13, Jane, a servant to Will. Bone.
" 22, James, son of Nicholas Roberts.
" 26, Martyn Champion.
Mar. 20, John Rawe, Sen.
" 21, Richard Saundrye.
" 24, Henery, son of Rich. Rosomorran.
" 24, John, son of Garrett Launder.
1616.
April 2, Joane, wife of John Chirgwine.
May 13, John, son of James Pendeene.
" 20, William Duke.
" 22, Mrs. Jane Chinalls.
" 25, Jane, wife of Joseph Lympanye.
" 28, Kathren, wife of John Friggens.
June 2, Gregorye, son of John Friggens.
July 8, Key, wife of Henery Game.
Sept. 10, Mary Mitchell.
" 23, John Doodowe.
Oct. 22, George Lanyon, gent.
Nov. 25, John Tremethack.
Dec. 2, Richard Harrye, Sen.
" 9, Richard Hawes.
" 10, Samewell Randall, gent.
" 19, Alice, daughter of John Chirgwine.
" 25, Richard Game, Sen.

[1617.]

Jan. 2, Edward, son of Joseph Limpanye.
" 6, Thomas Lawrence.
" 28, Marye, daughter of John Davy.
" 3,† Margarett Lawrence.
1617.
May 4, Margerye Willowe.
" 8, Germayn Morish.
" 24, Jane Duke.
" 26, Elizabeth, wife of John Davye.
" 26, Walter Bosaverne.
Sept. 13, Thomas Pendeene.
" 28, John Hoskyn, *alias* Trembath.
Nov. 6, Richard Cooke.
" 9, William Rawlyn.

* *Sic.*
† *Sic.* This should probably be 30, the naught having perhaps been accidentally omitted, or the entry may be simply misplaced. If intended for 3 and not 30 it possibly belongs to May, the month of the succeeding entry, which in the original follows without any break.

REGISTER OF BURIALS.

Dec. 1, Thamasin, daughter of Bennett Harry.
,, 9, Joan, daughter of Joane Hill, spur.
,, 16, Simon, son of William Launder, spur.

[1618.]

Jan. 28, Ann, wife of Richard Game.
Feb. 3, Walter Tresyes.
,, 18, Ralph Beecum.
1618.
April 6, John Davye, of Pensane.
,, 7, William, son of William Castell.
May 20, Thomas, son of Emanuell Bluett.
June 10, Mary, daughter of Walter Tresies.
July 25, Jane Toocker.
Aug. 16, Jane Francis.
,, 22, Jane, wife of Rich. Alexander.
,, 28, Elizabeth, daughter of Jermayn Mor[i]sh.
Nov. 12, Silvester Williams.

[1619.]

Jan. 8, William, son of John Stone.
Feb. 14, John Chine.
,, 17, John Valentine.
Mar. 14, Christopher, son of Bartholomew Edye.
1619.
May 12, Ann Searle.
June 16, Ellenor Tolvan.
,, 24, Henery, son of William Greene.
,, 28, Elizabeth, daughter of Rich. Tome.
July 6, Kathren Chinalls.
Aug. 4, Blauch, daughter of William Boas.
Sept. 10, Richard, son of William Bone.
,, 14, Sybell Bellyn.
Oct. 29, Elizabeth, wife of Rowan Marke.
Nov. 20, Henery, son of Christopher Wills.
Dec. 6, Marye, daughter of Christ. Wills
,, 20, Elizabeth, wife of John Lethibye.
,, 26, Edward, son of William Kestell.

[1620.]

Jan. 20, John Boskeninge.
,, 26, John Champion.
,, 30, Ambrous Robins.
Feb. 4, Richard Tratt.
,, 10, Thomas Mulford.
,, 24, John Phillipps.
Mar. 12, Steephen Pomeroy.
1620.
May 16, Joseph Lympanye, gent.
Aug. 20, Jane, wife of Saundry Maddren.
Sept. 14, Maddren Champion.
Oct. 9, Thomas Mitchell.
Nov. 18, John Hammett.
Dec. 22, Ann Rowland.
,, 30, —— a child to Maddren Lego.
,, 30, John Lego.

[1621.]

Jan. 19, John Bentlett, gent.
,, 24, Richard Randell.

Jan. 25, Elizabeth Williams.
Feb. 28, Joane, wife of Robert Duncken.
March 7, John Mathew.
,, 14, Jenney Cock.
1621.
April 30, John Champion.
May 30, Elizabeth, wife of Raph Bennett.
June 3, John Hugh.
,, 7, William Greene.
July 16, Ralph Bennett.
,, 20, Rebecka, wife of John James, Jun.
Aug. 30, John Maddren, Jun., gent.
Sept. 1, Elizabeth, wife of Walter Mitchell.
,, 6, Alice, wife of John Fynnye.
,, 29, Susan, wife of David Penleas.
Oct. 4, Ellen Launder.
,, 14, Thomas Hockine.
,, 16, Kathren, wife of Thomas Fynnye.
,, 18, William Harris.
,, 30, Ann, wife of Edward Vean.
Nov. 16, John Draper.
,, 19, Elizabeth, daughter of Tho. Baggs.

[1622.]

Jan. 13, Nicholas Roch.
,, 15, Amy Clies.
,, 20, Joane Rawlyn.
1622.
July 23, William, son of William Champion.
Aug. 20, Thomas Chesshoere.
,, 29, Jane Mitchell.
,, 29, Richard Jenekyn.
Oct. 14, Richard Hoskyn.
,, 19, Richard Bishopp.
,, 29, Mary, daughter of John Harbert.
Nov. 3, Jeane, wife of William Trewren.
,, 18, Ellen, wife of Teage Loudye.
,, 19, Elizabeth, wife of William Gyles.
,, 20, John Drews.
Dec. 20, William Maddren.

[1623.]

Mar. 14, Maurice, son of Maddren Lego.
,, 18, Martyn Meane.
,, 24, Umfrye Hughe.
1623.
May 28, John Chinalls, gent.: xo:
June 10, Elizabeth, daughter of John Clies, gent.*
Aug. 6, Henery, son of Edward Saundry.
,, 12, —— son of William Robins.
Oct. 26, John, son of Thomas Sudgeo.
Nov. 11, Margerye Rawe.
,, 16, William Tomekyn, Sen.
,, 29, John Clies, gent.

---

* This entry has been erased, and 1635 written over. A similar entry occurs in 1635, Aug. 16, but it is not possible that it refers to the same person (unless there were some very extraordinary blunder—such as burying alive); therefore, if the above has been struck out for no better reason than this, it has surely been done in error.

PARISH OF MADRON.

Dec. 24, Germon Geefe.

[1624.]

Jan. 6, Jane Porteere.
,, 12, Jane Trasye.
,, 12, Sisly Addam.
,, 21, Joane Meane.
Feb. 10, —— son of Joseph Baslye.
March 1, Thomas Bodye.
,, 24, John, the smith, of Pensance.
1624.
April 23, William Callye.
Aug. 12, Richard, son of Joseph Baslye.
,, 22, Richard Champion.
Sept. 21, Jane Calensowe.
,, 21, William, son of Robert Trewren.
,, 25, William, son of Alexander Lanyon.
,, 25, Ann, daughter of Davye Lanyon.
Oct. 2, Bennett Harrye.
,, 12, John, son of William Kelye.
Nov. 22, Kathren, daughter of Maddren Lego.
Dec. 13, John Webber.

[1625.]

Jan. 30, John Lethibye.
Feb. 4, Mrs. Alice Clies.
,, 17, Robert, son of Jermyn Luke.
,, 21, Marye, daughter of Jer. Luke.
,, 28, Elizabeth, wife of John Mulfra.
March 7, Jennett Wolcock.
,, 10, Joane, daughter of John Trenhayle.
,, 20, Marye, wife of Will. Sommer, gent.
,, 20, Blanch ——
1625.
April 11, Susan, wife of Edward Jencken.
,, 20, John James, Sen., of Churchtowne.
,, 26, Alice Penquite, widow.
Aug. 10, Richard Lawrence.
,, 20, Richard, son of Bennett Cotha.
Sept. 29, Nicholas Game.
Oct. 10, Emmett, wife of William Hooper.
,, 19, Symon Robbyns.
,, 26, George Waymoth.
Dec. 20, John Chinalls, Jun.

[1626.]

Jan. 8, Kathren Howe.
Feb. 1, The child of Gabriell Sommer.
,, 1, Jane Tompekyn.
,, 11, Grace, daughter of Tho. Millard.
,, 22, Grace, wife of Rodger Polkinghorne.
,, 22, Margerye, wife of Will. Maddren.
1626.
May 31, Robert Hammett.
June 23, Thomas Newton.
July 16, John Maddren, Sen.
Aug. 11, Constance, wife of Thomas Lavelis.
Sept. 27, William Blachford.
Oct. 17, Florence, daughter of John Harbert.

Oct. 24, Ann, daughter of John Holla.
,, 27, Margarett, wife of John Morish.
Dec. 4, Kathern Harris.
,, 14, John Sampson, ye smith.

[1627.]

Jan. 10, John, son of Erasmus Pascowe.
Feb. 14, Joaue, servant to Mrs. Clyes.
Jan.* 24, Jane Sandrye.
Feb. 24, Henery, son of William Davye.
March 4, Annis, daughter of Thomas Treganhorne.
,, 12, Thomas Drewe.
,, 16, Robert Pender.
,, 22, Dina, daughter of Emanewell Bluett.
1627.
April 15, Alezander Maddren.
May 14, Henery, son of Stephen Pomeroy.
Aug. 19, Nicholas, son of Richard Tome.
Sept. 8, Addam Rawlyn.
Nov. 14, William Lanyon, gent.
,, 15, Michell Sparnan.
,, 20, Ursula, daughter of John Sampson.

[1628.]

Jan. 10, Mary, wife of Edward Luddra.
,, 14, Christover Game.
,, 20, Robert Luke.
Feb. 8, William Daddowe.
,, 20, Cornelius, son of Cornelius Crosse.
Mar. 17, John Polkinghorne.
1628.
June 3, John Rawe.
,, 24, Thomas Baggs, John Thomas, & Emanewell Offall, killd wth the breaking of a peece of C....
July 21, Elizabeth Daddowe.
Sept. 4, Two Dover men.
Nov. 16, Peter Nickles, Sen.
,, 23, John Ellis.
,, 23, Sampson, son of Anthony Gubbs.
,, 29, Alice Legg.
Dec. 10, Jane, wife of Richard Bennett.

[1629.]

Feb. 21, John Sampson, Jun.
,, 29, Richard Mulfra.
1629.
Mar. 30, Ellynor Luke.
[+] May 12, Alice Nickles, widow.
June 16, John, son of Sampson Noye.
July 4, Elizabeth, wife of John James, the elder.
Aug. 10, Richard Bossence.
Sept. 5, Ann, wife of Richard Penrose, gent.
Nov. 27, Grace, daughter of Nicholas Maddern, gent.
Dec. 27,† Phillip, daughter of Nicholas Maddern, gent.

---
* Sic.
† This was originally written Dec. 2; the 7 is an addition.

REGISTER OF BURIALS.

[1630.]

Jan. 3, Robert Dunkyn, Sen., gent.
,, 10, James and Joane, children of Nicholas Mitchell.
,, 15, John, son of John Tompkyn.
,, 22, Alice, wife of Thomas Mitchell.
Feb. 19, Paskoe Barnes.
,, 22, William, son of Thomas Sudgyow.
Mar. 22, Pacyence Russell.

1630.

April 23, Richard Fynny, the elder.
June 10, A child to Nicholas Ginver.
,, 17, Edward Lawrye.
,, 20, Richard Thomas.
,, 26, Em. Creode.
,, 28, A child to Ananyas Hosford.
,, 30, William, son of William Keylie.
July 10, Mitchell, son of Mitchell Sparnan.
Aug. 12, A child to Richard Bennett.
,, 22, Henry Rawe.
Oct. 16, Three seamen that were drowned.
Nov. 24, John James Tremethack, Sen.
Dec. 2, William Legoe, Sen.
,, 29, John, son of Nicholas Mitchell.

[1631.]

Jan. 4, Mary Shillinge, widow.
Feb. 6, Tamzine Angeare.
,, 17, William Reskymmer, gent.
,, 20, Richard, son of Symon Sincock.
Mar. 24, Henry Thomas.

1631.

April 17, Mary, daughter of William Watkins.
,, 30, Thomas Carne.
May 8, Christabell, wife of Lewis Hockyn.
,, 16, Elizabeth, wife of John Cowlinge, Sen., gent.
,, 22, Mawd, wife of James Finny.
June 14, Thomas Flemmynge, gent.
July 4, John, son of John Jacea.
,, 12, Alice, daughter of Mitchell Sparnan.
,, 17, Bartholomewe Edye.
Aug. 16, William Bennet.
,, 23, William, son of William Bennet.
Oct. 4, Thomas Cowlinge, gent.
,, 31, William Sommer, gent.
Nov. 28, A child to Henry Tremenheere.
Dec. 10, Blanch, daughter of Peter Elford.
,, 28, John Finny.

[1632.]

Jan. 12, Elizabeth Jocan, widow.
Feb. 2, William Trewren, gent.
,, 7, William, son of Robert Trewren, gent.
,, 10, William, son of Christopher Nickles.
Mar. 14, Elizabeth Trolill, widow.
,, 14, A poore man, of Buryan.
,, 18, Agnis Bickam, widow.
,, 20, Roger Parker.

1632.

April 12, Jane Redwood, widow.
May 6, John Cowlinge, Sen., gent.
,, 21, Ann, daughter of Thomas Legoe.
June 13, Katheren, wife of Roger Frost.
,, 20, A child to Richard Ludra.
,, 28, Richard Edward.
July 16, Thomas Robert.
Aug. 5, Richard, son of Henry Pencast.
Sept. 9, Ann, daughter of Thomas Noy.
Oct. 10, John, son of Walter Stone.
Nov. 18, Jacob, son of Alexander Daniell, gent.
Dec. 4, Margaret, wife of Ralph Boas.
,, 16, Eppow Willow, widow.

[1633.]

Jan. 15, William Levelis, gent.
,, 22, Jane, wife of John Rooan.
Feb. 15, Mr. Thomas Miller.
,, 28, Honor, wife of William Lavelis, gent.
Mar. 23, James Thomas, of Newlan, in Wales, who died at Pensanc.

1633.

June 3, Constance, daughter of Thomas Lavelis, gent.
,, 18, Alice Penhellick, widow.
Aug. 12, Henry Hooper.
Sept. 10, Nicholas Maddern, gent.

[1634.]

Jan. 12, Elizabeth Boas, widow.
Mar. 13, Margaret, wife of John Battyn.

1634.

April 13, John Lanyon, gent.
,, 29, Margarett Drewe, widow.
May 12, Roger Bowes.
June 12, Grace Walker, widow.
Aug. 14, Phillip Davye.
,, 19, John, son of Nicholas Rawlyn.
,, 19, Mary, daughter of John Trick.
Sept. 24, Thomas Hutchens.
,, 28, Richard Bennett.
Oct. 18, Richard George.
Nov. 25, Chesten, wife of Thomas Penrose, gent.
Dec. 7, Elizabeth Jenckyn, widow.

[1635.]

Jan. 9, William Mulfra.
Feb. 1, John Bone.
,, 2, William Gyles.
,, 10, Ann Bone.
,, 15, Francis Glover, gent.
Mar. 19, William Tregellas.

1635.

April 12, Jane, wife of Richard Clyes.
,, 20, Alice, daughter of Bennett Angwino.
July 17, Jane, daughter of Jane Luke.
Aug. 2, Florence, wife of Phillipp Periam.
,, 4, Margarett Tom, widow.

PARISH OF MADRON.

Aug. 16, Elizabeth, daughter of John Clyes, gent.
Nov. 6, James John.
,, 7, Honor, wife of Richard Lander.
,, 10, Pasquos Lawrence.
,, 12, Francis, son of John Cowlinge, gent.

[1636.]

Feb. 12, James, son of John Bodye, ye second.
,, 20, Ann, daughter of Nowell Argoll.
,, 23, Richard, son of John Randall.
March 3, Thomas Champion.
,, 16, Elizabeth, daughter of William Kelly.

1636.

May 20, Mary, daughter of Thomas Hutchens.
,, 22, Mary, daughter of John Thomas.
June 10, Blanch, daughter of John Lamerton.
,, 13, Richard Nicholas.
,, 14, Gregorye, son of John Beaver.
,, 20, Elenor, wife of William Cardewe.
,, 21, Blanch, wife of Halnight Stephen.
July 2, Mary, daughter of William Treneere.
,, 8, Peeter Tolvan.
,, 11, Lewes Hockon.
,, 11, John, son of John Umfrye.
,, 15, Alice, daughter of Sampson Lake.
,, 16, Richard, son of Nicholas John.
,, 18, Thomas, son of John Umfrye.
,, 20, William, son of William Jeffrye.
Aug. 14, Marye, daughter of William Treneere.
,, 14, Ann, wife of Edward Lego.
,, 16, Ann, daughter of Thomas Lego.
Sept. 5, Christian, daughter of Thomas Sudgeo.
Oct. 22, Richard Limpanye.
,, 26, William, son of William Jeuckyn.
,, 30, Thomas, son of Thomas Jeuckyn.
,, 31, John, son of John Polsowe.
Nov. 16, John Porthia.
Dec. 28, Edward Lego.

[1637.]

Jan. 9, Thomas Barbar.
Feb. 2, Joane, wife of Richard George.
,, 22, Ralph Bowes.
Mar. 22, Samuel, son of Tho. Noye.

1637.

April 11, Thomas, son of John Lamerton.
,, 18, Margaret Lawrence.
,, 21, John Boas.
May 5, John, son of Mr. Robert Trowren.
,, 22, John Hoskyn.
,, 25, Mr. David Ponlease.
June 21, Clarence, wife of William Prust.
July 10, Alice, wife of John Jeffrye.
Aug. 12, Margaret, daughter of John Batten.
Sept. 8, Katheren, daughter of William Rawlyn.
,, 10, Thomas Releigh.
Oct. 4, Mr. Robert Luke.
,, 9, Thomas, son of William Nighton.
,, 10, Katheren Finny, widow.

Nov. 16, Alice Watkins, widow.
,, 18, Margaret Edwards, widow.
,, 20, Christabell, daughter of Symon Francis.
Dec. 28, Elizabeth, wife of Henry Clise.

[1638.]

Jan. 4, Joane Mitchell, widow.
Feb. 9, Ruith, daughter of John Melderne.
March 5, Teag Loadye.

1638.

,, 28, William White, a seafaring man, bound for St. Christop[her's.]
April 10, Charls, son of John Toncken.
,, 15, Prissilla, wife of Ralph Williams.
May 4, Mary Gover, alias Skinner.
,, 17, Robert, son of Phillip Paskoe.
June 3, Margaret, wife of Garret Lauder.
,, 4, Joane Hammet, widow.
July 29, Mary, daughter of John Boddy.
Aug. 5, Elizabeth Nennis.
,, 6, Ann, wife of William Boskeninge.
,, 23, Maddern, son of John Champion.
,, 24, John, son of John Tonckyn.
Oct. 15, William Hooper.
,, 15, Dorothye, daughter of John James, alias Dreauegles.
,, 26, Digorye, son of Henry Launder.
,, 29, William Harry.
Nov. 16, Margaret, wife of James Pears.
,, 26, Katheren Long.
Dec. 26, Edward Satchell.

[1639.]

Jan. 10, Dorothye Champion.
,, 20, Elizabeth Penticost.
Feb. 2, Mr. William Leagoe.
,, 2, John Hoskyn.
,, 2, John, son of Rooan Davye.
,, 10, Elizabeth, daughter of John Rawe.
March 2, Thomas George.
,, 12, Richard Robert.
,, 16, Joane, wife of John Hoskyn.
,, 18, John, son of Thomas Pryor.
,, 22, John Sampson, of Tolcarno.
,, 22, Edward Hutchens.
,, 23, Gavrigan Game.

1639.

April 5, Ann, wife of Nicholas Flemyngo, gent.
,, 6, Mary Penmenith, widow.
,, 14, Blanch, daughter of Thomas Bennet, tanner.
June 9, Paskoe Elis.
,, 14, Redigon, daughter of Willm. Younge.
,, 21, Margaret, wife of Thomas Lavelis, gent.
,, 27, Joane Blechford, widow.
,, 28, Katheren, wife of George Cloke.
,, 28, Katheren Symons, widow.
,, 31, Alice, wife of Richard Geiles.
July 10, Elizabeth, wife of Robert Carne.
Aug. 18, Margaret, wife of Hercules Ash.

REGISTER OF BURIALS.

Nov. 1, Agnes, daughter of John Kete, gent.
,,   21, Mary, wife of Reignald Bose.
,,   25, Richard, son of Reignald Bose.
Oct. 28,* Margery Curry, widow.
Dec. 14, Robert, son of James Trenwith.
,,   16, John, son of James Trenwith.
,,   18, Francis Bouden.
† ,, 20, Ralph Lawrence.
,,   22, Elizabeth Reseigh, widow.

[1640.]

Jan. 12, Margaret, wife of Henry Paskoe.
,,   20, William Thomas.
,,   20, Joane Oliver, widow.
,,   25, Mary Champion.
Feb. 20, Katheren Pears, *alias* Beagoe.
,,   29, James Pears.
March 8, Garthered, wife of Robert Covye.

1640.

May 8, Elizabeth, daughter of Richard Luddra.
,,   10, William Edmonds.
,,   10, Margaret Hoskyn.
June 12, John, son of Richard Rosemorran.
,,   20, Katheren Polseiwe.
July 11, Arthur Leagoe.
Nov. 13, Elizabeth Hooper, widow.
,,   28, John Toll.
Dec. 1, Richard John.
,,   28, John Tonkyn, Sen.
,,   30, Mary, wife of John Sandrye.

[1641.]

Feb. 13, Alice Morise, widow.
,,   14, Elizabeth Bartell.
,,   19, Sampson Noye.

1641.

Mar. 28, Thomas Penrose, gent.
[+] April 5, John Trelill.
May 7, Jane, wife of William Digens, merchant.
,,   18, Synobea, daughter of Francis Jones, Esq.
June 22, Robert, son of John Cowlinge, gent.
Sept. 14, Robert, son of John Lanyon.
Oct. 5, Elizabeth Ellis, widow.
‡ ,, 8, Joseph Baseley.
,,   — Hercules Ash.
,,   29, Charles Sudgeo.

[1642.]

Jan. 4, Charitye Boddye, widow.
,,   22, David Lanyon.
,,   24, John Fenny.
Feb. 14, John Toucken.   [gent.
,,   24, Blanch, daughter of Henry Polkinghorne,
,,   28, Winnyfrid Draper, widow.
March 7, Kathrein Rowland, widow.

* *Sic.*
† The five entries which follow are placed in the original according to the numbers to the right.
‡ The three following entries, evidently belonging to the year 1641, are in the original placed after the 21st March, at the end of the year, old style.

March 7, Elizabeth, wife of Isack Newton.
,,   13, Phillipp Peryam, Sen.
,,   14, Ann, daughter of Robert Duncken.
,,   20, John, son of Richard Treneere.
,,   21, Mawde, wife of William Champion.

1642.

April 16, Elizabeth, wife of Thomas Grosse, gent.
,,   20, Mrs. Ann Maddren, widow.
June 24, Luce, wife of John Beryman.
,,   28, Isack Newton, Clerke.
July 4, William Chinalls.
,,   20, Henery Tremenheere.
,, ... Thomas Noye.

* * * * * * * * * * * * * *†

[1644.]

June 16, ...
Aug. 10, Sara, wife of Nicholas Hosken.
,,   20, John Saundry.

1645.

April 10, Grace, wife of Walter Stone.
,,   17, Prudence, daughter of Isack Newton.
June 7, William Holla.
,,   23, Richard Stephens.
July 3, William Williams.
Aug. 26, Maddren Ambone.
,,   29, Thomas, son of Thomas Pike.
,,   — Sampson, son of Ralph Noye.
Dec. 10, Alice, daughter of Sir Thomas Faushowe.

[1646.]

Jan. 20, Mary Hosken, widow.
Feb. 7, Robert, son of Robert Coleman.
March 1, John Hawas.

1646.

,,   31, English Stephens, widow.
May 26, Anne, wife of John Monallack.
June 3, Elizabeth Games, widow.
,,   3, Richard, son of Richard Luddra.
,,   5, Richard Howes.
,,   5, Tom, son of Richard Noye.
,,   24, Anne, wife of James Tregerthen.
,,   26, Grace, daughter of Thomas Prior.
,,   24,* Thomas Nighton.
,,   28, Robert Clemow.
,,   14,* Julian Trick, widow.
July 6, Anne Cloake, widow.
,,   7, Anne Christopher.
,,   15, Richard, son of Richard Treneere.
,,   18, Elizabeth, wife of John Tregunnow.
,,   20, Mary, daughter of Maddern Legoe.
,,   25, Alice, wife of Christopher Glasan.
Aug. 4, John George.
,,   12, Steven Shearme.
,,   12, Dina, daughter of Reynold Bose.
,,   16, Elloner, wife of Reynold Bose.

† A leaf missing.   * *Sic.*

PARISH OF MADRON.

Sept. 3, Thomas, son of James Tregerthen.
„ 3, Margarett, daughter of John P[rior.]
„ 5, Thomas Levelis, gent.
.... 14, Roger Polkenhorne, gent.
„ 24, Arthur Wolcock.
.... 5, John, son of Thomas Morish.

[1647.]

Jan. 3, John Pawley.
„ 4, Elizabeth Lawrey, widow.
Feb. 19, John Howes, Jun.
„ 20, William, son of Thomas Bonithon.
Mar. 10, Grace, wife of Thomas Bonithon.

1647.

April 2, Grace Foster.
„ 5, Peter Foster.
„ 15, Susan, daughter of Thomas Williams.
„ 17, Prudence, wife of Thomas Williams.
„ 17, Ezechiell, son of Tho. Williams.
„ 20, Anne Bond.
„ 22, Jone, daughter of Thomas Robarts.
„ 22, Sara Humfry, widow.
„ 30, Anne, wife of Thomas Stephens, alias Trevawin.
„ 30, Thomas Robarts.
„ 30, Susan, daughter of Thomas Robarts.
„ 30, Sackvell, son of Thomas Robarts.
May 1, Katherine, daughter of Thomas Stephens.
„ 2, John, son of Thomas Stephens, alias Trevawin.
„ 4, Gerrard Launder, Sen.
„ 6, Anne Hocken.
„ 7, Mary, daughter of John Barnes.
„ 9, Mary, wife of Henry Launder.
„ 12, Anne Allyn.
„ 15, Othnell Humfry.
„ 17, Thomas Barbor.
„ 17, Alexander Ricar.
„ 19, Jone Bonithon.
„ 24, Garrerd, son of Henry Launder.
„ 28, Elizabeth, daughter of Martyn Bosavern.
June 3, Nicholas, base child of William Fosse.
„ 5, Ellonor Nicholas.
„ 8, Martyn, son of Martyn Bosavern.
„ 19, John R[awlen?]
„ 21, Martyn Boddy.
„ 22, John Hosford.
„ 22, William Giles.
„ 23, Jone, daughter of William Rawlen.
„ 24, John Pormeere.
„ 25, Bridgett, wife of William Fosse.
„ 26, Elizabeth, daughter of David Penleaze.
„ 27, Henry Fosse.
„ 27, Robart, son of Martyn Boddy.
„ 28, William Diggens.
„ 29, Mary, daughter of John Touken.
July 1, John, son of John Tonken.
„ 2, Honor Rawlen, widow.
„ 3, Anne Pormeere, widow.
„ 3, Alice, wife of John Tonken.

July 6, John James, alias Treneglos.
„ 6, Amy Bosekarne.
„ 7, Thomas Kallway.
„ 8, Roger Pearse.
„ 8, Jane Wolcock, widow.
„ 8, Jane Roode, widow.
„ 9, Richard Sampson.
„ 9, Jane, daughter of William Fosse.
„ 10, William Launder.
„ 10, Margaret Pearse.
„ 11, William, son of James Earle.
„ 12, William Harries, alias Ankow.
„ 12, Elizabeth Prior.
„ 13, Charles Game.
„ 16, John Jowan.
„ 16, Anne Tonken, widow.
„ 18, Henry Barnes.
„ 19, Robert James.
„ 20, Petherick Edwards.
„ 20, Richard Lambrick.
„ 20, Margarett Champion.
„ 20, Mary, base child of John Anbone.
„ 21, Thomas . . . . . .
„ 22, Ellonor Penhall.
„ 22, Henry, son of Morish Carne.
„ 23, Thomasine, daughter of Richard Sampson.
„ 24, William Rawlen.
„ 24, James, son of John James, alias Treneglos.
„ 25, Michaell, son of Michaell Skinner.
„ 28, Peter Nicholas.
„ 28, John Boddy, the second.
„ 29, Katherine Fosse, widow.
„ 29, John Lambrick.
„ 30, Mary Tonken.
„ 30, William Tonken.
„ 30, William Warren.
„ 31, Margarett, wife of Richard Newhall.
„ 31, Henry Paschow.
„ 31, Jone, daughter of Robart James.
Aug. 1, Jane, daughter of Arthur Noye.
„ 3, Othnell Earle.
„ 3, Elizabeth, wife of Thomas Somer.
„ 4, Jane Champion, widow.
„ 6, Jane, wife of George Blewett.
„ 8, Phillipp Nicholas, widow.
„ 10, Ellizabeth Warren, widow.
„ 10, Jone, wife of Arthur Noye.
„ 10, Anne, daughter of William Tonken.
„ 11, Honor Symons, widow.
„ 12, Florence Collins, widow.
„ 13, John Trenhaile.
„ 14, Richard Hitchens.
„ 15, Elizabeth, daughter of Zacharias Gregar.
„ 23, Elizabeth Wearne.
„ 23, Anne Jasper.
„ 23, Samuell Fynny.
„ 26, Anne Collins.
„ 31, Jane Trenhaile.
Sept. 1, Mary, daughter of Robart Tonken.

REGISTER OF BURIALS.

Sept. 5, Honor, daughter of William Giles.
,, 6, Ursula Cocke.
,, 6, ... son of Abraham Gegar.
,, 7, Jone Jasper.
,, 7, Nicholas Jasper.
,, 8, Elloner Elford, widow.
,, 10, Margarett, wife of Gabriell Somer.
,, 11, John Thomas.
,, 12, Jane, daughter of Robart Tonken.
,, 14, Elizabeth Rowe.
,, 17, Grace Giles.
,, 21, Jone Tremenheare.
,, 27, William Luddy.
,, 27, Jane Sise.
,, 27, Elizabeth, daughter of Gabriell Somer.
,, 28, Elloner Tremenheare.
,, 29, Avis, wife of John Edy.
Oct. 2, Margarett, wife of Paschow Tincombe.
,, 3, Richard Giles.
,, 4, John Somer.
,, 6, Alice, wife of George Renowden.
,, 9, Jane, daughter of Robart Harrie.
,, 10, Peter Gregar.
,, 12, Thomas Jasper.
,, 12, Alice, daughter of Nicholas Rawlen.
,, 17, Mr. John Kete, Vicar.
,, 18, Jane, daughter of Mr. John Kete.
,, 22, John, son of Robart Harrie.
,, 23, Richard, son of Robert Harrie.
,, 25, Anne Fynny.
,, 30, Robart, son of Mr. John Kete.
Nov. 1, Elizabeth, wife of Nich. Rawlen.
,, 7, Anne, wife of German Luke.
,, 7, Anne, daughter of Luke Stephen.
,, 15, Elizabeth Tregerthen.
Dec. 2, Edward Box.
,, 8, Frances, wife of John Cocke.
,, 16, Robart Connell.
,, 20, Simon, son of [Simon Francis ?]
,, 26, Mary, daughter of Reynold Boase.
,, 27, Anne Francis, widow.
,, 29, William Shilling.

[1648.]

Jan. 5, Richard Steven.
,, 14, Reynold Boase.
,, 23, William Anbono.
Feb. 5, Katherine Wall, widow.
,, 6, John, son of James Earle.
,, 6, Amy, wife of James Earle.
,, 8, Henry Penticost.
,, 10, Jone, daughter of Richard Harris.
,, 11, James Earle.
,, 13, Margarett Harris, widow.
,, 16, Robert, son of Morish Connell.
,, 20, Charity, daughter of James Earle.
,, 25, John Symon.
,, 27, Rebecca, daughter of John Tremenheare.
,, 28, Honor, daughter of George Noye.
March 6, Richard Ellis.

March 8, Elizabeth Mawgan.
,, 8, Richard Tremellyn.
,, 9, Mary Tremellyn, widow.
,, 10, John Howes, alias Cally.
,, 11, Margarett, wife of John Cock.
,, 15, Tho., son of James Earle.
,, 15, Sara, daughter of Walter Cory.
,, 22, John Tailor.
,, 23, Mary Tremellyn.

1648.

,, 30, John Synkow, alias Bond.
April 2, Elizabeth Olliver.
,, 10, Elizabeth, daughter of William Penticost.
,, 13, Jane Howes, widow.
,, 14, Anne Lamyn, widow.
,, 25, William Landy, alias Teage, and Kay, his wife.
,, 25, Bennatt, son of Thomas Bennatt.
May 2, Walter and Jone, children of Nicholas Phillipp.
,, 5, Margery, wife of John Sennen, alias James
,, 6, John Sennen, alias James.
,, 9, Agnes Lamyn.
,, 9, Morish Landy, alias Teage.
,, 13, Agnes, daughter of Thomas Bennatt.
,, 16, Elizabeth Nicholls, widow.
,, 19, Elizabeth Hubhart.
,, 20, Mary, daughter of William Treneere.
,, 24, Thomas Prior.
,, 30, Temperance Tull.
June 1, William, son of William Penticost.
,, 4, Jone Bosekennen, widow.
,, 6, Hugh Chinalls, gent.
,, 16, Jone, daughter of John Maiear.
,, 18, Edward Seese.
,, 24, John Harberte.
July 1, Henry, son of Joseph Wannell.
,, 6, Margarett, daughter of John Cocke.
,, 16, Jane Legaw, widow.
,, 17, Jane, daughter of Joseph Wannell.
Aug. 4, Katherine, wife of John Mulfra.
,, 13, Elizabeth Alexander.
Sept. 10, Elizabeth Laity.
,, 30, Jermyn Luke.
Nov. 1, Margery, daughter of William Couchie.
,, 21, Anne Chamberlaine.
,, 23, John, son of John Sampson, the younger.
,, 27, Henry Foster.
,, 27, Jane Bennatt, widow.
Dec. 5, Thomas Michell.

[1649.]

Jan. 3, Blanch Polkenhorne, widow.
,, 5, Oates Nicholas.
,, 15, Barbary, wife of John Harrie.
,, 28, Margarett, daughter of Thomas Foster.
Feb. 6, William Treneere.
,, 8, Grace, wife of Luke Steven.
,, 11, Jone Gregar, widow.

PARISH OF MADRON.

March 3, Grace, wife of John Tonken.
1649.
„ 26, Phillipp, son of Phillipp Lanion.
April 18, Othnell, son of Othnell Wall.
„ 18, Charles, son of John Luke.
„ 24, Alice, wife of John Bosewarrack.
„ 26, Phillipp, daughter of Degory, the cooper.
„ 26, Jane, daughter of William Hall.
„ 28, Nicholas Connack.
„ 30, Nicholas Trick.
May 26, Margarett, daughter of John Barnes.
June 11, John, son of Ralph Morish.
„ 15, Thomas, son of Martyn Sampson.
July 29, Martyn Thomas.
Aug. 22, Elizabeth, daughter of Nich. Rawlen.
„ 26, Jane Rowe.
Sept. 12, Jone, daughter of Thomas Rawlen.
Oct. 13, Sara, daughter of John Cowling, gent.

[1650.]
Jan. 25, Mary Noall, widow.
Feb. 27, James Tredennack.
March 3, Richard Jacka.
1650.
May 6, Walter Cory.
„ 12, Margery, daughter of Henry Dunkin.
June 4, Margarett, daughter of John Maddern.
„ 9, Robart Fynney.
„ 15, Jane Michell.
„ 15, Grace, daughter of Henry Edmonds.
„ 23, Margarett, wife of George Blewett.
July 21, Nowall Argoll.
„ 23, Stephen, son of William Jenken.
Aug. 11, Arthur Charter.
Sept. 2, Elizabeth Fleming, widow.
„ 12, Jone, wife of John Nowall.
Oct. 3, Jane Williams, widow.
„ 9, Abraham Holla.
Nov. 24, Mary, wife of Leonard Rowe.
„ 27, John Bosewarrack.
Dec. 4, John Stone, Sen.
„ 4, Jone Legaw.
„ 5, Grace, daughter of William Michell.
„ 18, Thomasine Clemow.
„ 19, Prudence Foster.
„ 30, Bennatt Anbone.

[1651.]
Jan. 8, Katherine, wife of William Noseworthie.
„ 12, Edmond Saundry.
„ 18, John Argoll.
„ .. .... daughter of .... Anbone.
„ 22, Anne Barber, widow.
1651.
April 11, John Luke, Sen.
May 3, Thomasin Cosen.
„ 4, Francis, child of Francis Lawrey.
„ 19, Jone Rawling.
June 12, Jane Edy, widow.

July 22, John, son of John Ellis.
Aug. 11, John, son of John Maddern.
„ 13, Elizabeth Sudgeow, widow.
Sept. 27, Ebbatt, wife of William Noye.
Oct. 2, John, son of William Noye.
„ 3, Robart Covy.
Nov. 19, Elizabeth, wife of Ralph Morish.
Dec. 24, —— wife of John Hooper.

[1652.]
Jan. 8, John Stone, Jun.
„ 9, Rebecca, daughter of William Penticost.
„ 10, Blanch, daughter of John Battyn.
March 7, Anne, wife of John Lanion.
„ 8, Agnes, wife of Robart Colman.
„ 24, Francis Lawrey.
1652.
May 19, William Ceely, gent.
„ 26, Blanch, daughter of Martyn Sampson.
June 20, Martyn Sampson.
„ 26, Robart Watchins.
July 6, Anne, wife of Richard Cardew.
Aug. 4, Elizabeth, wife of Thomas Sudgeow.
„ 4, James Teage.
„ 4, Robart, son of Robart Watchins.
Sept. 30, Christian Saundry, widow.
Dec. 20, Thomas Chinalls, gentleman.*

[1653.]
Jan. 19, Mary, daughter of Walter Noye.
„ 26, George Noye.
Feb. 6, Anne Jeffry, widow.
„ 21, Jone, wife of William Michell.
„ 28, Jane, wife of Thomas Hacker.
March 6, George Cock.
1653.
April 12, John Banfeild.
May 5, Christian, wife of Francis Glover.
„ 6, Jonathan James.
„ 27, Margarett Chinalls, widow.
July 14, Agnes Edmonds, widow.
„ 22, Thomasine, daughter of Henry Polkenhorne gent.
„ 30, Mary, daughter of John Barnes.
Nov. 14, Anne Tregerthen.
„ 28, Grace Robarts.
„ 29, Anne, daughter of Hugh Edwards.
Dec. 14, John, son of John Tonken.
„ 17, Margery Tregerthen.

[1654.]
Jan. 18, Judith, daughter of Thomas Pike, gent.
„ 19, Jone Tailor, widow.
Feb. 8, John, son of Richard Stone.
„ 10, Anne, daughter of John Boskennen.
March 3, John Battyn.
„ 12, Sicely Humfry.

* Written on erasure.

REGISTER OF BURIALS.

Mar. 19, Jane Holla, widow.
,, 21, Mary, daughter of John Michell.
1654.
,, 28, Humfry Hutchens.
April 14, Margarett, wife of Richard Tom.
,, 21, Roger, son of John Cossens.
May 15, Jane, daughter of James Newhall.
June 22, Francis, son of William Tregeow.
July 5, Sampson, son of Walter Noye.
,, 10, Christopher Glasan.
,, 16, Mary, daughter of John Lanion.
Aug. 23, Anne Skinner.
Sept. 21, Ralph Noye.
Oct. 24, John James.
,, 27, Mildred Box, widow.
Nov. 1, John, son of John Harrie.
,, 10, Thomas Robart.
,, 16, John Benmer, the younger.
Dec. 6, Elizabeth, wife of Oliver Wolcock.

[1655.]
Jan. 3, Degory Duke.
,, 10, Will., son of John Tregenhorne.
,, 16, Richard Harrie.
Feb. 1, Ursula Barnes, widow.
,, 6, William Young.
,, 7, Florance, wife of William Gife.
,, 26, Thomas Becarlock.
March 1, Jone, daughter of Tonken Boase.
,, 10, Nicholas Fleming, gent.
,, 15, Sampson Thomas.
1655.
,, 26, Mathew Howes.
April 2, Alice, wife of Thomas Chirgwin.
,, 9, John Davy.
,, 10, Richard, son of Salamon Carvarth.
,, 12, John, son of Thomas Morish, the younger.
May 3, Alexander Tregerthen.
,, 6, Elizabeth, daughter of John Anbone.
,, 11, Elizabeth, wife of John Saundry.
,, 17, William, son of Robart Touken.
,, 18, Elizabeth Benny, widow.
,, 31, Anne, wife of Michaell Nicholas.
June 26, Avis Bennatt.
,, 21, Phillipp, wife of Morish Collens.
,, 26, Joane, daughter of William Angove.
Aug. 3, Anne Edwards, widow.
,, 22, Agnes, wife of John Angwin.
,, 25, Joane, daughter of Robart Watkins.
,, 28, Sicely, daughter of John Luke.
,, 31, William, son of William Nicholls, gent.
Oct. 18, Mary Game, widow.
,, 26, Mary, wife of Thomas Holla.
Nov. 6, James, son of Gabriell White.
,, 14, Thomas Sudgeow.
,, 25, Elloner, daughter of William Christopher.
Dec. 23, William Jeffry, alias Nighten.
,, 26, Alice Edy, widow.

[1656.]
Jan. 8, Hanna Robarts, widow.
,, 10, Edward Jenken.
,, 13, William, son of Henry Saundry.
,, 16, William, son of John Saundry.
,, 20, Elizabeth Clyes, widow.
,, 24, John Hooper.
,, 25, Andrew, son of Thomas Tyack.
,, 25, Elizabeth, wife of Francis Lanion.
,, .. Susan, wife of John Williams.
,, 30, Thomas Maddern.
Feb. 4, Jonathan, son of Francis Lanion.
,, 6, Peter Chirgwin.
,, 20, Chesten Champion, widow.
,, 22, Joane Robarts.
,, 25, John Seiscell.
March 5, Dorithie Nicholls.
,, 7, Alice, wife of Michaell Tredennack.
,, 18, William, son of John Thomas.
,, 20, Robart Colman, gent.
1656.
,, 28, Elizabeth Hoskyn, widow.
April 9, Jone, daughter of John Maddern.
,, 10, John James, alias Mulfra, the younger.
,, 12, Reynold Harrie.
,, 18, Honor Thomas, widow.
,, 24, William Lemin.
,, 30, Joane, daughter of William John.
May 2, Elizabeth, daughter of Samuell Edye.
,, 4, Elizabeth, wife of John Rundle.
,, 26, Joane, daughter of William Williams.
June 17, David, son of John Lanion.
,, 19, John, son of John Treucere.
,, 25, Thomas, son of Thomas Foster.
July 1, Avis Rawling.
,, 5, Henry Polkenhorne, gent.
,, 13, Peter Foster.
,, 16, William, son of William Trewren, gent.
,, 19, Thomas, son of John Magor.
,, 20, Rodigon, daughter of John Saundry.
Aug. 25, Elizabeth Whitefeild.
Sept. 4, Anne, daughter of Phillipp Argall.
,, 18, Joane, wife of James John, the elder.
,, 21, Joane James, otherwise Mulfra.
,, 28, Thomas, son of Richard Osbern.
Oct. 29, Hugh Suger.
Nov. 10, Elizabeth Ralph, widow.
,, 11, Francis Michell.
Dec. 7, Prudence Glasan, widow.
,, 10, Anne Cowling.
,, 16, Henry Fosse.
,, 20, Leonard Rowe.
,, 26, Jane Luke, widow.

[1657.]
Jan. 5, Ralph Duke.
,, 12, John Bennatt.
,, 24, Amy Anthony, widow.
,, 29, Ursula Thomas, widow.

PARISH OF MADRON.

Feb. 1, Margarett Giles.
,, 8, Nicholas Edwards.
,, 1.. Joane Anbone, widow.
,, 13, Thomasine Dee.
March 4, William, son of James Noye.
,, 8, Grace, daughter of Walter Stone.
,, 15, Joane Fallenton.

1657.
,, 29, Thomasine, daughter of William Anthony.
April 5, William Rodda.
,, 6, John James, otherwise Mulfra.
,, 13, Robart, son of Roger Covye.
,, 19, Anne Leddra.
,, 19, Wearne Tremenheare.
,, 29, John Nowall.
May 5, Elizabeth, wife of Rich. Leddra.
,, 18, Anne, wife of John Barnes.
June 3, Alice Giffo.
,, 10, Thomas Lovelis, gent.
,, 10, Robart Fison, gent.
,, 10, Thomas Rawling.
,, 21, Joane, daughter of Thomas Hew.
July 28, Richard Champion.
Aug. 2, William, son of Gilbert Thicke.
,, 4, Anne, daughter of Mathew Reede.
,, 6, Maddern Pearse.
,, 13, John Tregunnow.
,, 17, Margery Duke, widow.
Oct. 6, John Jacka.
,, 17, Grace, daughter of John Williams.
Nov. 24, Joane, wife of Nicholas Jasper.
Dec. 13, Richard Duke.
,, 20, Peter, son of Thomas Chirgwin.

[1658.]
Jan. 20, John Jeffry.
,, 24, Margarett, wife of James Fynny.
Feb. 2, Anne Legawe.
,, 7, John Hitchens.
,, 12, James, son of Peter Williams.
,, 14, Mary, wife of Edward Rawling.
,, 17, Tho. Young.
,, 19, Joane Mumford, widow.
,, 21, Robart Hocken.
Mar. 14, Joane Victor, widow.

1658.
,, 31, Mary Treneere, widow.
April 4, Grace Edyo.
,, 11, Nicholas, son of Edward Rawling.
,, 21, Jane, wife of Henry Lutye.
May 3, Elizabeth, wife of William Michell.
,, 3, Charity, daughter of William Michell.
,, 7, Jane Williams, widow.
,, 9, John Roberts.
,, 22, Elizabeth, wife of John Wolcock.
,, 24, John, son of John Houichurch, gent.
,, 29, Margarett, wife of William Legawe.
June 2, Jane Harbert, widow.
,, 4. Alexander Clies, of Gulvall.

June 13, Peter, son of Peter Cloake.
July 20, Ursula, wife of William Chirgwin.
Aug. 1, Thomas, son of Thomas Benmer.
,, 20, Susan, wife of Thomas Stephens.
,, 22, Roger Covie.
Oct. 7, Margarett, wife of John Manly.
,, 16, Elizabeth, wife of Humfry Stone.
,, 20, Jacobb, son of Francis Poultry.
,, 29, George Davy.
,, 30, Gartered Blewett, widow.
Nov. 13, Catherine, wife of Gilbart Thick.
,, 22, Grace, wife of William Rodda.
,, 30, Grace, daughter of Salamon Carveth.
Dec. 1, Ursula Nicholas, widow.
,, 5, Margarett, daughter of Gilbart Thick.
,, 11, Margarott Sakerley, widow.
,, 29, Catherine Chirgwin.

[1659.]
Jan. 3, Mary Treneere, the younger, widow.
,, 6, Jane, wife of Walter Saundry.
,, 9, William, son of William Pearse.
,, 10, Anne, wife of Michaell Nicholas.
,, 11, John Pollard.
,, 14, Catherine, daughter of John Williams.
Feb. 26, Alice Roleigh.
March 6, Blanch Garrett, widow.

1659.
April 18, Anne, wife of William Bosekennon.
,, 22, Blanch, wife of Salamou Carveth.
,, 22, Margery, daughter of Nathaniell Treneerry.
,, 26, Margery, daughter of Thomas Jonken.
,, 29, Mary, daughter of William Young.
May 1, Henry, son of Thomas Jeffrey.
,, 5, Joane, daughter of William John.
,, 6, Marke Thomas.
,, 11, Constance, daughter of John Tregunnow.
,, 13, Esabella, daughter of John Foster.
,, 20, Margarott Boddye, widow.
,, 22, Thomas Legawe.
,, 29, Ralph, son of John Pollard.
,, 30, Mary James, *alias* Mulfra, widow.
June 14, John, son of John Thomas.
,, 19, Sara, wife of Martyn Gwennapp.
,, 20, Joane, daughter of Bennatt Davy.
July 4, Jane, daughter of Thomas Drew.
,, 8, James, son of Walter Richard.
,, 8, Anne, daughter of Richard Symons.
,, 10, Willmott, daughter of John Harrie.
,, 21, Duke, son of John Hitchens.
Aug. 4, Elizabeth, wife of John Lamerton.
Sept. 1, Joane Young, widow.
,, 4, Elizabeth Launder, widow.
,, 11, —— son of Walter Collombe.
,, 18, William Legawe.
,, 30, Jane, daughter of Thomas Baynard.
Nov. 1, Jane, daughter of William Chirgwin.
Dec. 12, Elizabeth, daughter of Arthur Noye.
,, 24, Margarett Davy, widow.

REGISTER OF BURIALS.

[1660.]

Jan. 18, William Noseworthy, gent.
 ,, 29, William Brathery.
Feb. 5, Sampson Noye.
 ,, 5, Thomas Trencere.
March 3, William Michell.
 ,, 21, Alice, wife of Richard Connack.
1660.
 ,, 26, John Cowling, the younger, of Poltegan.
April 12, Margarett, daughter of Jo. Gilbart, Jun.
 ,, 18, Elloner Maddern, widow.
May 13, Blanch, wife of Richard Legawe.
 ,, 20, Rebecca, daughter of Jo. Maddern.
 ,, 27, Tho. Trelill.
June 12, Agnes, wife of Phillipp Lanion.
 ,, 12, Christian, daughter of Hugh Baggs.
 ,, 19, Anne, daughter of Jo. Barnes.
July 4, Tho. Esham.
Aug. 7, Richard, son of Samuell Edye.
 ,, 22, Mary, wife of Robart Luty.
Sept. 22, Alexander Lanion.
 ,, 23, Jane Jacka, widow.
 ,, 28, Charles, son of William Chirgwin.
Oct. 2, Richard Connack.
 ,, 19, Elizabeth Wannell, widow.
 ,, 28, William Williams.
Nov. 1, Margarett Noye, widow.
 ,, 4, William, son of John Williams.
 ,, 20, John Robarts.
 ,, 28, Earth Sampson, widow.
Dec. 14, William Rodda, Sen.
 ,, 17, Sicely, wife of Walter Stone.

[1661.]

Jan. 3, John Aubone.
 ,, 10, Margarett Champion.
 ,, 20, Mawde, wife of Alexander Lanion.
 ,, 28, Frances, wife of John Cowling, gent.
Feb. 1, William, son of John Harrie.
 ,, 5, William Lanion, gent.
 ,, 21, Joane Thomas, widow.
Mar. 19, Edward Anboue and Thomasine, his wife.
 ,, 21, Alice John, widow.
 ,, 22, Joane Williams.
1661.
 ,, 31, Richard Martyn.
April 5, Jane, daughter of William Angove.
 ,, 10, Agnes Suger, widow.
 ,, 12, Anne, daughter of Sampson Lanion.
 ,, 28, John Tonken.
 ,, 30, Nich.,* wife of Nich. Kinsham.
May 4, Henry Tremearne.
 ,, 22, Francis Lanion, gent.
 ,, 24, Margarett, daughter of Sampson Lanion.
 ,, 24, Alice Wearren, widow.
July 14, Joane Michell, widow.

Aug. 14, Nich. Skinner.
 ,, 21, John Daniell.
 ,, 23, James Fynney.
Sept. 22, Richard Hoskin.
 ,, 25, Sara, daughter of Rich. Martyn.
Oct. 7, Elizabeth, wife of William Trowren.
 ,, 13, Phillipp Rawling, widow.
 ,, 22,* Margaret, wife of Sciprian Burnow.
 ,, 23, Elizabeth,† alias Noale. widow.
Nov. 10, Anne Tremenheare, widow.
 ,, 24, Julian, wife of John James.
Dec. 30, Michaell Tredennick.

[1662.]

Jan. 31, Margarett Burlace, widow.
Feb. 3, Alice, daughter of William Giles.
 ,, 7, John Harries, alias Martyn.
 ,, 20, Henry Luty.
Mar. 11, Richard Lanion.
 ,, 23, Bennat Lanion.
1662.
 ,, 28, Maddern Hugh.
April 21, —— child of Lawrence Geare.
May 27, John, son of Tho. Benmer.
June 22, Christian Dune.
 ,, 23, Anthony Gubbs, marchant.
July 9, John Boddye, Sen.
Sept. 6, John, son of John Luke.
 ,, 8, William, son of Edward Nicholas.
 ,, 10, John, son of Sciprian Burnow.
 ,, 23, Thomas Holla.
 ,, 24, John Manly.
Oct. 9, Robart Carne.
 ,, 15, Anne Somery, widow.
Nov. 28, Phillipp Anbone, widow.
 ,, 29, Joane, wife of John Sudgeow.
Dec. 25, Anne Noye, widow.

[1663.]

Feb. 5, Catherine, wife of Richard Hall.
 ,, 13, Ananias Hosford.
 ,, 22, Mary Lanion, widow.
 ,, 27, Tho. Fleming, gent.
March 6, Robart Welmenton, of Chidick, neere Crookehorne, in Somersett Scire.
 ,, 15, Jane Launder, widow.
1663.
April 1, Richard, son of Jo. Kete, gent.
 ,, 15, Eloner James, widow.
 ,, 17, Elizabeth Hutchens, widow.
 ,, 28, Alice Hitchens.
May 5, William Maddern. gent.
 ,, 17, John Benmer.
 ,, 23, Margarett, daughter of Lewis Gennens.
 ,, 25, Joane, daughter of Richard John.
 ,, 31, James, son of Peter Cloake.

* Sic. * Query 23, the second figure being partly cut off. † Sic.

PARISH OF MADRON.

Oct.* 16, Elizabeth, wife to William Maddron, gent.
June 8, Mathew, son of John Thomas.
 ,, 30, —— daughter of Ralph Shoale.
 ,, 30, Mary, wife of John Maddern.
July 1, Mary Howes, widow.
 ,, 1, John Anbone.
 ,, 20, Eliz., wife of Nich. Keygwin.
Aug. 4, William, son of Thomas Esham.
 ,, 13, Elloner, wife of William Pearse.
 ,, 19, Margarett James.
Sept. 2, Ellonor, daughter of Will. Pearse.
 ,, 15, Jane, wife of Henry Edmonds.
Oct. 8, Sicely, daughter of Nicholas Launder.
 ,, 16, Elizabeth Maddern, widow.
 ,, 16, Mary, daughter of Lawrence Geare.
 ,, 18, Dorothie, daughter of Lawrence Geare.
 ,, 27, Alice Pryor, widow.
 ,, 28, Beniamyn, son of Richard Paule.
 ,, 29, Elizabeth, wife of Jo. Edwards, *alias* Portcere.
 ,, 31, Humfry, son of Bennatt Champion.
Nov. 2, Edward, son of Nich. Launder.
 ,, 3, Julian, daughter of John Fynny.
 ,, 4, Elizabeth, daughter of Mathew Skinner.
 ,, 8, Mary, daughter of William Anthony.
 ,, 29, Jo., son of John Badcock.
Dec. 6, Mary Blewett.
 ,, 27, Agnes Mildren, widow.

[1664.]

Feb. 8, Jo. Randell.
Mar. 12, Anne, daughter of John Gilbart.
 ,, 13, John James, *alias* Rosemorran.
 ,, 15, Joane, daughter of Will. Edye.
 ,, 18, Walter Cennack.
 ,, 19, John Borriman.
1664.
 ,, 28, Jane, wife of Zacharias Gregar.
 ,, 28, —— child of Ralph Hacker.
April 3, William Chirgwin.
 ,, 4, Charles, son of John Luke.
 ,, 5, Tho. Lake.
 ,, 5, Margarett Tredennick, widow.
May 15, Jane, daughter of Tho. Cardew.
July 10, Grace Wale, widow.
 ,, 12, Anne Boase, widow.
 ,, 20, Henry Edmonds.
Aug. 9, Thomasine, wife of Tho. Cardew.
 ,, 12, Alice, wife of Richard Stone.†
 ,, 21, Phillipp Argall.
 ,, 28, Rich., son of Richard Paule.
Sept. 2, Joane Cowling.
 ,, 12, Jane Chinialls.
 ,, 22, John Fleming, gent.
Oct. 23, William Fosse.
 ,, 30, Sampson Thomas.

Nov. 6, Tho. Holla.
 ,, 8, John Michell.
 ,, 20, Jane, wife of Tho. Hacker.
Dec. 6, Elizabeth Champion, widow.
 ,, 6, Anne Richard, widow.
 ,, 30, Anne Player.

[1665.]

Jan. 15, Elizabeth Rawling, widow.
Feb. 18, James, son of Peter Cloake.
 ,, —— Elloner Avery, widow.
1665.
Mar. 31, Arthur Noye.
April 12, —— child of Henry Saundry.
 ,, 19, Bridgett, wife of Arundell Sackarley.
June 26, Leonard, son of Mr. Robart Harrie.
July 11, Constance, wife of Robart Cowling, gent.
Oct. 3, Anne, wife of Jo. Tremenheare, marchant.

[1666.]

Feb. 28, Arthur Rawling.
Mar. 17, Richard Lanion.
 ,, 18, John Cowling, gent.
1666.
 ,, 25, Christopher Creede.
[+] April 22, Leonard, son of William Pearce.
 ,, 22, Elizabeth Phillipps, widow.
May 5, Elloner, wife of Nicholas Rawlings.
 ,, 22, Hugh, son of William Michell.
 ,, 31, Kathraine Bose.
June 3, Dina, daughter of Sampson Rodda.
 ,, 4, Elizabeth, wife of James Loase.
 ,, 29, Thomas, son of William Honichurch, gent.
July 1, David Penlease.
 ,, 3, George Cloake.
 ,, 9, William, son of Richard Trevailor.
Aug. 13, Giles Thomas.
 ,, 17, Salamy, wife of Joseph Benmer.
Sept. 2, Richard Lanion.
Oct. 2, Thomas Morish.
 ,, 27, Thomas Somer, gent.
 ,, 29, Joane, daughter of William Calleusow.
Nov. 20, Alice, wife of John Cock.
Dec. 19, Bennett Nicholas.
 ,, 23, John George.
 ,, 30, Robart Hearle, of Lansullos.

[1667.]

Jan. 5, Emanuell Drew, of Gulvall.
 ,, 11, Richard, son of Richard Treviler.
 ,, 15, Mary Jenken.
 ,, 17, Joane, wife of Zacharias Champion.
Feb. 17, Lidea, daughter of James Gilbart.
 ,, 22, Phillipp Gilbart, widow.
 ,, 25, Ralph Morish.
March 6, Kathraine James, widow.
[+] ,, 8, Mary Couche, widow.
 ,, 15, Degory Nicholls.

---

* *Sic.* This entry is an addition in a different hand. See Oct. 16.
† This entry is an interlineation.

REGISTER OF BURIALS.

1667.
April 16, John Champion.
,, 23, Mary, daughter of Richard Saundry.
,, 24, Anne Barnes, widow.
May 26, Mary, daughter of John Mathew.
,, 29, Dorothie, daughter of Thomas Baynard, of Sancre[ed.]
June 1, Tho. Games, gent.
,, 12, Henry Chinialls, gent.
July 7, Will. Luke.
,, 9, William, son of John Rogers.
,, 10, Jane Rodda.
,, 28, John Cleverdon, marchant.
Aug. 1, Bennatt Jennens.
Dec. 15, Tho. Hacker.

[1668.]
Jan. 2, Walter Rodda.
[+],, 2, Elizabeth Elis.
,, 3, Jane, daughter of Richard Leagow.
,, 18, Anne Games, widow.
,, 25, Sara, daughter of Jacob Penhallow.
,, 30, Luke Stephens.
Feb. 3, Halnight Stephens.
,, 5, William Jenken.
Mar. 16, John Benetts.
1668.
April 8, William Bosekennen.
,, 13, Ellenor Nicholas, widow.
,, 14, Alexander Daniell, gent.
May 9, Bridgett, daughter of James Benn[ett.]
,, 12, Margarett Hosford, widow.
July 4, The child of Nicholas Richard.
Aug. 24, Edward Nicholas.
,, 28, Anne, wife of Thomas Callensow.
,, 28, Robart Glendening, of Kirconbree, in Scotland.
,, 30, Humfry Pearce.
,, 30, Mary, wife of Robart Trewren.
Sept. 13, Alice, daughter of John Williams.
,, 14, —— child of Marten Gwennapp.
,, 15, Salamon Beumer.
Oct. 5, Thomas, son of Nathaniell Trenerrey.
,, 6, Nicholas Fleming, gent.
,, 13, Henry, son of Robart Lutey.
,, 17, Margarett, wife of George Humfrye.
,, 24, Enoch, son of James Thomas.
Nov. 3, Richard Tom.
,, 3, Robart Thomas.
,, 17, Julian, wife of Luke Chamberlaine.
,, 25, Mary, daughter of Robart Colman, gent.
Dec. 9, Katherine Stone, widow.
,, 10, John Fynny.
,, 25, Andrew Connell.

[1669.]
Jan. 1, Margarett, daughter of James Carpenter.
,, 1, John Mathew.
,, 19, John Smyth, of Hamton.

Jan. 19, Richard, son of Will. Rawling.
,, 22, Jane, daughter of Nicholas Michell.
Feb. 7, Milchezedick Thomas.
,, 9, Elizabeth Rodda, widow.
,, 12, John, son of Bennett Champion.
,, 13, John, son of James Perrow.
,, 16, John, son of Richard Osbern.
,, 20, Peter, son of Nicholas Rawling.
,, 23, John Sampson.
Mar. 21, John Cock.
1669.
April 24, Anne, wife of Marten Bosavern.
May 12, Anne, wife of Nicholas Tregerthen.
June 5, Thomasine, wife of Thomas Stephens.
,, 30, Mary, wife of Robart Colman, gent.
July 1, Mary, daughter of Mathew Skinner.
,, 6, Jane Gregar, widow.
,, 14, Bredgett, daughter of James Bennett.
Aug. 8, William Rawling.
1671.*
Oct. 24, Alexander Lanion, gent.
.... Nicholl, wife of William Lawry, of Penzance
* * * * * * * * * * * * *†
1673.
April 2, Elizabeth, wife of William Pentichost.
,, 10, Ann, daughter of Humphry Jaccah.
,, 21, James Rawling.
,, 23, William, son of William Michell.
,, 27, Jone, wife of Thomas Osbarn.
,, 29, Elizabeth, daughter of William Cowling, gent.
May 7, Margarett, daughter of Reginald Ladnar.
,, 19, Ann Fosse, widow.
,, 28, Cordeliah, daughter of Thomas Fleming, gent.
,, 29, Mary, daughter of Bennett Lanyon.
June 25, William, son of William Penlease.
July 23, Mary Sandry.
Aug. 23, Christophar Boddye.
Sept. 7, Dorothie Phillipps.
,, 9, Marten, son of William Sampson.
,, 23, Thomas Hugh.
Oct. 13, English Boggow.
,, 21, William, son of John Kegwin, gent.

[1674.]
Jan. 3, Elizabeth Phillipps.
,, 8, Kathrayn Vanson, widow.
Feb. 11, Mathew Reed.
,, 12, Elizabeth Leagow.
,, 14, Thomas Cardew.
,, 15, Jone Heddy.‡
,, 18, Elizabeth Jackson.
,, 19, Grace Tonken.
March 1, Jone George, widow.

* *Sic.* There being no break.
† A leaf missing here.   ‡ *i.e.* Eddy.

PARISH OF MADRON.

Mar. 12, Jane Glasse, widow.
 „ 24, William, son of Stephen Luke.
1674.
April 7, Ann Addams, widow.
 „   8, Emaniwell Hosken.
 „ 12, James Thomas.
 „ 16, Salomon Cock.
 „ 26, Margarett, daughter of Bennett Champion.
May 1, Elizabeth Fostar.
 „ 10, Alice, daughter of Sampson Harrie.
 „ 23, Edward Dagwell, of the Ille of Wight, marinor.
 „ 25, William Lanyon.
June 15, Thomas Ellis, gent.
July 5, William, son of John Barns.
 „ 15, Margarett Maddarn.
 „ 16, Richard Trelill.
 „ 19, John Eddye.
Aug. 4, Elizabeth, wife of William Chirgwin.
 „   4, Ellenor, wife of William Williams, of Paule
 „   6, Jone, daughter of William Pearce.
 „ 13, Jane, daughter of William Pearce.
 „ 14, Jone, wife of Thomas Pearce.
Sept. 10, William Chirgwin.
 „ 15, Mrs. Blanch Bonithan.
 „ 27, Katheren, wife of Davied Gift.
 „ 28, Margarett, wife of John Pedwell.
 „ 30, Blanch George, widow.
Oct. 3, Richard Leddra.
 „   7, Elizabeth, wife of John Luke.
 „ 29, Honor Chirgwin, widow.
Nov. 8, Richard, son of Jacob Cock.
 „   9, —— wife of George Renowden.
 „ 10, Mary, daughter of Robart Whitt.
 „ 10, William, son of William Leagow.
 „ 30, Elizabeth Newton.
Dec. 23, Joseph, son of Sampson Gubbs, marchand.
 „ 28, Kathren, wife of Robart ——

[1675.]
Jan. 5, John Corrie.
 „ 10, Blanch Sudgow.
 „ 18, Mary, daughter of John Barnes.
 „ 26, Edward, son of Edward Jones.
Feb. 4, Margery, daughter of George Christophars
 „ 17, Nathanuell Trenery.
 „ 17, —— Trewren, of Sancread.
 „ 18, Honor Chinalls.
 „ 19, Christian Corry.
 „ 20, The child of William Chirgwin.
 „ 28, William, son of Nicholas Richards.
 „ 28, The daughter of Thomas Hugh.
Mar. 14, Elizabeth Noye, widow.
1675.
 „ 28, John, son of Richard Row.
 „ 29, Mrs. Alice Gubbs.
 „ 30, Elizabeth, daughter of William Lanyon.
April 25, Mary Sampson.
May 29, Humphry Nicholas.

June 10, Elizabeth Legaw.
 „ 17, Margery, wife of Thomas Row.
 „ 30, The daughter of Frances Benetts.
July 12, Thomas Tyagg.
 „ 13, Mary Hosken.
 „ 19, Mr. Caswin.
Aug. 26, Elizabeth Dun.
 „ 27, Mary, daughter of Marten Rodda.
Sept. 4, Katheren Collam.
 „ 14, Alise, wife of William Anthony.
 „ 14, John, son of John Dawe.
 „ 21, Avise Dun, widow.
Oct. 3, Samwell, son of Mr. Ralph Beard.
 „   6, Susanah, wife of William Christophars.
 „   7, James, son of Richard Osbarn.
 „ 10, —— son of Edward Jones.
Nov. 26, Alise, daughter of Thomas George.
 „ 29, Margarett Luke.
Dec. 10, Alise, wife of Thomas Fynnis.
 „ 11, Jane Boswarrack.
 „ 12, Thomas Champion.
 „ 13, Vernan, son of Michaell Brown.
 „ 21, Mathias, son of William Rawling.
 „ 27, William Noye.

[1676.]
Jan. 2, Thomas Osbarn.
 „   4, —— —— of Edward Jons.
 „ 25, William, son of Jacobb Cock.
 „ 27, William, son of Michaell Brown.
Mar. 16, Jane Whitt.
 „ 22, —— —— of Somar Honichurch, gent.
1676.
April 10, —— —— of Sampson Harrie.
 „ 29, Susanah, wife of William Lanyon.
 „ 30, Agnes Cowling, widow.
May 1, Humphry, son of Humphry Lanyon.
 „ 10, Mary Burrows.
 „ 14, Tobias, son of Thomas Luddra.
 „ 28, Ann, wife of William Luke.
June 18, Elenor, wife of Ralph Hackar.
 „ 21, Thomas, son of James Somons.
 „ 22, Noye Champion.
 „ 24, Garthred, daughter of George Blewett.
 „ 25, Marten, the Blackmooar.
 „ 28, Grace, daughter of Thomas Lanyon.
July 4, Mary Fleming, widow.
 „ 19, Sciprian Stephens.
Aug. 8, Bridgett, wife of Mr. Beniamen Penhallow
 „ 18, James, son of James Bennetts.
 „ 25, ————
Sept. 6, Richard, son of Thomas Leagow.
 „ 17, Maddarn Leagow.
 „ 30, Joane, wife of Petar Cloak.
Oct. 2, John, son of Henry Tremenhear, gent.
Nov. 16, Anthony Gubbs, gent.
Dec. 2, Davied Gift.
 „   6, Jone Rise.
 „ 17, Elizabeth, wife of John Davies.

Q

REGISTER OF BURIALS.

[1677.]

Jan. 6, Avies, wife of Richard Noye.
Feb. 5, Alise, wife of Marten Rodda.
 ,, 9, Mary, daughter of Bennett Lanyon.
 ,, 10, Gabrell Sommar, gent.
 ,, 15, Jane Dunken.
Mar. 11, Thomas, son of Charles Pike, gent.
 ,, 18, Richard James.
 ,, 19, Mary, wife of John James.
 ,, 20, John Williams.
 ,, 21, Kathrayne, wife of Nicholas Connack.
1677.
 ,, 27, Edward Rawling.
 ,, 27, Jane, wife of Jaspar James.
 ,, 27, Kathrayne, daughter of Thomas Pearce.
 ,, 28, Marratt Furse.
 ,, 30, Jane Robarts, widow.
April 5, George Blewott.
 ,, 5, Clarance, wife of Petar Trelill.
 ,, 5, Elizabeth Anny.
 ,, 12, Humpry, son of Humpry Lanyon.
 ,, 12, Elizabeth Duke, widow.
 ,, 22, William Michell.
 ,, 24, Nicholas Landar.
 ,, 29, Mathew, son of Alexandar Reed.
May 7, Ann Usticke, widow.
 ,, 10, Thomas Fenne.
 ,, 13, Margarett Michell, widow.
 ,, 14, Jane, wife of Waltar Harrie.
 ,, 18, Grace, wife of John Eddye.
 ,, 22, Elizabeth Boase.
June 12, Sciprian Digory.
 ,, 13, John Nicholas.
 ,, 24, Paskow Tincom.
July 1, Alise, daughter of Marten Richards.
 ,, 9, Jane Hugh, widow.
 ,, 9, George, son of Mr. Reginald Trenhayle, vicar
 ,, 17, John, son of Degory Marshall.
 ,, 20, Sarah, wife of John Trenerre.
Aug. 3, Alise, daughter of Mr. Anthony Gubbs.
 ,, 12, Kathren, daughter of Petar Jenken, gent.
 ,, 24, John, son of George Treweek, gent.
Sept. 2, Ann Prade.
 ,, 3, Petar Trelill.
 ,, 10, —— son of Peter Jenken, gent.
 ,, 17, —— son of Peter Jenken, gent.
 ,, 23, Frances, son of Richard John.
 ,, 26, —— daughter of Henry Hutchens.
 ,, 28, Jane, daughter of Davied Hall.
Oct. 13, John Sudgow.
 ,, 28, William, son of William Calensow.
Nov. 5, The son of William Nickles.
 ,, 9, George Safgard, of St. Ives.
 ,, 12, Richard, son of George Pearce.
 ,, 17, —— daughter of Thomas Calensow.
 ,, 18, Brudgett, wife of Richard Mildarn.

[1678.]

Jan. 8, Elizabeth Holla, widow.

Feb. 8, Mrs. Grace Daniell, widow.
 ,, 25, John, son of Richard Row.
 ,, 30, Grace Treloweth, widow.
Mar. 18, Simon Noye.
 ,, 21, Robart Wallish, gent.
 ,, 21, Francis, daughter of William Cowling, gent.
1678.
 ,, 30, Honor, wife of John Veale, gent.
 ,, 31, Elizabeth Pike.
April 11, —— son of John Draneglos.
 ,, 25, Grace, daughter of John Williams.
 ,, 26, William Christophers.
[+] 28, Susan Lanion.
May 5, The child of Thomas Brush.
 ,, 10, William, son of John Gift.
 ,, 14, Mary, daughter of Emaniwell Hall.
 ,, 20, English Legow.
 ,, 23, Honor, wife of Marten Richards.
 ,, 25, Mary, wife of Henry Tregerthen.
 ,, 25, Thomas Harvye.
 ,, 29, —— son of Nicholas Lander.
June 13, Kathren, daughter of John Cowling.
 ,, 18, Isack Spredles.
 ,, 26, Kathren, wife of Richard Osbarn.
 ,, 29, John, son of Richard Giles, Jun.
July 17, Solomon Carverth.
 ,, 24, Mary Sampson, widow.
 ,, 26, Precella, daughter of William Calensow.
 ,, 29, Jane, wife of Peter Cloake.
Sept. 3, Elizabeth, wife of Robartt Harry, gent.
 ,, 7, Elizabeth, wife of Nicholas Hosking.
 ,, 27, Elizabeth Penlease, widow.
Oct. 3, George, son of George Sampson.
 ,, 6, Richard, son of John Rogars.
 ,, 19, Mary, daughter of John Prior.
 ,, 26, Mrs. Grace Angwin, widow.
Nov. 10, Henry Scissell.
 ,, 16, Margarett Trembath.
 ,, 17, Alice, daughter of John Jenings.
Dec. 30, Thomas Lanion.

[1679.]

Jan. 5, Mary, daughter of Richard Williams.
 ,, 7, Jane, wife of Thomas Legow.
 ,, 8, Charles Pike, gent.
 ,, 14, Alice, daughter of Nicholas Connack.
 ,, 16, Mary, daughter of Roger Robins.
 ,, 16, John Harry.
 ,, 21, William Jenkens.
 ,, 26, Jone Jenkens, widow.
 ,, 27, Nicholas Phillipps, Sen.
Feb. 9, Thomas Bennetts.
 ,, 14, John Trelever.
 ,, 16, Jone, daughter of Nicholas Phillipps.
 ,, 16, Ann, daughter of Thomas Legow.
 ,, 18, Elizabeth, wife of Nicholas Phillipps.
 ,, 21, Mary Bennetts, widow.
March 4, Andrew, son of Thomas Robarts.
 ,, 8, Thomas George.

PARISH OF MADRON.

Mar. 11, Susanna Williams.
 „ 23, Walter Richards.

1679.
April 6, Kathren, wife of William Knebone.
 „ 11, Ann, wife of Richard Saudars.
 „ 11, Susanna, daughter of Richard Sandan.
 „ 17, William Prust.
May 2, Elizabeth Hodge, widow.
 „ 13, Mr. William Penhallow.
 „ 13, Jone Pearce, widow.
 „ 31, James, son of James John.
June 5, Sarah, wife of Gabrell Whitt.
July 17, Patience, daughter of Mr. Ralph Lanion.
 „ 21, James James.
 „ 21, —— son of Thomas Pearce.
 „ 31, William, son of Peter Cloake.
Aug. 27, —— daughter of Arthur Tonken.
Sept. 7, Margary, daughter of George Christophers
Oct. 6, Margaret Polglase, widow.
 „ 23, Margarett, daughter of Stephen Eddye.
Dec. 14, George Richards.
 „ 27, Ann, daughter of John P'sons.*

[1680.]
Jan. 3, John Edwards, *alias* Porteure, Sen.
 „ 3, James, son of John Parsons.
 „ 8, Charles Pike, gent.
 „ 19, Kathren, wife of Thomas Grose, gent.
 „ 19, James Bennetts.
 „ 26, Agnes, daughter of Nicholas Lander.
Feb. 2, Sarah Legow, spinster.
 „ 26, Kathren, daughter of John Cock.
 „ 27, —— son of Mr. Trestean.
March 9, Eliz. Barns, spinster.

1680.
April 7, Honnor, wife of John Legow.
 „ 21, Jane Guye, widow.
 „ 29, Robart Polard, of ye Pish. of Klovelly, in yo County of Devon, marinor.
May 4, Richard Osbarn.
 „ 14, Thomas, son of Thomas Benver, marchaud.
 „ 14, Mary, daughter of George Stephens.
June 4, Digory, son of Thomas Borch.
 „ 5, Bennett Champion.
 „ 16, Alice Phillipps, widow.
 „ 16, Ann, daughter of James Tricke.
 „ 18, Aves, daughter of Arondell Elary.
 „ 21, Richo Lonard, widow.
 „ 22, Alice, daughter of Richard Connack.
 „ 24, Mary, daughter of Thomas John Holior.
 „ 28, Eliz., daughter of Richard Giles.
July 2, Thomas, son of Mr. John Piller.
 „ 6, Nicholas, son of John Boddye.
 „ 30, Jone Hall, spinster.
Aug. 5, Margary, wife of David Penlease.
 „ 11, Jacobb, son of Acobb† Cock.

* *i.e.* Parsons. Sic. † *i.e.* Jacob

Sept. 27, Cathren, wife of William Osbarn.
Oct. 4, —— daughter of Nicholas Phillipps.
 „ 9, Dorithie, wife of Mr. Oliver Trestcane.
 „ 12, Jane, daughter of Richard Legow.
Nov. 12, Michell Govor.
 „ 22, Henry Carn.
Dec. 8, Jane, wife of William James.
 „ 11, Marten, son of Nicholas Cloake.
 „ 15, Thomas Stinian.
 „ 24, Thamson, wife of Samwell Nicholas.
 „ 28, Elizabeth Sampson, widow.

[1681.]
Feb. 4, James Rogers.
 „ 20, —— daughter of William John.
March 5, Morrish Carn.
 „ 8, Arthur Paynter, gent.
 „ 8, —— son of John Geles.
 „ 9, Ann, wife of William Boase.

1681.
May 6, William Sommars, gent.
 „ 9, —— daughter of Mr. Petar Jenken.
 „ 28, George, son of Marten Davye.
June 5, Sechem, son of James Trick.
 „ 13, Kathren, wife of John Knobone.
 „ 28, Mrs. Jane Game.
July 3, —— daughter of Sampson Rodda.
 „ 4, —— daughter of Mr. Somar Honichurch.
 „ 31, Jenken, son of Arthur Payuter, gent.
 „ 31, Charles, son of Thomas Noye.*

---

* Here the Register of Burials, so far as it is contained in the first book, finishes with the book itself. One stray entry is however written on the fly-leaf at the end, and is as follows:—

"September ye 15th, in the yeare 1702, was buried Mary, the wife of Alexander Reade."

Beneath which is written in another hand "*See ye Register Book*, THOS. ROWE, *Vicar*." It evidently does not belong to the first book at all, and the same may be said of the few eighteenth century entries which occur at the end of the Register of Baptisms. These, together with the above, are moreover entered in the succeeding volume, which commences with the year 1700; but it is worthy of note that the dates do not in all cases coincide.

It is greatly to be regretted that the old Registers of this Parish are partially deficient, not that they are more so however than those of many neighbouring Parishes. The Baptisms, though irregularly entered towards the latter part of the seventeenth century, are nevertheless comparatively complete at this time, but are missing before the year 1592; whilst the Registers of Marriages and Burials, which are sufficiently well kept in their early portions, are altogether wanting as to their later years, at a period corresponding with the time of the irregular entries among the Baptisms. The entries in this volume therefore—except in so far as they may have been preserved (originally in duplicate) at Exeter Cathedral, or be hidden elsewhere—represent the whole of the Registers of the Parish of Madron that are extant from the year 1577 to the year 1700.

Fig. 5. Interior of Minden Church.

Appendix.

The following entries relating to persons connected with the Parish of Madron, at a period corresponding to that comprised in the first book, will be found in the several Registers of the Parishes named. Undoubtedly much additional information might be obtained through such extracts from these and other Registers, since the entries here given are but a few which have been collected without any thorough search, showing how very materially the records of one Parish may help and elucidate those of another. In more than one case it will be noticed that a Marriage is registered in a neighbouring Parish as having taken place at Madron,—once at a time when the Madron Marriage Register is missing. Some few of these entries are here given merely on account of the similarity of names, and as a guide to the direction in which more may be found. Possibly there may have been no relationship between the persons mentioned in the Registers of Madron and those referred to below, but the occurrence of such combinations of names as Solomon Cock, Ephraim Weymouth, Isaac Newton, &c., seem to point to some probable connection.

Baptisms.

1610. April 15, Ann, daughter of Arthur Wolcoke, of Pensans, at Gulval.
" Nov. 4, William, son of William Bose, of Pensans, at Gulval.
1626. May 7, Zenobia, daughter of Henry Fosse, of Penzance, at Gulval.
1628. Aug. 9, Phillip, son of Henry Fose, at Gulval
1630. Oct. 1, Thomas, son of Henry Fose, at Gulval.
1632. May 27, Thamsin, daughter of William Boskenninge, at Gulval.
1633-4. Feb. 24, Elizabeth, daughter of Henry Fosse, at Gulval.
1635. Nov. 1, Emmanuell, son of William Boskeyning, at Gulval.
" Dec. 16, Alice, daughter of William Coocke, *alias* Hoile, at Gulval.
1637. May 14, Thomas, son of James Earle, of Penzance, at Gulval.
1638. July 8, Richard, son of Willm. Boskenninge, at Gulval.
1642-3. Jan. 15, Phillip, son of Thomas Burch, [of] Penzance, at Gulval.
" .. Elizabeth, daughter of Richard Trencare, [of] Penzance, at Gulval.
" 18, William, son of William Luke, of Penzance, at Gulval.
1643. Dec. 10, Margaret, daughter of John Polmcare of Penzance, at Gulval.
1644. Nov. 17, Thomas, son of Thomas Nighten, of Penzance, at Gulval.
1645. June 1, Dorothy, daughter of John Chambers of Penzance, at Gulval.
" 1, John, son of Juell Garrett, of Penzance, at Gulval.
1646. April 18, Joane, daughter of Henry Edmonds, of Penzance, at Gulval.
1650-1. Feb. 16, William, son of William Couchee, of Penzance, at Paul.
1651-2. Jan. 30, John, son of John Batten, of Maddron, at Paul.
1661. June 23, Ephriam, son of William Waymouth and Elizabeth, at Buryan.
1662. Oct. 19, Edmund, son of Robert Harrie, of Penzance, at Gulval.
1663-4. Feb. 28, James, son of Peter Cloake, of Penzance, at Gulval.
1667. Dec. 15, Katherin, daughter of Solomon Cock, at Gulval.
1669. Oct. 3, Elizabeth, daughter of Solomon Cock, at Gulval.
1670. Sept. 25, Katherin, daughter of Thomas Bennetts, of Maddern, at Gulval.
1671. May 14, William, son of Solomon Cock, at Gulval.
1673. April 4, Mary, daughter of Solomon Cock, at Gulval.
1676. Sept. 16, John, son of Frances Bennetts, of Penzance, at Gulval.

APPENDIX.

1676-7. Jan. 20, Beniamin, son of Solomon Cock, at Gulval.
1679. Aug. 3, Solomon, son of Solomon Cock, at Gulval.
1680. Sept. 5, Solomon, son of Solomon Cock, at Gulval.
1681-2. Feb. 12, Nicholas, son of John Batten, at Gulval.
1683. Nov. 30, John, son of Solomon Cock, at Gulval.
1686. Dec. 7, Adama, daughter of Solomon Cock, at Gulval.
1688. Nov. 30, Ane, daughter of Mr. Phillip Hicks, Vicar of Gulval, at Gulval.
1689. April 5, Philippa, daughter of Francis Lanion, gent., at Buryan.
1690. April 22, William, son of Mr. Phillip Hicks, Vicar of Gulval, at Gulval.
Nov. 23, John, son of Alexander Reed, at Gulval.
1692. Oct. 2, Ann, daughter of Andrew Tonken, of the Parish of Maddern, at Gulval.
1693. July 9, Elizabeth, daughter of Alexander Reed, at Gulval.
Sept. 5, Margarett, daughter of Mr. Phillip Hicks, Vicar, at Gulval.
1695. May 11, Lydia, daughter of Mr. Phillip Hicks, Vicar, at Gulval.
1696. Nov. 17, Philippa,* daughter of Phillip Hicks, Cler., at Gulval.
1697. Dec. 31, Lydia, daughter of Phillip Hicks, Cler., at Gulval.
1699. June 18, Margaret, daughter of Edmund Luke, at Gulval.
Dec. 10, Margaret, daughter of William Finnicomb, at Gulval.
1700. Sept. 8, Grace, daughter of Edmund Luke, at Gulval.
Oct. 6, Sampson, son of Rawlen Bons, Gallici, (born 1st Oct.) at Gulval.

1700. Nov. 1, Ann, daughter of William Cock, of the Parish of Maddern, (born 7th Oct.) at Gulval.
1700-1. March 4, Sara, daughter of Alexander Reed, (born 7th Feb.) at Gulval.
1703. April 10, Henry, son of Alexander Reed, (born 1st March) at Gulval.
,, 3, Margaret, daughter of Edmund Luke, at Gulval.
1708. Oct. 24, William, son of William Halse, at Paul.
1709. May 28, Joel and Maria, twins of Alexander Reed, at Gulval.
1710-11. Mar. 16, Nicholas, son of Peter Tom, of ye Town of Penzance, at Buryan.
1713. June 14, Dorothy, daughter of Ephriam Weymouth, at Morvah.
1714. Aug. 22, Christopher, son of Thomas Daddow, alias Thomas, at Morvah.
1718. June 3, Charles, son of William Bonse, of Penzance, at Paul.
1720. Aug. 11, Elizabeth, daughter of Martin Roddah, of Maddern, at Morvah.
1721. Oct. 24, Phillis, daughter of John Pollard, of Maddern, at Paul.
Dec. 28, Lydia, daughter of the Rev. Walter Borlase, Vicar of Maddern, at Paul.
1722-3. Jan. 14, Mary, daughter of the Rev. Walter Borlase, Vicar of Maddern, at Paul.
1723-4. Feb. 11, Margaret, daughter of the Rev. Walter Borlase, Vicar of Maddern, at Paul.
1724-25. Jan. 3, Mary, daughter of John Maddern, of Maddern, at Morvah.
1725. Nov. 7, Dorothy, daughter of Thomas Warren, of Madren, at Morvah.
1728. April 30, Margaret, daughter of James Woolcock, of Madren, at Morvah.

Marriages.

1583. May 12, John Clyse and Elizabeth, at Ludgvan.
1592. April 9, Harry Mellett and Margaritt, at Ludgvan.
1595. Sept. 1, German Geive, of Penzance, and Margerie, at Paul.
1596. Oct. 21, John Champion, of Maddren, and Elizabeth, at Paul.
1598. Oct. 3, Tom Tremba, of Madderne, and Cristen, at Paul.

1598. Nov. 19, Martin Harrie and Margaret, of Maderne, at Paul.
1599. Nov. 17, John Chinne, of Madderne, and Margaret Nicholas, at Paul.
1624. Nov. 14, John Size and Ellina Stevens, at Gulval.
1627. Aug. 6, William Nycolys, gent. [of Trereife, Madron], and Jane, [daughter of Nicholas Godolphin, Esq., of Trewarveneth, Paul], at Paul.
1640. Aug. 23, Alexander Clyes and Alice, at Ludgvan.

* Re-written.

APPENDIX. 71

1617. Oct. 23, Richard Scaddan and Joan Cossen, of Penzance, at Stowford, in Devonshire, by Mr. Roger Ashton. *See the Parish Register of Ludgvan.*

1655-6. Jan. 26, Nicholas Flomen and Elizabeth Veale, at Gulval.

1656-7. Jan. 19, Anthony Gubbs, gent., and Mrs. Ann Keigwin, at Paul.

1658. Dec. 1, Thomas Fleming, gent., [of Madron] and Mary Harris, at Gulval.

1663-4. Feb. 5, Richard Trevilour and Katherin Jacka, of Penzance, at Gulval.

1664. Aug. 12, Nicholas Richard, of Senuen, and Jane Rowling, of Penzance, at Buryan.

1666-7. Jan. 18, Solomon Cock and Adama Ladnor, at Gulval.

1667. Oct. 11, John Gennings and Elizabeth Cloak, of Penzance, at Gulval.

1671. April 24, Francis Blake, of Helston, and Amye Rowling, of Penzance, at Buryan.

" 29, Mr. Martin Mellett, of St. Just, and Mrs. An Burlace, of Penzance, at Buryan.

June 3, John Kneebone, of Maddern, and Catherine Hugh, of Saucrett, at Buryan.

Aug. 26, Mr. Christopher Pender and Mrs. Jaquilina, at Buryan.

1675. Sept. 6, John Trenery and Sara Connack, of Penzance, at Gulval.

1676. June 30, Robert Tonken, of Penzance, and Elizabeth Nicholls, of Gulval, at Gulval.

1677. Aug. 4, William Richards, of Gulval, and Mary Morrish, of Maddern, at Gulval.

1678. April 27, John Batten, of Penzance, and Alice Nicholls, of Gulvall, at Gulval.

1678-9. March 4, William Anthony and Margaret Tonkin, both of the Town of Penzance, at Buryan.

1679. April 28, Richard Tonken and Margarett Bennets, of Penzance, at Gulval.

1682. July 31, John Kneebone, of Maddern, and Grace Hinson, of Gulvall, at Gulval.

1683. April 16, Isaac Newton and Margery Daniell, of Zenner, at Gulval.

1683-4. Feb. 17, Phillip Lanion, gent., and Mary, daughter of Henry Edwards, gent., at Ludgvan.

1685. April 21, Andrew Tricke and Elizabeth Gubbs of Penzance, at Buryan.

1685-6. Feb. 16, Robert Davy and Ann Kitt, at Maddern. *See the Parish Register of Ludgvan.*

1686. Oct. 16, James Muddern, of Maddern, and Elizabeth Sandry, of Gulvall, at Gulval.

1687. April 8, John Carveth, gent., and Mary Tremenheere, of Penzance, widow, at Ludgvan.

1687-8. Jan. 24, Phillip Hicks, Vicar of Gulvall, and Mrs. Phillip Harris, at Gulval.

1690. April 29, Frances Sentaubyn, Esq., of Crowan, and Mrs. Ane Arundell, of Maddron, at Gulval.

1691. April 16, Mr. Nuall Tonken and Mrs. Lydia Hicks, both of the Parish of Paule, at Gulval.

1696. Dec. 30, Richard Luddra, of Maddern, and Jone Hosking, of this Parish, at Paul.

1699. June 29, Rawlon Boas, *Gallicus*, and Janet Nichols, at Gulval.

1701. Aug. 26, Oliver Woolcock, of Penzance, and Ursula Tonkin, of this Parish, at Paul.

1701-2. Jan. 25, John Russell and Honor Pike, of Penzance, at Paul.

1704. April 22, Philip Thomas, of Maddern, and Philippa Thomas, at Gulval.

" 26, Jacob Jenken, of Maddern, gent., and Ursula Vibert, at Gulval.

" 29, Richard Harry, of this Parish, and Francis Johns, of Penzance, at Paul.

July 8, Tristram Rawling, of Penzance, and Ann Ealy, at Gulval.

Aug. 16, Arthur Boase, of Penzance, and Ruth Boase, of this Parish, at Paul.

Dec. 23, William Baynard and Jane Bennets, of Penzance, at Gulval.

1705. July 2, Martin Bromble, of Penzance, and Jane Tremearn, of this Parish, at Paul.

Oct. 19, Richard Guy, of Morvah, and Grace Daniel, of Maddern, at Morvah.

Nov. 6, Thomas Wills, of this Parish, and Margaret Batten, of Maddern, at Paul.

1706-7. Feb. 24, Roger Ellis, of Maddern, and Frances Hicks, of this Parish, at Paul.

1707. May 5, Jonathan James, of Maddern, and Elizabeth Hanifor, of this Parish, at Paul.

1707-8. Jan. 6, John Calinsow, of Maddern, and Bridgit Harry, of this Parish, at Paul.

1708. June 30, Samuel Lamerton, of the Town of Penryn, and Grace Bramble, of this Parish, at Paul.

APPENDIX.

1708. Oct. 11, John Rogers, of Maddern, and Mary Mathews, of this Parish, at Paul.
1708-9. Jan. 14, Clement Carleen, of Breag, and Margaret Rogers, of Penzance, at Gulval.
1709. July 8, Mr. Thomas Row, Clerk of Maddern, and Mrs. Elizabeth Pearce, of Penzance, by John Penhollick, Vicar of Gulval, at Morvah.*
1709-10. Jan. 2, William Gift, of Penzance, and Margarett Edmunds, at Buryan.
1710. June 27, Mr. John Denncard, of Bideford, and Mrs. Ann Treminheer, of Penzance, at Morvah.
July 3, Richard Batton, of Penzance, and Susan Tremearn, of this Parish, at Paul.
1712. June 28, William Bainard, of Maddern, and Avis Garland, at Gulval.
Oct. 1, Charles Pennecke, of St. Hilary, gent., and Lydia, daughter of John Borlase, of Maddern, Esq., at Morvah.
„ 25, Thomas, son of Matthew Daniel, of Morvah, and Jane, daughter of William Carvosow, of St. Just, at Maddern. Registered at Morvah.
1713. Nov. 25, Deogry Nichols, of Penzance, and Ursula Bonse, of this Parish, at Paul.

1713-14. Feb. 9, William Pollard, of Maddern, and Joan Tremearn, of this Parish, at Paul.
1715. July 5, John Richards, of this Parish, and Ann Skewes, of Penzance, at Paul.
Aug. 10, Mr. Francis Lanyon, Jun., of Sancred, and Mrs. Jane Edwards, of Penzance, at Morvah.
Nov. 5, Thomas Lutey, of Penzance, and Elizabeth Biskay, of this Parish, at Paul.
1717. June 9, Martin Davy, of Penzance, and Elizabeth Richards, at Buryan.
1719. June 9, John Prior, of ye Burrw. of Holstone, and Alice Stone, of ye Town of Penzance, at Morvah.
1720. Feb. 21, Walter Borlase, Vicar of Maddern, and Margaret Pendarves, of this Parish, at Paul.
1723. Dec. 31, Mr. John Penrose and Mrs. Margery Ustick, both of Penzance, in Madderne, at Morvah.
1727. May 1, George Cara and Elizabeth Martin, of Maddern, at Paul.
1728. Nov. 30, Beavis Harris, of Maddern, and June Pearce, of this Parish, at Paul.
1728-9. Feb. 7, Martin Gwenap and Constance Veale, both of Penzance, at Morvah.

Burials.

1574. Dec. 30, John Clyse, at Ludgvan.
1589. April 17, John Clyse, at Ludgvan.
1592. Oct. 16, Jane, daughter of Nicholas Batton, at Ludgvan.
1595. Oct. 14, James, son of Henry Tremenheere, at Ludgvan.
1600. Nov. 15, Nicholas Batton, at Gulval.
1607. April 6, Elizabeth, daughter of Mr. George Hutchens, at Ludgvan.
1627. May 22, Mr. George Hutchens, Parson of Ludgvan and Vicar of Madderne, Preacher of God's Worde, at Ludgvan.
1644. Dec. 31, Joane, wife of George Hutchens, gent., at Ludgvan.
1657. —— — Counstance, daughter of Nicholas Flemen, (died 8th Aug.) at Gulval.
1660. Aug. 18, Ebat Laveles, (died 14th Aug.) at Buryan.

1661-2. Feb. 2, Margery Pascow, widow, of Penzance, at Gulval.
1664-5. Feb. 6, John Jelbert, of Maddern, at Gulval.
1667. Oct. 4, William, son of John Lenyne, at Gulval.
1670. Sept. 19, John, son of John Lenyne, at Gulval.
1672-3. Mar. 17, Thomas, son of Nicholas Simons, of Penzance, at Gulval.
1673. Nov. 17, Stephen Thomas, of Penzance, at Gulval.
1674. Sept. 14, William, son of William Thomas, of Penzance, at Gulval.
1675-6. Jan. 17, Isaac Nuton, at Gulval.
1678. Aug. 15, Mrs. Jane Nicholls, widow [of William Nicholls, gent., of Trereife, Madron], at Paul.
1679. Aug. 9, Peter Oliver, of Penzance, at Gulval.
„ 23, Solomon, son of Solomon Cock, at Gulval.
1682. Aug. 28, John Nicholls, *alias* Trevello, at Gulval.
1683. June 1, Mrs. Mary Tratt, at Gulval.

* This Marriage is also registered at Gulval as having taken place at "Morva."

APPENDIX.

1685. April 10, Ducns, wife of Robert Goble, at Gulval.
Oct. 8, Mary, wife of William Nenys, of Penzance, at Gulval.
1686-7. Feb. 3, William Thomas, of Penzance, at Gulval.
1687. Mar. 25, Richard Bennetts, of Penzance, at Gulval.
July 20, —— son of Nicholas Genver, of Penzance, at Gulval.
1691. Oct. 16, Ane, wife of Richard Eva, of the Parish of Maddern, at Gulval.
1692. Mar. 28, Roger John, of Maddern, at Gulval.
June 4, An Thomas, of Madarn, at Paul.
1694. Dec. 9, Elizabeth, daughter of George Richards, gent., of the Town of Penzance, at Gulval.
1695. April 24, Margaret, daughter of George Richards, gent., of the Town of Penzance, at Gulval.
May 11, Lydia, daughter of Mr. Phillip Hicks, Vicar, at Gulval.
Dec. 17, Blanch Noy, of Penzance, widow, at Paul.
1696. Dec. 21, Mary, wife of John Bolithoe, in ye Church, at Helston.
1698. Aug. 3, Mr. Christopher Cock, in the Chancel, at Helston. * * * "Tho year when small pox was very mortal."
1699. June 18, Richard Tonkin, of Penzance, at Paul.
1700. May 18, Elizabeth Nouton, of Penzance, at Gulval.
July 7, George Veal, of Penzance, at Gulval
1701. June 5, Honor, wife of Richard Veal, of Maddern, gent., at Paul.
1702. May 16, Martin Luke, at Gulval.
„ 21, Charles Roberts, of Maddern, at Gulval.
1703. May 10, Richard Cowling, of Penzance, at Gulval.
1703-4. Feb. 1, Mrs. Cornish, alias Payan, at Breage.
1705-6. March 9, Thomasin Lanyon, at Gulval.
1706. Oct. 25, Avis Pedwell, at Helston.
Dec. 24, John Brey, of Maddern, at Gulval.
1706-7. Feb. 8, Ann, wife of Tristram Rawling, of Penzance, at Gulval.
1707. May 14, Juliana, wife of Mr. Grose, nec non prætoris of Penzance, at Gulval.
1708. June 15, Mrs. Mary Cock, at Helston.

1708. June 18, Thomas Deckerlegg, of Maddern, at Paul.
Sept. 4, Dorothy Nowman, of Penzance, at Gulval.
„ 27, Robert Boase, of Penzance, at Paul.
Oct. 16, Margery, wife of George Veale, of Penzance, at Gulval.
„ 18, Bridget, daughter of Mr. Francis Penneck, at Helston.
Dec. 9, James, son of Mr. John Tremenheere at Helston.
1710. Nov. 5, Mr. Richard Bullock, at Helston.
Dec. 12, Richard Door, of Maddern, at Gulval.
1710-11. Jan. 31, Hosea, son of Thomas Roberts, of Penzance, at Paul.
Feb. 1, Jaquet John, of Maddern, at Gulval.
1711. Dec. 7, John Bray, of Maddern, at Gulval.
1711-12. Feb. 6, Elizabeth Coswin, at Gulval.
1714. Nov. 11, Mr. Lionell Jons, at Sennen.
1715. Dec. 14, Hugh Jones, Esq., at Sennen.
1716. July 1, Elizabeth, wife of Richard Gilbert, of Maddern, at Morvah.
1717. Sept. 7, Mrs. Mary Floming, at Helston.
1717-18. Mar. 22, Elizabeth Cowling? of Maddern, at Paul.
1718. Dec. 14, Margaret, daughter of Thomas Germin, of Maddern, at Morvah.
1718-19. Mar. 20, Catherine Hoskin, of Maddern, at Paul.
„ 21, Beaumont Walrond, Captain of His Majesties Man of War, at Paul.
1720. Aug. 11, Joan, wife of Martyn Roddah, of Maddern, at Morvah.
1722. May 16, Mrs. Anne Bullock, at Helston.
1722-3. Mar. 20, Mr. Francis Penneck, at Helston.
1724. May 4, Ruth Boas, of Penzance, at Paul.
Dec. 16, Francis Tremenheere, at Helston.
1725. Aug. 30, Jenefer Jelbert, widow, of Maddern, at Morvah.
1725-6. Feb. 9, William Gelbert, of Maddern, at Morvah.
1726. Nov. 23, Ann, daughter of Phillip Elford, of Penzance, at Paul.
1727. Nov. 2, Mr. John Fleming, at Helston.
1730. May 14, John Angwin, of Maddern, at Morvah.
1730-1. Mar. 16, John Clies, at Paul.

With regard to the spelling of many names in the foregoing entries, the rule of copying the original, letter for letter, could not conveniently be observed. In some Parishes the Registers are written almost entirely in Latin,—in Gulval for instance; and, in passing, the idea suggests itself that it must have puzzled the brains of many a by-gone Clerk to Latinize some of the very extraordinary names in which the "old people" of this neighbourhood rejoiced.

APPENDIX.

The Registers of St. Mary's Chapel, Penzance, in 1693.

In the Parish Chest in Madron Church is a small folio volume—or rather the covers of one, with a few loose leaves—which dates from the year 1693. It was originally designed as a Register Book for the Chapel of St. Mary, in the Town of Penzance, lying within the same Parish, about two miles distant in a south-easterly direction from Madron Church; but unfortunately its contents are almost entirely gone, and this is the more to be regretted, since the earlier entries would have helped to fill up the blanks, which occur in the Registers of the mother Church at the latter part of the century. The entries on the few pages which are left, being of later date than the year 1700, have been embodied in the second book at Madron, and this practice of amalgamating the two Registers was long continued, there being no separate book kept at St. Mary's until a comparatively recent date. One interesting fragment however remains in the leaf which is affixed to the inside of the first cover, for on it is inscribed in a bold hand, with a highly flourished heading in black letter, the lines which are here set forth after the manner of the original:—

A Register

Of the Marriages, Christnings, and Buryalls within the Towne of

Penzance,

In the County of Cornwall, Taken and Began Annoq. Dmi: 1693, in the Fifth yeare of the Reign of King William and Queene Mary.

THE MAJESTRATES OF THE SAID TOWNE THEN.

The Wirpll. Thomas Eastlake, Mayor; The Wirpll. George Richards, Justice; John Groase, gent.; John Tremenheere, Marchant; Richard Pearce, gent.; Peter Jenken, Marchant; John Pellow, gent.; James Loase, Velmonger; Daniell Hawkey, Mercer.

THE ASSISTANTS OF THE SAID TOWNE THEN.

Tonkin Boas, Velmonger; Thomas Pearce, Yeoman; John Pike, Cooper; William Penlease, Shoomaker; Samuell Williams, Marchant; John Pedwell, Habadasher; Tristram Phillipps, Bucher; Martin Gwennopp, Marchant; William Ninnis, Shipwt.; William Tonkin, Shopkeeper; William John, Blacksmyth.

THE WIRSPLL. JAMES PRAED, ESQ., RECORDER.

Francis Paynter, of Boskenna, ye Towne Clerke; The Reverend Reginald Trenhayle, Vic. of the Parish of Madderne and Penzance; and Mr. Thomas Billott, Curate of the said Towne then.

OTHER OFFICERS IN THE SAID TOWNE.

John Pedwell, John Pike, Alexr. Reedo, and Wm. John, Constables; Thomas Vigurs and Edward Jones, Chaple Wardens; John* Yeale and John Stone, Overseeres of the poore; John* Rawling and Thomas Stone, Sarjeants at Mace.

* Doubtful.

Monumental Inscriptions.

There are several interesting memorials of former inhabitants of the Parish in Madron Church, and, inasmuch as their inscriptions corroborate the entries in the Registers, or supply additional particulars, it will not be out of place to introduce them here.

The oldest and one of the most curious is that of John, son of John Maddern, gentleman. It is a large oblong slab of black marble or slate, upon which are carved in low relief two kneeling figures, in Elizabethan costume, a man and a woman, perhaps intended to represent the deceased and his wife, or possibly his disconsolate parents. To the right of the man, on a sort of table, is a large book with clasps, and above it is engraved "Aetatis sue 1595," and again, in another place, "Aetatis sue 23" appears near the head of the woman, who holds a closed book before her with both hands, whilst to her left is a massive pillar with a base and capital ornamented with roses, dividing the surface of the slab into two parts,—the one containing the carving mentioned, and the other the eulogistic verse. Three shields are conspicuous in the spaces between, and on either side of the heads of the figures: one is charged with the arms,—*Ermine, a chevron* . . . ; the second bears,—. . . *on a fesse between two chevrons* . . . *three escallops* . . . , *with a crescent for cadency in the first quarter* ;* and the third,—. . . *on a chevron between three stags* . . . *three mullets* . . The colours are not shown, this rude specimen of heraldic engraving being older than the system of delineating blazon by lines. The first part of the inscription runs borderwise round the slab—a fleur de lys in one angle marking the spot where it commences and ends, whilst the versified remainder, together with the figures, arms, &c.—which are cut across the breadth, and not with the length—occcupy the central space. This slab is now fixed near the chief door, against the south wall of the Church, showing its middle portion to advantage; but whether this is its original position seems very doubtful, since the lower part of the bordering inscription is upside down. It appears as if intended to have been placed horizontally, and probably once formed the top of an altar tomb; or it may have lain flush with the flooring, though the uneven surface presented by the rough sculpture would have been unsuitable for treading on,—moreover it does not seem to have suffered, severely at least, from such ill treatment. The inscription—the letters of which have been whitened—is as follows:—

 Here lieth the Body of John, the sonne of John Maddern, Gentleman, who departed this life in the feare of God the XXth† day of August, Anno Domini 1621. Aetatis Sue 1595. Aetatis Sue 23.

If teares the dead againe to life could call,
thou hadst not slept with in this earthly ball.
If holy vertues could aransome bue,
Soe sone corrupcion had not wrapt thee in.
But thou were ripe for god, and god didst crave;
Soo gavest agladsome wellcome to the grave.
Assuring still that thou with god dost dwell;
Thy ond soe good; thy life was led soe well.

The next memorial, which also appears to have been originally intended for the horizontal position,‡ is similar in style and material to the foregoing, but is more comprehensive in detail, the principal figures being shown at full length, and with the length of the stone. In its upper portion it displays the representations of Thomas Cock, of Bodmin, and Alice, his wife. Between them is a shield bearing the arms of Cock,—*Lozengy, arg. and gu., on a fesse of the first, three cocks of the second,§ impaling* . . . . *on a chevron between three garbs* . . . *five roundels* . . . Lower down are the figures of Thomas Fleming, of Landithy, on whose right is a drawn sword (much too large for the sheath which hangs from his belt by the way), and his wife, Elizabeth, daughter and heiress of the said Thomas Cock, who, like the lady on the last slab, clasps a book to her breast. Another shield is

---
* Or, on a fesse between two chevrons gu. three escallops arg. are the arms of De Hemenhale. *See* BOUTELL's *English Heraldry*, p. 51.
† XXᵒ was originally cut here, but the ⁹ has been filled up and *th* engraved over it.
‡ See the second line in the epitaph, over leaf.   § The colours are not shown on the slab in either case.

APPENDIX.

between them, on which are impaled the arms of Fleming,—*Vairé, a chief checky or and gu.*, and Cock, as before. The dress of the last two figures has more ornamentation than that of the first two. At their feet their ten children are pourtrayed kneeling in two rows, one above the other; each of these—as well as the larger figures—have initials in close proximity to their heads, but instead of setting down these letters here it will be more desirable to give the names. There were three sons, Nicholas, Thomas, and John; and seven daughters, Frances, Grace, Anne, Elizabeth, Mary, Phillipa, and Jane; all of whom were living, with the exception of John, at the time of the Herald's visitation in 1620, when the pedigree of the family was signed by the first-mentioned Thomas Fleming. This slab is placed against the east wall in the south aisle, and the borderlike inscription—the commencement and ending of which are marked by a rose of heraldic fashion—is as follows:—

 Here lyeth ye Bodyes of Thomas Fleming, gent., who was buried ye 14th day of June, 1631, Thomas Cock, gent., was buried ye 9th day of December, 1601. Alice, his wife, was buried ye 5th day of January, 1610.

On a smaller slab near by, on the south wall, is the following epitaph, with the arms of Fleming engraved on a shield in the upper left-hand corner.

An epitaph to ye memorye of ye deceased Thomas Fleming, gent.

Fleming, ye ayde to neighbours poore opprest,
interred here beneath that tomb doth rest.
His wydowes teres, nor Phisicks helpe could save,
nor childrens cries, his body from ye grave.
But that from greved hearts they sigh and saye,
lamentinge oft, they wante their only staye.
His sonnis and daughters and his wife withal,
even syde by syde doe with one funerall.
His neighbours, soldiers, kinsman, and ech one,
doe deck hs. herse with sadnes mourneful mone;
Sayinge, hees gon whome we must needs commend,
a true peace maker, and a faithfull freind,
Beloved of all, not hated once, whose pure
and good report for ever shall endure.
Concludinge thus, his soule to heaven did fly;
that well did live, and ended gloriously.

A monumental brass, to the memory of an early Mayor of the Borough of Penzance, occupies a prominent place on the eastern extremity of the north wall. Inlaid upon an oblong slab of black marble are full length figures of John Clies and his wife. The first is attired in a long cloak turned out with fur, such as might be worn by an Alderman at the present day; and the second in a costume very similar to that of the ladies represented on the other monuments,—the hat and ruff being conspicuous in all, though this good dame's ruff is somewhat larger than the others. At their feet are the laudatory lines given below, and beneath these their only son is represented in a short cloak, a little apart from his five sisters who appear in a graduated row, whilst the following inscription on a narrow border of brass surrounds the whole.

 Here lyeth buried the body of John Clies, Marchant, twice Maior of Penzance, who had to wife Blanch the onely daughter of Hugh Trevanion, Esq., by whome he had issue one sonne and five daughters, and left this life for a better upon ye 27th day of November, in ye yere of or. Lord God 1623; when he had lived to ye full age of 55 yeares.

Here underneath this marble stone doth rest,
The corpes of him whom God in goodnes blest.
In whose faire courses we may freely find,
The lively patterne of a vertuous mind;

APPENDIX. 77

> As Penzour well approves when he was found
> Unto that towne a stay both sure and sound.
> Where he had place and creddit with the best;
> Till death him of his life had disposest.
> So Blanche his wife, this monument propar'd,
> In love to him, for love to her declar'd.
> God hath his soule, her heart his love still keepes;
> The odds betwixt thim breath, thus all flesh sleapes.

C. S. Gilbert, in his "Historical Survey of the County of Cornwall," published in the year 1820, after quoting the inscriptions of several monuments in the Church (vol. ii. p. 734), says:—"Another marble monument is inscribed as follows:—

> "Here lyeth the body of Francis Arundell, of Trengwainton, who departed this life the 10th day of August, Anno Domini 1697; and was buried the 13th day of the same month; who married Dorothy the daughter of John Saffin, of Sutton, in the County of Devon, Esq., by whom he had one son and two daughters."

This monument however is not now to be seen in the Church, nor do the oldest inhabitants of the Parish remember its being there; but a dark marble slab inscribed to the memory of Francis Arundell is remembered in the Churchyard, on the south side, where it has long since been hidden by the mould, from the gradual accumulation of which, many tomb-stones lie buried almost as deeply as the persons whose memories they were intended to perpetuate. Moreover Mr. Gilbert speaks of "other small monuments in the Church," inscribed to Mary Jenkins, Martin Gubbs, William Rawles, &c., which are undoubtedly in the Churchyard.

On the south wall, over the Trereife pew, is a chaste monument, commemorating a distinguished member of an ancient family long resident at Trereife, in this Parish—a family which became extinct in the eldest line, just sixty years ago, in the person of William John Godolphin Nicholls, who died unmarried on the 9th of May, 1815. (The property then passed by marriage to another family, the mother of the last representative having become the wife of the Rev. Charles Valentine Le Grice, who was for several years perpetual Curate of St. Mary's, Penzance; and their son Day Perry Le Grice, Esq., M.A., is the present proprietor.) Black and white marble—the latter richly carved and relieved with gilding—are blended in a harmonious design, finished in detail and unobtrusive in effect. Slender columns of highly polished black marble support a handsome cornice, on which rests a shield—festooned with flowers, and flanked by two flaming urns—bearing the arms of Nicholls,— *Arg. three pheons sa.* An exquisite piece of Italian workmanship[*] is empannelled in the lower part of the monument; it is composed of rare and brilliantly coloured stones, lapis-lazuli, jasper, &c., inlaid so as to represent flowers and fruit, advantage having been taken of the natural tints to give force to the form and shading of the group. With such skill has this been done, that at a little distance it is difficult to believe the fact that the flowers and fruit are not in relief, so real and rounded do they appear. On the entablature, forming the middle of the monument, the following inscription is engraved.

> Near this place, in the Grave of his Fathers, whom he Honour'd, lyes Interr'd the body of John Nicholls, of *Trereife, Esquire,* Who being born in the Year of our Lord 1663, was sent to LONDON in the Year 1680, and having served a laborious *Clerkship,* was in 1688 sworn one of the *Clerks* of the high Court of Chancery; And having with great Industry and Integrity increased the Paternal Estate of his Family, was in the Year 1705 call'd to the Bar by the Society of the Middle Temple, where having for some Years practiced with Success He retired to the Seat of his Ancestors, and having made many improvements, departed this Life the 3rd Day of August, 1714; in the 5jst Year of his Life, leaveing three Sons and one Daughter, of whom Jael, his

---

[*] C. S. Gilbert in the work before mentioned (vol. ii. p. 755), with regard to the above says: "The north"—"it should be the south—"aisle is graced by an elegant monument, the foliage of which, with other ornamental work, was executed in Italy."

T

APPENDIX.

Daughter, and Samuel his youngest Son (by whose Order this Monument is erected) lye here likewise interr'd.

Et cum Christus, Qui est vita nostra apparebitt,
Nos etiam cum illo Apparebimus in Gloria.

The most pretentious monument in the Church is that which commemorates the Rev. Duke Pearse and the Rev. Thomas Rowe, the latter having been nearly 16 years Vicar of this Parish: it is on the north wall of the chancel within the altar rails, which, by the way, were presented to the Church by Vicar Rowe, as is stated in the inscription. Two pillars of white marble with gilded capitals support an effective pediment, the central ornament being an urn—from the top of which flames issue—with figures of angels, one on either side. Coloured slabs enrich the entablature, and moulded scroll-work adds to the embellishment of the composition. On a base of black marble upheld by supports of polished porphyry, terminating in gilded fir cones, are two effigies, kneeling face to face, with a draped reading desk—on which are two open books—between them. The first, facing eastward, is probably the representation of the Rev. Thomas Rowe; his hair is long, and lank when compared with the flowing wig of the opposite figure, which, judging from a portrait of him now in the possession of a member of his family, it may be presumed represents the Rev. Duke Pearse, who died at the early age of 27 years. Both these reverend gentlemen wear bands and surplices, and with uplifted faces raise their hands in an attitude of prayer. On the principal pannel, forming the centre of the monument, is the following inscription.

Juxta hic jacent corpora Reverendi Duke Pearse, qui obiit die decimo septimo Novembris, A.D. 1712; Ætatis suæ 34; necnon Reverendi Thomæ Rowe, hujus parochiæ annos prope sexdecem Vicarii qui hos Cancellos anno 1702, propriis sumptibus erexit; obiit Vigesimo octavo die mensis Augusti et tricesimo primo sepultus erat A.D. 1716; ætatis suæ 40. Elizabetha Rowe Vidua, in memoriam mariti et fratris hoc monumentum mœrens posuit A.D. 1720.

Siste pedem, lacrymisque solum perfunde Viator,
    Durius hoc saxo tu nisi pectus habes;
Nobile par fratrum jacet heic ea terra recondit
    Quæ peperit Studiis iugenioque pares.
Alter adhuc juvenis, Musas Veneratur amœnà
    Quá, tu, Came Pater, litura lambis aquâ.
Nec mora; divulsum petit alter anhelus amicum
    Hospitioque ambos excipit una domus.
Ast ubi promeritâ rediuuiti tempora Lauro,
    Visere jam patrios gestit Uterque Lares.
Heic Utriusque sacros complectitur Infula crines
    Hic pueros monitis erudit, ille Viros;
Heic magis ardenti tandem ferventia motu
    Pectora fraterno fœdere junxit amor.
Patria quos, eademque domus, quos cura, Venusque,
    Uniit, hos tumulus non Sinit esse duos.

On the north side of the middle aisle, over the Castle Horneck pew, is a handsome memorial inscribed to Lydia, wife of John Borlase, Esq., M.P. for St. Ives, the first of his family who took up his residence in this Parish, he having become the proprietor of Castle Horneck, but lived and died at Rosealgwell. His eldest son, Dr. Walter Borlase, who is mentioned hereafter, built the main portion of the present house at Castle Horneck, and there resided. A convex entablature—elliptical in shape—of veined and polished marble bears the inscription, and this is surrounded by carved drapery and scroll-work, with here and there a cherub. In the upper part of the design is an achievement displaying the arms of Borlase,—*Ermine, a bend sa., charged with two arms, armed, issuing out of the clouds arg. (or rather proper), pulling asunder a horse shoe or,* impaled with those of Harris,—*Sa. three crescents arg. within a bordure arg.,* with the crest,—*A wounded wolf arg. regardant, biting with agony an arrow or fixed in his neck, blood proper dropping from the wound,*—all being fully blazoned, though the artist has not evinced that love of accuracy shown in the description of the arms and crest by Dr. Borlase, from whose MS. the foregoing exemplification is taken. Other portions of the ornamental sculpture are also enlivened with colour and gilding. The inscription is as follows:—

Memoriæ Sacrum Lydia Borlase, Christoph. Harris de Hayne, Arm. Natæ, Johan. Borlase de Pendoen, Arm. Uxoris. Bis duos filios in Ecclesia de St. Just Sepultos posuit; Quinque filii et quatuor filiæ Supersunt. Piissimam ejus et bene præparatam animam Mors non abripuit Sed Cœlo reddidit Julii 28, Anno Salutis 1725; Ætatis vero Suæ 54. Amans, amabilis, amata tam formosissima quam dilectissima Sui generis Viduum reliquit, charissimum viventis, hic laborantem et Suam dissolutionem expectantem, nullo modo post mortem dividendum, sed volente Deo, Sub hac Sede adjungendum cineribus Suis.

Animam fugientem curet Jesus.

A small marble tablet nearer the chancel, in the same aisle, is inscribed:—

John Borlase, gent., son of John Borlase, of Pendeen, Esq., died in 1775; aged 71. Dorothy his wife, daughter of James Keigwyn, Esq., died in 1788; aged 86.

Our birth not mean, our age unsullied ebb'd;
Content our bliss, eternity our care.
Te digna sequere.

Another marble monument on the south wall of the Church commemorates Dr. Walter Borlase, who for nearly half a century was Vicar of Madron. It is surmounted by a small shield bearing the arms of Borlase, with those of Pendarves,—*Sa. a falcon rising between three mullets or*, on an escutcheon of pretence. The following is the inscription.

Here lie the remains of Walter Borlase, LL.D., Vice-warden of the Stannaries of Cornwall, Justice of the Peace, and for upwards of fifty Years Vicar of this Parish, The Duties of which several Stations he discharged to the Close of a long-extended Life with unwearied Attention and approved Ability. A devout, upright, liberal Demeanour distinguished his whole Conduct, and rendered him a pattern worthy of the most reverent Observance. He died April 26th, 1776; aged 81 years and 6 Months. Here likewise lieth interred, his amiable and affectionate Wife, Margaret, only Daughter of Henry Pendarves, Vicar of Paul; She died April 8th, 1743; aged 42 years, leaving a very numerous, and for the most Part young Offspring, to lament the untimely Loss of a virtuous and accomplish'd mother.

There are many other monuments and tablets within the Church, as well as several memorial windows, but since they are of later date than the period comprised in the first book of the Registers, it will be unnecessary to consider them now.

In the Churchyard there are not many very old inscriptions. One of the most interesting is that of Alexander Daniel, of Lariggan, which, together with an imperfect representation of the arms of Daniel, has been re-cut upon a slate forming the upper surface of an altar tomb, standing south of the Church, between it and the school which his son endowed. It is as follows:—

Here lieth the body of Alexander Daniel, gent., who departed ys. life in the year of our Lord 1668.

Belgia me Birth, Britain me Breeding gave,
Cornwall a Wife, ten Children, and a grave.

A grateful posterity unites in laudable remembrance of George Daniel, gent., the son of the above-mentioned Alexander. The adjoining free school and its liberal endowment witness his charity and reward. He was buried near this tomb May 4th, 1716.

APPENDIX.

Repaired. Uriah Tonkin, George Treweeke, Saml. Borlase, Thomas Robyns, William Borlase, Vicar, Trustees 1780.

Wm. Tremenheere, Vicar, John Borlase, M.D., Thos. Pascoe, Richd. Hichens, Richd. Oxnam, John Batten, Trustees 1813.

M. Nowell Peters, Vicar, Samuel Borlase, Day Perry Le Grice, John Batten, Edward Bolitho, E. H. Rodd, Trustees 1858.

An ancient looking grave-stone, formed by one large block of granite, is now built into the south wall of the Churchyard, between the lych gate and the school before mentioned. The inscription in large letters runs borderwise round the stone, the middle surface being blank. It is as follows:—

Mary · wife · of Jas · Jenkin · of Alverton · Gent · Buried · Sep · 25 · 1699.

The last figure of this date is doubtful; it has the appearance of a nine but is of a different style to that which immediately precedes it, and might possibly be a nought with a dash underneath. Mr. C. S. Gilbert—who however is not exact in the other part of the inscription—reads it as a seven.

A large slate, covering a grave somewhat south of the Daniel tomb, is inscribed much after the manner of the older slabs within the Church—the first part of the inscription forming a border to the remainder, which occupies the central space, headed in this case by an heraldic achievement, for the most part obliterated; but judging from the position, it might be supposed to have displayed the arms of Rawles, impaled with those of Honychurch, a crescent for cadency being visible where the two coats unite. The dexter coat, which has surely been engraved without due regard being paid to the rules of heraldry, appears to have been intended for *Ermine (the surface of the shield being divided pilewise), a chevron* ... Of the second coat not a trace remains, and the mantling and helmet—which probably once supported a crest, no longer visible—are more or less indistinct. The following is inscribed:—

Heer lyeth the body of Elisabeth Honychurch, dau[ghter] of John Honychurch, who dyed the 8th day of July, 1713, aged 23 years.

Here lies the Body of Mary Rawles, daughter of John Honychurch, of Lerigon, in this Parish, who departed this life for a better April 16, 1751, in the 63rd year of her age.

Also of William Rawles, Surgeon, son of William Rawles, of the Town of Penzance, who departed this life for a better October 25, 1774, in the 21st year of his age.

He pleased God and was beloved of him, so that liveing amongst sinners, he was translated; yea speedily was he taken away, least that wickedness should alter his understanding, or deceit beguile his soul.

A slate very similar in style to the last is affixed to the south wall of the Church, having the following inscription.

 Here lies the bodies of ye Family of Thos. Hosking, of Landithy, with in this Parish.

Our tears attend you to the shades below,
Badge of our love and monuments of woe;
Tears at your Tomb, deep flowing tears are paid,
Yet fruitless all, since in the dust you'r laid.
Alas! where is your youth and blooming years?
Relentless Death would not be stay'd by tears.

Your ripening years now fades in putrid dust,
Then gentle Mother Earth receive thy trust.
Within thy Bosom easy let them sleep;
Their tender ashes unpoluted keep.

Mary his daughter was burd. the 30th of May, Anno Dom. 1726, in the first year of her age.

Christr. his son burd. Octr. 16, 1742, in the 20th year of his age.

Thos. Hosking, of Landithy, died 22nd April, 1769, aged 76.
Memento Mori.

Jane, his wife, Died July 10th, 1772, aged 75.

In the angle formed by the Church tower and the west wall of the south aisle is an altar tomb, beneath which rest the remains of several members of the family of Gubbs. The name appears early in the Registers; and one Anthony Gubbs was twice Mayor of Penzance, just two-and-a-quarter centuries ago. The inscription, which is engraved on a slate on the upper surface of the tomb, is comparatively modern,—the latter portion decidedly so; and except that it relates to an ancient and —in this neighbourhood at least—extinct family, which was formerly influential in Penzance, as the Borough records attest, it is of little interest. It is as follows:—

In Memory of the ancient family of Gubbs's of the Town of Penzance.

Here lieth the Body of Martin Gubbs, gentleman, who departed this life March 13th, 1770, aged 56 years. He was a very good Uncle: a Father to the Fatherless and surported the widow in all her distress. Also of his nephew George Mathews, who departed this life March 6th, 1795, aged 55 years. * * *

A block of granite which appears to have formed part of an ancient tomb, now quite out of its proper position, protrudes itself cornerways from the soil, west of the south aisle. On it is inscribed in large well formed letters, A · CHIRGWIN·, though only the first part of the name is visible. A somewhat similar block, jutting out at a little distance from the other, is supposed to be a fragment of the same tomb.

Many of the oldest memorials in the Churchyard are without doubt deeply buried, and thus much information, interesting and perhaps valuable to particular persons, is lost.

St. Mary's Church, Penzance, formerly a Chapel of ease to Madron, has few monumental inscriptions of more than a hundred years old, and none of an earlier date than the commencement of the last century. Its oldest and most imposing monument is that erected to the memory of one of the Tremenheere family, which has been long and honourably connected with the town and neighbourhood. It occupies a somewhat elevated position on the south side of the chancel, and originally was placed over a pillar on the wall space between the arches, directly opposite the most eastern of the two southern doors in the south aisle of the old Chapel, the demolition of which was begun in July, 1832. It is composed of various sombre-hued marbles, well cut, and effectively ornamented with carving—the whole design bearing a general resemblance to that of Duke Pearse and Vicar Rowe, at Madron, though it is less pretentious and upon a smaller scale. In the upper part an achievement appears displaying the arms of Tremenheere,—*Sa. three columns (menhirs) arg.*, impaled with those of Worth, here shown as,—*Arg. a two-headed eagle displayed sa.** A helmet with mantling supports the crest,—*A man's head and shoulders couped, proper.* In the lower part, between the brackets which support the base, is carved a winged Death's head crowned with laurel, the leaves being gilded, as are the crest and accessories to the shield above mentioned. The inscription, engraved upon a central panel of black veined-marble, is as follows:—

---

* Messrs. Lysons give as the arms of "Worth of Tremough in Mabe," near Penryn, "*Erm., an eagle displayed with two necks Sable, armed Guls.*" —*Magna Britannia*, vol. iii., p. clxiii.

APPENDIX.

Near this Place Lyes the Body of Mr. John Tremenheere, Merchant, who Exchanged this life for A Better the 23rd of July, 1701, in the 51st year of his Age, Being the son of Mr. John Tremenhoere, of Penzance, the only Person that Endowed this Chappell, and an affectionate Husband of Sybella, Daughter of Thomas Worth, of Penryn, Gent. She in respect to his Memory hath caused this Monument to be erected.

On the north wall of the present Church is a tablet in memory of a descendant of the above-named John Tremenheere, and since the inscription alludes to the foregoing (the persons commemorated too being also connected with two Vicars of Madron), it will scarcely be out of place here, though it is more modern than others already described. It is composed of pure white marble on a darker background, shaped after the manner of a sarcophagus, on the upper surface of which rests a partly unrolled scroll with a pen lying across it, whilst branches of cypress droop over either side; above all are placed the arms and crest of Tremenheere. On the sarcophagus is engraved :—

In the vault of his Ancestors, in the middle aisle of this Church, lies interred WILLIAM TREMENHEERE, Esquire, an eminent Attorney, a friendly father and an affectionate husband, who died on the 14th day of June, A: D: 1780, aged 48 years, a lineal descendant of the gentleman who alone endowed the ancient Chapel (here built) of this town, (which about this time was called Buriton). Also with him CATHERINE, his wife, a most amiable woman, a kind mother and an affectionate wife, who died on the 12th day of October, A: D: 1812, aged 79 years, a daughter of the Revd. WALTER BORLASE, L: L: D: of Castle Horneck. This tablet to the memory of his parents, as a tribute of filial respect, regard, and affection, is dedicated by their eldest son WILLIAM, A: M. and Vicar of Madron.

Just outside the north-east door of St. Mary's Church are two fine old slabs of limestone—locally known as Plymouth marble—precisely alike in size and style, which are now laid down end to end as pavement. They are somewhat injured, yet still present a tolerably perfect appearance; and are remembered to have been formerly affixed to the east wall of the extension of the old Chapel, on the outside beneath the windows, but probably were originally laid in the flooring within the building, being evidently intended for the horizontal position. The inscriptions run border-fashion round the stones; that of the first, the most southern of the two, encroaches a little upon the central space, and is as follows :—

Here lie the bod[ies] of Christopher Pendar, who died the 12th Xber, 1709, and Anne Pendar, who died the 7th of January after, Son and Daughter of Mr. Christopher Pendar, of Penzance.

May one so bloomy, years thus nipt enga[g]e
Early Repentance to ye future age.

The other slab is inscribed :—

Here lieth ye Body of John Pellow^e, Jun., of this town, Me[rchant w]ho died ye .... March, 1713, In ye 36th year of his age: he married Mary, ye Daughr. of Francis Newman, of this Town, Gent.

No other older inscriptions are known to be in the Churchyard, though there can be but little doubt that the sod hides many an old memorial stone.

Before leaving the subject of monuments and grave-stones altogether it is almost necessary to say that the eccentricities of spelling, and other apparent inaccuracies, which will be noticed in the foregoing transcripts, are not printers' errors, but are faithfully copied from the original inscriptions; though with regard to pointing and accentuation, which for the most part remain unaltered, it has not been thought objectionable to introduce stops or accents whenever the sense might have otherwise become ambiguous through the want of them.

A List of the Incumbents of the Parish of Madron.

THOMAS DE CHIMELLY, *Rector Ecclesiæ Sci. Maderni de Rydwori*, 1st June, 1203.
There is no record of this Incumbent in the Exeter Registers, which commence A.D. 1257.
'In the Charter Rolls in the Tower will be found a charter of King John, dated 1st June, 1203, granting *Ecclesiam Sci. Maderni de Rydwori*, to Thomas de Chimelly for life.'—*Rotuli Chartarum, fol.* 163. 'There is also a record dated 9th March, 1203, which says that it had been determined by the oath of twelve men of the neighbourhood of Runery, in Cornwall, that the Church *Sci Maderi de Runeri*, about which there had been a dispute between the King and the Knights Hospitallers, belonged to the latter, having been given them by the predecessor of the then Henry de Pomeroy, and the King therefore declared that the rights of the Knights of S. John should not be disputed after the death of Thomas de Chimelly, because Thomas had been admitted to that Church on the King's presentation, at a time when the land of Runeri and other lands of Henry de Pomeroy were in the King's hands.'*
In the *Rotuli de Liberate of John, fol.* 52, it is said that John had named Robert de Clifford, but yielded to the claim of the Knights of S. John in the year 1203. Madron was not finally appropriated to S. John of Jerusalem until the 30th October, 1336, and in a grant, dated as recently as the 24th March, 1612, from James I. to Francis Morris and Francis Philips, Esquires, the Rectory and Tithes of S. Madernus and Penzance are mentioned as being late the property of the Prior and Convent of S. John of Jerusalem. Thomas de Chimelly was perhaps related to William de Chymeleis, Bishop of Avranches, 1196—8, and he may have become connected with this neighbourhood through the Priory at S. Michael's Mount,—the Norman Abbey of that name being in the diocese of Avranches.

The Manor of Alverton, which included Penzance and a large district around, was held successively by Alward, (*temp.* Edward the Confessor); Robert, Earl of Moretain; Pomeroy; Richard, Earl of Cornwall; Henry le Tyes, (who in the early part of the 13th century endowed the Chapel of "our Ladye," at Penzance, "dystaunte from the parishe churche ij myles and halff"); † De Lisle; Berkeley; the Crown; Whitmore and others; Keigwin; and Veale, of Trevaylor. It has since been held by Tonkin, of Lelant, and Halse, of St. Ives; the latter being followed by Ley, who was succeeded by Bolitho, of Trewidden.

GYRARDUS, *Rector Ecclesiæ S. Maderni*, 8th Sept., 1276. There is no record of the institution of Gyrardus, but *Bronescombe's Register, fol.* 74, contains a copy of a testimonial by the Bishop to the effect 'that he was capable of discharging the duty of residence,' from which it is presumed that he was aged or infirm. The Bishop further testifies *inter alia* that Gyrardus "*bona gaudebat prosperitate in festo nativitatis beatæ virginis anno gratiæ* 1276."

JOHN DE METINGHAM, 'admitted by Bishop Bronescombe 5th June, 1278, *Vicar ad Ecclesiam Sci. Maderni in Cornubia ad presentationem fratris Josep de Chauncy, Prioris Hospitalis Jerusalem, in Anglia.*'—*Bronescombe's Reg., fol.* 87.

NICHOLAS ARTHUR DE TYNTAGEL, 'instituted 3rd November, 1309, on the Presentation of Prior William de Tottehale.'—*Stapleton's Reg., fol.* 45. 'This Vicar was to be allowed all the glebe with its manse thereon, and all the small tithes of the Parish, *excepta decima Piscariæ*: but was under an engagement to afford lodging to the Prior, or his brethren, or Procurator, when they visited the Parish, but who were maintained at their own costs. This arrangement proving inconvenient to the Vicar, it was agreed, 1st July, 1336, with the Prior Philip de Tame, that an angle of the glebet of sixty-two feet square, and looking to the south and west should be given up, *Pro horreo et aliis necessariis domibus construendis cum libero ingressu et egressu ad portam suam, ac ducendi temporibus debitis Bigam vel plaustrum facultate.*'—*Grandison's Reg., vol. ii., fol.* 12. "*Alucarton cum capella*" forfeited in 1322.—*Inquisitiones Post Mortem, vol. i., p.* 301.

---

* In preparing this List of Incumbents, that printed in the *Parochial History of Cornwall*, (published by Mr. Wm. Lake, of Truro, 1867—72', rol. iii. pp. 210-11, has been taken as a foundation : certain paragraphs, here appearing between single inverted commas, being extracted from it. Several alterations and corrections have been made, and much additional matter, together with references, introduced—the references to the Bishops' Registers being chiefly supplied by Arthur Burch, Esq., Secretary to the Bishop of Exeter, who has not only revised this List, but has taken much trouble in searching the Cathedral records for the purpose.   † Oliver's *Monasticon*, p. 490.   ‡ Vicar's "Sanctuary."

APPENDIX.

During the incumbency of Nicholas Arthur de Tyntagel the Church was dedicated to S. Madernus on the 10th July, 1336.—*Grandison's Reg., vol. ii., fol.* 12. "About this time namely 1338 the great tithes of this Parish were valued at 44 marks, equal to £29 · 6 · 8 and the glebe at 9d. per annum."

WILLIAM OF YORK. His institution is not recorded, but he exchanged for the Rectory of Redruth with the next Incumbent 20th September, 1344.

STEPHEN DE RESWALSTES, instituted 20th September, 1344; Patron, Prior Philip de Thame.—*Grandison's Reg., vol. iii., fol.* 52. He resigned, and was succeeded by

RALPH ROSKASTEL, instituted 16th June, 1349; Patron, Prior Philip de Tame. *Grandison's Reg., vol. iii., fol.* 82. He probably was a native of, or came from, the village of Rosekestal, in St. Levan. He also resigned, and was succeeded by

HENRY REDON, admitted 31st July, 1363; Patron, Prior John Pavely. *Grandison's Reg., vol. iii., fol.* 149. He was probably of a Buryan family; the name of John Reddon, of Buryan, occurs in November, 1328.—*Oliver's Monasticon, p.* 11.

ROGER MELEDER. No information as to the institution of this Incumbent is to be found in the Bishops' Registers, but at his death he is mentioned in the record of the institution of his successor.

LAWRENCE TREWYTHGY, instituted 7th February, 1391-2, on the Presentation of Prior Hildebrand Juge.—*Brantingham's Reg., vol. ii., fol.* 129. During his incumbency the Chapel of S. Mary, at Penzance (where a chantry had been founded with a salary of £4 by Sir Henry le Tyes, Lord of the Manor of Alverton before the year 1223), was licensed by Bishop Stafford, 15th June, 1397.—*Oliver's Monasticon, pp.* 441, 490. On his death he was succeeded by

JOHN BURDET, instituted 17th January, 1407, on the Presentation of Prior Walter Grendon.—*Stafford's Reg., vol. ii., fol.* 99. During his incumbency the Chapel of S. Morwetha, in the neighbourhood of Penzance, was licensed by Bishop Stafford, 17th April, 1409; as well as the Chapel of S. Gabriel and S. Raphael, at Penzance, by Bishop Lacy, 12th August, 1429, who also licensed that of S. Bridget, at Mousehole, 28th October, 1437.—*Oliver's Monasticon, p.* 441.

RICHARD ACTON, *alias* BROUAMP, admitted September, 1431; Patron, Prior William Hullys.—*Lacy's Reg., vol. ii., fols.* 106, 191. On the 11th August, 1440, he exchanged for S. Matthews' Church, "*Friday-strete, Ciritatis Londoniensis,*" with its Rector.—*Lacy's Reg., vol. iii., fol.* 206. Friday Street is in Cheapside, and S. Matthews' Church is still in existence.

RALPH DREW, instituted 11th August, 1440; Patron, Prior William Halls.*—*Lacy's Reg., vol. ii., fol.* 191; *vol. iii., fol.* 206.

ROBERT PASCHOW *or* PASLEW. There is no record of the institution of this Incumbent, but in that of the Vicar who, upon his death, succeeded him, he is called "Paslew."

BENEDICT TREGOOS *or* TREGOSE, admitted 21st November, 1498; Patron, Prior John Kendall.—*Redmayne's Reg., fol.* 6. He was also Vicar of St. Just, Penwith, being admitted 15th May, 1492. He was succeeded by

JOHN JACKES *or* JAKYS, instituted 19th November, 1534; 'Patron, *pro hac vice* John Arundell, Esq., of Trorice, by a grant of the Prior and his brethren.'—*Voysey's Reg., vol. i., fol.* 76. On his death he was succeeded by

THOMAS MARLESTON, LL.D., instituted 22nd March, 1536; Patron, the Prior.—*Voysey's Reg., vol. i., fol.* 80. This Vicar resigned on a pension from the living of £16 : 13 : 4 (the living being then rated at £50 per annum), and was succeeded by

---

* *Halls* and *Hullys*—the Prior last named—are probably the same, but the names are thus written in the Register.

APPENDIX. 85

JOHN SANDRE, instituted 2nd October, 1540; Patron, *hac vice*, Richard Roberd de Althorpe, Gent., of the County of Lincoln, 'by the grant of Richard Layton, Archdeacon of Bucks, who had acquired the right of the next presentation from the Prior by deed dated 30th May, 1536.'—*Voysey's Reg.*, *vol. i. fol.* 102. The name Sandry, or Saundry, appears frequently in the Parish Register.

EDMUND POWTON, 'a student at Oxford, was admitted by William Alley, Bishop of Exeter, *ad vicariam legitimé vacantem* 18th February, 1567;' Patroness, Queen Elizabeth.—*Alley's Reg., fol.* 21. Among the Communion plate at Madron is a silver chalice which bears the date 1576.

ANTHONY WHITEROWE, instituted by Bishop Bradbridge 20th August, 1577, *ad vicariam perpetuam de Madderne cum capella de Morva*; Patroness, Queen Elizabeth.—*Bradbridge's Reg., fol.* 39. He was succeeded by

RALPH HARBERTE (*i.e.* HERBERT) instituted by Bishop Woolton, 14th January, 1583-4; Patroness, Queen Elizabeth.—*Reg. of Woolton and others, vol. xxi., fol.* 14. He was buried at Madron on the 2nd February, 1600-1.

GEORGE HUTCHINS, M.A., instituted 12th June, 1601.—*Reg. of Woolton and others, vol. xxi., fol.* 72. He was also Rector of Ludgvan. During his incumbency a transcript of the old Registers of the Parish of Madron was made, according to the Act of Parliament, 2 James I. "Mr. George Hutchins, Parson of Ludgvan and Vicar of Madderne, Preacher of God's Worde," was buried at Ludgvan on the 27th May, 1627.

JOHN KEATE or KEATT. There is no entry as to the institution of this Incumbent in the Bishops' Registers, but in the records of the Episcopal Visitations, held 15th March, 1630-1, and 27th August, 1638, he is mentioned as the then Vicar of Madron. Isaac Nuton is also mentioned as being Curate of Morvah, and this name occurs in the Registers of Madron and Gulval: in the latter there is an entry, "Isaac Nuton, Buried 17th January, 1675-6." In the year 1645 John Keate collected and paid to the agents of Charles I. £2:5:6 for Madron, £2:5:6 for Penzance, and £0:10:4 for Morvah.—*Calendar of Clarendon State Papers in the Bodleian Library, edited by Macray, vol. i., p.* 293, No. 2.067. (N.B. Henry Keet, Vicar of Gulval, collected £2:4:6.) He died at Nanceglos, as was supposed of the plague, 16th October, 1647—*Daniel MSS., (Brief Chronological Observations, p.* 10*),*—and was buried at Mad on, as appears by the Parish Register, on the 17th October, 1647.*

SYMON LAND, intruded in 1647 by the Puritans. His institution is not recorded in the Bishops' Registers, but in the record of the Episcopal Visitation, held 21st November, 1662, his name appears thus:—"*Simo: Land abest.*"
The following, from another source, relates to him:—"Lew Symon, Madern V. (unless I misread it for Land, and he be the same person with Mr. Land, of Penzance, and so lost two Livings. Quære.)" "He was likewise Robb'd of his Horse, which at that time was his All, and threatned with *Imprisonment,* which oblig'd him to confine himself to his own House. He had no other Title than that of the *Times;* because he came not to this Living till 1647.† I think he lived to be Restored."—*Walker's Sufferings of the Clergy, p.* 291. He resigned the living in the year 1662, and was succeeded by

REGINALD TRENHAYLE, instituted 22nd November, 1662, 'to S. Maddern, with its annexed Chapels of Penzance and Morva, on the presentation of John Cowling, gent., of Trengwainton.'—*Registers, vol. i., New Series, fol.* 42. At the Episcopal Visitation, held on the 23rd July, 1665, John Zackrey is mentioned as Curate, and in the year 1693 Mr. Thomas Bellott was Curate of Penzance, as appears by the fragment of the St. Mary's Chapel Register. Vicar Trenhayle signed the terrier 19th April, 1680. It will be observed that the name Trenhayle, spelt in a variety of ways, appears early and not unfrequently in the Parish Registers of Madron: the name occurs also in the Registers of St. Erth and Constantine, and a Reginald Trenhaile was Vicar of Newlyn East in 1697,—possibly the same person. If he were a pluralist it would in some measure account for, though it would in nowise excuse, his neglect of the Parish Registers, which during the latter part of his incumbency were most irregularly kept, or not kept at all. He died in London in the year 1699 or in the early part of 1700, as is stated on a fly-leaf (page 93) in the fourth book of Registers at Madron, and was succeeded by

---

* In consequence of the leaf on which this entry is written having been accidentally bound wrong side out, this date has been erroneously given in Lake's *History of Cornwall*, before mentioned. The day too is clearly the 17th, and not the 19th.
† A further corroboration of the statement with regard to the date of the last Vicar's death.

V

APPENDIX.

THOMAS ROWE, instituted 16th March, 1700-1, on the presentation of Faith Rowe, widow and executrix of Thomas Rowe, of Breage.—*Reg., vol. iv., N. S., fol.* 60. He in the year 1702 presented to the Church the handsome and substantial communion rails, which are composed of polished teak or some other hard wood having the appearance of mahogany; and erected the oak pulpit and sounding board,—there being carved and gilded round the latter the words, " Blessed are they which hear the Word of God and keep it. Thos. Rowe, Vicar." He died on the 28th August, 1716, aged 40 years, and was buried on the 31st of the same month in the chancel at Madron, where a fine monument to his memory—with effigies of himself and his brother-in-law, the Rev. Duke Pearse, also commemorated—was set up by his widow.—*Ante., p.* 78. John Keigwin was Curate at Madron in the years 1716-17.

GEORGE WILLIAMS, instituted 15th April, 1717; Patron, Thomas Fleming, Gent., of Landithy.— *Reg , vol. v., N. S., fol.* 106. He resigned the living in favour of the next Incumbent.

WALTER BORLASE, LL.D., instituted 27th September, 1720; Patron, John Borlase, Esq., of Pendeen.—*Reg., vol. v., N. S., fol.* 133. This Vicar—the elder brother of Dr. Borlase, the Antiquary—eventually became Patron of Madron, and was also Vicar of Kenwyn, a Prebendary of Exeter, and Vice-warden of the Stannaries. He was baptised on the 5th November, 1694, and dying on the 26th April, 1776, aged 81 years and six months, was buried in the chancel at Madron, where a monument is erected to his memory.—*Ante., p.* 79. By his last Will and Testament he gave the next presentation to his third son, William, who had acted as his Curate from the year 1765. Previously, 1754—56, Nicholas Carkeet had been Curate.

WILLIAM BORLASE, M.A., instituted 19th July, 1776; Patrons, Henry Penneck and Joseph Hankey, trustees and devisees of the Will of the last Vicar.—*Reg., vol. ix., N. S., fol.* 121. 'At this time the reputed value of the benefice, including the Chapels of Penzance and Morvah, was £200.' This Incumbent, who was also Vicar of Zennor, died on the 15th November, 1812, aged 71 years. Thomas Modell Hawker was Curate here in the early part of this century.

WILLIAM TREMENHEERE, M.A., instituted 25th November, 1812.—*Reg., vol. xi., N. S., fol.* 49. So say the Records at Exeter, yet the following, written with his own hand, will be found at Madron. "His uncle, the said William Borlase, dying 15th November, 1812, when he the said William Tremenheere was instituted conformably to the last Will and Testament of his grandfather, Walter Borlase, into the next presentation, at Exeter, 18th November, A.D. 1812; inducted 21st November, and read himself in 22nd November, in the same year."—*See fly-leaf (page* 93*) in the fourth book of Registers.* Patron, Henry Penneck, M.D., of Penzance, acting under the provisions of the said Will. This Vicar died on the 26th June, 1838, aged 81 years, as is stated on the fly-leaf just mentioned, and was buried at Madron on the 4th July following.—*See Registers.* But a tablet with the following characteristic inscription—a blank being left for the date of his death, which curiously enough has been incorrectly filled in, *Id.* being engraved instead of *Kal.*—had place near the south side of the chancel before his decease :—

> M · S · Gulielmi · Tremenheere · A · M · qui · Reverendi · Gualteri · Borlase
> L : L : D : Nepos · (hic · juxtim · inhumati) · et · hujus · Parochiæ · Vicarius · non
> vocors · a · decimo · septimo · calendas · Decembres · MDCCCXII · usque · ad
> VI · Id · Jul · MDCCCXXXVIII · vitæ · discedentis · mortis · adventum · æter-
> nitatis · expectandæ · haud · immemor · octogenarius · lapidem · sepulcralem
> ipso · poni · curavit · A · S · MDCCCXXXVII ·   " Memento · Mori."

During his incumbency the following were Curates at Madron :—James Carne, 1818—20; George Treweek, 1820—22 ; Henry Tonkin Coulson, 1822—28 ; Francis Gregory, 1828—34 ; J. S. Cox, 1834 —36 ; and George Pinnock, 1836—38.

MICHAEL NOWELL PETERS, M.A., instituted on his own petition 25th September, 1838.—*Reg., vol. xii., N. S., fol.* 143. He married Anne, only daughter and heiress of the late Rev. William Borlase, Vicar of Madron, and in her was vested the right of presentation. The following have been Curates of Madron during the present incumbency :—J. A. Wood, 1842-3 ; John R. Bishop, 1843—45 ; William Wood, 1845—48 ; V. R. Vade, 1849—51 ; Michael Morgan Humble, 1851-2 ; Frederick William Poland, 1852-3 ; Edward Norman Coles, 1853-4 ; Philip Hedgeland, 1854—60 ; George Richard Scobell, 1860—67 ; John Jones, 1867-8 ; E. M. Griffiths, 1868-9 ; Jevon James Muschamp Perry, 1869—72 ; John Smith, 1872—74 ; Charles Holt Ensell, 1874—76.

Extended Transcripts from Documents, relating to the Parish of Madron, preserved at the Record Office.

[*Lease, in reversion, of the Tithes of Madron, Penzance, and S. Clare, for 21 years from 24th June, 1585, granted 8th January, 1574.*]

PATENT ROLL, 16 ELIZ. PART 3, MEMB. 13.

De Concessione ad firmam pro Coryton et Hogben. } Regina Omnibus ad quos &c. salutem.

Sciatis, quod nos pro fine centum librarum legalis monete Anglie, ad Receptam Scaccarii nostri ad usum nostrum per dilectos subditos nostros Petrum Coryton Armigerum et Willielmum Hogben solutâ, ac non diversis aliis causis et considerationibus nos ad presens specialiter moventibus, de gratia nostra speciali, ac ex certa scientia et mero motu nostris, tradidimus concessimus et ad firmam dimisimus, ac per presentes pro nobis heredibus et successoribus nostris tradimus concedimus et ad firmam dimittimus prefato Petro Coryton Omnes* illas Rectorias et Ecclesias nostras Sancte Clare, Madron et Pensaunce, in Comitatu Nostro Cornubiensi, ac omnes decimas bladorum garbarum granorum et feni nostras, annuatim et de tempore in tempus crescentes provenientes sive renovantes in Sancta Clera, alias Clare, Madron et Pensaunce, in eodem Comitatu Nostro Cornubiensi, cum eorum juribus et pertinentibus universis, modo in tenura sive occupatione dicti Petri Coryton vel assignatorum suorum, parcellas Preceptori de Trebight† in eodem Comitatu ac nuper Prioratui Sancti Johannis Jerusalem in Anglia modo dissoluto quondam spectantes et pertinentes, ac parcellas possessionum inde quondam existentes, Ac omnia, domos, edificia, horrea, stabula columbarum, hortos pomarios, gardinos, terras, globas, decimas garbarum, bladorum, granorum et feni, ac omnes alias decimas nostras quascumque tam majores quam minores, necnon oblaciones, obvenciones, fructus, proficua, commoditates, advantagia, emolumenta, et hereditamenta nostra quocunque dictis Rectoriis et decimis seu eorum alicui aut alicui inde parcelle quoque modo spectantia vel pertinentia, aut cum eisdem seu aliqua inde parcella antehac dimissa, locata, usitata, sive occupata existentia, cum omnibus et singulis et eorum pertinentibus universis * * * * * * * * * * Ac advocationibus vicariarum Ecclesiarum predictarum, Habendum et tenendum predictas Rectorias decimas ac cetera omnia et singula premissa dicto Petro Coryton per presentes, ut prefertur, dimissa et concessa cum omnibus et singulis eorum pertinentibus universis (exceptis preexceptis), prefato Petro Coryton executoribus et assignatis suis a festo Nativitatis Sancti Johannis Baptiste quod erit in anno Domini Millesimo quingentesimo octuagesimo quinto usque ad finem termini et per terminum viginti et unius annorum extunc proximo sequentem, et plenariè Complendum. Reddendum‡ extunc et abinde annuatim nobis, heredibus et successoribus nostris, de et pro predicta Rectoria Sancte Clare, octo libras et tresdecim solidos, Ac de et pro predicta Rectoria de Madron et Pensaunce, triginta et tres libras legalis monete Anglio, ad festa Sancti Michaelis Archangeli et Annunciacionis beate Marie Virginis, ad receptam scaccarii nostri seu ad manus Ballivorum vel Receptorum premissorum pro tempore existentium, per equales porciones solvendas durante termino predicto.

Et predictus Petrus Coryton executores et assignati sui sufficientem Ministrum et Curatum ad divina celebranda et Curam Animarum observandam in Ecclesiis predictis de tempore in tempus sumptibus suis propriis et expensis providebunt et invenient, Ac nos heredes et successores nostros inde exonerabunt, acquietabunt et indemnes conservabunt, durante termino per presentes (ut prefertur) concesso Quod quoque idem Petrus Coryton et Willielmus Hogben executores et assignati sui Cancellum Ecclesiarum predictarum ac omnia, domos, et edificia, necnon omnia, sepes, fossata, inclausuras, littoraria, ripas, et muros marittimos Ac cetias omnes alias necessarias reparationes premissorum

---

* All these our Rectories and Churches of St. Clare, Madron and Penzance, in our County of Cornwall, and all tythes of corn and hay accruing in St. Clare, *alias* Clare, Madron and Penzance, in the same our County of Cornwall, with their rights and appurtenances whatsoever now in the tenure or occupation of the said Peter Coryton, or his Assignes, Parcels formerly belonging and pertaining to the Preceptory of Trebigh, in the same County, and lately to the Priory of St. John of Jerusalem, in England, now dissolved.

† The Preceptory of Trebigh was in St. Ive, near Liskeard.

‡ To pay them and thenceforth annually to us, our heirs, and successors, for the aforesaid Rectory of St. Clare £8 : 13, and for the aforesaid Rectory of Madron and Penzance £33, of legal money of England, at the festivals of St. Michael the Archangel and the Annunciation of the Blessed Virgin Mary, at the receipt of our Exchequer, or into the hands of our Bailiffs or Receivers, &c.

APPENDIX.

in omnibus et per omnia de tempore in tempus tociens quotiens necesse et oportunium* fuerit, sumptibus suis propriis et expensis bene et sufficienter reparabunt, supportabunt, sustinebunt, escurabunt, purgabunt, et manutenebunt durante termino predicto Ac premissa sufficienter reparata in fine termini illius dimittent Et volumus ac per presentes concedimus prefato Petro Coryton et Willielmo Hogben executoribus et assignatis suis quod bene licebit eis de tempore in tempus capere percipere, et habere, de in et super premissis crescentem, competentem et sufficientem housebote, hedgebote, fyrebote, et ploughbote, et cartebote, ibidem et non alibi annuatim expendendum et occupandum durante termino predicto Et quod habeant maeremium in boscariis et terris promissorum crescens ad et versus reparacionem domorum et edificiorum premissorum, per assignacionem et superviciouem Senescalli seu Subsenescalli aut aliorum officiariorum nostrorum ibidem pro tempore existentium durante termino predicto. *   *   *   *   *   *   *   *   *   *   *
In cuius rei, &c. Teste Regina apud Westmonasterium viij die Januarii.
Per breve de privato sigillo.

[*Lease to Thomas Betts for* 50 *years from Michaelmas*, 1584.]

TRANSCRIPTS OF LEASES (AUGMENTATION), 27 ELIZ. No 24.

Regina Omnibus ad quos &c. salutem.

Sciatis, quod nos de avisamento dilectorum et fidelium nostrorum Consiliariorum Willielmi Baronis de Burghley Thesaururius noster* Anglie et Walteri Mildmay, militis, Cancellarii Curie Scaccarii nostri Tradidimus, concessimus, et ad firmam dimisimus ac per presentes tradimus, concedimus, et ad firmam dimittimus dilecto nobis Thome Betts, generoso,   *   *   *   *   *   *   *   *   *
Ac totam illam peciam terre adiacentem Pinfoldo‡ nostram infra Manerium nostrum de Alwarton et Pensaunce, in dicto Comitatu Cornubiensi, modo vel nuper in tenura sive occupatione Ricardi Lanyne junioris vel assignatorum suorum Annualis redditûs duorum solidorum, Ac unam vacuam parcellam terre nostram vocatam Ropers' place adiacentem ville de Pensaunce predicte annualis redditûs sex denariorum Ac totam illam Capellam nostram cum pertinentibus in medio ville de Moushole, parcellam Manerii de Alwarton et Pensaunce predicti, annualis redditûs sex denariorum, Ac unam vacuam parcellam terre nostram cum pertinentibus adiacentem cuidam Capelle scituate infra regiam viam inter Pensaunce et Madderne in Comitatu predicto, annualis redditûs quatuor denariorum, Necnon unum gardinum nostrum cum pertinentibus ibidem, vocatum le hempe garden, adiacentem prope domum cuiusdam Johannis Beachym, generosi, modo vel nuper in tenura sive occupacione Thome Clise vel assignatorum suorum, annualis redditûs sex denariorum, Que quidem premissa in Alwarton et Pensaunce predictis sunt parcella Manerii de Alwarton et Pensaunce in predicto Comitatu nostro Cornubiensi, ac nuper fuerunt parcella terrarum et possessionum Henrici nuper Comitis Rutland, Ac omnia et singula, domos, edificia, structuras, horrea, stabula, hortos pomarios, gardinos, vacua, fundos, semitas, vias, introitus, exitus, aesiamenta, proficua, comoditates, advantagia, emolumenta, et hereditamenta nostra quecunque dictis tenementis et gardinis et ceteris premissis seu eorundem alicui parcelle ullo modo spectantia vel pertinentia, aut cum eisdem seu eorum aliquo vel aliquibus antehac usualiter pro vel sub separali annuali redditu superius mencionato dimissa, locata, usitata, occupata seu gavisa existentia, cum eorum pertinentibus universis Habendum et tenendum predicta tenementa, mesuagia, gardinos ac cetera omnia et singula promissa superius expressa, et spectantia, ac per presentes dimissa cum eorum pertinentibus universis prefato Thome Betts executoribus et assignatis suis a festo Sancti Michaelis Archangeli ultimo preterito usque ad finem termini et per terminum Quinquaginta annorum extunc proxime sequentem, et plenarie complendum Reddendum annuatim nobis, heredibus et successoribus nostris de et pro predictis terris et ceteris premissis in villa Circoucestrio predicta in tenura dicti Ricardi Pachett, ut prefertur, Tresdecim Solidos et quatuor denarios ac de et pro tenementis ibidem in tenura dicti Johannis Cooke, ut prefertur, Tresdecim solidos, Ac de et pro predictis mesuagiis, tenementis, gardiuiis et ceteris omnibus et singulis premissis cum eorum

---

* Sic.
† And all that our piece of land adjoining Pinfold, within our Manor of Alwarton and Pensaunce, in the said County of Cornwall, now or lately in the tenure or occupation of Richard Lanyne, Jun., or his Assigns, at an annual rent of 2s. And one waste parcel or piece of our land called Ropers' Place, adjoining the town of Penzance aforesaid, at an annual rent of 6d. And all that our Chapel with its appurtenances, in the middle of the town of Moushole, a part of the Manor of Alwarton and Penzance aforesaid, at an annual rent of 6d. And one waste parcel of our land with its appurtenances, adjoining a certain Chapel situated within the high road between Penzance and Madderne, in the County aforesaid, at the annual rent of 4d.; and a garden, * * * at the same place, called the Hemp Garden, adjoining the house of one John Beachym, gent., now or lately in the tenure or occupation of Thomas Clies, or his Assigns, at the annual rent of 6d. * * * lately parts of the lands and possessions of Lord Rutland. * * * (And for the aforesaid premises Thomas Betts is to pay 45s. 8d., legal money of England, at the same period and in the manner mentioned in the previous document.)   ‡ Cattle Pound.

APPENDIX.

pertinentibus universis in dicto Comitatu nostro Cornubiensi quadraginta quinque solidos et octo denarios legalis moneto Anglie ad festa annualia beate Marie Virginis et Sancti Michaelis Archangeli, ad Receptam Scaccarii nostri Westmonasterii seu ad manus Ballivorum vel Receptorum promissorum pro tempore existentium, per equales porciones solvendos durante termino predicto. Et predictus Thomas Betts executores et assignati sui omnes domos et edificia ac omnes alias necessarias reparaciones premissorum in omnibus et per omnia de tempore in tempus tociens quociens necesse et opportunum fuerit sumptibus suis propriis et expensis bene et sufficienter reparabunt, supportabunt, sustinebunt, oscurabunt, purgabunt, et manutenebunt durante termino predicto, Et premissa sufficienter reparata et manutenta in fine termini illius dimittent: Proviso semper quod si contigerit predictos separales redditus aut eorum aliquem a retro fore non solutos in parte vel in toto per spacium Quadraginta dierum post aliquod festum festorum predictorum, prout prefertur solvi debeant, quod tunc et deinceps hec presens dimissio et concessio, quoad illam partem et parcellam promissorum unde separales redditus sic a retro fuere insoluti tantummodo, vacua sit ac pro nullo habeatur, aliquo in presentibus in contrarium inde non obstante, aliquo Statuto &c.
In cuius rei &c.

W. BURGHLEY. WA. MILDMAYE.

Exr per CHRISTOFERUM SMYTH.

Gloucestria } Thomas Betts,* dimissio cortorum tenementorum et gardinorum in villa Cirencestrie
Cornubia. } et alibi pro certo assiso Redditu per annum lxxij solidos. Fine nil.

[Endorsed.] Teste * * * secundo die Decembris, 1584, Anno Regni Regine Elizabethe xxvij.†

PARTICULARS FOR LEASES (AUGMENTATION); ELIZ. CORNUBIA. ROLL 2, MEMB. 42.

Comitatus Cornubiensis.

Parcella possessionum nuper Hospitalis Sancti Johannis Jerusalem, in Anglia.

Rectorie Sancte Clare,
Madron et Peusaunce, } Firma omnium illarum Rectoriarum et Ecclesiarum Sancte Clare et Pensaunce in Comitatu predicto Ac omnium illarum decimarum bladorum,
valent in garbarum, granorum, et feni annuatim et de tempore in tempus crescentium, provenientium, sive renovantium in Sancta Clare, alias Clere, Madron et Pensaunce, cum eorum iuribus, membris, et pertinentibus universis Sic (inter alia) dimissarum Petro Corrington per literas patentes Domine Elizabethe Regine Datas viij die Januarii Anno Regni sui xvj pro termino xxj annorum Incipiendo in Anno Domini 1585, Reddendo inde per annum pro predicta Rectoria Sancte Clare viij libras, xiij solidos et pro predicta Rectoria de Madron et Pensaunce predicte xxxiij libras. In toto per Annum * * * xlj libras, xiij solidos.

xviij yeares to come.

xij° Maij, 1589.
xj° Maij, 1589.   Exr per Willielmum Neale,
Auditorem.

PATENT ROLL OF 9 JAMES I. PART 10, No. 12.

Grant to Robert, Earl of Salisbury.

The King To all to whom &c. greeting * * * * * * * * *

Sec. 42. Know ye that we of our special grace and of our certain knowledge and mere motion have given and granted, and by these presents for us; our heirs, and successors, give and grant to (the aforesaid) Robert, Earl of Salisbury, his heirs and assigns.

Sec. 43. Omnes decimas granorum et feni ac alias decimas quascunque tam majores quam minores annuatim crescentes renovantes sive emergentes in Peusaunce in Comitatu nostro Cornubiensi.

---

* The name of Thomas Betts occurs in Edward Jones' *Index to Records*, 1793, vol. i.,—"Originalia Elizabethae," "Firmae dimis-ac in Com. Cornubiae et Southamptoniae. 5 Pars original. Anno 25. Rotulo 16."
† There is at the Record Office a similar grant to Nicholas Coleman, dated 32 Eliz.

W

APPENDIX.

Sec. 46. Ac* Dominium, Manerium, Firmas, Mesuagia, terras, tenementa, redditus liberorum tenencium, et hereditamenta quocunque, scituata jacentia et existentia in parochia, villa, hamletto seu campis de Pensaunce * * * * in Comitatu nostro Cornubiensi, nuper Prioratui Sancti Michaelis ad Montem quoquo modo spectantia, pertinentia, incidentia, appendentia vel incumbentia.

Sec. 62. Exceptis† tamen semper, et nobis heredibus et successoribus nostris omnino reservatis, omnibus advocationibus donacionibus liberis disposicionibus et juribus patronatûs omnium et singularum ecclesiarum &c., predictarum firmarum vocatarum Saincte Michaells Mounte et predictorum dominiorum &c., superius per presentes preconcessorum in dicto Comitatu Cornubiensi.

Sec. 63. Habendum tenendum et gaudendum omnes et singulas predictas decimas &c. * * * * prefato Roberto Comiti Sarisburiensi heredibus et assignatis suis ad solum et proprium opus et usum prefati Roberti Comitis Sarisburiensis heredum et assignatorum suorum in perpetuum.

Sec. 64. Tenenda predicta firma Sancti Michaelis ad Montem et cetera omnia et singula premissa in predicto Comitatu Cornubiensi de nobis, heredibus, et successoribus nostris, ut de honore nostro de Hampton Courte in Comitatu Middlesex, per servicium quadragesime partis unius feodi militis, pro omnibus aliis redditibus serviciis exactionibus et demandis quibuscunque proinde nobis heredibus vel successoribus nostris quoquo modo reddendis solvendis seu faciendis.

Sec. 76. Teste Rege apud Westmonasterium secundo die Marcii.

per ipsum Regem.

Patent Roll, 10 James I. Part 2, No. 1.

Grant to Francis Morrice and Francis Phelipps.

Rex Omnibus ad quos &c. salutem.

Sciatis quod nos ad humilem peticionem nominacionem et requisitionem dilectorum subditorum nostrorum Anthonii Cope &c. * * * * qui grandes pecuniarum summas ad Receptam Scaccarii nostri apud Westmonasterium ante datum harum literarum nostrarum patentium ad usum nostrum bene et fideliter persolverunt, unde fatemur nos plenariè esse satisfactos et persolutos, eosdemque Anthonium Cope &c. * * * * inde acquietatos et exoneratos esse in perpetuum per presentes, quam pro diversis aliis bonis causis et considerationibus nos ad presens specialiter moventibus, de gratia nostra speciali ac ex certa scientia et mero motu nostris, dedimus et concessimus, ac per presentes pro nobis heredibus et successoribus nostris damus et concedimus, Francisco Morice et Francisco Phelips generosis, heredibus et assignatis suis in perpetuum * * * * * * * *

Memb. 17. Omnes illas Rectorias et ecclesias vocatas de Madron et Pensaunce in Comitatu Cornubiensi cum eorum juribus membris et pertinentibus universis.

Ac† omnes illas decimas garbarum bladorum granorum et feni annuatim et de tempore in tempus crescentes provenientes sive renovantes in Madron et Pensaunce predictis in dicto Comitatu Cornubiensi cum eorum juribus membris et pertinentibus universis, modo vel nuper in tenura sive occupacione Petri Cureton Armigeri vel assignatorum suorum, annualis redditûs sive valoris triginta trium librarum, ac quondam parcellam possessionum nuper Hospitalis sive Prioratûs Sancti Johannis Jerusalem, in Anglia.

Necnon advocacionem donacionem liberam disposicionem et jura patronatuum omnium et singularum ecclesiarum vicariarum et Capellarum predicte Rectorie et ecclesie de Madron et Pensaunce, vel eorum alterius alicui vel aliquibus quoquo modo spectantia pertinentia incidentia appendentia vel incumbentia.

Memb. 20. Habendum tenendum et gaudendum omnia et singula predicta, Rectorias ecclesias &c. * * * * prefatis Francisco Morice et Francisco Phelipps heredibus et assignatis suis ad solum et proprium opus et usum ipsorum Francisci Morice et Francisci Phelipps heredum et assignatorum suorum in perpetuum.

---

* And the demesne, manor, farm, messuages, lands, tenements, rents of free tenants, and hereditaments situate, lying, and being in the Parish, town, hamlet, or plains of Pensaunce, in our County of Cornwall, in any way belonging to the late Priory of St. Michael, at the Mount.

† Nevertheless, always excepted and altogether reserved for ourselves, our heirs, and successors, all advowsons, donations, free dispositions, and rights of patronage of all and each of the Churches, &c., of the aforesaid farms of St. Michaell's Mount, and of the aforesaid demesnes, &c., above granted by these presents, in the said County of Cornwall.

‡ And all those tythes of corn and hay in Madron and Pensaunce aforesaid, in the said County of Cornwall, with their rights and appurtenances whatsoever now or lately in the tenure or occupation of Peter Cureton, Esq., or his Assigns, at an annual rent or value of £33, and formerly a part of the possessions of the late Hospital or Priory of St. John of Jerusalem, in England. Also the advowson * * * and rights of patronage of all and each of the Churches, Vicarages, and Chapels of the aforesaid Rectory and Church of Madron and Pensaunce, or in any way belonging or pertaining to either or any of them.

APPENDIX.   91

Tenendum de nobis heredibus et successoribus nostris ut de Manerio nostro de Eastgreenwich in Comitatu nostro Kancie, per fidelitatem tantùm in libero et Communi socagio et non in Capite nec per servicium militare.
Memb. 27.   Teste Rege apud Westmonasterium vicesimo quarto die Marcii.

per breve de privato sigillo.

Conveyance of Glebe for the Augmentation of the Curacy of Penzance, 1762.

BOWN TO MARSHALL.

This Indenture of four parts made the sixteenth day of April in the second year of the reign of our Sovereign Lord George Third by the Grace of God of Great Britain France and Ireland King Defender of the Faith and so forth and in the year of our Lord one thousand seven hundred and sixty-two Between Peter Bown of the Town of Falmouth in the County of Cornwall Esquire of the first part The Reverend Richard Pearse of the Parish of Saint Levan in the County of Cornwall Clerk of the second part The Governors for the Bounty of Queen Anne for the augmentation of the maintenance of the poor Clergy of the third part and The Reverend John Marshall Clerk Curate of the Curacy of Buriton or Penzance in the County of Cornwall and Diocese of Exeter of the fourth part Witnesseth that for and in consideration of the sum of four hundred pounds of good and lawful money of Great Britain by the said Governors at or before the sealing and delivery of these presents to the said Peter Bown in hand well and truly paid by the direction of the said Richard Pearse (testyfied by his being a party to and executing these presents) being the same sum of four hundred pounds as is mentioned to be paid to him in and by a certain Indenture of Release of five parts bearing even date herewith the receipt of which said sum of four hundred pounds he the said Peter Bown doth hereby acknowledge and thereof and of and from every part thereof as well as of and from all claims and demands whatsoever on account of a certain Mortgage or Security in the said Indenture of Release mentioned and recited he the said Peter Bown doth hereby acquit release and discharge the said Governors and their Successors and the said John Marshall and his Successors and also the messuage or dwelling-house closes or parcels of Land and heredits. hereinafter mentioned and intended to be hereby and by the said Indenture of Release Granted and conveyed and also in consideration of the sum of five shillings apiece of like lawful money by the said John Marshall at the same time in hand paid to the said Peter Bown and Richard Pearse the receipt of which said sums they do hereby respectively acknowledge and for conveying assuring and settling the same messuage or dwelling-house closes or parcels of Land and heredits. for the perpetual augmentation of the Curacy of Buriton or Penzance aforesaid He the said Peter Bown by the direction of the said Richard Pearse testyfied as aforesaid and also with the approbation and by the direction of the said Governors (testyfied by their common seal being hereunto affixed) Hath bargained and sold and by these presents Doth bargain and sell and the said Richard Pearse with the like approbation and direction of the said Governors (testyfied as aforesaid) Hath granted bargained sold ratified and confirmed and by these presents Doth grant bargain sell ratify and confirm unto the said John Marshall and his Successors Curates of the Curacy of Buriton or Penzance aforesaid All that one messuage or dwelling-house and garden thereunto belonging situate lying and being in Alverton Lane within the said Town of Penzance now in the holding of Ezekiel Trengrove Clovier which said house and garden Plott was formerly taken out of part of a field or close of Land called Tonkin's Weith Tonkin's Land or Park-an-vounder And also all and singular those two fields or closes of Land with the appurts. commonly called or known by the name or names of Tonkin's Weith or Tonkin's Land otherwise Park-an-vounder situate lying and being in the said Town of Penzance bounded towards the East with a field called Park-an-grouso towards the west with a Driving Lane (formerly taken out of the said field called Park-an-vounder and leading to the fields now of George Veale and John Sandford Gentlemen other part of Tonkin's Weith or Tonkin's Land which they purchased of the late Richard Pearse Gentleman deceased) towards the North with a field or close of Land (part of the said Lands called Tonkin's Weith now belonging to the said John Sandford) and towards the South with the Highway leading from Penzance to Alverton which said two closes or fields of Land called Tonkin's Weith Tonkin's Land or Park-an-vounder contain by estimation three acres of ground or thereabouts (be the same more or less) and are now in the tenure holding or occupation of the said Ezekiel Trengrove as tenant thereof or by whatsoever other name or names the said messuage or dwelling-house fields or closes of Land have been or may be called or known or howsoever otherwise abutted bounded distinguished or described together with all houses outhouses edifices buildings barns Stables

APPENDIX.

Orchards Gardens ways paths passages waters watercourses timber and trees woods underwood gates hedges fences and enclosures Commons Common of Pasture and Turbary advantages privileges emoluments heredits. and appurts. whatsoever to the said messuage or dwelling-house closes or parcels of Land heredits. and premises or any part thereof belonging or in anywise appertaining or to or with the same now or at any time heretofore usually held occupied or enjoyed or accepted reputed deemed or taken as part parcel or member thereof or appurtenant thereunto and the reversion and reversions remainder and remainders rents issues and profits thereof and all the estate right title interest use trust property claim and demand whatsoever both at Law and in Equity of them the said Peter Bown and Richard Pearse or either of them out of in or to the said premises and every part and parcel thereof To have and to hold all and singular the said messuage or dwelling-house closes or parcels of Land heredits. and premises hereinbefore granted bargained sold and confirmed or intended so to be with their and every of their appurts. unto and to and for the only use and behoof of the said John Marshall and his Successors Curates of the Curacy of Buriton or Penzance aforesaid for ever for the perpetual augmentation of the said Curacy and to and for no other use intent or purpose whatsoever And whereas the said messuage or dwelling-house closes or parcels of Land heredits. and premises hereinbefore granted bargained and sold or intended so to be do arise from the Bounty of her late Majesty Queen Anne and have been purchased with the sum of four hundred pounds arising from such Bounty Now the said Governors by virtue and in pursuance of the last Clause in an Act of Parliament passed in the first year of the reign of his late Majesty King George the first entitled an act for making more effectual her late Majesty's Gracious intentions for augmenting the maintenance of the poor Clergy do hereby allott and apply to the Church or Chappel of Buriton or Penzance aforesaid All and singular the said messuage or dwelling-house closes or parcels of Land heredits. and premises with their appurts. and do hereby declare that the same shall for ever hereafter be annexed to the said Church or Chappel of Buriton or Penzance and shall be from henceforth held and enjoyed and go in succession with such Church or Chappel for ever In witness whereof the said Governors have caused their common seal to be hereunto affixed and the said other parties to these presents have hereunto set their hands and seals the day and year first above written.

JOHN MARSHALL.   PETER BOWN.   RICHD. PEARCE.

Signed sealed and delivered by the within named Peter Bown Richard Pearce and John Marshall in the presence of Jos. Tonkin of Penzance, Clerk, Abrahm. Hall of Falmouth Attorney at Law.

Received the day and year first within written of and from the within named Governors the sum of four Hundred pounds being the full consideration money within mentioned to be paid by them to me and for which I have also signed a Receipt upon another part of this Indenture and likewise signed another receipt for the same sum of money upon an Indenture of Release bearing even date herewith—PETER BOWN.

Witness Js. Tonkin, Abrahm. Hall Attorney at Law in Falmouth.

And be it Remembered that the sixteenth day of April in the year of our Lord 1762 the aforesaid Richard Pearse Clerk came before our said Lord the King in his Chancery and acknowledged the Indenture aforesaid and all and every thing therein contained and specified in form above written and also the Indenture aforesaid was stamped according to the tenor of the Statute made in the sixth year of the reign of the late King and Queen William and Mary of England and so forth.

Inrolled the twenty-seventh day of May in the year of our Lord one thousand seven hundred and sixty-two.

I certify that the above is a true copy of the original enrolment in Chancery, made there under the 1 Geo. 1., Cap. 10.   HENRY GROVE.   (Extracted from the Close Roll, 2 Geo. III., Part 4, No. 11.)

N.B. The foregoing documents are from copies of the originals. Those in Latin have been here set forth *in extenso*, with an occasional free translation. Certain inaccuracies, due to the original writer or to the transcriber, which it is almost impossible to avoid and seemed unadvisable to interfere with, will be noticed.

Notes.

Register of Baptisms.

1592. [? Sept.] "BOSSAVERNE." Surnames were commonly assumed in this part of the County, until a comparatively recent period, from the name of the place at which the persons resided. This James or his fathers most probably lived at Bosavern, in the adjoining Parish of St. Just, and when he took up his abode in Madron was still known by the name of his old home. Numerous names of this class will be found in these Registers. Occasionally two surnames occur, as Edwards, *alias* Porteare, James, *alias* Mulfra, &c.

Sept. 24. "RAW, SPUR." *Raw* the vulgar pronunciation of Rowe at the present day; Rowe being probably derived from Ralph. *Spur*. This abbreviation is that most frequently used whenever it is intended to mark illegitimacy. In one place it is written in full, *Spurius* (See Burials. 1588, July 22), and occasionally it is represented by an *S* only.—See Baptisms, 1606, Feb. 9.

Nov. 30. "JERMYN," or German, a favourite christian and surname throughout this book, probably introduced by some one from Germany.

Dec. 17. "RAWE DAVYE." Possibly in this case Rawe is an abbreviation for Rowan.—See Baptisms, 1601, Sept. 3.

1592-3. Jan. 21. "MADERNE," a surname derived after the manner above mentioned from the Parish of Madron, which formerly was, and vulgarly is still, so pronounced. As might have been expected perhaps no surname is of more frequent occurrence in the Registers than this.

Feb. 17. "HEXT." This is probably John Hext, of Kerris, in Paul.

Feb. ... "BENNET" appears to be an abbreviation of Benedict. Some of the contracted or altered forms of names are curious, such as Bendigo—from Abednego, and Arclas—from Hercules. These are favourite names in West Cornwall, and Bendigo, in Australia, was so called after a Cornishman who settled there in the present century.

1593. April 22. "BUSKEYNING." There are two estates of this name in the Parish, Higher and Lower Boskenning.

June 3. "JOHN JAMES TREMETHACK." Here is an instance of two christian names at a time when such a thing was very uncommon, but does it not rather mean John James, of Tremethack? He is evidently not the same person as John Tremethack, whose name occurs in the same year (Nov. 25); and perhaps the third name in the first case was used to distinguish the one from the other.

Aug. 12. —— Very frequently, as in this case, a blank has been left. Probably the transcriber was unable to decipher the ancient Registers from which the present were copied, down to about the year 1607.

Sept. 2. "WILLIAM TREVE," *i.e.* William Nicholls, of Trereife. Trereife is usually pronounced, as here spelt, Treve.

Sept. 2. "JOHN, THE ROPER." Surnames appear to have been scarcely settled even at this time, and seem often to have been assumed in allusion to trade or calling, or from some personal peculiarity, as well as from residence.

x

NOTES.

1594. April 7. "LANYON," or Lanion, signifying John's enclosure. *Lan* more or less relates to the Church, and this property probably formerly belonged to the Knights of St. John of Jerusalem, who had an establishment at Lanclithy, in this Parish, near the Church, which had been appropriated to them. The correct pronunciation of this name is Lanion or Lanine, but it is often when used as a surname pronounced, as most usually written, Lanyon; the *y* being sounded as in *beyond*. It has sometimes been called Lan John also, and this would seem to add force to the supposition that this place appertained to the Knights Hospitallers.

1597. Sept. 1. "COWLINGE." A family of this name resided at Trengwainton.

1598-9. Mar. 11. "ANDRILLIER," or Andryllier. Query, Audry, Clerk; possibly an error of the transcriber.—See Marriages, 1587, Nov. 19. Awdry occurs as a christian name.—See Baptisms, 1601, Sept. 15.

Mar. 18. "ROWAN." This name occurs frequently, spelt in a variety of ways, both as a christian and surname. *Rohan* is not unknown in Brittany.

1599. July 22. "SUDGIOW." This name (which the Rev. William Tremenheere persistently writes Gudgeon) frequently occurs in these Registers. It was not extinct in the neighbourhood at the latter part of the last century. A person of the name—from whom by the way the late Rev. Henry Penneck received the first rudiments of his education—lived and died in Penzance.

1600. July 15. "PERES," a distinct name from Pearce, and formerly known in Gulval.

1601. Sept. 3. "ROAN."—See Baptisms, 1592, Dec. 17.

1601-2. Feb. 21. "BAUDE." Possibly this name may be Band which occurs in the Gulval Registers, but as the bearer of it usually figures here under the same circumstances perhaps the more objectionable appellation is the most suitable.—See Baptisms, 1609-10, Jan. 7.

1602. April 5. "CHARELLS," a not unfrequent vulgar pronunciation of Charles at the present day.

1602. Sept. 5. "FYNNIE" appears to have been sounded as Feeny. The family was influential in Penzance in the 17th century.

1602-3. Jan. 6. "DAWDIN," a contraction of St. Aubyn—sometimes further reduced to Dobbin.

1603. Aug 28. "TREF," *i.e.* Treriefe, *alias* Nicholls.

1604. Dec. 12. "EDWARDE," or Edwardes.—See Baptisms, 1609, April 14.

1605. July 6. "PENZANC," an early instance of the name being spelt with a *s*.

1605-6. Feb. 23. "DODO," (or Dadowe—See Marriages, 1587, June 12), a curious surname, but one very similarly sounded was not unknown in Penzance about the commencement of the present century.—See Le Grice's *Petition of an old uninhabited house in Penzance*.

1606. Sept. 21. "ALCE." This might almost be supposed to be a distinct name from Alice, or perhaps is only a variation of it. Possibly this pronunciation of it may not have died out even yet, but in the last century there was a poor foolish girl at the Quay, Penzance, who was fond of talking of "John * * * * and Alice, Tom, Hugh, and Alce (sounded Ailsey), Titzy, Mammy, and I."

1606-7. Jan. 25. "JEELES," a very clear exemplification of the ancient pronunciation of Giles, confirming the supposition that *i* was most frequently sounded as *e* in this neighbourhood.—See Baptisms, 1610-11, March 3.

1607-8. Feb. 7. "TREREIFE," *i.e.* Nicholls, of Trereife.—See Baptisms, 1628, June 15, and Appendix to Marriages, 1627, Aug. 6.

1608-9. Jan. 13. "Mr. JOHN CLIES," twice Mayor of Penzance.—See Monumental Inscriptions, p. 76.

1609-10. Jan. 7. See Baptisms, 1601-2, Feb. 21.

1610. July 13. "LANYON, Esq." Esquires are remarkably rare in this book.

1610-11. Jan. 1. "LAVELIS," or Levelis, then of Castle Horneck, afterwards of Trewoof, Buryan.

Jan. 20. "OTES," whether here intended as a christian or a surname is uncertain.

March 3. See Baptisms, 1606-7, Jan. 25.

1611. Oct. 13. "BOODEN." The *o* is probably doubled to intensify its sound, and not to represent *oo* as in fool; so this name would be pronounced Bowden. Similar instances occur in the older part of the Register—as Loose for Louse, Nooal for Nowell, Portear, Feeny, &c.

Nov. 28. "PHILLIP" is frequently used as a woman's name as well as a man's.

1617. July 20. "NOSEWORTHYE." In the MSS. of Alexander Daniel, of Lariggan, written about the middle of this century, this name frequently occurs, and always written *Norsworthy*.

1625. Dec. 30. "ANTHONY GUBBS," twice Mayor of Penzance. He is frequently mentioned in the Daniel MSS., and issued a farthing token in Penzance in 1667.

1628. May 18. "SISSELL," *i.e.* Cecil.

June 15. "NICHOLLS," of Trereife.—See Baptisms, 1607-8, Feb. 9; Appendix to Marriages, 1627, Aug. 6.

1631. Dec. 7. "JICHOLAS." Query a fanciful name or a slip of the pen.

1632-3. Jan. 22. "ELIASSAPH DANIELL," born on the 10th of the same month.—See Daniel MSS.

1634. Sept. 12. "JOHN, my sixth son, was born in Noye's house, at Penzance, about sun rising, being ye Lord's day, 1634." "Aug. 19. My son John dyed at Larigan circa three a clock afternoon, and was buried 21st in Madr. Chur. 1661."—Daniel MSS.

1635. May 2. "KETE."—See p. 85.

1636-7. Feb. 18. "TOLLAR." This name probably was originated by the occupation of a Toller or Bounder, one whose duty it is to renew Bounds of Tin Works.

1637. June 3. "AGNIS." This is the first time the name of the wife is given in the Register of Baptisms.

June 7. "HALENIGHT," a man's name: its antithesis, "LOVEDAY," occurs as a woman's.

Aug. 6. "Aug. 1, GEORGE, mine eighth son, was born at Penzance, in Noye's house circ. two a clock after midnight, Tuesday, 1637.—Daniel MSS. He was the founder, in 1701, of the Free School at Madron for poor children of that Parish, and of its Chapelries of Morva and Penzance.

1637-8. Mar. 18. "KERROWE," signifying in the Cornish language a plough, an old form of *Carew*; though in this Register the name occurs early spelt as at present.—See Marriages, 1587, June 5.

    "*Carew* of ancient *Carru* was,
       And *Carru* is a plowe;
    Romanes the trade, Frenchmen the word,
       I doe the name avoue."
          Carew's *Survey of Cornwall*, fol. 103, (Ed. 1769).

1644-5. Feb. 7. "PRIMROSE." Persons of this name lived in Newlyn, near Penzance, as lately as at the commencement of the present century; and the fine old house, the present residence of the Misses Leah, at Newlyn, was formerly the seat of the Primroses.

1647. April 25. "NICHOLL." This name, spelt in a variety of ways, occurs as a female christian name.

Aug. 29. "BLAZERIS." Query a corruption of Lazarus.

Dec. 26. "EMETT." (Emmet=ant.) Query a male or female name.

1648-9. Mar. 20. "GILBERT FICKS." This is undoubtedly the same as Gilbert Thick, whose name occurs several times at later dates.

NOTES.

1649-50. Jan. 5. "FOSSE." This name, which still exists in this neighbourhood, was familiar to Penzance people in the first half of the present century through an artist—"little Tom Foss."

1679. June 27. "HERCULES PEDWELL." This name occurs also in the old Parish Register of St. Hilary.

1681. Mar. 27. "COVN MAKER." The Rev. William Tremenheere reads this *comb* maker.

1686. Dec. 12. "ADDAMA, daughter of Solomon Cock, of Golval."—See Appendix to Baptisms, 1686, Dec. 7. It would appear from this that the same child had been twice baptised—at Gulval on the 7th Dec., and then at Madron on the 12th; but the first may have been private baptism.

1674. Nov. 3. See Appendix to Marriages, 1671, Aug. 26.

1682-3. Mar. 11. "FENNE," *i.e.* Fynny.—See Burials, 1577, May 20, and Baptisms, 1600, May 15.

1699-1700. *N.B. The entries after this date have been as already mentioned chiefly embodied in the second book of the Registers, but certain variations and additions will be found there which are here noted.*

1699-1700. Mar. 11. "ANN," daughter of James Harry, *alias* Penreeth, baptised April 1.—See second book.

1700. Sept. 19. This is probably the date of birth. According to the second book baptism took place on the 18th Oct.

1700-1. Feb. 26. Baptised March 8.—See second book.

1701. April 7. Baptised April 21.—See second book.

    June 7. Agrees with entry in second book.

    Aug. 1. This entry not found in second book.

    Oct. 17. Not found in second book.

    Oct. 24. Agrees with entry in second book.

    Nov. 20. Probably date of birth. Baptised Dec. 1.—See second book.

1702. April 21. Entered as baptised on the 20th April in the second book, and Hamond is there written *Hamen*.

    July 24. This date agrees with that in second book, but, instead of Row, Chepy is entered, and this name has been re-written or re-touched.—See Note to Baptisms, 1705, July 7.

    Aug. 10. In the second book the date of baptism is Aug. 2, and John Davye is entered as of Penzance.

    Nov. 28. Agrees with entry in second book, in which Robart Harry, Jun., is entered as of Madron.

1703. May 24. Baptised June 3.—See second book.

    May 24. The entry in the second book is as follows:—"Ann, a base child of Magdalene Freind, of Scilly, baptised May 24, 1703."

    June 17. Baptised July 2; and Christopher Williams is entered as of Penzance.—See second book.

    Aug. 21. Date agrees. "THOMAS JAMES," the tanner, of Penzance.—See second book.

    Sept. 13. Date agrees. Hamond is entered as "*Hamen*, of Penzance," in the second book.

    Nov. 25. Baptised Nov. 29.—See second book.

    Nov. 30. This entry not found in second book.

1704. Aug. 8.	Agrees with entry in second book.	
1704-5. Feb. 2.	"ROBART HARRYE, JUN.," of Madron.—See second book.	
1705. July 7.	"WILLIAM ROW," *alias* Chepy.—See second book.	
Aug. 28.	The date of birth. Baptised Sept. 17.—See second book.	
Nov. 5.	This entry not found in second book.	
1705-6. Feb. 16.	Agrees with entry in second book.	
1707. Dec. 28.	Probably the date of birth. Baptised Dec. 29. "Matthew Hall" is entered as of Madron.—See second book.	
1724-5. Jan. 20.	This entry not found in second book.	
1726. July 18.	This entry not found in second book.	

Register of Marriages.

The letters which appear in a somewhat puzzling arrangement on either side of the title page to the Marriages in the original, form the following:—

GEORGIUS HUCHINS, in Artibus Magister, Predicator verbi Dei, et Vicarius Sancti Paterni.

1578. Aug. 4. "DOVE." Query Done, *i.e.* Dunn.

Aug. 10. "WEYMUOWTHE," certainly intended for Weymouth; but it is almost impossible to be exact in representing such a word as this, for the strokes of *m*, *n*, and *u* being all alike, and without any division between the letters, it might be read in several ways. Perhaps the design was to have written *Weymmowethe*, but one of the strokes of the double letter was omitted.

1581. April 10. "NEALE." Clearly so written but perhaps intended for Noall, *i.e.* Nowell.

Nov. 5. "ROWAN." Query a christian or surname.—See Baptisms, 1598-9, March 18.

1584. Oct. 11. "SISELIE." The Rev. William Tremenheere in his MS. copy of the Register frequently writes this name "Grislie," and Miss Yonge in her work on Christian Names quotes this as a curious name, evidently having referred to the copy of the Register mentioned.

1587. June 5. "CAREW."—See Baptisms, 1638, March 18.

June 12. "DADOWE."—See Baptisms, 1605-6, Feb. 23.

Nov. 19. "OLERE." This is undoubtedly *Clere*, and does not stand for *Clericus*.—See Burials, 1585, June 28, and 1604, June 2.

1588. Oct. 19. "JOHN COWLINGE," or Cowlin, of Trengwainton, and Alice, daughter of John "Parmere" (Query Palmer), of "Sunner," *i.e.* Zennor, his second wife.—See *Visitation of Cornwall*, 1620.—See Marriages, 1605, June 10.

1598-9. Jan. 22. "SYSE," pronounced *Seese*.—See Marriages, 1608, March 28.

1600. Nov. 23. "GELES," *i.e.* Giles.—See Baptisms, 1606-7, Jan. 25.

1601-2. Feb. 16. " + + " The reason for these crosses being on either side of this entry does not appear.

1602. May 25. "ANBROSE," or Ambrose. *N* and *m* are frequently interchanged in such names, as Anbone, &c.

1605. June 10. "GARTERED," *i.e.* Gertrude, daughter of John Cowlinge, or Cowlin, before mentioned, of Trengwainton, by Christian, daughter of Robert "Rosetor, of Kestenton," *i.e.* Coustantine, his first wife.—See *Visitation of Cornwall*, 1620.—See Marriages, 1588, Oct. 19.

NOTES.

1607. July 5. "Mr. ROGER POLKINHORNE," of Penzance, and Grace, daughter of John Cossen, alias Maddern, of Penzance, 30 years of age in 1620.—See *Herald's Visitation of Cornwall*, 1620.

July 6. "Mr. JOHN CLIES," of Penzance, who is commemorated on a brass in Madron Church.—See p. 76. A branch of the Trevanion family resided in this Parish, and Hugh Trevanion, Esq., is mentioned in the Charter of Penzance, dated 1614, as is also Mr. John Clies. The Trevanions had probably intermarried with the Madderns since their arms *(arg. on a fesse between two chevrons gu. three escallops or)*, though without blazon, appear on the monument of the latter family.—See p. 75.

1608. Mar. 28. "SEESE."—See Marriages, 1598-9, Jan. 22.

1615. Sept. 25. "FRANCIS." In the *Herald's Visitation of Cornwall*, 1620, Christian and Alice are given as the names of the wives of John Cowlinge, whose son John by the second wife was then 20 years of age.—See Marriages, 1604, May 16; 1605, June 10; and 1628-9, Jan. 5.

1624. Sept. 25. "MADREN CHAMPEN," or Champion.—See Baptisms, 1598, Feb. 12. CHESTEN, daughter of Sampson Noye and Jane.—See Marriages, 1587, July 22; Baptisms, 1600, Dec. 24, and 1626, June 21.

1628-9. Jan. 5. See Marriages, 1615, Sept. 25; and Marriages, 1605, June 10.

1646. Nov. 30. "GRACE," daughter of Thomas Fleming.—See Baptisms, 1602, Dec. 7.

1649. Nov. 17. "JAQUILINA," daughter of Alexander Daniel, of Lariggan. "1649, Nov. 17, my daughter Jaquilina was married to Wm. Paynter, ye son of Richd. and Honor P. his wife."— See Daniel MSS.

1650. It will be noticed that Marriages are fewer in proportion during the time of the Commonwealth. This is to be accounted for in a great measure by the fact that Marriage was then regarded more especially as a civil contract, and could be legally celebrated elsewhere than in the Parish Church.

1653. By an Act of the Commons, passed 24th August, 1653, Marriages were solemnized by Justices of the Peace. In Parish Registers at this time it is not uncommon to find such an entry as the following, which occurs in the first book of those of the Parish mentioned :—

"Paul Parish.

"Wee whose names are subscribed doe think Wm. Badcock to bee a fit man for our prish to be regrstar, and wee desire your approbation in it.

"Martin Keigwin.   Nic. Boson.   William Harry.
"Wm. Keigwin.   Richard Tremearne.   John Huchens.
"William Boson.   Edward Tonkin.   John Harry.
"Js. Marack.

"Redruth, 2th 9ber, 1653.   Sworne and allowed by   P. Ceeley.   Ja. Daniell."

This was in consequence of an Act passed during the administration of Cromwell, directing that Parish Registers should be placed in better hands than those of the Clergy; and frequently they were given over to some village tradesman whose chief recommendation to the office was perhaps the zeal he had shown in the destruction of the ancient registers.*

It does not appear, however, that the Register Book at Madron changed hands: there is no such entry as the above, nor does the writing during the time of the Commonwealth differ from that which immediately precedes and follows. The only alteration is that the date of Birth is registered instead of the date of Baptism.

1653. Dec. 17. "JOHN BLUNT." A farthing token was issued in Penzance by a person of this name. It bore on the obverse JOHN · BLVNT *three lions rampant regardant*, 2 and 1; on the reverse IN · PENZANCE · 1665 · 1 · I · B ·

---

* Sim's *Manual for the Genealogist, Topographer, and Antiquary*, p. 352.

"1665. Dec. 7. My son Eliasaph was married to Jane Penrose, ye daughter of J. Penrose, Esq., at Maddren."—See Daniel MSS. It does not appear that this marriage was ever registered; there happens to be a blank about this time, no entries having been made in the Register after the 25th June, 1665, until the early part of the following year.

Register of Burials.

1577. May 20. "FYNNY, FYNNIE." In this, the earliest entry in the Madron Register, occurs an instance of a surname being differently spelt in the same line; not a very unusual circumstance, by the way, nor perhaps in all cases accidental, since it was formerly common, especially among the wealthier classes, to spell a surname in as many different ways as possible in the same document.

1578. June 7. A plague or fatal sickness appears to have commenced about this time, and prevailed during several months. It will be noticed that whole families seem to have been swept away in some instances.

July 7. "ELIZABETH, quædam, morbo convitiali laborans." Does this simply mean that the deceased laboured under a disease of reproach? Do these words in any way refer to the plague which had just commenced, or did some priest, with more wit than reverence for Parish Registers—finding the line unfinished—complete it with the words in italics, inferring that the deceased Elizabeth had been a scold, and was suffering at the time of her death from the scolding disease instead of the "*morbus comitialis;*" but was there such a disease as "*morbus convitialis?*"—See *Notes & Queries*, vol. iii., p. 128, fifth series.

1585. June 28. "HARBYE, *alias* CLEARE." This explains other entries.—See Marriages, 1587, Nov. 19, and Burials, 1604, June 2. The extreme north-west of Penzance is known as St. Clare, or Chapel St. Clare; a chapel dedicated to that saint having formerly stood near the high road to Madron where it crosses the borough boundary.—See p. 87.

1595. July 23. It is worthy of note that through the Spaniards on this unlucky day an ancient Cornish prophecy became fulfilled. It was—

"Ewra teyro a war meano Merlyn
Ara Lesky Pawle, Pensanz, ha Newlyn;"

which may be translated—

"There shall land on the rock of Merlyn
Those that shall burn Paul, Penzance, and Newlyn."

Possibly the gap which occurs in the Parish Registers of Madron at this time is more or less due to the marauding invaders; at least the fact of there being no Registers of Baptisms, Marriages, or Burials for the year 1595 is suggestive. That the Spaniards destroyed much valuable property in this neighbourhood is certain: they set fire to many houses on the day mentioned, and returned to their galleys intending to land again on the following day, but were prevented from doing so; for the old prophecy having been fulfilled, they were driven from these shores by the inhabitants. The first book of the Registers of the Parish of Paul commences with the following:—

"Pawle Register.   Jesu spes et Salus nra.   1595.

"A Register of the names of all those that were Baptized, Married, or Buried in the Prish "of St. Pawle, in the Countie of Cornwall, from the 23rd daye of Julie, in the yeare of our Lord "God 1595, on the wh. daie the Church Towre, Bells, and all other things pertaining to the same, "together with the houses and goods, was burn'd and spoil'd by the Spaniards in the saide Prish, "beinge Wensdaie, the daie aforesaide, in the 37th yeare of the reign of our Sovereigne Ladie "Elizabeth, by the grace of God of England, France, and Ireland, Queen, Defender of the Faith, &c.

"Per me Johnem Tremearne, Vicarium ejus."

In the same book, the first entry in the Register of Burials is—

"Jenken Keigwin, of Mowsholl, being kild by the Spaniards, was buried the 24th July, 1595."

NOTES.

1600-1. Feb. 1. "RAPHE HARBERTE."—See p. 85.

1601. July 20. "BLAUNCHE."—See Baptisms, 1594, Aug. 27. The christian names are clearly different, but it must be remembered that this portion of the Register is a transcript, and inaccuracies as to a letter or so might easily creep in.

Dec. 9. "COX," or Cock.—See Fleming monument, p. 76.

1602. April 4. "JENYE MY FRINDE." Query Anhoy.—See Burials, 1597-8, Feb. 27.

1604. June 2. "CLERE."—See Baptisms, 1587, Nov. 19; Marriages, 1587, Nov. 19.

1605. Dec. 10. "COZEN." This surname, variously spelt, occurs several times in these Registers. A family named Cossen, *alias* Maddern, resided at Penzance at the time of the Herald's Visitation, 1620.

1610-11. Jan. 5. "MISTRIS ALSE COCKE."—See Fleming monument, p. 76.

1614. Oct. 6. "LAUNCE," *i.e.* Launcelot.

1623. Nov. 29. "JOHN CLIES, GENT." One of those chiefly instrumental in procuring the Charter for Penzance in 1614, a member of the original Corporation, and an early Mayor of that Town.—See Marriages, 1607, July 6; Clies monument, p. 76.

1632. Nov. 18. "JACOB DANIELL." "Nov. 5. My son Jacob died at Penzance, in K. Colan's house, aged 3 y. and almost a ¼, buried in Madr. Chur. 1632."—See Daniel MSS.

1641. April 5. "JOHN TRELILL." Possibly this is the person to whom Bishop Hall, of Exeter, alludes in his *Devotional Works*, vol. vi., p. 465. Speaking of the invisible world and the insensible helps of good spirits, he says, "Of this kind was that no less than miraculous cure which, at St. Maderne's, in Cornwall, was wrought upon a poor cripple (one John Trelill); whereof, besides the attestation of many hundreds of the neighbours, I took a strict and personal examination, in that last Visitation (at Whitsuntide) which I either did or ever shall hold. This man, that for sixteen years together was fain to walk upon his hands, by reason of the close contraction of the sinews of his legs, was, upon three monitions in his dream to wash in that well, suddenly so restored to his limbs that I saw him able both to walk and get his own maintenance. I found here was neither art nor collusion: the thing done, the author invisible."

1642. June 28. "ISACK NEWTON, CLERKE," Curate of Morvah.—See p. 85.

1647. Oct. 17. "Mr. JOHN KETE, VICAR."—See p. 85.

1660-1. Jan. 28. "FRANCES."—See Marriages, 1615, Sept. 25, and 1628-9, Jan. 5.

1661. Aug. 21. "JOHN DANIELL," son of Alexander Daniel, of Lariggan, died 19th Aug.—See p. 95.

1674. Sept. 15. "Mrs. BLANCH BONITHAN." Among the communion plate at St. Mary's Church, Penzance, there is "one chalice of silver, weighing twelve ounces and half and half quarter, with this inscription:—Ex dono Blanchæ Bonithon Viduæ Sacello Penzantiensi Collato 1670;" and "two salvers of silver, weighing nine ounces and half and half quarter,—one of them marked with the letters B. B."—See Terrier for the Parish of Madron, Morvah, and Penzance, dated 1st May, 1746.

1677. July 9. "Mr. REGINALD TRENHAYLE, VICAR."—See p. 85. In the Westminster Abbey Registers, *Harleian Society's Publications*, 1876, p. 247, the following will be found:—"Burials, 1700, Sept. 23, Mr. Reginald Trenhayle, in the south cloister, near the west end thereof."

1677-8. Feb. 8. "Mrs. GRACE DANIELL," widow of Alexander Daniel, of Lariggan. She appears to have died on the same day according to an entry in a different hand in the Daniel MSS., *Brief Chronological Observations*, which is—"Feb. 8. My mother Grace Daniell departed this life 1677."

Index.

Names of Persons.

A full stop (.) following a figure indicates the first column, and a colon (:) the second, in the page referred to. *Surnames* are here spelt as in the Register, and the various ways of spelling the same name are given, with a reference to the page where the variation first occurs. With regard to the *christian names* the intention has been, as far as possible, to spell them according to the most usual manner. Names occurring in the Notes and Appendix are distinguished by italics.

ABBOTT 43:
   Joan 43:
   Thomas 43: 44:
Acton, alias Bechamp, 84.
   Richard 84.
ADAMS 45: ADDAM 53.
   Ann 65.
   Cicely 53.
   Thomas 45:
AGEARE 43.
   Elizabeth 43.
ALEXANDER 32: ALLEXANDER 45.
   Alice 49.
   Elizabeth 58:
   Jane 32: 32: 52.
   Richard 32: 32: 49. 52.
   Saundry 45.
ALFORDE 31:
   John 31:
   Margaret 31:
ALGER 5: ALGAR 49. ALLGER 45:
   Agnes 50:
   Alexander 5: 49.
   Charity 50.
   Mary 45:
   Nowell 50.
   William 5: 45: 49. 50:
ALLEN 50. ALLAN 38. ALLYN 57.
   Ann 50: 57.
   Elizabeth 38.
   Henry 50. 50:
   Thomas 38.
Alley 85.
   William 85.
Althorpe 85.
   Richard Roberd de 85.
Alward 83.
AMBELL 7. AMBLE 33.
   Ann 33.
   Jane 50:
   Joan 7.

   John 7. 7: 7: 33. 50:
AMBROSE 4: ANDROSE 32:
   Elizabeth 4:
   John 4: 5: 32: 49: 50:
   Margery 32:
   ——— 5:
AMMEARE 3: AMEARE 5. AMMEAR 31:
   alias JAMES 5.
   English 31:
   John 5.
   Richard 3: 5. 31:
   William 3:
AMYE 13. See Anny.
   Elizabeth 13. 13.
AMYS 30. AMES 46: *alias* ASH 51.
   Jane 30.
   John 45. 46:
   Richard 45. 46: 46: 51.
ANBONE 1. AMBONE 4: See Bone.
   Bennet 1. 59.
   Edward 62.
   Eleanor 38.
   Elizabeth 4: 60.
   Jane 44:
   Joan 32: 61.
   John 6: 17: 38. 38. 57: 60. 62. 63.
   Maderne 1. 56:
   Mary 57:
   Noye 32:
   Paschas 38.
   Peter 4: 17:
   Philippa 62:
   Richard 7:
   Susan 31: 48:
   Thomas 3. 3. 4: 31: 43: 48:
      (Margaret, his servant, 43:)
   Thomasine 62.
   William 4: 6: 7: 44: 48: 50: 58.
   . . . . 59. 59.

ANBROSE 97. See Ambrose.
ANDERTON 26:
   Jaquito 26:
   Richard 26:
ANDRYLLIER 3.
   Richard 3.
   Thomas 3.
ANGEARE 54.
   Thomasine 54.
ANGOSSE 42.
   James 42.
   John 42.
ANOOVE 3. *alias* THOMAS 7:
   Bennet 44:
   Edward 47.
   Elizabeth 3.
   James 3. 30. 44.
   Jane 38. 62.
   Joan 30. 60.
   Nicholas 7:
   Ponticoste 42:
   Robert 42:
   William 38. 60. 62.
   ——— 7:
ANGWIN 37. ANGWINE 12. ANGWYN 35.
   Agnes 60.
   Alice 12. 39. 54:
   Andrew 39.
   Bennet 12. 35. 54:
   Grace 37. 66:
   Jane 35.
   John 60. 73:
   Richard 37.
ANHAYE 3. ANHEY 47.
   Eme 47.
   Jenny 3. 47.
   William 3.
ANKOW *alias* HARRIES 57:
   William 57:
ANNY 66. See Amye.

z

INDEX.

Elizabeth 66.
ANTHONY 22: ANTHONYE 42:
  ANTONY 34. ANTONYE 12.
Agnes 32.
Alice 42: 65:
Amy 60;
Ann 47.
Henry 43:
Jane 30.
John 10: 11: 30. 32. 48.
Margaret 71.
Mary 10. 16: 19. 63.
Philippa 34.
Prudence 4.
Ralph 34.
Richard 12.
Stephen 42: 42:
Thomasine 61.
Wilmot 22:
William 10. 10: 11. 11. 11:
  12. 16: 19. 22: 43: 43:
  47. 61. 63. 65: 71.
——— 43:
ARGALL 2. ARGOLL 8. *alias*
  CARPENTER 45:
Agnes 31.
Alice 38.
Ann 5: 10. 10: 17. 33: 55. 60:
Catherine 34. 49.
Charity 32:
Cheston 17:
Elizabeth 18. 33:
Hugh 29. 45.
James 6. 45.
Jane 9:
Joan 3. 29. 30: 45. 48. 51.
  51:
John 20: 30: 45: 59.
Mary 8:
Nowell 5: 8. 8: 9. 9: 10. 10:
  11: 32: 33: 51: 55. 59.
Olsett 29.
Philip 17. 17: 18. 38. 60: 63.
Richard 8: 11:
Sampson 8. 51:
Thomas 2. 3. 8: 9. 29. 33:
  34. 48. 51:
William 2. 3: 3: 6. 20: 29.
  31. 47: 47: 49.
ARNOLDE 45:
John 45:
ARTHUR 19.
Nicholas 83. 84.
Philip 19. 19.
Arundell 71:
  Ann 71:
  Dorothy 77.
  Francis 77.
  John 84.

ASH 51. *alias* AMES 51.
Hercules 55: 56.
Margaret 55:
Richard 51.
Ashton 71.
  Roger 71.
ASKOT 31.
Mary 31.
William 31.
ASYE 42:
Amy 43.
Christopher 42: 43.
ATKYNS 30.
Elizabeth 30.
John 30.
AVERY 35:
Eleanor 63:
Ellen 35:
Henry 35:
BABELL 32.
Jane 32.
Roger 32.
BADCOCK 19.
John 19. 19. 63. 63.
William 98.
BAGG 9. BAGGS 9:
Christian 62.
Elizabeth 34. 52:
Hugh 62.
Margaret 9:
Thomas 9. 9. 9: 34. 52: 53:
BALE 6: BAYLE 26.
Agnes 6:
Andrew 6:
Elizabeth 26.
John 27.
Samuel 26. 27.
BALIFFE 50:
BANFIELD 15: BANFEILD 59:
Eleanor 15:
John 59:
Richard 15:
BARAGWANATH 6. BARAGWANNATHE
  45.
John 6.
Thomas 45.
——— 6.
BARBER 1.
Agnes 1. 45:
Ann 59.
Barnard 43.
Catherine 42: 43.
Elizabeth 7: 12:
Helen 42:
Jane 47.
John 42: 45: 45: 47. 49:
Margaret 45:
Richard 12:.

Robert 1.
Sampson 42: 42: 42: 42 :
Stephen 7:
Thomas 43: 55. 57.
BARLEIGHE 43.
Alice 43.
BARNARD 1.
Philippa 1.
Thomas 1.
BARNELL 33:
Clarence 33:
James 33:
BARNES 13: BARNE 7: BARNS 22.
Amy 23.
Ann 13: 17: 36: 61. 62. 64.
Anquite 22:
Catherine 9.
Elizabeth 11. 67.
Frances 7: 36:
Henry 57:
Isabel 16.
James 21:
Jane 16: 22.
John 8. 10. 13: 13: 15. 16.
  16: 16: 17: 20. 20. 21. 21:
  22. 22: 23. 36: 39. 43. 57.
  59. 59: 61. 62. 65. 65.
Margaret 15. 59.
Mary 16: 57. 59: 65.
Pascoe 7: 8. 9. 10. 11. 33: 54.
Thomasine 39.
Ursula 33: 60.
William 21. 43. 65.
BARNICOTT 42. BARNYCOTE 3.
  BARNYCOTTE 48.
Catherine 4.
Jane 3.
John 3. 4. 48.
William 42. 42.
BARTELL 56.
Elizabeth 56.
BARTLET 6.
Elizabeth 49:
Giles 6. 32. 49:
Joan 6. 49:
Lucy 32.
Thomas 49:
BASELEY 56. BASSLYE 35. BASLYE 53.
Grace 35.
Joseph 35. 53. 53. 56.
Richard 53.
——— 53.
BASSETT 43.
Agnes 43.
John 43.
BASTIAN 31:
Mary 31:
Richard 31:
BATHE 42.

INDEX.

Maud 42.
William 42. 44.
BATTEN 12. BATTYN 11. BATYN 15.
 BETTEN 36:
 Alice 71.
 Blanch 16. 59;
 Elizabeth 13. 34. 39.
 Grace 36;
 Jane 72.
 John 12. 12; 13. 14. 15. 16.
  20. 22; 22; 37. 54; 55. 59;
  59; 60; 69; 70. 71. 80. 80.
 Margaret 12; 14. 15. 54; 55.
  71:
 Mary 12.
 Maud 37.
 Nicholas 70. 72. 72.
 Ralph 20. 39.
 Richard 72.
 Sampson 11.
 Susan 72.
 William 11. 15. 15. 34.
BAUDE 4.
 Ann 4. 6;
 Elizabeth 4.
 Jane 6;
 Nan 6;
BAWDEN 4. BOWDEN 5. BOODEN 7;
 BODEN 49. BOUDEN 56.
 Ann 7;
 Elizabeth 37.
 Florence 32.
 Francis 56.
 Jane 5. 49.
 Joan 4. 49.
 John 37.
 Nicholas 6; 50.
 Orpheus 7;
 Prudence 6.
 Richard 49.
 Thomas 4. 5. 6. 6. 6; 7; 32.
  49. 49; 50.
 William 6. 49;
BAYNARD 17. *Bainard* 72.
 Avis 72.
 Dorothy 64.
 Grace 17.
 Jane 17; 61; 71;
 Thomas 17. 17; 18; 18; 61;
  64.
 William 71; 72.
BAZAW 35.
 Catherine 35.
 Walter 35.
BEAGOE 56. *alias* PEARS 56.
 Catherine 56.
BEARD 19;
 Elizabeth 20;
 Hannah 28;

Joan 20.
Joseph 28; 28;
Ralph 19; 19; 20. 20; 65;
Samuel 65;
Susannah 28;
Bechamp 84. *Beachym* 88. *alias*
 Acton 84.
 John 88.
 Richard 84.
BECKERLEGG 23; BECCALEGGE 10;
 BECALEGG 9. BECARLECK 60.
 BECALEGGE 33; BECCALEGG 36.
 Charles 23; 26. 26; 26; 26;
  27. 27. 27;
 Elisha 23;
 Henry 26.
 Honor 27.
 Joan 36.
 Mary 10; 26;
 Oliver 27;
 Thomas 9. 10; 33; 36. 60. 73;
 William 9. 27.
BEECUM 52.
 Ralph 52.
BEGGOW 64; BEGOE 48; *alias*
 GEORGE 48;
 English 64;
 John 48;
BELL 1.
 Alice 30.
 Ann 1.
 Catherine 31;
 Emanuel 1. 31;
 Lodovicke 42.
 Robert 45;
 Roger 45;
 Sampson 30. 45;
 Tyrracke 42;
BELLAMYE 12; BALLAMYE 35;
 Jane 35;
 Joseph 12;
 William 12; 35;
Bellott 85. *Billott* 74.
 Thomas 74. 85.
BELPIT 30.
 Catherine 30.
 Samuel 30.
BENALLACK 13.
 John 13.
 Launcelot 13.
BENMER 11;
 John 11; 11; 60. 62; 62;
 Joseph 25. 63.
 Mary 19?
 Nicholas 11;
 Othniel 19; 20; 25.
 Rebecca 18;
 Salamy 63;
 Solomon 11; 20; 64.

Thomas 18; 61; 61; 62;
BENNE 33; BENNY 60.
 Elizabeth 33; 60.
 Robert 33;
BENNETTS 22; DENNET 43. BENET 42.
 BENNATT 16; BENNATTS 18.
 BENNETT 2. *Bennets* 71. *alias*
 HARRIE 4;
 Agnes 17. 58;
 Alexander 2. 9. 9. 9; 10.
 Alice 8;
 Ann 10; 22; 35. 38.
 Avis 4; 60.
 Benjamin 24;
 Bennet 58;
 Blanch 55;
 Bridget 64. 64;
 Catherine 69;
 Charity 23.
 Christian 13; 44.
 Cyprian 31.
 Dorothy 39.
 Edward 10;
 Elizabeth 31. 36. 42. 52;
 Ellis 36.
 Frances 65;
 Francis 5. 50. 69;
 Henry 4; 48;
 Honor 20.
 James 18. 19; 20. 20. 21; 21;
  24; 64. 64; 65; 65; 67.
 Jane 9. 21; 31; 32; 49; 53;
  58; 71;
 Jennet 45.
 Joan 3. 17. 23; 35. 38. 42. 48.
 John 6; 9. 9; 13; 16; 16; 17.
  20. 20. 38. 39. 43. 43. 45.
  60; 64; 69;
 Lewis 17. 38.
 Lydia 19;
 Margaret 6; 71.
 Margery 23.
 Mary 10. 18. 39. 66;
 Philippa 17.
 Ralph 52; 52;
 Richard 2. 2. 2; 2; 3. 4; 4;
  6; 8; 9. 9; 31; 35. 48. 48;
  49; 53; 54. 54; 73.
 Robert 13; 21; 23. 24. 24.
 Simon 9.
 Thomas 2. 2; 20. 39. 55; 58;
  58; 66; 69;
 William 5. 6; 8; 8; 9; 22; 23.
  23; 32; 35. 50. 54. 54. 54.
  ....54.
BENTLETT 52.
 John 52.
BENVER 10.
 Gregory 55.

INDEX.

John 10. 12. 13. 13. 34: 55.
Joseph 12.
Rebecca 34:
Thomas 10. 67. 67.
Berkeley 83.
BERRIMAN 63. BERYMAN 56:
John 56: 63.
Lucy 56:
Betts 88.
Thomas 88. 89.
BEWFORDE 31:
John 31:
Mary 31:
BIGGS 23.
John 23.
Warner 23.
BILLEN 2: BELLYN 49.
Agnes 30.
Catherine 49.
David 47.
Henry 2: 48.
Sybell 52.
Teage 2: 30. 48. 49. 49.
BISHOPP 13. *Bishop* 86.
Cicely 14.
Gilbert 13. 13. 14.
John 86.
Richard 34. 52:
Thomasine 34.
Biskay 72:
Elizabeth 72:
BLACHFORD 53. BLECHFORD 55:
Joan 55:
William 53.
BLACKE 29. BLACK 30. BLACHE 32:
Blake 71.
Amy 71.
Christian 44.
Edward 30. 45.
Francis 71.
Jane 29. 32:
Joan 30.
William 32:
Blackamore, The, 65:
Martin 65:
BLAGROWE 45:
Simon 45:
BLAUNCHE 48.
Agnes 48.
BLA..CH 2:
Agath 2:
....2:
BLAZERIS 14:
John 14:
Martha 14:
BLECHFORD, See BLACHFORD.
BLEWETT, See BLUET.
BLIGHE 2. BLIGH 46.
Elizabeth 2. 46.

William 2. 46.
BLUET 5: BLEWETT 8. BLEWET 13.
BLEWATT 16. BLUETT 8:
Blanch 8.
Dinah 10: 53:
Elizabeth 7. 23.
Emanuel 5: 7. 8. 8: 9. 10:
32: 49. 52. 53:
Frances 8:
Garthorod 21: 32: 61: 65:
George 10: 10: 13. 16. 21: 22.
22. 23. 23: 24: 37: 57: 59.
65: 66.
Jane 16. 57:
John 5: 24: 49.
Margaret 37: 59.
Mary 23: 63.
Thomas 9. 13. 52.
BLUNT 38.
Joan 38.
John 38. 98.
Blynde man, The, 44:
Teage 44:
BOASE 15. BOWES 1. BOES 6. BOSE
13. Bossy 41. BOAS 52. *alias*
GYMDALE 48.
Agnes 45:
Ann 18: 37: 63. 67:
Arthur 21: 71:
Blanch 52.
Catherine 63:
Charles 70:
Dinah 14. 56:
Edward 45:
Eleanor 56:
Elizabeth 6: 19: 54: 66.
Florence 31:
Gavrigan 6.
Jacob 19: 20.
Jane 15.
Janet 71:
Joan 41. 60.
John 25: 41. 55.
Joseph 13.
Margaret 9. 54:
Martin 26:
Mary 16. 34: 56. 58.
Peter 1. 15. 19. 48.
Ralph 54: 55.
Rawlen 70. 71:
Reginald 14. 34: 56. 56. 56:
56: 58. 58.
Richard 13. 31: 56.
Robert 73:
Roger 54:
Ruth 71: 73:
Sampson 70.
Thomas 1. 5. 8:
Tonken 18: 19: 20. 60. 74.

Ursula 43.
William 5. 6. 6: 8: 9. 16. 19.
19: 21: 22. 22 25: 26: 37:
43. 52. 67: 69. 69. 70:
BODENNAR 18. BODENNER 38:
BODENAR 30: BODYNAR 42.
alias NOY 30:
Beatrice 39:
Christopher 18. 38:
Henry 46.
Jenkin 39:
John 42.
Maderne 42.
Robert 30: 46.
Sarah 38:
Thomas 18. 42. 42.
Thomasine 30:
BODYE 2. BODDY 17. BODDYE 22.
BODIE 4:
Ann 16:
Charity 31. 56.
Christopher 16. 16: 17. 64:
Edward 16.
George 17.
Henry 23:
James 9: 55.
Jane 14.
Joan 14:
John 2. 5. 9: 14. 14: 21. 21.
22. 23. 23: 55. 55: 57: 62:
67.
Margaret 61:
Martin 57. 57.
Mary 55:
Nicholas 22. 67.
Rebecca 2:
Robert 57.
Susan 4:
Thomas 2. 2: 4. 4. 4: 5. 6:
14. 31. 53.
Thomasine 6:
William 23.
BOES, See BOASE.
BOLITHOE 37: *Bolitho* 80.
Edward 80.
John 73.
Mary 73.
Philippa 37:
Richard 37:
BOLLENOWE 47.
George 47.
———— 47.
BOLLOCK, See BULLOCK.
BOND 12: *alias* SYNKOW 58:
Ann 57.
Blanch 14:
Jane 35:
John 58:
Margaret 12:

INDEX. 105

Thomas 12; 14; 35;
BONE 3; See ANBONE
  Ann 54:
  Bennet 10.
  Edward 7; 8. 33;
  Elizabeth 33; 44.
  James 5;
  Joan 30;
  John 3; 9; 10. 33; 44. 54;
  Maderne 30;
  Margaret 44.
  Mary 8.
  Susan 3;
  Richard 52.
  Thomas 7;
  Thomasine 33;
  William 5; 9; 44. 51; 52.
  (Jane, his servant, 51;)
BONETTOW 25; BONETTO 26.
  Catherine 26.
  Elizabeth 25;
  John 25; 26. 26. 26; 26;
  William 26.
BONITHON 10. BONITHAN 65.
  Blanch 65. 100.
  Grace 10. 57.
  James 10.
  Joan 14; 57.
  Thomas 14; 57. 57.
  William 57.
BONNSYE 47;
  Margery 47;
  Richard 47;
BORCH, See BURCH.
BORLASE 27. BURLACE 62;
  Ann 71. 86.
  Catherine 82.
  John 72. 78. 79. 79. 80. 86.
  Lydia 70; 72. 78. 79.
  Margaret 62; 70; 72; 79.
  Mary 70;
  Samuel 80. 80.
  Walter 70; 70; 70; 72; 78.
    79. 82. 86.
  William 27. (Dr. 79.) 80. 86. 86.
BOSAVERN 13. BUSSAVORNE 44.
  BOSSAVERNE 1. BOSAVERNE 7;
  BOSAVARNE 33;
  Ann 35; 64;
  Clarence 8.
  Elizabeth 34; 57.
  James 1. 31. 93.
  Joan 31.
  John 10. 34; 44.
  Margaret 12; 33;
  Margery 10.
  Martin 7; 12. 12. 12; 13. 35;
    57. 57. 57. 64;
  Richard 44.

Walter 7; 8. 13. 33; 51;
  .... 1.
BOSCENCE 34; BOSSENCE 36.
  Clarence 34;
  Earth 36.
  Richard 34; 53;
  Sampson 36.
BOSE, See BOASE.
BOSEKARNE 57;
  Amy 57;
BOSHOBER 29.
  Hellynor 29.
BOSKENING 51. BOSKENNINGE 2;
  BUSKEYNING 1. BOSKENEN 19.
  BUSKENING 2. BUSKENNING 32.
  BOSKENNEN 59; BUSKENINGE
    3. BOSKENINGE 10. BUSKENNEN
    17. BOSEKENNEN 16; *Boskeyning*
    69. BUSKENNINGE 47;
  Agnes 48;
  Ann 16; 33; 37; 55; 59; 61;
  Elizabeth 2. 17. 47;
  Emanuel 69.
  Frances 18.
  Henry 3.
  Jane 32. 50.
  Joan 17; 31. 58;
  Jodua 48;
  John 1. 2. 10. 16; 17. 17; 18.
    19. 31. 32. 47; 48; 50. 51.
    52. 59;
  Mary 3.
  Mathew 1.
  Richard 69.
  Thomas 2;
  Thomasine 69.
  William 10. 19. 33; 37; 55;
    61; 64. 69. 69. 69.
  ——— 2;
BOSON 25;
  Amy 26.
  Bathrem 25; 26. 26. 26.
  Jonathan 26.
  Julian 25;
  Nicholas 98.
  William 98.
BOSORE, See BUSSOORE.
BOSSAVA 42;
  Henry 49;
  John 42;
  Mellyor 49;
BOSSOLLACK 7.
  Margaret 7.
  Thomas 7.
BOSSY 41. See BOASE.
  Joan 41.
  John 41.
BOSVINE 5;
  John 5; 49.

——— 5; 49.
BOSWARRACK 65; BOSEWARRACK 15.
  Alice 15. 59.
  Jane 65;
  John 59. 59.
  Nicholas 15.
BOSWARTHEN 46; BUSWARTHEN 2;
  Elizabeth 2; 46;
  George 2;
  Jane 44;
  John 44.
  Sampson 2; 46;
BOSWATHACK 8. BUSWATHACK 6;
  Alice 36.
  Jane 12;
  Joan 6;
  John 6; 8. 8; 10. 13; 50.
  Nicholas 8. 12; 13; 36.
  Reynauld 10.
  Robert 8;
  William 50.
BOSWEDNAN, See BUSWEDNAN.
BOWES, See BOASE.
• *Bown* 91.
  Peter 91. 92.
Box 14;
  Edward 14; 58.
  Mildren 14; 60.
BOYER 30;
  Catherine 30; 31;
  Petherick 30; 31; 45;
  William 45;
Bramble 71; BREMBLE 21;
  Grace 21; 71;
  Jane 71;
  John 21;
  Martin 71;
BRATHERIE 17. BRATHERY 62.
  BRATCHERIE 37;
  Blanch 37;
  Stephen 17.
  William 17; 37; 62.
Bray 73; *Brey* 73.
  John 73. 73;
BREACH 1.
  Mary 31;
  Ralph 1.
  Richard 1. 31;
BREMBLE, See BRAMBLE.
BRITTAYNE 43; Britton, The, 44;
  BRITTON 45;
  Elizabeth 44;
  Jane 43;
  Joan 45;
  John 43; 45;
  Oliver 44;
  Peres 47.
BROCKHURST 1. BROCKHURSTE 47;
  BROCKEHURSTE 2;

A A

Joan 46:
John 1. 2. 2; 3; 31; 47; 47:
Margaret 31:
Simon 2:
William 1. 3:
.... 2.
BROKER 5.
John 5. 46;
Simon 46:
Walter 5.
BROMWELL 18. BROMEWELL 38;
See BRAMBLE.
Ann 26:
Constance 38;
Elizabeth 26.
Grace 18. 27.
John 18. 19. 21. 38;
Martin 19. 21.
Walter 26. 26; 27. 27; 27;
Bronescombe, Bishop, 83.
BROWN 23; BROWNE 24;
Michael 24; 24; 65; 65;
Vernon 24; 24; 65;
Wilmot 23;
William 23; 65;
BRUSH 22; BRUSHE 43.
John 43.
Thomas 22; 22; 66;
BUCKLER 12;
Richard 12; 12;
Bullock 73; BOLLOCK 26;
Ann 73;
John 26; 26;
Richard 73;
BURCH 12; BORCH 67.
Arthur 83.
Digory 22; 67.
Grace 24;
Nicholas 12;
Philip 69.
Thomas 12; 20. 20; 20; 22;
24; 67. 69.
Winifred 20.
Burdet 84.
John 84.
Burghley 88.
William, Lord, 88. 89.
BURLACE, See BORLASE.
BURNOWE 2; BURNOW 32.
Alice 32.
Cyprian 62; 62;
Jane 46;
John 62;
Margaret 62;
Ralph 46;
Rebecca 2;
Thomas 2; 32. 46;
BURROWS 65; BURROES 13;
Edward 13;

Mary 65;
Thomas 13;
BURYAN 10;
John 10;
William 10;
A poor man of, 54.
BUSKENING, See BOSKENING.
BUSSOORE 45.
John 45.
BUSWARTHEN, See BOSWARTHEN.
BUSWATHACK, See BOSWATHACK.
BUSWEDNAN 43.
Sampson 43.
BUTTAMORE 33; BUTTEMORE 8.
Jane 8.
Jellian 33;
Thomas 8. 33;
BUTTLER 43;
John 43;
BYCKHAM 4. BYKHAM 2. BICKAM 4;
Agnes 54.
Alexander 3.
Elizabeth 2.
John 4. 48.
Ralph 2. 3. 4. 4; 4; 48.

CALENSO 27. CALLYNSOWE 44;
CULENSOE 36. CALENSOWE 8
CALENZOE 13. CALENSOW 21;
CALLENZEOW 14. CALLENSOW
15. *Calinsow* 71;
Ann 64.
Bridget 71;
Catherine 36.
Edward 21;
Eleanor 25.
James 14.
Jane 8. 49; 53.
Jemima 26;
Joan 20. 63;
John 25. 27. 44; 71;
Margaret 14;
Mary 26.
Nicholas 22;
Patience 23.
Philippa 16.
Priscilla 66;
Robert 25.
Thomas 8. 13. 14. 14; 15. 16.
21; 21; 21; 22; 23. 27.
36. 64. 66.
Ursula 14.
William 13. 20. 25. 26. 26;
63; 66. 66. 66;
———— 15. 66.
CALLAWAY 21. KALLWAY 57;
Abraham 21. 27; 27; 28;
Ann 21.
Jane 28;

Thomas 57;
CALLY 31; CALLYE 35. See KELLY.
Alice 31;
Elizabeth 48.
Jane 46.
Joan 35.
John 35.
Margaret 44.
William 31; 44. 46.
CALVENNYTH 46;
David 46;
Henry 46;
CAPTENN 48.
William 48.
Cara 72;
Elizabeth 72;
George 72;
CARDEWE 2; CARDEW 30;
Ann 59;
Annis 34;
Eleanor 30; 55.
Elizabeth 32;
Jane 63.
John 32; 49.
Ralph 2; 47.
Richard 34; 59;
Thomas 63. 63. 64;
Thomasine 63.
William 2; 30; 47. 55.
CAREW 30; KERROWE 13. KEROWE
30.
Elizabeth 30. 30;
John 13;
Richard 30. 30; 49;
Robert 13. 13.
Thomas 13;
CARGEASE 45. CARGEAS 45.
Margaret 45.
William 45.
Carket 86.
Nicholas 86.
Carleen 72.
Clement 72.
Margaret 72.
CARLYON 3.
Elizabeth 3.
———— 3.
CARNE 3; CARN 67;
Agnes 42.
Ann 10. 11. 36;
Blanch 36.
Catherine 3; 11; 15. 31;
Christian 42;
Elizabeth 4; 55;
Henry 57; 67;
James 86.
John 42.
Morish 15. 57; 67;
Pascoe 43;

INDEX. 107

Philip 7; 36.
Robert 10. 11. 11; 36; 55;
  62;
  Thomas 3; 4; 7; 31; 54.
CARPENTAR 25. CARPENTER 25;
  alias ARGALL 45;
  Cuthbert 42.
  Elizabeth 26.
  James 39. 64.
  Joan 39.
  John 26; 42. 45;
  Margaret 25. 64.
  Margery 25;
  Nicholas 42. 42. 42.
  Peter 25. 25; 26. 26;
CARPESACK 38.
  Jane 38.
  Richard 38.
CARTER 6; CHARTER 59.
  Arthur 6; 59.
  Elizabeth 6;
CARTHEWE 3.
  Marke 3. 3.
CARVANELL 30. CARVANNELL 46.
  Margaret 30.
  Philippa 46.
CARVETH 61; CARVARTH 60.
  CARVERTH 66;
  Blanch 61;
  Grace 61;
  John 71;
  Mary 71;
  Richard 60.
  Solomon 60. 61; 61; 66;
Carvosow 72.
  Jane 72.
  William 72.
CASWIN 65; *Coswin* 73;
  Elizabeth 73;
  Mr. 65;
CAUNTER 30.
  Florence 30.
  William 30.
CECIL, See SISSELL.
CEELY 59;
  Peter 98.
  William 59;
CHALWILL 32;
  Mary 32;
  Thomas 32;
CHAMBERLAINE 5; CHAMBERLYN 32.
  CHAMBERLEYNE 48.
  CHAMBERLEN 4;
  Agnes 31; 48.
  Ann 58;
  Jane 32.
  Joan 5;
  John 4; 5; 31; 32. 48. 50;
  Julian 64.

Luke 64.
Richard 4; 50;
Chambers 69;
  Dorothy 69;
  John 69;
CHAMPION 2. CHAMPTON 2. CHAMPEN
  8. CHAMPIAN 20;
  Agnes 42; 44.
  Alice 6. 43.
  Amy 47;
  Ann 8. 9;
  Benedict 38;
  Bennet 3; 18. 20; 44. 63. 64;
  65. 67.
  Catherine 3;
  Chesten 34; 60; 98.
  Christopher 37.
  Dorothy 55;
  Edward 33;
  Eleanor 37.
  Elizabeth 2; 33; 33; 36. 42;
  43. 63; 70.
  Faith 18.
  Henry 3;
  Humphry 63.
  James 2. 2;
  Jane 2; 57;
  Joan 20; 31; 36. 38. 49; 49;
  63;
  John 3; 5; 6. 7. 7. 8. 9; 9;
  11; 31; 33; 38. 44. 50. 52.
  52; 55; 64. 64; 70.
  Lawrence 49;
  Maderne 3. 10; 34; 52. 55;
  98.
  Martin 5; 7. 50. 50; 51;
  Margaret 5; 33. 57; 62. 65.
  Margery 30.
  Mary 2. 56.
  Mathew 44.
  Maud 56;
  Nicholas 7.
  Norowe 43.
  Noye 10; 38; 65;
  Ralph 30. 47.
  Redigon 38;
  Richard 9. 9; 37. 43. 53. 61.
  Sacharie 43. 43. 43; 50;
  Susan 37.
  Thomas 20; 20; 21. 33. 55.
  65;
  Wany 5;
  William 2. 3. 3. 9. 11; 21.
  42; 52; 52; 56;
  Zacharias 63;
  .... 2. 38;
  ———— 43; 50;
Chauney 83.
  Joseph de 83.

CHENHALLS, See CHINALLS.
Chepy, alias Row, 97.
  William 97.
CHESHEERE 8; CHESSHEERE 52;
  Noy 8;
  Richard 8;
  Thomas 8; 8; 52;
Chimelly 83. *Chimeleis* 83.
  Thomas de 83.
  William de 83.
CHINALLS 7; CHINALS 7; CHENALLS
  33. CHINALLCE 45. CHINIALLS
  63.
  Catherine 52.
  Christopher 45.
  Ebbott 8;
  Elizabeth 51;
  Henry 15. 36; 64.
  Honor 36; 65.
  Hugh 7; 58;
  James 45;
  Jane 9. 51; 63.
  John 52; 53.
  Margaret 9; 15. 33. 59;
  Mary 7;
  Richard 46.
  Thomas 7; 7; 8; 9. 9; 33.
  45. 45; 46. 46; 47. 59;
  (Jane, his servant, 46;)
  William 56;
CHINGE 7. CHINE 52. *Chinne* 70;
  Amy 33.
  Frances 7.
  John 7. 33. 52. 70;
  Margaret 70;
CHIRGWIN 9. CHIRGWINE 9; CHIRGWYN
  10; CHERGWINE 12. CHERGWIN
  34.
  A. 81.
  Abraham 23; 24. 24.
  Alice 51; 60.
  Catherine 61;
  Charles 62.
  Elizabeth 23; 34. 65.
  George 19;
  Honor 65.
  James 24;
  Jane 38. 61;
  Joan 19; 24; 51;
  John 19; 20. 20. 22; 23. 26;
  34. 51; 51;
  Margaret 20.
  Mary 9. 23.
  Peter 12. 60; 61.
  Richard 22;
  Sarah 20.
  Thomas 9; 18; 18; 19; 26;
  38. 60. 61.
  Ursula 61;

INDEX.

William 9. 9; 10; 10: 12. 61;
61; 62. 63. 65. 65. 65.
—— 65.
CHRISTOPHER 15; CHRISTOPHARS 22;
CHRISTOPHERS 67.
Ann 56;
Barbary 39.
Catherine 44:
Eleanor 60.
George 22: 39. 65. 67.
James 44.
John 29. 44. 44;
Margery 22: 65. 67.
Olsett 29.
Susan 15;
Susannah 65;
William 15: 60. 65; 66:
CLEARKE 21; CLEARK 22.
John 21: 21: 22. 23. 25.
Mary 25.
Sibella 22.
—— 23.
CLEMOW 56;
Robert 56;
Thomasine 59.
CLERE 30; CLEARE 44; *alias*
HARRYE 44;
Bennet 44;
Jane 30;
Richard Henry 30;
Wilmot 49.
CLEVE 32;
Elizabeth 32;
Henry 32;
CLEVERDON 64.
John 64.
CLIES 4. CLYES 9. CLISE 35.
Clyse 70.
Alexander 6: 12. 12. 61. 70;
Alice 7: 44; 50; 50; 53. 70;
Amy 52;
Ann 35.
Annis 6;
Anthony 32.
Arthur 44. 44;
Blanch 33. 76. 77.
Catherine 9;
Edmond 5; 6; 6; 32; 50;
Elizabeth 8; 30. 52; 55. 55;
60; 70.
Eleanor 4. 48.
Henry 7. 55;
Jane 4. 48. 49; 54;
Joan, servant to Mrs. Clyes, 53;
John 6; 7; 8. 8; 9. 9. 9; 33.
35. 44; 50; 52; 52; 55. 70.
72. 72. 73; 76. 94. 98. 100.
Margaret 9. 32; 44; 49;
Mathew 4;

Michael 48;
Philip 12.
Richard 4; 12. 49. 54;
Richoe 32.
Susan 9.
Thomas 8. 30. 42. 48. 88.
(Alice, his servant, 30.)
Thomasine 12.
William 12. 42. 44; 47.
—— 5; 6; 7. 49.
Clifford 83.
Robert de 83.
CLOKE 5; CLOAKE 15; CLOAK 65;
Ann 36. 56;
Catherine 55;
Elizabeth 71.
George 15: 15; 55; 63;
James 62; 63; 69;
Jane 66;
Joan 65;
John 5; 35. 36.
Margaret 35.
Martin 67;
Nicholas 67;
Peter 5; 7; 61; 61; 62; 63;
65; 66; 67. 69;
William 67.
—— 7;
CLYMMOWE 3;
John 3;
William 3;
COCK 11. COCKE 16. *Coocke* 69. Cox
48. *alias Hoile* 69.
Addama 24. 70. 71. 96.
Alice 13. 36; 50; 63; 69. 75.
76. 100.
Ann 22. 70;
Benjamin 70.
Catherine 22; 67. 69;
Christopher 73.
Edward 22.
Elizabeth 24; 38. 38. 69;
Emanuel 18;
Frances 34; 58.
Francis 15.
Gabriel 38.
George 24; 59;
Grace 34. 37;
Honor 16.
Jacob 21; 22. 65. 65; 67. 67.
James 22. 39;
Jane 21.
Jenny 52;
Joan 34.
John 15. 20. 21; 21; 22; 23.
34; 58. 58; 58; 63; 64;
67. 70.
Margaret 15. 58; 58;
Mary 17; 39; 69; 73.

Nicholas 17. 17; 18; 21. 21;
38.
Richard 11. 20 21; 34. 34. 65.
Solomon 16. 24. 37; 65. 69;
69; 69; 69; 70. 70. 70. 70.
70. 70. 70. 71. 72; 72; 96.
Stephen 15.
Thomas 11. 13. 17. 36; 48.
75. 76.
Ursula 58.
William 21; 23. 65; 69. 69;
70;
COCKWELL 42; COKEWELL 42;
Jane 42;
John 42; 42;
Simon 42; 42; 42;
COHONE 49.
Margaret 49.
COLEMAN 12; COLMAN 15.
Agnes 59;
Charles 15.
Francis 14;
Mary 16; 35; 64. 64;
Nicholas 89.
Robert 12; 12; 14; 15. 16;
35; 56; 56; 59; 60; 64. 64;
COLENSO, See CALENSO.
Coles 86.
Edward Norman 86.
COLLAM 65; COLLOMBE 61;
Catherine 65;
Walter 61;
—— 61;
COLLAN 44; CULLAN 32;
Alice 33; 44;
Bennet 32; 33; 50;
Florence 32; 50;
Grace 44;
COLLERK 39;
James 39;
Mary 39;
COLLET 25. COLLETT 25.
Edward 25. 25. 27;
James 25. 25. 25; 26. 26.
Mary 25; 27;
COLLINS 7. COLLINGS 22; COLLENS 60.
Ann 57;
Florence 57;
John 7. 7. 22;
Morish 60.
Philip 22; 60.
CONNELL 7.
Andrew 64.
Dennis 9.
Ellen 7.
Joan 9;
Maurice 8; 15; 58.
Robert 7. 8; 9. 9; 58. 58.
. . . . 15;

INDEX.

CONNOCK 3; CUNNACKE 11. KONNACK
21. CONNACK 11. CONACK 39:
  Alice 22 : 62. 66 : 67.
  Ann 11 :
  Catherine 39 ; 66.
  John 11.
  Mary 11.
  Nicholas 3: 32. 39 : 59. 66. 66;
  Philippa 32.
  Richard 3 : 11. 11. 11 ; 21. 22 ;
    27 : 27 ; 62. 62. 67.
  Sarah 71.
  Walter 63.
COOKE 29.
  Agnes 29.
  Hugh 29.
  John 88.
  Richard 51 :
COOME 43:
  John 43 : 43 :
Cooper, The, 15.
  Digory 15. 59.
  Philippa, daughter of, 15. 59.
CORDEG 41.
  Jellian 41.
  Nicholas 41.
CORNEWALL 44 :
  Jane 44 :
CORNISH 1. CORNISHE 47 : *alias*
  Payan 73.
  Joan 1. 47 :
  John 1.
  Mrs. 73.
Cornwall, Richard Earl of, 83.
CORRY 65. CORY 58 : CORRIE 65.
  CURRY 56.
  Christian 65.
  John 65.
  Margery 56.
  Sarah 58 :
  Walter 58 ; 59.
Coryton 87. *Corrington* 89. *Carreton*
  90.
Peter 87. 88. 89. 90.
COSSENS 15 : COSEN 2 : COSSAN 34 :
  COZEN 49. *Cossen* 98. *alias*
  Maddern 98.
  Alice 46.
  Ann 15 :
  Eleanor 37.
  Grace 98.
  Henry 34.
  Jane 47 :
  Joan 71.
  John 5 ; 5 : 15 : 37 : 49. 49.
    60. 98.
  Margaret 44.
  Reynold 2 ; 31 :

Richard 41. 44. 45.
Roger 2 : 60.
Thomasine 31 : 59.
———— 34.
COTHA 10. COATHE 50 : GOATHE 49 :
  alias SAKARIA 50 :
  Ann 10.
  Bennet 10. 53.
  Clarence 49 ;
  John 50 :
  Richard 53.
COUCHE 63 : COUCHIE 15. *Couchee* 69:
  John 15.
  Margery 58 :
  Mary 63 :
  William 15. 58 ; 69 : 69 :
Coulson 86.
  Henry Tonkin 86.
Covn maker, The, 23.
  Joan, daughter of, 23.
COVYE 56. Covy 59 :
  Garthered 56.
  Robert 56. 59 ; 61.
  Roger 61.
COWLINGE 2 : COWLEN 4 : COWLYN 5 :
  COWLING 16.
  Agnes 12 ; 35. 65 :
  Alice 2 ; 9 ; 30 : 35. 49 : 97. 98.
  Ann 6 ; 35 ; 51. 60 ;
  Catherine 11. 22. 32 : 38 : 66 ;
  Christian 46. 97. 98.
  Constance 13. 63 :
  Eleanor 48 :
  Elizabeth 11 : 12. 16. 54. 64 :
    73 :
  Frances 19. 34. 35. 62. 66 ; 98.
  Francis 12. 55.
  Gertrude 97.
  Honor 6.
  Joan 63.
  John 2 : 4 ; 5 : 11. 11. 11 ;
    11 : 11 ; 11 : 12. 12. 12 ; 13.
    13 : 18 : 21. 22. 30 : 34. 35.
    35. 35. 38 ; 46. 49. 49 : 51.
    51. 54. 54 : 55. 56. 59. 62.
    62. 63 ; 66 : 85. 97. 97. 98.
    98.
  (Alice Eva, his servant, 51.)
  Margaret 44 :
  Mary 4 ; 44 ; 49.
  Mildren 19.
  Philippa 23. 37.
  Richard 73.
  Robert 9. 19. 43 ; 56. 63 :
  Sarah 11. 59.
  Simon 44 :
  Thomas 5 ; 6. 6 ; 7 ; 9. 9 ; 11 ;
    12 : 18 ; 19. 32 ; 35 ; 54.
  Tobias 14 :

William 7 ; 13 : 14 ; 16. 21.
  23. 37. 49 : 61 : 66 :
COYLE 3.
  John 3.
  Mary 3.
Cox 86. See COCK.
J. S. 86.
  Thomas 48.
CRANKAN 3. CRANKANN 42 ; *alias*
  SYMON 31 :
  Jane 45.
  Joan 31 :
  John 3. 31 : 45. 46 :
  Richard 3. 42 :
CREEDE 54.
  Christopher 63 :
  Em 54.
CRIPPS 37 :
  Ann 37 :
  John 37 :
Cromwell 98.
CROSS 10 : CROSSE 53 :
  Cornelius 10 : 10 : 53 : 53 :
CROWELL 18 :
  Catherine 18 :
  George 18 :
CRUDGE 3. CRUDG 44.
  Awdry 4. 48.
  John 3. 46 :
  Richard 48 :
  Thomas 3. 4. 48 : 48 :
CUNTYES 30.
  Joan 30.
CURRY, See CORRY.

DADOWE 30 : DODO 5 : DOODOWE 44.
  DODOWE 48. DADDOWE 53 :
  Daddow 70: *alias Thomas* 70 :
  Christopher 70 :
  Elizabeth 30 : 53 :
  John 5 : 5 : 44. 45 : 45 : 48.
    51 :
  Thomas 44. 70 :
  William 30 : 53 :
  ———— 48.
DADGIELL 45.
  Charles 45.
DAGWELL 65.
  Edward 65.
DANIELL 11 : *Daniel* 71 :
  Alexander 11 : 12. 12 ; 54 : 64.
    79. 95. 98. 100. 100.
  Daniel 22.
  Eliassaph 11 ; 95. 99.
  George 12 ; 79. 95.
  Grace 66 ; 71 : 100.
  Jacob 54 : 100.
  James 98.
  Jane 72. 99.

INDEX.

Jaquilina 98.
John 12. 21. 22. 24: 27: 27:
  27: 62: 95. 100.
Margaret 20.
Margery 71.
Mathew 72.
Mathias 27:
Phœbe 24:
Richard 20.
Thomas 21. 72.
DAVIDES 30. DAVYDE 44.
  Ralph 44.
  Simon 30.
DAVIES 21:
  Elizabeth 21: 65:
  John 21: 65:
DAVY 11. DAVYE 1. DAVEY 24.
  DAVIE 29. *alias* ROWAN 7.
  Ann 24. 27: 71.
  Bennet 17. 18. 61:
  Blanch 18.
  Cicely 30.
  Constance 31.
  Edward 3:
  Elizabeth 1. 4. 28. 29. 46:
    51: 72:
  George 38. 61: 67:
  Henry 7. 10: 53;
  Honor 19.
  James 23:
  Joan 61:
  John 2. 2: 4. 7. 11. 17. 23:
    24. 24: 24: 27: 28. 29. 43:
    43: 51: 51: 52. 55: 60. 96.
  Margaret 61:
  Martin 19. 19: 19: 67: 72:
  Mary 2: 51:
  Penelope 38.
  Philip 54:
  Rawe 1.
  Richard 2. 31.
  Robert 71.
  Rowan 3: 4. 4. 55:
  Thomas 30. 42. 42.
  William 10: 11. 53:
DAWBYN 1. DAWBIN 4: DAWBYNN
  48:
  Alice 4: 31. 49.
  Blanch 3:
  James 1. 3: 4: 31. 47: 47:
    48: 49. 50:
  Mary 1.
  Prudence 47:
  William 47: 48:
DAWES 21. DAWE 21:
  Joan 21.
  John 21: 21: 65: 65:
  Richard 21.
DEE 37:

Joan 37:
Thomas 37:
Thomasine 61.
De Lisle 83.
Denneard 72.
Ann 72.
John 72.
DENNYCE 29. DENNYS 42. DYNNICE
  45. DENNYC 31. DYNNIS 45:
  Catherine 31. 49.
  Chesten 45.
  Edward 42.
  Margaret 29.
  William 29. 42. 45:
DEWEN 43.
  Alice 45:
  Elizabeth 45:
  Jane 45.
  Jennet 45:
  John 45:
  Margaret 43.
  Richard 45: 45: 47.
  Thomas 43. 45:
  William 45:
DIGGENS 14. DIGENS 36:
  Ann 36:
  Jane 56.
  John 14.
  Mary 14:
  William 14. 14: 36: 56. 57.
DIGORY 66. DEGORY 16.
  Alice 37:
  Catherine 16.
  Cyprian 16: 66.
  Peter 16. 16: 37:
DINGLEY 6: DINGLE 7:
  James 6: 7: 10:
  Mary 6:
  Tiberia 7:
  Thomas 10:
DODO, See DADOWE.
DONITHORN 20:
  Honor 20:
  William 20:
DONNALL 2. DONNOLL 46:
  Christopher 47.
  Jane 47. 48:
  Joan 2. 30.
  John 3: 44.
  Rebecca 46:
  Richard 2. 3: 30. 44. 46: 47.
    47.
  Sampson 48:
Door 73:
  Richard 73:
DOVE 29.
  Margaret 29.
Dover men, two, 53:
DOWNING 32:

Catherine 32:
Robert 32:
DRAKE 30:
  Amy 30:
  William 30:
DRANEGLOS, See TRENEGLOS.
DRAPER 4:
  Elizabeth 4:
  John 4: 4: 4: 5: 6. 32: 48.
    49: 49: 52:
  Lucy 6.
  Margaret 5:
  Margery 48.
  Winifred 32: 56.
DREW 17. DREWE 2: DREWS 52:
  Elizabeth 31.
  Emanuel 17. 33: 63:
  Grace 33:
  Jane 61:
  John 52:
  Margaret 54:
  Mathew 17.
  Ralph 84.
  Susan 2:
  Thomas 2: 31. 53: 61:
DRYVER 47.
  Michael 47.
Dry woman, The, 50.
  Paskus 50.
DUKE 3:
  Catherine 5:
  Digory 3: 5. 5; 6: 7. 8. 8:
    9. 32. 33. 36. 36: 48. 49:
    50: 60.
  Elizabeth 6: 12: 13. 32. 35:
    49: 66.
  Emanuel 9.
  Grace 33.
  Jane 36: 51:
  Joan 7.
  John 7. 7. 9: 9:
  Margery 8. 36. 61.
  Mary 3:
  Mathew 8:
  Ralph 60:
  Rebecca 48.
  Richard 5. 12: 13. 35: 61.
  William 9: 9: 51:
  ——— 50:
DUN 23. DUNE 62: *Done* 97. *Dunn* 97.
  Avis 65:
  Christian 62:
  Elizabeth 65:
  John 23.
  Martin 23.
DUNKYN 1. DUNKIN 6: DUNCKEN 8.
  DUNCKING 9: DUNKYNNE 4.
  DUNKEN 66. DUNKINGE 30:
  DUNKING 15:

INDEX. 111

Ann 8. 56:
Anthony 6:
Catherine 4:
Elizabeth 9:
Henry 15. 15: 37. 49: 59.
Jane 66.
Jenefred 37.
Joan 9: 30: 52:
John 1. 4: 8. 9: 9: 15.
Margaret 9: 51:
Margery 15: 59.
Mary 5:
Orpheus 4.
Robert 1. 3. 3. 4. 4: 4: 5:
  6: 9: 30: 46: 49: 52: 54. 56:
——— 46:

EARLE 34:
Amy 34: 58.
Charity 58.
James 34: 57: 58. 58. 58. 58.
  58: 69.
John 58.
Othniel 57:
Thomas 58: 69.
William 57:
Eastlake 74. EASTLACK 25.
Joan 26:
Martha 25:
Mary 25:
Richard 27:
Samuel 27.
Thomas 25. 25. 25: 25: 26:
  26: 27. 27: 74.
William 26:
EDMONDS 6. EDMONDES 4:
Agnes 59:
Ann 32.
Blanch 37.
Catherine 8:
Grace 15: 59.
Henry 7: 14. 14: 15: 27: 36:
  59. 63. 63. 69:
Jane 6: 36: 63.
Joan 14. 69:
Margaret 5. 72.
Robert 4: 14: 27: 37.
William 4: 5. 6. 6: 7: 8:
  32. 50: 56.
——— 6.
EDWARDS 11: EDWARD 3. EDWARDES
  4: EDWARDE 5. *alias* PORTEER
  4:
Ann 4. 16: 35. 48. 59: 60.
Catherine 7:
Christian 20:
Cicely 17:
Edward 11: 23: 35.
Elizabeth 23: 35. 63.

George 18. 23:
Henry 71.
Hugh 16: 17. 17: 59:
Jane 50. 72:
Joan 17. 34: 38.
John 4: 4: 5. 5. 6: 7: 17:
  17: 18. 18: 27. 35. 50. 63. 67.
Margaret 31: 55:
Margery 18:
Martha 23:
Mary 3. 19: 23: 27: 71.
Nicholas 11: 19. 25. 61.
Petherick 34: 57:
Richard 3. 4. 31: 38. 48. 48:
  54:
Sarah 18: 23.
Thomas 18: 19. 19: 20. 20:
  25.
Walter 46:
William 6: 20. 23. 23: 23:
  27. 27. 27. 27:
——— 48:
EDYE 6. EDIE 5: EDDYE 20: EDES
  7: EDY 16: HEDDY 64:
Eady 71:
Alice 33: 60,
Ann 7: 19. 71:
Arthur 8. 8: 9: 9: 33: 51.
Avis 23. 36. 58.
Bartholomew 5: 6. 7. 8. 9.
  32: 50: 50: 52. 54.
Bathsheba 22:
Christopher 9. 52.
Eleanor 20:
Elizabeth 8. 17. 17: 21. 21:
  39. 47: 51. 60:
Grace 37: 61. 66.
Hannibal 6.
Helen 30.
Honor 16:
Jane 5: 7. 21: 32: 38: 59.
Joan 18. 38. 50: 63. 64:
John 9: 9: 11. 21: 30. 36.
  37: 49: 58. 65. 66.
Jowannat 50:
Margaret 8: 9: 17: 22: 67.
Mary 10. 10: 22.
Mathew 7:
Nicholas 47:
Peter 22: 23:
Philip 20: 20:
Philippa 23:
Ralph 20: 21. 21: 22. 23. 23.
Richard 17: 62.
Samuel 9. 9: 10. 10: 11. 16:
  17. 17: 17: 38. 60: 62.
Stephen 19: 22: 23. 67.
Thomas 19: 39.
William 8. 17: 18. 19. 38: 63.

——— 50:
ELFORDE 49. ELFFORD 7: ILLEFORDE
  5. ELFORD 54.
Ann 73:
Blanch 54.
Eleanor 58.
Ellen 49.
Humphry 7:
Peter 5. 7: 49. 54.
Philip 73:
William 5.
ELLARY 16. ELARY 67.
Arundell 16. 22: 39: 67.
Avis 22: 67.
John 16.
Mary 39:
ELLIS 6. ELIS 55:
Ann 15:
Charles 6. 7: 49: 49:
Elizabeth 33: 56. 64.
Frances 71:
Hugh 6. 49:
John 8. 15: 16. 16. 16: 16:
  17: 24: 33: 53: 59: 59:
Mary 49:
Pascoe 55:
Richard 58.
Roger 8. 17: 24: 71:
Thomas 7: 65.
Ensell 86.
  Charles Holt 86.
ESCOTT 2.
Joan 2.
William 2.
ESHAM 62. ESHAME 16.
Thomas 16. 16. 62. 63.
William 63.
ESTLIGH 1. ESLYE 45.
John 1. 45.
William 1. 45.
ETHAW 36.
Francis 36.
John 36.
EVA 16. EVAH 22.
Alice 51.
Ann 73:
Christian 44:
Edmond 22.
Elizabeth 26:
Henry 16.
Jaquite 22:
John 26:
Richard 22. 22: 73.
Solomon 26:
Thomas 16.
——— 44:

FALLENTON 61.
Joan 61.

INDEX.

FANSHOWE 56:
  Alice 56:
  Thomas, Sir, 56:
FELL 50.
  James 50.
FENYE 3. FENNYE 3: FYNNIE 4:
  FYNNYE 5. FENNY 14. FINNY
  15. FYNNEY 16. FENNE 25:
  FYNNY 41. FYNNIS 65: FEENY
  43.
  Alice 34. 36. 52: 65:
  Ann 58.
  Brian 25: 25: 27.
  Bridget 9. 10.
  Catherine 52: 55.
  Elizabeth 37.
  Henry 43.
  James 8: 9. 33. 35: 54. 61.
    62:
  Joan 37.
  John 3: 4: 8: 14. 15. 34. 36.
    37. 41. 52: 54. 56. 63. 64.
  Julian 37: 63.
  Margaret 14. 35: 61.
  Margery 36.
  Mary 10. 25: 33:
  Maud 33. 54.
  Phineas 27.
  Richard 3. 5. 8. 41. 43. 45:
    45: 47. 54.
  Robert 8. 10. 15. 33: 37. 59.
  Samuel 57:
  Thomas 3. 3: 4: 5. 14. 16. 36.
    46. 47. 52: 65: 66.
  Walter 16. 25: 37:
  ——— 46.
FICKS 15: FIX 37: See THICK.
  Catherine 37:
  Gilbert 15: 37:
  Mary 15:
FIGHT 37.
  Arthur 37.
  Priscilla 37.
Finnicomb 70.
  Margaret 70.
  William 70.
FISON 61.
  Robert 61.
FLEMING 4. FLEMINGE 8: FLEMYNG
  31: FLEMYNGE 11. *Flemen*
  71. FLEMMYNGE 54.
  Ann 5: 13. 35. 55: 76.
  Blanch 13.
  Catherine 30. 46:
  Christopher 19.
  Constance 72.
  Cordelia 21. 64:
  Elizabeth 6. 12: 16: 18. 31.
    35. 38. 38: 49. 59. 71. 75. 76.

Frances 76.
  Grace 4: 76. 98.
  Jane 8: 16. 31: 38. 76.
  John 9: 12. 18. 63. 73. 76.
  Mary 7. 17: 35: 38: 65: 71.
    73: 76.
  Nicholas 4. 11. 11: 11: 12.
    12. 12: 13. 13. 18. 18: 19.
    19: 19: 31. 35. 38. 38: 55:
    60. 64. 71. 72. 76.
  Philippa 7: 76.
  Prudence 17.
  Robert 43:
  Roger 2.
  Thomas 4. 4: 5. 5. 5: 6. 7.
    7: 8: 9: 11. 16. 16: 17.
    17: 17: 17: 18. 18: 19. 19.
    21. 31: 35. 35: 38. 38: 43:
    47. 54. 62: 64: 71. 75. 76.
    76. 86. 98.
  ——— 43: 47.
FLYNN 30: FLINOE 33.
  Helen 30:
  Jane 33.
  Morgan 30:
  Peter 33.
  William 51.
FORSE 32. FURSE 35:
  Alice 32.
  Christian 35:
  James 48:
  Marret 35: 66.
  Thomas 32. 48:
FOSKUE 30. *Fortescue* 30.
  Florence 30.
FOSSE 8. FOSE 69.
  Ann 33. 64:
  Bridget 57.
  Catherine 57:
  Elizabeth 69.
  Henry 8. 33. 60: 69. 69. 69.
  Hugh 15:
  Jane 8. 23. 57:
  Margaret 23. 23: 37:
  Nicholas 57.
  Philip 69.
  Thomas 17: 23. 23: 69. 96.
  William 15: 16: 16: 17. 17:
    23. 37: 57. 57. 57: 63.
  Zenobia 69.
  . . . . 17.
FOSTER 2. FOSTAR 30:
  Agnes 45:
  Alice 6:
  Catherine 31.
  Elizabeth 37. 41. 65.
  Grace 14. 57.
  Hellinor 42:
  Henry 6: 9. 33. 41. 42. 45:

    45: 45: 58:
  Isabella 61:
  Jane 39:
  John 61:
  Margaret 15. 58:
  Margery 42.
  Mary 14.
  Peter 57. 60:
  Prudence 33. 59.
  Richard 45:
  Robert 2.
  Thomas 9. 15. 37. 39: 58:
    60: 60:
  William 2. 31.
FOX 28.
  Armanell 28.
  James 28.
  William 28.
FRANCIS 10.
  Ann 34: 58.
  Christabel 10. 55:
  Jane 52.
  Simon 10. 34: 55: 58. 58.
FRAUNCKE 42:
  John 42:
FREINDE 28. Frinde, my, 48:
  Freind 96.
  Ann 28. 96.
  Jenny 48: 100.
  Magdalen 28. 96.
  Modlen 28.
  Modlen 28.
  Frenchman, a, 46:
  John 47: 47:
  Peter 47: 47: 47:
FRIDGESS 64.
  Catherine 34. 51:
  Gregory 51:
  John 34. 51: 51:
FROSSE 11:
  Henry 11: 11:
FROST 35:
  Catherine 35: 54:
  Roger 35: 54:
FURSE, See FORSE.

GAME 3. GAMES 56:
  Agnes 32.
  Alice 45:
  Ann 5: 48: 52. 64.
  Catherine 3.
  Charles 57:
  Christopher 32. 41. 42: 44:
    45: 47. 53:
  Elizabeth 56:
  Ellen 7:
  Gavrigan 7. 55:
  Grace 6. 50.
  Henry 3: 31. 41. 44. 47: 51:

INDEX. 113

Jane 3: 44. 67:
Joan 4.
John 3. 3: 4. 5. 5: 6. 6: 6:
  7: 8. 8: 31. 44: 48: 48:
  49. 50. 50. 50.
  (Henry, his servant, 49.)
Key 51:
Margaret 47.
Mary 7: 31. 60.
Nicholas 3: 53.
Richard 6: 7. 7: 7: 42: 50. 51:
  52:
Roger 5. 6: 48: 50.
Sarah 8.
Thomas 8: 64.
William 7:
GARBYE 46:
  Catherine 46:
GARDEAGE 45: *alias* MICHELL 45:
  John 45:
GARLAND 2: GARLANDE 46:
  Ann 44:
  Avis 72.
  Cordelia 22:
  Edward 21.
  Elizabeth 2:
  Joan 46:
  John 44.
  Launcelot 2: 3. 32. 44. 44:
    46: 47: 48. 51.
  Margaret 47:
  Robert 22:
  Thomas 3. 48.
  Tryphena 32. 51.
  William 21.
GARRATT 15: GARROW 37: *Garrett*
  69:
  Blanch 37: 61:
  John 69:
  Joel 15: 37:
  Juell 69:
  Roger 15:
GARROW, See GARRATT.
GAYE 42. GAAYE 10:
  John 42. 42:
  Margery 10:
  Thomas 42. 42:
  William 42:
  ——— 10:
GEARE 19.
  Dorothy 19. 63.
  Lawrence 19. 62: 63. 63.
  Margaret 37.
  Mary 19. 63.
  Richard 37.
  ——— 62:
GEGAR, See GREGOR.
GEIFE, See GIVE.
GELES, See GILES.

GENDALL 28.
  Alexander 28. 28.
GENE 43: GRINE 43: GRENE 50. *alias*
  SUDGIOW 44: See JANE.
  Elizabeth 50:
  Geoffrey 43:
  Joan 43:
  John 43: 44. 44:
  Thomas 50.
GENVER 10. GINVER 54.
  John 10.
  Nicholas 10. 54. 73.
  William 19: 19:
  ——— 54. 73.
GEOFFRIE, See JEFFRY.
GEORGE 10. GEORG 2. *alias* BEGOE 48:
  Agnes 47:
  Ann 37:
  Alexander 3: 48.
  Alice 21. 65:
  Blanch 36: 65.
  Charity 30.
  Charles 24:
  Deborah 14.
  Edward 15:
  Elizabeth 2. 44.
  Grace 11:
  Jane 34: 46:
  Jermyn 13.
  Joan 18: 30. 44. 55. 64:
  John 13. 14. 15: 30. 36: 36:
    47: 48: 56: 63:
  Mary 17: 33:
  Peter 12: 20.
  Richard 2. 3: 16: 30. 44. 44.
    46: 48. 54: 55.
  Thomas 10. 10. 11: 16: 17.
    17: 18: 19. 19. 20. 21. 24:
    33: 34: 37: 55: 65: 66:
  Zacharias 12: 17.
GERMIN, See JERMYN.
GEVE, See GIVE.
GIES 15.
  Alice 15.
  William 15.
GIFT 21.
  Catherine 39: 65.
  David 39: 65. 65:
  Elizabeth 25:
  Florence 22.
  Jeremiah 21: 21:
  John 21. 66:
  Margaret 39: 72.
  Thomas 21: 21: 22. 25: 25:
    39:
  William 21. 25: 66: 72.
GILBERT 17: GILBART 18. *Jelbert* 72:
  Ann 18: 21. 63.
  C. S. 77.

Elizabeth 17: 20. 73:
Honor 18. 38:
James 17: 18. 18. 18: 19. 19:
  20. 38: 63:
Jennifer 73:
Joan 19.
John 18. 18. 18. 19: 20. 21.
  22. 24: 38: 62. 63. 72:
Lydia 20. 63:
Margaret 18. 62.
Philippa 18. 63:
Richard 24: 73:
William 22. 73:
  .... 38:
GILES 2. GELES 5. JEELES 6. JELES
  44: GYLES 51. GEILES 55:
  GEELES 7. JEILES 30.
  Alice 32: 55: 62:
  Ann 37. 39:
  Barnard 8. 51.
  Catherine 2. 47.
  Elizabeth 30. 45: 52: 67.
  Grace 58.
  Honor 58.
  Jane 44: 46:
  Joan 44:
  John 2. 27. 37. 47. 51. 52:
    66: 67:
  Margaret 61.
  Paul 6.
  Richard 5. 6. 7. 7. 8. 25. 25.
    27. 32: 39: 51. 51. 55: 58.
    66: 67.
  Thomas 63:
  William 5. 8. 30. 45: 46: 46:
    46: 51. 54: 57. 58. 62:
  ——— 67:
GILLARD 42. GILLARDE 50: GILLERD
  46: GILLERDE 47:
  Helen 47:
  Leonard 42. 48: 50:
  (Joan, his servant, 48:)
  Thomas 42.
  William 46:
GIVE 3. GEVE 47: GEEFE 53. GIFFE
  61. GEIFE 2: GEIFFE 6: GIFE
  60. GYVE 44. *Geive* 70.
  Alice 61.
  Elizabeth 2:
  Florence 60.
  Jane 33. 44.
  Jermyn 2: 3. 6: 33. 47: 47:
    53. 70.
  Margaret 47:
  Margery 70.
  Simon 3. 47:
  William 6: 60.
GLANVYLE 36. GLANFIELD 35:
  Digory 35:

cc

INDEX.

Jane 35:
Joan 36.
GLASAN 37.
  Alice 56:
  Christopher 37. 56: 60.
  Prudence 37. 60:
GLASSE 36:
  Jane 65.
  Joan 36:
  John 36:
GLENDONING 64.
  Robert 64.
GLOVER 10. Glover, The, 11:
  Ann 10. 38:
  Christian 59:
  Francis 35: 54: 59:
  Hannah 34.
  Jane 42:
  Joan 35:
  John 38:
  Mary 36.
  Susan 11:
  Elizabeth 10. 11: 34.
GOATHE, See COTHA.
Godolphin 70:
  Jane 70:
  Nicholas 70:
GONDRY 26:
  Ann 26:
  Henry 26:
GOOBLE 16. GOBBLE 18. *Goble* 73.
  Duens 38: 73.
  Jane 16.
  Richard 18.
  Robert 16. 18. 38: 73.
GOODALE 30.
  Christian 42.
  Joan 30.
  John 42. 42. 42. 42. 42. 42.
  Jonathan 42.
  Nicholas 42.
  William 42.
GOVER 55: *alias* SKINNER 55:
  Mary 55:
  Michael 67:
GREENE 52.
  Henry 52.
  William 52. 52:
GREGOR 4: GREGAR 14: GREGAR 18:
  Abraham 14: 58.
  Clarence 5.
  Elizabeth 26: 57:
  Frances 20.
  Grace 22. 39.
  Jane 32. 45. 63. 64:
  Joan 26. 36. 48: 58:
  John 4: 5. 6: 7: 19: 21. 26. 26: 32. 45. 47: 48:
  Lewis 20:

Lois 38:
Margaret 24:
Peter 14: 18: 24: 58.
Thomas 4: 18: 21. 22. 38: 48:
William 6: 49.
Zacharias 7: 19: 20. 20: 36. 39. 57: 63.
.... 58.
Gregory 86.
  Francis 86.
GRIFFEN 32:
  Margaret 32:
  Thomas 32:
Griffiths 86.
  E. M. 86.
GROMOHALL 49:
  Jellian 49:
GROSSE 12. GROSE 22: GROSS 36:
  Ann 36: 36:
  Catherine 67.
  David 12.
  Elizabeth 56:
  Jane 36:
  John 36: 74.
  Juliana 73.
  Mary 22:
  Thomas 12. 22: 56: 67.
  William 36; ——— 73.
Grove 92.
  Henry 92.
GUBBS 10. GUBBES 24:
  Agnes 18:
  Alice 14: 65. 66.
  Ann 71.
  Anthony 10. 10. 10: 11: 12. 53: 62: 65: 66. 71. 81. 95.
  Elizabeth 71.
  Joan 10:
  Joseph 14: 18: 24: 65.
  Martin 77. 81.
  Roger 11:
  Sampson 12. 24: 53: 65.
GUY 20: GUYE 30.
  Bernard 20:
  Elizabeth 30.
  George 20:
  Grace 71:
  Jane 67.
  Richard 71:
  Thomas 30.
GWENNAPP 15: *Gwenap* 72:
  Gwennapp 74.
  Catherine 26:
  Constance 72:
  John 26:
  Martin 15: 18: 18: 26: 37: 61: 64. 72: 74.

Mary 15:
Nicholas 26:
Richard 26: 26:
Sarah 37: 61:
——— 64.
GYMBALL 3: GYMBOLL 30.
  Elizabeth 3: 30.
  Joan 34:
  Peter 3: 30. 46:
  Roger 34:
  Thomas 46:
Gyrardus 83.

HACKER 13. HACKAR 65:
  Eleanor 65:
  Jane 18. 24. 59: 63:
  Marian 14.
  Mary 24.
  Peter 15:
  Ralph 18. 19: 24. 24. 63. 65:
  Richard 19:
  Thomas 13. 13. 14. 15: 59: 63: 64.
  ——— 63.
HAKE 30.
  Jenny 30.
HALGARRACKE 48:
  Richard 48:
HALL 14:
  Abraham 92.
  Avis 22.
  Bishop of Exeter 100.
  Catherine 19. 62:
  Chesten 38:
  David 21: 22. 22: 22: 66.
  Diana 19.
  Elizabeth 20:
  Emanuel 66:
  Hugh 18. 19.
  Jane 14: 21: 59. 66.
  Joan 67.
  Margery 21.
  Martin 21. 21: 22. 22: 22:
  Mary 22. 66:
  Mathew 28: 28: 97.
  Richard 19: 62:
  Samuel 18.
  Tabitha 21:
  Thomas 19. 19: 20: 38:
  William 14: 59.
Halls 84. *Hallys* 84.
  William 84.
Halse 70:
  William 70: 70:
HAMBLING 30: HAMBLYE 46.
  Andrew 30: 46.
  Joan 30:
HAMETT 3: HAMMETT 34: HAMMET 48:

INDEX.   115

Eleanor 34:
Elizabeth 48.
James 3: 34:
Joan 55:
John 52.
Richard 4. 48:
Robert 3: 4. 48. 48: 53.
HAMOND 28.
 Edward 28.
 Elizabeth 28.
 James 28. 28.
HANCOCK 25.
 Deborah 26.
 Elizabeth 25: 36.
 Grace 27.
 John 25. 25: 25: 26. 26. 26.
  26. 27.
 Mary 26.
 Rebecca 25.
 Wilmot 25:
HAND 23:
 John 23:
 William 23:
Hanifor 71:
 Elizabeth 71:
Hankey 86.
 Joseph 86.
HANN 31.
 Jane 31.
 William 31.
HARBERT 5. HARBERTE 6. *Herbert* 85.
 Florence 53.
 Grace 6. 49:
 Jane 32. 61.
 John 5. 6. 6: 7: 7: 8. 8. 8.
  8: 10. 10. 11. 32. 49: 50.
  50: 50: 51. 51. 52: 53. 58:
 Mary 5. 8. 11. 50. 52:
 Ralph 6: 48. 85. 100.
 Robert 10.
 Thomas 7. 7. 10.
 William 8: 48.
HARRIS 6: HARRIES 57: *Harriss* 37. *alias* ANKOW 57: *alias* MARTYN 62: See HARRY.
 Amy 34.
 Beavis 72:
 Catherine 53:
 Elizabeth 6: 50.
 Gilbert 6: 7. 50.
 Jane 72:
 Joan 58.
 John 19: 37. 62:
 Margaret 58.
 Margery 37.
 Mary 38: 71.
 Philip 19:
 Philippa 71:

Richard 58.
Sampson 7.
William 34. 38: 52: 57:
HARRY 14: HARRYE 3. HARRIE 14:
 HARREY 21. HERRY 41. *alias*
 BENNET 4: *alias* CLEARE 44:
 alias Penrceth 96. See HARRIS.
 Alice 14: 21. 22: 30. 65.
 Ann 27: 96.
 Barbara 36: 58:
 Bennet 9. 9: 41. 44: 52. 53.
 Bridget 9: 71:
 Christian 36.
 Christopher 8.
 Edmund 69:
 Elizabeth 33: 66:
 Frances 71:
 Gilbert 33.
 Henry 4: 41. 48:
 Hugh 18.
 James 27: 96.
 Jane 14: 23: 38. 58. 66.
 Jemima 21.
 John 8: 9. 11. 12. 14: 16.
  18. 21. 36: 58. 58: 60. 60.
  61: 62. 66: 98.
 Leonard 63:
 Lowdy 33.
 Margaret 16. 70:
 Martin 70:
 Mary 9: 28. 28: 41.
 Nicholas 8. 21: 22. 24: 30.
 Ralph 12:
 Richard 3. 3: 3: 4: 5: 8. 8:
  33: 41. 42. 46: 48: 51:
  58. 60. 71:
 Reynold 60:
 Robert 5: 14: 21. 28. 28: 36.
  58. 58. 58. 63: 66: 69: 96.
  97.
 Sampson 21. 21. 21: 22. 22:
  23: 65. 65:
 Thomas 10: 28:
 Thomasine 62.
 Walter 19: 38. 66.
 William 3. 8. 9: 10: 11. 11.
  11. 12. 19: 28. 55: 62. 98.
 Wilmot 46: 49. 61:
 —— 24: 65:
HARVY 29. HARVYE 66:
 Grace 29.
 Thomas 66:
HASE 43.
 Anthony 43.
 Barnard 43.
 George 43.
HATHERLEY 10:
 William 10: 10:
HAWES 2. HAWAS 56:

Agnes 3.
Ann 2.
Blanch 8. 36.
Jane 31:
John 34: 56:
Margaret 34:
Mathew 8. 36.
Prudence 5.
Richard 2. 3. 5. 31: 51:
HAWKE 42.
 Jane 42.
 Rodigon 42.
 Thomas 42.
 William 42. 42. 42. 42.
Hawker 86.
 Thomas Medell 86.
Hawkey 74.
 Daniel 74.
HEAREN 46.
 Catherine 46.
HEARLE 9:
 James 9:
 Robert 63:
 William 9:
Hedgeland 86.
 Philip 86.
HEIDEN 49: HIDEN 6.
 Richard 6. 49: 49:
 Sampson 6.
HELLIER 11. HELIOR 67.
 Mary 67.
 Robert 11:
 Sampson 11:
 Thomas John 67.
Hertfordshire man, a, 47:
 George 47:
HEXT 1. HIXT 2: See HICKS.
 Arthur 1.
 John 1. 2: 44. 93.
 Robert 2:
 William 44.
HICHEN 6: HITCHENS 7: See HUTCHINS.
 Alice 62:
 Duke 17: 61:
 Edward 7:
 Emanuel 6:
 Grace 15.
 Henry 16:
 John 15. 15: 16: 17: 61. 61:
 Richard 6: 7: 57: 80.
 Thomasine 15:
HICKS 5: HIKX 32: HEEX 33:
 Alice 32:
 Ann 34. 70.
 Catherine 38:
 Frances 71:
 John 5: 32: 38:
 Lydia 70. 70. 71: 73.

INDEX.

Margaret 70.
Mary 33:
Philip 70. 70. 70. 70. 70.
  71: 73.
Philippa 70. 71:
  Susan 5:
  Thomas 33: 34.
  William 70.
HIDEN, See HEIDEN.
HILL 52. HILLS 31.
  Catherine 31.
  Joan 52. 52.
  Thomas 31.
HINGSTONE 32:
  John 32:
  Mary 32;
Hinson 71.
  Grace 71.
HITCHCOCKE 39.
  Blanch 39.
  John 39.
HOARE 46.
  Clarence 50.
  Joan 46.
HOBBS 37:
  Hugh 37:
  Joan 37:
HOCKEN 9. HOCKYN 11. HOCKKEN 46. HOCKINE 52:
  Alice 8:
  Ann 11. 57.
  Christabel 54.
  Gillian 11:
  John 46.
  Lewis 9. 35: 54. 55.
  Nathaniel 9.
  Robert 61.
  Thomas 52:
  William 11. 11:
HODGE 37.
  Ann 37.
  Elizabeth 67.
  John 37.
  Mary 38.
  Walter 38.
Hogben 87.
  William 87. 88.
Hoile 69. *alias Cock* 69.
  Alice 69.
  William 69.
HOLBERT 38.
  Alice 38.
  Thomas 38.
HOLLA 1.
  Abraham 59.
  Alice 10; 11. 13;
  Ann 8; 53;
  Bennet 43.
  Blanch 13.

Dinah 13.
Eleanor 51.
Elizabeth 9. 37: 44: 66.
Jane 29. 60.
Joan 13:
John 1. 10: 13: 34. 37: 43:
  44: 46: 48. 53:
Margery 47.
Mary 10: 32: 60.
Richard 47.
Robert 23:
Thomas 8: 9. 9: 9: 10: 11. 32: 43. 60. 62: 63:
William 1. 23: 41. 56:
———— 34.
HONICHURCH 7: *Honychurch* 80.
  Alice 26.
  Avis 27.
  Catherine 7:
  Elizabeth 16: 25: 80.
  John 7: 17. 18: 27. 61. 61. 80. 80.
  Lydia 26:
  Margery 39:
  Mary 25. 80.
  Nicholas 19:
  Somer 16. 25. 25: 26. 26. 26: 39: 65: 67:
  Thomas 63:
  William 15: 16. 16: 17. 17: 17: 18: 19: 26. 63:
  .... 15:
  ———— 65: 67:
HONYWELL 2. HONIWELL 51.
  Agnes 2.
  Alice 50.
  John 2. 50. 51.
HOOPER 2:
  Agnes 43.
  Elizabeth 2: 34. 35. 56.
  Emmet 53.
  Henry 2: 2: 3: 5: 6. 7: 31. 54:
  John 34. 59: 60:
  Margaret 38: 44:
  Mary 35:
  Nicholas 2: 7: 35: 38:
  Richard 5:
  Stephen 44: 45:
  Simon 43.
  Ursula 31.
  William 3: 35. 53. 55:
  ———— 6. 59:
HOPENSACK 48:
  Gysbrecht Mychelsoon 48:
HORSFORD 10. HOSFORD 11.
  Annanias 10. 11. 12. 12. 34: 39. 51. 62:
  Catherine 11.

John 10. 57.
Margaret 34: 64.
Mary 39.
———— 54.
HOSKING 66: HOSKYN 5. HOSKYNS 2: HOSKIN 4: HOSKYNN 32. HOSKEN 9: HOSKYNE 48: *alias* TREMBAII 6. *alias* TREMBATII 51: *alias* KIGWIN 50.
  Agnes 6:
  Alice 2: 36.
  Ann 12: 36. 39:
  Blanch 39:
  Catherine 35: 39: 73:
  Christopher 81.
  Edward 51.
  Elizabeth 31. 33. 36: 60: 66:
  Emanuel 8: 19. 20. 65.
  Ennee 50.
  Grace 20.
  Hannah 19.
  Henry 14. 39:
  Honor 15.
  James 2: 24:
  Jane 81.
  Joan 36. 55: 71:
  John 4: 5. 5: 5: 6. 6: 7. 8: 8: 8: 9: 9: 10. 11. 11: 32. 33. 33. 33: 36. 51: 51: 51: 55. 55: 55:
  Margaret 33: 56.
  Margery 32. 48:
  Mary 19. 56: 65: 81.
  Mathew 4: 12: 35:
  Nicholas 14. 15. 16: 36: 36: 56: 66:
  Penticost 11:
  Ralph 48: 49. 49.
  Richard 10. 31. 39: 49. 52: 62:
  Sarah 36: 56:
  Silvester 6.
  Susan 9:
  Thomas 7. 9: 19. 24: 80. 81.
  Thomasine 16:
  William 5. 11. 39:
  .... 33.
HORSEY 26:
  John 26:
  Mary 26:
HOWES 33: *alias* CALLY 58:
  Jane 58:
  John 57. 58:
  Mary 33: 63.
  Mathew 35: 60.
  Richard 56:
HUBBARD 37: HUBBORD 13: HUBBART 58:
  Elizabeth 35. 58:

INDEX.   117

Thomas 13: 13: 35.
Winifred 37:
HUGH 11: HEWE 4. HUGHE 6:
    HEW 4:
Ann 17:
Blanch 14.
Catherine 12: 31: 53. 71.
Elizabeth 16.
Hannibal 6: 50.
Humphry 52:
Jane 66.
Joan 4. 17: 61.
John 4. 4: 5. 5. 6: 7. 8. 11:
    12: 14. 16. 16: 31: 48. 48.
    48: 50. 51. 52:
Maderne 4: 11: 19. 62:
Mary 18:
Sampson 4. 4: 48. 49.
Thomas 17: 17: 18. 18. 18:
    19. 48. 61. 64: 65.
William 4. 4: 7. 8. 16: 32.
    49. 51.
——— 32. 65.
Humble 86.
    Michael Morgan 86.
HUMFREYS 20. HUMFRY 57. UMFRY
    8: UMFRYE 9. UMPHRYE 12:
    HUMFRYE 64.
Alice 11.
Cicely 59:
George 12: 20. 64.
James 8:
John 9. 11. 11: 12: 20. 55.
    55. 55.
Margaret 64.
Othniel 57.
Richard 11:
Sarah 57.
Thomas 55.
William 8: 9.
HUTCHINS 7. HUTCHENS 7: HUCHINS
    29. *Huchens* 72. See HITCHENS
Catherine 34:
Christian 35:
Digory 17.
Edward 55:
Elizabeth 9. 33. 34: 62: 72.
George 7: 29. 29. 51. 72. 72.
    72. 85. 97. .
Henry 66.
Humphry 7. 9. 33. 60.
Jane 8.
Joan 34: 72.
John 7: 17. 37. 51. 98.
Margery 37.
Mary 9. 55.
Richard 8. 8: 8: 9. 34: 34:
Thomas 7. 31: 35: 54: 55.
——— 66.

H .... 37.
John, Sir, 37.
Mary 37. 37.

ILLEFORDE 5. See ELFORD.
    Peter 5.
    William 5.
IRISHE 42.
    Catherine 42.
    John 42.
    Owen 45:
Irish man 42. Irish woman 42.
    Irish soldier 47:
    George 47:
    Helen 47.
    John 42.
    Margaret 42.
    Michael 42.

JACKA 13. JACCA 54. JACCAH 64:
    Ann 20: 64:
    Benjamin 19:
    Catherine 13. 71.
    Humphry 19: 19: 20: 39. 64:
    Jane 19: 62.
    John 13. 54. 54. 61.
    Margaret 39.
    Maud 35.
    Richard 35. 59.
Jackes 84. *Jakys* 84.
    John 84.
JACKSON 64:
    Elizabeth 64:
JAGOE 33.
    Mary 33.
    Robert 33.
JAMES 1. *alias* AMEARE 5. *alias*
    DREANEGLES 13. *alias* MULFRA
    17. *alias* TREMETHACK 2. *alias*
    TRENEGLOS 57: *alias* SENNEN
    58: *alias* ROSEMORRAN 63.
Amy 42:
Ann 17: 26: 27. 38.
Bartholomew 6:
Bernard 15.
Catherine 27: 31. 44: 50: 63:
Charles 26:
Clarence 3:
Dorothy 55:
Drew 31: 46:
Edward 41. 43. 43.
Eleanor 62:
Elizabeth 29. 46. 46: 49. 53:
    71:
Emmet 45.
Francis 6.
Gillian 6: 50.
Grace 3. 41. 47.
Helen 34:

Honor 13.
Hugh 18.
Jael 39:
James 57: 67.
Jane 2. 4: 15. 31: 33: 35:
    46. 66. 67:
Jasper 15. 35: 66.
Jennet 30.
Joan 1. 5: 7. 31. 33: 43. 47.
    57: 60:
John 2. 2: 3. 3: 4. 4: 5. 5:
    6. 6. 6. 6: 11. 13. 14: 19:
    22. 22. 23. 23. 30. 31: 31:
    33: 34: 38. 38. 43. 44. 44:
    46. 47. 48: 49: 50. 50: 52:
    53. 53: 55: 57: 57: 58: 58:
    60. 60: 61. 62: 63. 66.
Jonathan 23. 59: 71:
Julian 38. 62:
Maderne 42: 43. 43. 43: 45.
    47. 48. 50:
Maderne John 46. 46.
Margaret 5. 31: 36: 63.
Margery 17. 58:
Mary 11. 44. 61: 66.
Michael 33:
Peter 22: 22: 39:
Ralph 23.
Rebecca 27: 45: 52:
Reynold 4: 5.
Richard 1. 5. 27: 28. 31. 66.
Robert 6: 7. 14: 31. 36: 57:
    57:
Roger 27.
Sampson 43.
Thomas 4. 4: 18: 19: 26: 26:
    27. 27. 27. 27. 27: 28. 48:
    96.
Wilmot 31: 50:
William 2: 15. 17. 17: 18.
    43: 67:
    ....18:
JANE 26. See GENE.
Dyonice 44:
Joan 26: 31.
John 26. 26. 26. 26: 26:
Margaret 42:
Mary 26.
Peter 26:
Robert 31.
William 44:
JASPER 15. JASPAR 20.
Ann 57:
Jane 15.
Joan 58. 61.
John 20. 20.
Nicholas 15. 16. 16. 16: 58.
    61.
Phillis 16:

DD

Thomas 58.
JEELES, See GILES.
JEFFRY 1. JEFFRYE 4. JEFFRIE 4:
   JEOFFRYE 11: JEOFFRIE 50.
   GEOFFRIE 43; GEFFREY 18;
   JEOFERY 12: JEFFREY 61:
   JEFRIE 31. *alias* NIGHTEN 5.
Alice 31. 35. 55.
Ann 8. 32. 59:
Catherine 50;
Charles 18:
Elizabeth 39.
Henry 61:
James 5. 50.
Jane 4:
Joan 45: 49:
John 1. 8. 15. 35. 43: 45:
   46. 51. 55. 61.
Margaret 5:
Mary 2. 51.
Nighten 2.
Pascus 8.
Richard 46.
Thomas 4. 5. 8. 9. 9. 10: 12:
   15. 18: 32. 50. 51. 61:
William 1. 4. 4: 5: 10: 11:
   11: 12: 19: 19: 31. 39. 55.
   55. 60.
JENKIN 3; JENCKYN 2. JENKYN 3.
   JENKYNNE 4. GENKINGE 42:
   JENKEN 15. JENKYNNES 46:
   JENKYNNS 46: JENKENS 46;
   JENCKEN 11. JENCKYNGE 13.
   JENKINGE 30: JENKYNES 47.
   JENCKYNNES 46: *Jenkins* 77.
Agnes 48:
Alice 32. 42: 47.
Ann 9: 11: 14. 36.
Annis 5.
Barnard 45. 46: 47.
Blanch 46:
Catherine 11. 20: 66.
Edmund 50.
Edward 2. 3. 4: 4: 49. 53.
   60:
Eleanor 4.
Elizabeth 2. 3. 10: 11: 35.
   46: 49. 54:
Emanuel 15. 22.
Enoch 21:
George 27.
Henry 35.
Jacob 71:
James 19. 19. 20. 20: 39. 80.
Jane 34. 36:
Joan 34: 66:
John 3: 4. 4. 5. 5. 6: 9. 12.
   12. 14: 20: 22. 27. 32. 45.
   46: 46: 49. 50:

(John, his servant, 16:)
Joseph 13.
Margaret 30:
Margery 61:
Mary 10. 20. 20: 21: 39. 39:
   63: 77. 80.
Nicholas 30:
Peter 12: 20: 20: 24: 66. 66.
   66. 67: 74.
Prudence 3: 11.
Richard 5. 9. 9: 34. 39: 52:
Robert 4. 50:
Stephen 15: 59.
Susan 10: 11. 53.
Susanna 10.
Thomas 10. 10. 11. 11: 11:
   12. 12: 13: 14. 14. 14: 24:
   55. 55. 61:
Tiberia 13:
Ursula 71:
William 10. 10: 11: 11: 12.
   12. 13. 15. 15: 34: 36. 55.
   55. 59. 64. 66:
——— 6: 66. 66. 67:
JENNENS 64. JENINGS 66; GENNENS
   14: *Gennings* 71.
Alice 66:
Ann 14:
Bennet 14: 64.
Elizabeth 71.
John 66: 71.
Lewis 18: 62:
Margaret 18: 62:
JERMYN 1. JERMAN 44: JERMYNE 47.
   Germin 73.
Ann 1.
James 47.
John 1. 48.
Margaret 44: 73:
Morva 44:
Syve 48.
Richard 44:
Thomas 73:
JEWELL 27: GEWELL 20.
Bridget 39.
Dorothy 20.
Elizabeth 24:
James 20.
Walter 20. 27:
William 20. 20: 20: 24: 27:
   39.
JOHN 9. *Johns* 71:
Agnes 31.
Alexander 15:
Alice 15: 62.
Ann 11.
Barnard 45.
Bennet 34.
Edward 19.

Eleanor 32.
Elizabeth 11. 21. 31.
Frances 71:
Francis 25. 36: 66.
Grace 24: 36:
Henry 11.
James 17. 37: 38. 55. 60: 67.
   67.
Jane 9. 34. 41.
Jaquet 73:
Joan 18. 26: 35: 38. 60: 60:
   61: 62:
John 9: 15:
Margaret 10: 25: 37:
Margery 12: 39:
Mary 10. 19. 50:
Maud 37. 45.
Nicholas 13. 35: 55.
Peter 15: 17. 23: 24. 37.
Ralph 31. 31.
Reginald 9: 10: 11. 11. 12:
Richard 9. 10. 13. 16. 18. 18.
   25. 55. 56. 62: 66.
Robert 31.
Roger 18. 19. 73.
Thomas 14: 20. 20. 21. 24.
   27. 39:
Ursula 31.
Vincent 25: 27.
Wenrue 32.
William 14: 16. 19. 26. 26.
   26: 60: 61: 67: 74. 74.
——— 67:
Joiner, The, 43:
Nicholas 43:
JOLLYE 42.
Jane 42.
John 42.
JONES 19: JONS 65:
Arthur 19:
Edward 19: 65. 65. 65: 65:
   74. 89.
Francis 56.
Hugh 73:
John 86.
Lionel 73:
Zenobia 56.
——— 65: 65:
JOWAN 57: JOEAN 54.
Elizabeth 54.
John 57:
Juge 84.
Hildebrand 84.

KALLWAY, See CALLAWAY.
KEAT 11. KETE 12. KEATE 19. *Keet*
   85. *Kratt* 85. See KITT.
Agnes 12: 56.
Ambrose 27. 27.

INDEX. 119

Elizabeth 11. 35.
Francis 11 ;
Grace 13 :
Helen 20 :
Henry 85.
Jane 14 ; 58.
John 11. 11. 11. 11 ; 12. 12 ;
  13. 13 ; 14. 14 ; 18 ; 19. 20.
  20 ; 35. 56. 58. 58. 58. 62 ;
  85. 100.
Margaret 12.
Mary 13.
Philippa 20.
Richard 18 ; 27. 62 :
Robert 14. 58.
Sampson 19. 27. 27.
KEIGWIN 13 ; KEGWIN 64 ; KEYGWIN
  13. KEYGWYNE 42. KIGWIN
  50. KEIGWYNE 46. *Keigwyn*
  79. *alias* HOSKIN 50.
Ann 71.
Catherine 42.
Constance 13 ;
Dorothy 79.
Elizabeth 14. 25. 63.
Eunice 50.
Garthered 30.
Isabella 13 ;
James 79.
Jenken 99.
John 13. 13 ; 20. 24 ; 24 ; 25.
  42. 46. 64 ; 86.
Margery 13 ; 24 ;
Martin 98.
Mary 13 ; 24 ; 24 ; 25.
Nicholas 20. 39. 63.
Philippa 13. 13 ;
Porthesia 24 ;
Richard 13. 13. 13 ; 13 ; 14.
William 64 ; 98.
KELLY 55. KELYE 55. KEYLIE 11 ;
  alias HOWES 58 ; CALLYE 53.
  See CALLY.
Elizabeth 11 ; 55.
John 53.
William 11 ; 53. 53. 54. 54. 55.
KELTER 33.
Margaret 33.
Richard 33.
KEMP, See KIMPE.
Kendall 84.
  John 84.
KENSHEM 20 ; KINSHAM 62.
Nich 62.
Nicholas 62.
Priscilla 20 ;
Walter 20 ; .
KERRYS 47 ; KERIHS 33.
Elizabeth 33.

Richard 47 :
William 33.
KESTELL 10. CASTELL 52.
Chesten 10.
Edward 52.
Thomas 10.
William 10. 10. 52. 52. 52.
KIMPE 23 ;
Thomas 23 ; 23 :
KIMPTHORNE 36.
Edward 36.
Mary 36.
King Charles I. 85.
  „ *Edward the Confessor* 83.
  „ *George I.* 92.
  „ *George III.* 92.
  „ *James I.* 83. 85. 89.
  „ *John* 83.
  „ *William III.* 74. 92.
KINGE 41.
John 41.
Nicholas 41.
KITT 36 : See KEAT.
Ann 36 ; 71.
Henry 36 ;
KNEEBONE 19; KNEEBON 22. KNEBON
  21 ; KNEDONE 22.
Catherine 39 ; 67. 67 ; 71.
Elizabeth 22.
Grace 71.
John 22. 67 ; 71. 71.
Mark 21 ;
Richard 22.
Roger 19 ;
Stephen 19 ;
William 21 ; 22. 39 ; 67.
Knights Hospitallers, or Knights of
  St. John of Jerusalem, 83. 87.
  89. 90. 94.

LADNER 64 : *Ladnor* 71.
Adams 71.
Margaret 64 ;
Reginald 64 ;
LAITY 37 :
Ann 37 ;
Bernard 37 ;
Elizabeth 58 ;
LAKE 2. LAKES 30 ; *alias* LANE 50.
  See LEEKE.
Alice 50. 55.
Catherine 34 ;
Elizabeth 4. 34 ;
Joan 30 ;
Mary 34 ;
Sampson 2. 34 ; 55.
Thomas 2. 4. 30 ; 34 ; 34 ; 50.
  50. 63.
William 83.

LAMBRICK 57 :
John 57 ;
Richard 57 :
LAMERTON 11 :
Blanch 11 ; 55.
Elizabeth 35. 61 :
Grace 71 :
Honor 13 ;
John 11 ; 12. 12 ; 13 ; 35. 55.
  55. 61 ;
Roger 12.
Samuel 71 ;
Thomas 12 ; 55.
LAMYN 10 ; LEMYN 12 ; LEMIN 60 ;
  LAMONE 15.
Agnes 58 ;
Ann 12 ; 58 ;
Evelyn 35.
Humphry 15.
John 35.
Mary 10 ;
Richard 10 ; 14 ;
Thomas 15.
William 12 ; 14 ; 60 ;
Land 85.
Simon 85.
LANDY (LAUDY) *alias* TEAGE 58 :
Kay 58 ;
Morish 58 ;
William 58 ;
LANE, *alias* LAKE, 50.
Thomas 50.
LANYON 2. LANION 15. LANNYON 45:
  Lenyne 72 ; *Lanyne* 88.
Agnes 14. 15. 15. 36 ; 62.
Alexander 8 ; 8 ; 9 ; 10 ; 53.
  62. 62. 64 ;
Ann 8 ; 10 ; 13 ; 17. 17 ; 22.
  22. 36 ; 53. 59 ; 62.
Anthony 14.
Barnard 13. 20 ;
Bennet 8. 15. 16. 16 ; 17. 21.
  21 ; 22. 22. 23. 24 ; 25. 37 ;
  62 ; 64 ; 66.
Blanch 22. 33.
Constance 9 ; 17. 20.
David 9 ; 10 ; 11 ; 13. 16. 16.
  53. 56. 60 ;
Dorothy 17 ;
Ebbot 21.
Eleanor 20 ; 39.
Elizabeth 16 ; 17. 17. 20. 23.
  24. 33. 34. 37 ; 47. 60 ; 65.
Francis 8. 8 ; 15 ; 16. 16. 33.
  36 ; 37 ; 60 ; 60 ; 62. 70. 72 ;
George 5; 6; 32; 33. 49; 50. 51;
Grace 24 ; 65 ;
Honor 39.
Hugh 15. 22 ;

INDEX.

Humphry 21. 21: 21: 22. 22:
24. 65; 65: 66. 66.
Jane 6: 34: 35: 72:
Joan 9: 10: 15: 38.
John 3. 7. 13: 13: 15: 16.
17: 18; 19: 19: 21. 23. 24.
24: 27. 27. 29. 34: 36: 45.
45. 45: 54: 56. 59: 60.
60: 72: 72: 72:
Jonathan 60;
Margaret 15: 22: 29. 37. 62.
Margery 38.
Mark 15: 37:
Martha 37:
Mary 12: 16: 21: 21: 22. 25.
32: 35. 36. 38: 60. 62: 64:
66. 71.
Maud 8: 62.
Patience 39: 67.
Peter 9:
Philip 14. 22. 36: 59. 59. 62.
71.
Philippa 19: 70.
Prudence 5: 32: 49:
Ralph 2. 2: 3. 5. 21. 21: 23.
23. 39: 45: 49. 49. 67.
Rebecca 18:
Richard 2. 7. 9: 17. 17: 34.
38. 50: 51. 62: 63: 63: 88.
Robert 15: 56.
Rosamond 37:
Sampson 8: 15. 16: 17. 37.
62. 62.
Simon 5. 49.
Susan 36; 66:
Susanna 39: 63:
Thomas 2: 12: 14. 14. 16. 17.
20: 21. 22: 24. 24: 36. 65:
66:
Thomasine 73.
Ursula 20:
Walter 19: 23. 29. 38: 47. 49.
(Hellynor and Peter, his
servants, 29.)
William 6: 6: 11: 15. 16. 20.
20. 32: 35. 35: 39: 50. 53.
53: 62. 65. 65. 65: 72:
———— 50: 51.
LAUDY, See LODY.
LAUGHARNE 36; LAUGHORNE 36:
Ann 36: 36:
Theophilus 36: 36:
LAUNDER 3. LANDER 5: LAWNDER 6.
LANDAR 66.
Agnes 67.
Alice 4: 11: 12. 36. 36:
Ann 3:
Cicely 19. 63.
Digory 55:

Edward 63.
Ellen 52;
Elizabeth 61:
Garret 5: 6: 51: 55: 57. 57.
Gerrard 57. 57.
Henry 6: 35: 55: 57. 57.
Honor 35: 55.
Hugh 6.
Jane 62:
John 12. 51:
Margaret 55:
Mary 9: 35: 44: 57.
Nicholas 19. 63. 63. 66. 66;
67.
Philip 12.
Richard 5: 35: 36. 44: 55.
Simon 9. 52.
Thomas 11:
William 3. 3. 3: 4: 6. 9. 9:
11. 11. 12. 49: 52. 57:
———— 66:
LAVELIS 7. LAVELLIS 43. LEVELIS
54: *Laveles* 72.
Ann 32:
Catherine 32:
Constance 53. 54:
Ebbot 72.
Emanuel 7.
Hannibal 7. 32:
Honor 54:
Margaret 35: 55:
Mary 32:
Robert 43. 44.
(Rowe, his servant, 43.)
Thomas 35: 53. 54: 55; 57. 61.
William 54: 54:
Law 85.
Simon 85.
LAWRENCE 5: LAURENC 1. LAWRENC
7:
Agnes 32.
Alice 2:
Amy 7:
Annis 5: 29.
Edward 4. 32. 34:
Ellen 47.
Elizabeth 6. 12.
Grace 4. 45:
Joan 1. 13:
John 7: 47.
Margaret 12: 34: 51: 55.
Martin 12:
Nicholl 13: 36:
Otts 13:
Pasques 55.
Ralph 56.
Richard 5: 6. 12. 32: 53.
Thomas 51:
Ursula 32:

William 1. 2: 13: 13: 29.
36: 45:
LAWREY 17. LAWRYE 6: LAUREY
14: LAWRY 23. LAWRIE 48:
alias NOYE 48:
Alice 15: 48:
Ann 15:
Catherine 17.
Edward 6: 54.
Elizabeth 35. 57.
Francis 15: 59. 59. 59:
Hannibal 19;
Hugh 17: 23. 23: 23:
Joan 14:
Nicholl 22: 64:
Ralph 35. 49.
Thomas 49.
William 6: 14: 15: 17. 17:
19: 22: 23. 64:
Layton 85.
Richard 85.
LEAH, See LEHA.
LEATHE 6: LEATH 33.
Blanch 6:
Elizabeth 33.
Thomas 6: 33.
LEEKE 4. See LAKE.
Abraham 4.
Ann 4.
LEGG 12.
Alice 53:
Francis 12. 35:
Mary 12.
Philippa 35:
R. 25:
Robert 23:
LEGOW 2. LEGOWE 2: LEAGOE 11:
LEGOE 6. LEGO 7: LEGAWE
15. LEAGOW 21. LEGAW 37.
Agnes 29.
Alice 4: 14. 35.
Ann 2. 7: 17. 21: 28. 33. 33.
35: 51. 54: 55. 55. 61. 66:
Arthur 56.
Blanch 37: 62.
Catherine 53.
Charles 15: 23.
Clarence 2:
Edward 10. 33. 55. 55.
Elizabeth 3. 24. 49: 64: 65:
English 66:
Eve 22.
Honor 14. 23. 37. 67.
James 18.
Jane 11: 17. 21. 22: 31. 58:
64. 66: 67:
Joan 3: 16. 59.
John 2. 2: 9. 14: 15: 16: 16:
17. 22. 23. 28. 29. 37. 41:

INDEX.

49. 52. 67.
Maderne 2. 6. 9; 11; 12; 14.
15. 16. 35; 52. 52; 53. 56;
65;
Margaret 38; 61.
Mary 8. 14. 15. 23; 56;
Maurice 9; 52;
Paschas 39.
Peter 21;
R. 25;
Richard 8. 12; 15; 15; 16;
17. 21. 21; 21; 21; 21; 22.
22. 22; 23. 23. 23. 23; 23;
23; 24. 37; 62. 64. 65; 67;
Robert 25;
Sarah 7. 14. 67.
Sibyl 6. 7.
Thomas 14. 14. 16; 21; 22.
35. 54; 55. 61; 65; 66; 66;
Walter 18.
William 2. 3. 3; 4; 5. 5. 6.
6. 7. 7. 7; 8. 8. 9. 10. 14;
21; 22. 28. 31. 33. 38; 49.
49. 51. 54. 54; 55; 61. 61;
65. 65.
——— 39. 52.
Le Grice 77.
  Charles Valentine 77. 94.
  Day Perry 77. 80.
LENA 29. *Leah* 95.
  Annis 29.
  Margaret 30.
  Misses, The, 95.
LEIGH 8.
  Grace 8.
  Thomas 8.
LEMYN, See LAMYN.
LENARD 67.
  Richo 67.
LETCHFEILDE 44;
  James 44;
LEREBYE 30;
  Edward 30;
  Elizabeth 30;
LETHEBYE 32. LETHIBY 34;
  LETHIBYE 51.
  Dorothy 51.
  Elizabeth 32. 52.
  Grace 34;
  John 32. 34; 52. 53.
  William 42;
Le Tyes 83.
  Henry 83. 84.
LEVELIS, See LAVELIS.
LEWER 2. LUER 5; LEWAR 35. *alias*
  RICHARD 31.
  Agnes 35. 47;
  Annis 5;
  Dyonice 47.

Elizabeth 30;
  Honor 49;
  Joan 4.
  John 2; 30. 31. 41. 48.
    (Elizabeth, his servant, 30.)
    (Maryan, his servant, 41.)
  Mary 2. 31.
  Walter 7;
  William 2. 2; 4. 4. 4. 5; 7;
    30; 35. 49; 51.
  ——— 47.
LEWES 31;
  Jane 41.
  Joan 31;
  John 31;
LOCK 45;
  Christian 45;
LODY 34. LODDYE 7. LOADVE 55;
  LAVDY 58; LUDDY 58. LODYE
  14. *alias* TEAGE 58;
  Catherine 7.
  Ellen 52;
  Garret 34.
  Kay 58;
  Margaret 14.
  Morish 58;
  Robert 34.
  Teage 7. 52; 55;
  William 14. 58. 58;
LOGAN 41. LOGANN 42; LUGGON 43;
  Alice 45.
  Elizabeth 42.
  Henry 41. 42; 42;
  Margaret 42;
  Matilda 45.
  Richard 42;
  William 42. 43;
LOMME 44;
  John 44;
  Margaret 44;
LONDON 32;
  Catherine 49.
  Gillian 32;
  William 32; 49.
LONG 27; LONGE 27;
  Ann 27;
  Catherine 55;
  Elizabeth 27;
  Grace 28.
  John 27; 27; 27; 28. 28;
  Philip 27;
  Susanna 28;
LOASE 63; LOOSE 12;
  Elizabeth 35; 63;
  James 12; 35; 63; 74.
  Nicholas 12;
LOPPIER 49.
  Thomas 49.
LUDDRA 1. LUDRA 54; LEDDRA 21.

LUDDRAH 14.
  Ann 3; 22; 61.
  Catherine 30;
  Edward 1. 3; 30; 51. 53;
  Elizabeth 1. 11; 14. 22. 51;
    56. 61.
  Joan 71;
  Mary 53;
  Richard 11; 14. 54; 56. 56;
    56; 61. 65. 71;
  Robert 21.
  Thomas 14. 21. 21; 22. 22;
    65;
  Tobias 21; 65;
  William 51.
  ——— 54;
LUER, See LEWER.
LUKE 1.
  Agnes 3;
  Alice 2;
  Ann 34. 38; 58. 65;
  Charles 15. 18. 59. 63.
  Cicely 17. 60.
  Dorothy 36.
  Edmund 70. 70. 70;
  Eleanor 53;
  Elizabeth 1. 51. 65.
  Grace 70.
  Jane 32. 36. 54; 54; 60;
  Jermyn 1. 8; 10; 34. 53. 53.
    58. 58;
  John 4. 5. 6; 7. 7. 7. 8; 8;
    8; 15. 17. 18. 32. 36. 36;
    37; 46. 50. 59. 59. 60. 62;
    62; 63. 65.
  Julian 36;
  Margaret 37; 65; 70. 70;
  Martin 73.
  Mary 53.
  Pascoe 4.
  Reginald 49;
  Robert 1. 2; 3; 10; 46. 49;
    50. 51. 53; 55.
  Stephen 15. 21. 65.
  Thomas 1. 6; 46; 50. 50.
  William 15. 21. 36. 38; 49;
    64. 65. 65; 69. 69.
  ——— 5. 7.
LUTYE 9; LUTY 16. LUTEY 27;
  Elizabeth 72;
  Helen 38;
  Henry 9; 61. 62; 64.
  Hestor 18;
  Jane 16. 61.
  John 9;
  Mary 62.
  Nicholas 19;
  Robert 16. 18; 19; 38; 62.
    64.

INDEX.

Thomas 72:
Tristram 27: 27:
LYMPANY 4. LIMPENYE 6. LIMPANY
  33: LYMPANYE 8: LIMPENY
  50: LIMPANYE 6: LYMPANIE
  4: LYMPENYE 6.
Agnes 4. 32.
Alexander 33:
Alice 4:
Amy 5.
Ann 48.
Anna 5.
Aunis 48.
Edward 8: 51:
Elizabeth 7:
Hugh 6: 50:
Jane 6. 51:
John 6. 50.
Joseph 4. 4: 5. 6. 6: 7:
  8. 8: 32. 48. 48. 50. 50:
  51: 51: 52.
Philippa 33:
Richard 8. 55.
LYNNE 45.
  John 45.
  William 45. 46.

Mableston 84.
  Thomas 84.
MADERNE 1. MADREN 6: MADDREN
  7: MADDERN 8: MADDARN
  19: MADDERNE 36: MADEREN
  30. *alias* RICHARD 6: *alias*
  Cossen 98.
Alexander 53:
Ann 7: 19: 30. 34. 36: 36:
Arthur 19:
Bennet 18: 19: 19:
Cheston 47.
Clarence 2. 47.
Eleanor 33: 62.
Elizabeth 29. 63. 63. 71:
Grace 6: 8. 10: 11. 53:
Harris 16:
Henry 42.
James 18: 71:
Jane 31. 46: 52.
Joan 3. 8: 37: 47: 60:
John 1. 2: 15: 16. 16. 18:
  29. 30. 34. 37: 42. 43. 44.
  45. 46: 47: 52: 53. 59. 59:
  59: 60: 62. 63. 70: 75. 75.
  (Thomas Davie, his servant,
  42.)
  (Florence, his servant, 46:)
Margaret 10. 15: 44. 59. 65.
Margery 21. 22. 53.
Martin 16: 18: 19:
Mary 2: 38: 63. 70:

Nicholas 2: 4. 10: 10: 11. 53:
  53: 54:
Philippa 10: 53:
Rebecca 62.
Richard 6: 9: 18: 19: 21. 22.
  23. 23. 38: 42. 50.
Saundry 3. 34: 47: 52.
Thomas 33: 60:
Thomasine 34: 45.
Ursula 7:
William 1. 2. 2: 4. 6: 6: 7:
  7: 8. 8: 8: 8: 9: 10. 18:
  31. 46: 47. 48. 50. 52: 53.
  62: 63.
  ———— 47: 48.
MADDOX 36.
  Ann 36.
  Thomas 36.
MAGOR 60: MEAIOR 15. MEAGOR 15:
  MAIEAR 68:
  Joan 15. 58:
  John 15. 15: 58: 60:
  Thomas 15: 60:
MANEWELL 29.
  Elizabeth 29.
  John 29.
MANLY 14:
  John 35: 61: 62:
  Margaret 35: 61:
  Sarah 14:
  William 14:
MANN 45.
  Jennet 45.
MARKE 3.
  Avis 47:
  Elizabeth 32. 52.
  Gillian 34:
  James 34:
  Joan 30.
  John 30.
  Nicholl 36:
  Ralph 3.
  Rowan 3. 32. 47: 47: 52.
  ———— 47:
MARRACK 38. *Marack* 98.
  George 38.
  James 98.
  Susanna 38.
MARSHALL 22:
  Digory 22: 66.
  James 22:
  John 66. 91. 92.
MARTIN 42: MARTYN 1. MARTEN 6.
  MARTYNE 35: MARTYNNE 42:
  alias HARRIES 62:
  Agnes 32: 33.
  Cheston 37:
  Elizabeth 12. 42: 72:
  Humphry 12. 35:

Jane 43.
Jennet 46.
Jennyfret 35:
Joan 1. 17: 38: 43: 43:
John 1. 17. 33. 42: 42: 43.
  43: 43: 50: 62:
Philippa 16:
Richard 6. 15. 16: 17. 17:
  37: 62. 62:
Sarah 62:
Thomas 12. 12. 19: 19: 38:
William 6. 32: 42:
Wilmot 15.
Mason, The, 48.
  Henry 48.
MATHEWS 27: MATHEW 6. MATHIES
  27. MATHEWE 8:
  Dorothy 23:
  Elizabeth 6. 33. 42:
  Ellen 45:
  George 81.
  Jane 39.
  John 6. 6: 7. 8: 9. 14. 14.
  16. 23: 24: 33. 39. 42: 45.
  45: 50: 50: 50: 52: 64. 64.
  Margery 7. 50: 50:
  Martin 27.
  Mary 8: 9. 64. 72.
  Paskus 6:
  Ralph 10.
  Robert 27. 27: 27:
  Sampson 27:
  Thomas 10.
  William 16. 27:
  ———— 24:
MAWGAN 58:
  Elizabeth 58:
MAYE 42.
  John 42.
MAYNE 3: MEANE 52:
  Joan 53.
  Martin 3: 47: 52:
  Richard 3: 47:
MEANE, See MAYNE.
MEAIOR (Monjor), See MAGOR.
MELDERN, See MILDREN.
  Melcher 84.
  Roger 84.
MELYANNECK 2.
  Elizabeth 2.
  Henry 2.
  James 2.
MEREFELDE 5.
  Ann 5.
  John 5.
MERRYNNE 47:
  Mark 47:
Metingham 83.
  John de 83.

INDEX.

MICHELL 2. MYCHELL 3. MITCHELL 3. MICCHAELL 12: MECHELL 22. *alias* GARDEAGE 45:
Alice 6. 12. 32. 33. 48. 54.
Ann 3: 5. 36. 47: 50.
Blanch 7.
Catherine 34:
Charity 12: 61.
Christian 3:
Constance 37:
Dorothy 4:
Elizabeth 3: 4. 4. 6. 22. 31: 47: 52: 61.
Francis 21: 31: 60:
Garthered 20.
Grace 16. 59.
Henry 12.
Honor 39.
Hugh 19. 63:
James 2. 3. 3: 4. 11. 21: 44: 45. 46. 46: 48: 49: 54.
Jane 3. 20. 22: 33. 48: 52: 59. 64:
Jermyn 14.
Joan 11. 14. 46: 54. 55: 59: 62.
John 2: 3: 4. 7. 9: 16. 16. 16: 22. 25. 25. 31: 36. 38: 43: 44. 45: 47: 50. 54. 60. 63:
John Cotha 3.
John Thomas 43.
Julian 38:
Lawrence 6. 33.
Margaret 21. 38: 66.
Margery 3. 16:
Mary 3: 16: 20: 33. 38: 51: 60.
Nicholas 11. 15. 20. 20: 21. 21: 22: 34. 54. 64:
Pascha 31:
Pascoe 33.
Philip 16. 16: 37:
Philippa 45.
Richard 2: 4. 5. 6. 6. 7. 25: 32. 44:
Robert 3.
Samuel 2.
Susanna 21.
Thomas 3. 3: 4. 4: 6. 47: 52. 54. 58:
Thomasine 31:
Walter 9: 34: 52:
William 7. 12: 14. 15. 16. 16. 19. 19. 19. 20. 21. 21. 21: 21: 22. 22. 25: 25: 25: 33. 38: 38: 44. 59. 59: 61. 61. 62. 63: 64: 64: 66.
.... 39.
———— 34. 43:
MIDLAME 6. MIDLAM 7. MYDLAME 48.

James 32. 48.
Joan 32.
John 6. 7.
Mary 7.
Susan 6.
MILCOMB 43.
John 43.
Nicholl 43.
Mildmay 88. *Mildmaye* 89.
Walter 88. 89.
MILDREN 13: MELDREN 13. MELDERN 35: MILDARN 66.
Agnes 35: 63.
Ann 13:
Annis 13:
Bridget 66.
John 55:
Richard 66.
Robert 13. 13: 35:
Ruth 13. 55:
MILLARD 53.
Grace 53.
Thomas 53.
MILLER 42. 54: Tho, 2.
Ann 2.
George 2.
Henry 42.
John 42.
Thomas 54:
MILLETT 51: *Mellett* 70.
Ann 71.
Elizabeth 51:
Henry 70.
Margaret 70.*
Martin 71.
MINES 26.
Elizabeth 26.
Robert 26. 26: 26:
MONALLACK 37:
Ann 56:
Jane 37:
John 37: 56:
Moretain, Robert, Earl of, 83.
MORISH 2. MORISHE 3. MORRISH 14: See MORRIS.
Agnes 50.
Alice 7. 30:
Ann 5: 17:
Clarence 6.
Elizabeth 3. 4. 10: 18. 34: 51. 52. 59:
Gartered 5.
Grace 12:
Jane 12:
Jermyn 2. 3. 4. 5. 6. 7. 30: 51: 52.
Joan 43:
Job 20.
John 4. 4: 5: 12. 14: 17. 32.

35. 43: 49: 51. 53: 57. 59. 60.
Margaret 32. 35: 53:
Mary 16. 33. 71.
Philippa 4:
Ralph 4. 10: 12. 12. 12: 17. 33. 34: 59. 59: 63:
Richard 50. 50:
Robert 19.
Sampson 20.
Thomas 2. 12. 12. 12. 12: 14: 16. 17. 17. 17: 18. 19. 20. 20. 35: 38. 57. 60. 63:
Thomasine 35.
Wilmot 38.
———— 49:
MORRIS 31: MORISE 56. *Morice* 90. *Morrice* 90. See MORISH.
Agnes 31:
Alice 56.
Francis 83. 90.
Richard 31:
MOTE 5.
Thomas 5. 49.
William 5. 5: 5: 49.
MOVERA 30.
Geoffrey 30.
Joan 30.
MULFORD 8.
Judith 8.
Thomas 8. 52.
MULFRA 3: *alias* JAMES 17.
Ann 4. 17:
Catherine 35: 58:
Elizabeth 7. 43: 53.
George 9.
Henry 16: 25: 25:
Hugh 18.
James 32: 49.
Jane 9: 32:
Joan 3: 49: 60:
John 5. 12. 12. 12. 15: 35: 50. 53. 58: 60: 61.
Margaret 8:
Margery 17.
Mary 12. 14: 32. 61:
Mathew 44:
Pascha 44.
Peter 44:
Prudence 37.
Richard 6. 44. 53:
William 3: 4. 5. 6. 7. 8: 9. 9: 10. 10. 10. 10. 14: 15. 15. 16: 17. 17: 18. 32. 37. 43: 54:
.... 15:
MUMFORD 61.
· Joan 61.
MUNDAYE 9.

INDEX.

Edward 9.
Jane 9.
NANCOTHANN 46:
  Pascas 46:
NANKOLLAS 23:
  Elizabeth 23:
  Robert 23: 24.
  Samuel 24.
NASHE 43.
  Alice 43.
  Jane 46.
  William 43.
NEALE 30.
  Joan 30.
  John 30.
  William 89.
NENNIS 50. NENYS 4. NENES 5. NENIS 32. *Ninnis* 74.
  Agnes 49.
  Edward 48:
  Elizabeth 55:
  Grace 5.
  Jane 50.
  Mary 73.
  Milson 32.
  William 4. 5. 32. 48. 48. 73. 74.
  ———— 4.
NEROE 47.
  Helen 47.
NEWHALL 15: NUHALL 37. See NOWELL.
  Ann 37:
  James 60.
  Jane 60.
  John 15:
  Margaret 37. 57:
  Richard 15: 37. 37: 57:
NEWHAM 14:
  James 14: 16.
  Jane 16.
  John 14:
  Martin 16.
NEWMAN 12.
  Dorothy 20: 73:
  Francis 20: 20: 20: 82.
  Jane 12.
  John 12.
  Mary 20: 82.
NEWTON 10: *Nuton* 72: *Neuton* 73.
  Ann 36: 36:
  Catherine 34:
  Dinah 13.
  Elizabeth 10: 56: 65. 73.
  Henry 34. 36:
  Isaac 56: 56: 56: 71. 72: 85. 100.
  Margery 71.
  Prudence 56:

Richard 36:
Thomas 10: 34: 53.
———— 34.
NICHOLAS 12: NICKLES 5: NICKLIS 8: See NICHOLLS.
  Alexander 36.
  Alice 33. 53:
  Ann 23. 36: 38. 38. 60. 61:
  Bennet 63:
  Bridget 17:
  Catherine 8:
  Christopher 54.
  Digory 12:
  Edward 17. 17. 17: 18. 19. 21: 23. 23. 24. 62: 64.
  Eleanor 57. 64.
  Elizabeth 16: 29. 32: 42.
  Hugh 21.
  Humphry 18: 38. 65.
  James 16: 21: 21: 22: 23: 24: 24:
  Jane 24:
  Joan 9. 23: 30. 36.
  John 5: 12: 22: 44. 66.
  Lydia 21:
  Margaret 70:
  Mary 17: 38. 44.
  Michael 16: 17: 23. 38. 38: 60. 61:
  Nicholas 38.
  Oats 36: 58:
  Peter 9. 33. 34. 53: 57:
  Philippa 57:
  Richard 5: 8: 21. 32: 55.
  Samuel 16. 16: 21. 23: 37: 67:
  Tamer 19.
  Thomasine 37: 67:
  Ursula 34. 61:
  Vivian 29.
  William 18. 18: 21. 21. 22. 23: 24: 30. 54. 62: 66.
  .... 38:
  ———— 16. 22. 66.
NICHOLLS 10: NICHOLL 14. NICHOLS 39. *Nycolys* 70: alias *Trereife* 31. alias PORTEER 48: alias *Trevello* 72: See NICHOLAS.
  Agnes 35:
  Alice 71.
  Barbara 32.
  Digory 16. 63: 72.
  Dinah 13.
  Dorothy 12: 17. 60:
  Elizabeth 13: 31. 58: 71.
  Emanuel 27.
  George 39:
  Grace 12.
  Gregory 13.

Honor 14. 15:
Jael 77.
James 14: 15: 27. 27:
Jane 32: 39: 70: 72:
Janet 71:
Joan 14.
John 11. 13. 19. 32: 72: 77.
Julian 27:
Nicholas 11:
Paul 12. 35:
Peter 48:
Philippa 12. 18. 38.
Prudence 13.
Robert 13. 32.
Ruth 16.
Samuel 78.
Thomas 14: 20.
William 10: 10: 11. 11: 12. 12: 13. 13: 14. 17. 17. 17. 17: 17: 18. 19. 20. 31. 38. 60. 60. 70: 72: 93.
William John Godolphin 77.
NIGHTEN 5. NIGHTON 50: alias JEOFFRIE 5.
  Catherine 50:
  Duens 10.
  Ellen 6:
  Elizabeth 35.
  James 5.
  Thomas 5. 6: 10. 55. 56: 69: 69:
  William 35. 55. 60.
NINNIS, See NENNIS.
NOLAN 38:
  Alice 38:
  James 38:
NOLE, See NOWELL.
NORISHE 43:
  Joan 43:
  John 43:
NORTHIE 45.
  Emanuel 45. 48.
  Prudence 45.
NOSEWORTHYE 8: NOSEWORTNY 34. NOSWORTHY 36: NOSEWORTHIE 59. *Norsworthy* 95.
  Ann 9. 36:
  Catherine 34. 59.
  Francis 8:
  William 8: 9. 34. 36: 59. 62.
NOWELL 1. NOALE 2: NOWALL 59. NOLE 3: NOOALL 12. *Noall* 97. See NEWHALL.
  Agnes 1. 30:
  Alice 46.
  Ann 47:
  Christian 3:
  Cicely 32.
  Elizabeth 46: 62:

INDEX. 125

Jane 48.
Joan 2: 35: 59.
John 1. 2: 3: 12. 30: 32. 33
  35: 47: 59. 61.
Margaret 12.
Mary 33. 59.
Richard 46.
Noy 2. Noye 2. Noie 7: *alias*
  BODENAR 30; *alias* LAWRIE 48:
Alice 37. 48: 48:
Andrew 2.
Ann 3: 11: 17: 32. 49. 54:
  62:
Arthur 7: 13. 13: 15: 37. 57:
  57: 61: 63:
Avis 26: 66.
Blanch 73.
Charles 22: 67:
Chesten 4. 98.
Constance 16:
Ebbott 37. 59:
Edward 16.
Elizabeth 2. 6: 10. 17: 22:
  23: 35. 36: 61: 65.
English 8:
George 4: 12. 13. 16: 24. 35.
  58. 59:
Honor 12. 58.
James 16. 16: 17. 17: 37: 61.
Jane 3: 30: 48. 57: 98.
Japhet 17: 26:
Jennet 42. 45:
Joan 37: 57:
John 5: 15. 16. 43: 44. 49:
  53: 59:
Joseph 24:
Lowdye 44.
Margaret 8. 31: 32: 36: 37.
  38. 62.
Martha 17.
Mary 11: 14: 15. 16. 59:
Maud 2.
Michael 18. 18.
Philip 4:
Ralph 5: 7: 8: 10. 32: 42.
  49: 50. 56: 60.
Richard 2. 3. 3. 5: 14: 17.
  17: 44. 44. 44. 47. 56: 66.
Robert 2. 2: 30: 44.
Sampson 2. 2: 2: 3. 3: 4. 4:
  5: 5: 6: 7: 8. 8: 13. 16:
  24: 30: 32. 36: 36: 47. 48.
  53: 56. 56: 60. 62. 98.
Samuel 55.
Sarah 36:
Simon 66:
Thomas 2: 11: 11: 13. 13.
  13: 13: 14: 15: 22: 22:
  23. 23. 23. 23: 23: 24:

  42. 42. 54: 55. 56: 56: 67:
Thomasine 30: 49.
Walter 8: 11: 15. 16. 16: 16:
  16: 17: 37. 43: 59: 60.
William 3. 3: 4: 5: 7: 8: 13.
  13: 14: 14: 15. 16. 17. 23:
  24. 24: 25. 25. 31: 37. 38.
  45: 49. 49: 49: 59: 59: 61. 65:
  —— 50.

OFFALL 53:
  Emanuel 53:
OLERE, See CLERE.
OLIVER 4: OLLIVER 58: OLYVER 2:
  OLLYVER 47.
  Amy 21:
  Ann 35:
  Catherine 3:
  Elizabeth 5: 12. 23: 45. 58:
  Grace 4:
  Henry 23.
  James 21: 22: 23. 23:
  Jane 6:
  Joan 22: 33: 56.
  John 2: 3: 4: 5: 6: 12. 33:
    35: 45. 47. 48:
  Mark 41. 44.
  Margaret 45.
  Mary 2: 48:
  Peter 72:
  William 41. 47.
OSBORNE 46. OSBERN 17. OSBARN 23.
  Catherine 37: 66: 67:
  Charles 46.
  James 17: 65:
  Joan 23. 64:
  John 18: 23: 64:
  Nicholas 17:
  Ralph 23: 24. 24.
  Richard 17. 18: 37: 60: 64:
    65: 66: 67.
• Thomas 17. 60: 64: 65:
  William 23. 46. 67:
OTES 7.
  Ann 7.
  Richard 44: 44:
Oxnam 80.
  Richard 80.

Pachett 88.
  Richard 88.
PAINTER 37: PAYNTER 67:
  Arthur 67: 67:
  Francis 74.
  Honor 98.
  Jaquilina 37: 98.
  Jenken 67:
  Richard 98.
  William 37: 98.

PALMER 31. *Parmere* 97.
  Alice 97.
  Elizabeth 44:
  John 44: 97.
  Margaret 31.
  William 31. 50.
PARDEW 38.
  Sarah 38.
  Stephen 38.
PARKER 54.
  Roger 54.
Parmere 97. See PALMER.
  Alice 97.
  John 97.
PARRET 36.
  Ann 36.
PARSONS 21: PSONS 67.
  Ann 21: 67.
  Charles 22:
  James 22. 67.
  John 21: 22. 22: 67. 67.
PASCOWE 10: PASKOWE 11. PASKOE
  11. PASCHOW 57: PASCAWE
  44. *Pascow* 72: *Pascoe* 80.
  Bennet 10:
  Edward 11.
  Elizabeth 43:
  Erasmus 10: 53:
  Henry 11. 11. 36: 56. 57:
  John 11. 53:
  Julian 36:
  Margaret 56.
  Margery 72:
  Mary 44.
  Pascoe 10:
  Philip 13. 55:
  Richard 43:
  Robert 55: 84.
  Thomas 80.
  William 13.
Paslew 84.
  Robert 84.
PAULL 18: PAULE 22. PAWLE 35.
  Ann 22:
  Benjamin 18: 63.
  Helen 43:
  John 35.
  Mary 22.
  Richard 18: 19. 19. 22. 22:
    63. 63. 63.
  Sarah 35.
  William 43:
Pavely 84.
  John 84.
PAWGHE 33: PAWGYE 51.
  Wilmot 33: 33: 51.
  Woolph 33:
PAWLEY 57.
  John 57.

FF

INDEX.

Payan, alias Cornish, 73.
  Mrs. 73.
PEARCE 20: PERES 4. PEARSE 19.
  PEARS 50: PERSE 30: PEARES
  42: *alias* BEAGOE 56.
  Alexander 4.
  Ann 24.
  Catherine 56. 66.
  Dorcas 22:
  Duke, 78. 81. 86.
  Edward 45:
  Eleanor 19. 38. 63. 63.
  Elizabeth 20. 23: 30: 31. 39.
    45: 49. 72.
  English 23:
  George 23: 66.
  Humphry 19: 39. 64.
  James 49. 55: 56.
  Jane 42: 65. 72:
  Jedua 4.
  Joan 38. 42. 45. 50: 65. 65.
    67.
  John 26:
  Leonard 19: 63:
  Maddern 61.
  Margaret 42: 55: 57:
  Mary 39.
  Richard 23: 23: 26: 30: 31.
    42: 46. 46: 47. 66. 74. 91.
    92.
  Roger 57:
  Stephen 42: 42:
  Simon 42.
  Thomas 19: 38. 45. 65. 66.
    67. 74.
  William 19. 19: 20. 20: 20:
    22: 23: 24. 38. 39. 46. 61:
    61: 63. 63. 63: 65. 65.
    ———— 46: 67.
PEDENBUSSATH 2.
  Margaret 2.
  William 2.
PEDWELL 22: PIDWELL 25:
  Asia 73.
  Constance 25.
  Elizabeth 25:
  Grace 22:
  Hercules 22: 96.
  John 25. 25. 25: 25: 25: 65.
    74. 74.
  Justinian 39:
  Loveday 27.
  Margaret 25: 65.
  Martha 25:
  Mary 25:
  Peter 26: 27:
  Sarah 39:
  Thomas 25: 26. 26. 26: 27. 27:
  William 25.

PELLAMONTEN 36:
  Lucy 36:
Pellow 74. *Pellowe* 82.
  John 74. 82.
  Mary 82.
PENCAST 11.
  Ann 11.
  Henry 11. 54:
  Richard 54:
Pendarves 72:
  Henry 79.
  Margaret 72: 79.
PENDENE 3: PENDYNE 3. PENDEENE 8:
  Elizabeth 12:
  James 8: 33: 51:
  Joan 30:
  John 3. 8: 12: 47. 51:
  Margaret 33:
  Margery 3: 47:
  Pascoe 3. 3: 30: 47. 47:
  Thomas 51:
PENDER 9: PENDAR 22:
  Ann 50. 82.
  Christopher 22: 24: 25. 25.
    71. 82. 82.
  Gratiana 22:
  Jaquilina 24: 25. 71.
  Joan 24:
  John 47:
  Robert 53:
  Sampson 9:
  Ursula 34.
  Walter 9: 34.
PENHALL 8.
  Edward 8.
  Eleanor 57:
  John 8.
PENHALLOW 18.
  Benjamin 65:
  Bridget 65:
  Jacob 18. 18: 64.
  John 18:
  Margery 18.
  Sarah 64.
  William 67.
PENHELLICK 54:
  Alice 54:
  John 72.
PENLEASE 5: PENLEAS 7:
  Ann 5: 36.
  Constance 47:
  David 5: 7: 13. 13. 13. 35:
    47: 52: 55. 63: 67.
  Elizabeth 20. 35: 66:
  Margery 67.
  Susan 52:
  William 7: 13. 20. 64: 64:
PENMENITH 3. PENMENYT 30.
  PENMENYTT 30.

  Christian 3.
  Elizabeth 31.
  Helen 30. 45:
  Joan 30.
  John 30. 46.
  Margaret 45:
  Mathew 3. 31:
  Mary 31: 55:
  Thomas 31. 45: 46.
  Udye 45:
PENMINOW 42. PENMYNOW 42:
  PENMYNOWE 43.
  Catherine 42.
  Elizabeth 43.
  John 43.
  John 42. 42:
    (Margaret, his servant, 42:)
PENNALERICK 30:
  Elizabeth 30:
  John 30:
PENNALIVEAN 31. PANNALVEAN 42.
  PANALVIAN 42. PENNALVYAN 42.
  Barnard 31. 46:
  Elizabeth 42.
  June 31.
  John 42. 42. 42. 42. 42. 42.
  Margaret 42.
  Nicholas 42.
  Thomas 42.
Penneck 73. *Pennecke* 72.
  Bridget 73:
  Charles 72.
  Francis 73: 73:
  Henry 86. 94.
  Lydia 72.
PENNYN 16:
  Nicholas 45:
PENQUITT 31. PENQUITE 53.
  Alice 31. 53.
  Richard 31.
Penreeth, alias Harry, 96.
PENROSE 10.
  Agnes 48.
  Ann 53:
  Chesten 51:
  J. 99.
  Jane 99.
  John 72:
  Margery 72:
  Mary 10.
  Richard 10. 10: 53:
  Thomas 10: 54: 56.
PENTICOST 8. PENTICHOST 64:
  Elizabeth 36. 55: 58: 64:
  Henry 8. 58.
  Mary 16.
  Rebecca 15. 59:
  William 8. 14. 14. 15. 16. 36.
    58: 58: 58: 59: 64:

INDEX.

PERDEW 26:
  Bridget 27.
  Sarah 26:
  Stephen 26: 27.
PERES, See PEARCE.
PERROW 19: PERVE 29.
  Jane 29.
  James 19: 19: 20. 20: 64:
  John 20. 64:
  Lawrence 29.
  Margaret 20:
PERRY 36:
  Blanch 36:
  Jevon James Muschamp 86.
  John 36:
PERYAM 36. PERIUM 36: PERIAM 54:
  Elizabeth 36.
  Florence 54:
  Frances 36:
  Philip 36. 36: 54: 56:
PERYMAN 13.
  Benjamin 13.
  Philip 13.
PETER 30: PEETER 3: *Peters* 80.
  Bartholomew 30:
  Edward 3: 32. 48.
  Elizabeth 30: 48:
  Eleanor 3: 48. 48:
  George 43: 47:
  Jane 43:
  Joan 32.
  John 44. 44. 44: 44:
  Margery 47.
  Michael Norrell 80. 86.
  Thomas 44: 47. 48: 51.
PETHERICKE 45.
  Margaret 45.
PHILLIPS 7. PHILLIPP 15. PHILLIPPS
  8. PHILLIP 5: *Philips* 83.
  Phelips 90. *Phelipps* 90.
  Alice 35: 67.
  Avis 18.
  Dorothy 64:
  Elizabeth 21: 63: 64: 66:
  Francis 83. 90. 90.
  George 12. 35:
  Jane 8. 24.
  Joan 22. 58: 66:
  John 7. 8. 12. 15. 20: 24: 46.
    52.
  Mary 5: 20:
  Nicholas 7. 15. 20. 21: 22. 24.
    24: 46. 58: 66: 66: 66: 67:
  Thomasine 20.
  Tristram 18. 74.
  Walter 58:
  William 5:
  ——— 67:
PIDWELL, See PEDWELL.

PIKE 14:
  Ann 15: 16. 21:
  Catherine 24.
  Charles 20: 21. 21: 22. 24. 66.
    66: 67.
  Elizabeth 14: 66:
  Honor 22. 71:
  James 15: 37:
  John 74. 74.
  Judith 59:
  Julian 37:
  Mary 20:
  Thomas 14: 16. 21. 56: 56:
    59: 66.
PILLER 67.
  John 67.
  Thomas 67.
PILSON 37.
  Ann 37.
  Jonathan 37.
Pinnock 86.
  George 86.
PLAYER 63:
  Ann 63:
Poland 86.
  Frederick William 86.
POLGLASE 67.
  Margaret 67.
POLGOONE 47. POLGONE 49. *alias*
    THOMAS 48.
  Jane 47.
  John 48. 48. 49.
POLHORMALL 47.
  John 47. 49.
  Margaret 48.
  Robert 47.
POLKINGHORNE 3. POLKENHORNE 13:
  POLKINHORNE 6: POLKINGHOURN
    13:
  Ann 9. 36:
  Anthony 3.
  Blanch 13: 35. 56. 58:
  Ellen 34:
  Grace 13: 13: 33. 53. 98.
  Henry 6: 13: 13: 13: 31. 41.
    43: 43: 56. 59: 60:
    (James, his servant, 41.)
  Jane 31.
  John 8. 10. 10. 15. 34: 51. 53:
  Richard 14:
  Roger 6: 8. 9. 11. 11. 33. 35.
    36: 51. 53. 57. 98.
  Thomas 3. 14: 15.
  Thomasine 13: 59:
POLLARD 14: POLLERD 44. POLLARDE
    44:
  Elizabeth 32: 44:
  James 44. 44: 48: 49: 51.
    (Elizabeth, his servant, 48:)

  Jane 38:
  Joan 72:
  John 14: 14: 17: 18. 19: 32:
    38: 61: 61: 70:
  Margaret 19:
  Mary 18.
  Nicholas 44.
  Phillis 70:
  Ralph 17: 61:
  Robert 67.
  William 72:
Polmeare 69.
  John 69.
  Margaret 69.
POLPERE 45. POLPEERE 51.
  Agnes 45.
  Henry 45.
  John 51.
POLTEERE 29.
  Jane 29.
  Peter 29.
POLWIGEN 30:
  Elizabeth 30:
  Humphry 30:
POLSEWE 12. POLZEWE 10: POLZEW
    11. POLSEIWE 13.
  Catherine 12. 35. 56.
  John 10: 10: 11. 11. 12. 13.
    35. 55. 55.
  Richard 13.
POMEROY 52. POMERY 34. PUMBRYE
    48.
  Agnes 48.
  Alice 34.
  Henry 53: 83.
  John 34.
  Stephen 52. 53:
PORMEERE 57.
  Ann 57.
  John 57.
PORRIA 42. PORRYA 46:
  Jellian 46:
  Joan 42:
  John 42.
PORTEER 1. PORTERE 4. PORTEERE
    17: PORTEARE 27. *alias*
    NICHOLL 48: *alias* EDWARDES
    4:
  Elizabeth 63.
  George 18.
  Jane 1. 32. 50. 53.
  John 4. 4: 4: 17: 17: 18. 18:
    27. 32. 33. 50. 50. 63. 67.
  Margaret 33.
  Mary 27:
  Peter 1. 48:
  Sampson 4.
  Sarah 18:
  William 27. 27. 27: 27: 50.

PORTHIA 55.
  John 55.
Potter, Tho, 13:
  Stephen 13:
  Thomas 13:
POULTRY 61:
  Francis 61:
  Jacob 61:
Powton 85.
  Edmund 85.
PRADE 66. Praed 71.
  Ann 66.
  James 74.
PRETER 46. PREATER 46; PRETOR 31.
  Henry 46:
  John 45.
  Robert 31. 45. 46.
  Roger 46.
  Thomasine 31.
PRIMROSE 26. PRIMEROSE 14.
  Catherine 26.
  Edward 14. 14. 26. 26:
  Mary 26;
PROUSE 21.
  Catherine 21.
  Richard 21. 22:
  William 22:
PRUST 13:
  Ann 13:
  Clarence 55.
  Elizabeth 13; 36.
  John 15.
  Mary 15.
  Stephen 13:
  William 13: 13: 36. 55. 67.
PRYOR 13. PRIOR 56: PRYAR 20:
  PRYER 36.
  Alice 36. 63. 72;
  Annis 32;
  Elizabeth 57:
  Grace 56:
  John 13. 20: 20: 55: 57. 66:
    72:
  Margaret 57.
  Mary 66:
  Thomas 13. 36. 55: 56: 58:
  William 32:
PUMBRYE 48. See POMEROY.
  Agnes 48.
PUNGIOW 41.
  Maud 41.
Purrye 48.
  Agnes 48.
PURSHALL 49:
  Margaret 49:

Queen Anne 91. 92.
  ,, Elizabeth 85. 87. 88. 89. 99.
  ,, Mary II. 74. 92.

RABNETT 42.
  Agnes 42.
  Richard 42. 42. 42.
RALPH 60:
  Elizabeth 60:
RANDALL 11. RANDELL 52.
  Ann 33; 38.
  Blanch 34.
  John 11. 11. 38. 55. 63.
  Philip 33:
  Richard 52. 55.
  Samuel 34. 51:
RAW, See ROWE.
Rawles 77.
  Mary 80,
  William 77. 80. 80.
RAWLYN 1. ROWLYNN 3. RAWLIN 6:
  RAWLINE 13. RAWLYNE 13.
  RAWLINGS 14: RAWLEN 15:
  RAWLING 15; RAWLYNGE 30.
  RAWLINGE 30; Rowling 71.
  Adam 6: 6: 7: 32: 53:
  Alice 14: 58.
  Amy 71.
  Ann 10. 11. 12: 12: 71: 73.
  Arthur 63:
  Avis 60:
  Catherine 3. 12: 48: 55.
  Christian 43:
  Edward 16: 25: 37: 61. 61.
    66.
  Eleanor 37: 63:
  Elizabeth 15: 30. 39. 58. 59.
    63:
  Hellynor 29.
  Henry 12:
  Honor 33: 57.
  James 64:
  Jane 37: 71.
  Joan 1. 13. 15: 30: 52: 57.
    59. 59.
  John 7: 33: 37. 54: 57. 74.
  Margaret 16: 37.
  Mary 11. 37: 61.
  Mathias 65:
  Nicholas 1. 12: 13. 14: 15:
    37: 44: 54: 58. 58. 59. 61.
    63: 64:
  Peter 20. 29. 43: 64:
  Philippa 32: 62:
  Richard 25; 25: 26. 26. 64:
  Sarah 13.
  Thomas 13. 15: 37: 59. 61.
  Tristram 25; 28: 28: 71: 73.
  William 1. 3. 4; 4: 10. 11. 11.
    12: 20. 20: 20: 30: 39. 48:
    51: 55. 57. 57: 64: 64: 65:
READ 26. READE 67: REEDE 14:
  REED 22.

Alexander 16. 19. 22. 22. 25.
  25. 25. 25. 26. 26. 26: 39:
  66. 67: 70. 70. 70. 70:
  70: 74.
Ann 61.
Avis 14:
Elizabeth 70.
Henry 70:
Jane 57:
Joan 26: 37:
Juel 70:
John 19. 70.
Maria 70:
Mathew 16. 25. 25. 37: 61.
  64: 66.
Mary 26. 39: 67:
Sarah 70:
Susanna 26.
Walter 14:
Redon 84. Reddon 84.
  Henry 84.
  John 84.
REDWOOD 30; REDWOODE 50.
  Jane 30: 54:
  William 30: 50.
REIGNALD 10. See REYNOLD.
  Ann 10.
  John 10.
RELEIGH 9.
  Alice 61:
  John 9.
  Thomas 9. 55.
RELIGGYE 51.
  John 51. 51.
  ——— 51.
RENOWDEN 37:
  Alice 58.
  George 37: 58. 65.
  John 47:
  ——— 37: 65.
RESEIGN 56.
  Elizabeth 56.
RESKORLA 19:
  Charles 19:
  Robert 19:
RESKORLATH 13:
  John 13:
  Robert 13:
  William 13:
RESTORLATH 36:
  Alice 36;
  William 36:
Reswalstes 84.
  Stephen de 84.
REYNOLD 32. See REIGNALD.
  Edward 32.
  Joan 32.
RICAR 57.
  Alexander 57.

INDEX.   129

RICHARDS 5: RICHARD 1. RICHARDE
    6: RYCHARDE 46: RICHERDE
    47: *alias* WHITEWELL 4: *alias*
    MADREN 6: *alias* LEWER 31.
  Abraham 3:
  Alexander 39:
  Alice 20. 22: 37: 66.
  Ann 19: 27. 39; 63: 72:
  Charles 18: 46.
  Chesten 39:
  Christian 27.
  David 23: 24. 24. 27.
  Edward 16: 22:
  Elizabeth 5: 19: 31: 34. 47.
    72: 73.
  George 15. 67. 73. 73. 74.
  Grace 21: 29. 44:
  Hannibal 34.
  Honor 66:
  James 61:
  Jane 45. 46: 71.
  Joan 18: 30. 30: 31. 32. 47:
  John 1. 2. 3. 3. 3: 4: 5: 15.
    15: 16: 17: 18. 18: 19: 21:
    23: 30. 30: 31. 31. 31: 32.
    32. 37: 39: 39: 44. 44. 44:
    44: 46. 46. 47. 47: 47: 47:
    47: 47: 72:
  Margaret 23. 29. 73.
  Margery 1.
  Martin 19: 20. 20. 20. 66. 66:
  Mary 15: 31. 32. 39: 39: 71.
  Nicholas 19: 19: 64. 65. 71.
  Ralph 17: 22. 24. 24. 28:
  Richard 2. 6: 29.
  Ruth 3: 47:
  Sampson 1.
  Sampson John 29. 29. 44:
  Sarah 4:
  Thomas 2. 18. 18: 22. 23. 28:
    39: 46:
  Walter 44: 61: 67.
  William 1. 3: 6: 46: 65. 71.
  ——— 64.
RICHATT 43:
  Joan 43:
  John 43:
RICHOE 44.
  Eleanor 44.
RIDER 7.
  Alice 7.
  Nicholas 7.
RISE 65:
  Joan 65:
ROBBINS 6: ROBINS 7: ROBBYNS 53.
    ROBBYN 11.
  Ambrose 52.
  Ann 14: 21.
  Emmet 7: 14:

Henry 7: 48:
Jane 6:
John 11. 21:
Maddern 11.
Mary 22. 66:
Roger 21. 21: 22. 66:
Simon 53.
Thomas 80.
William 6; 7: 7: 10. 10. 33.
  52:
Wilmot 33.
——— 52:
ROBERTS 7. ROBERT 2: ROBARTS 27.
    RODARTT 42. *Roberd* 85. *alias*
    THOMAS 7.
  Alice 42.
  Andrew 66:
  Ann 14.
  Annis 11.
  Bennet 44:
  Charles 73.
  Duke 27:
  Elizabeth 12: 14: 27. 31:
  Grace 31: 59:
  Hannah 60:
  Henry 7. 31:
  Honor 38:
  Hosea 73:
  James 8. 51:
  Jane 34: 66.
  Joan 2: 32. 33: 43. 44. 57. 60:
  John 7. 14: 27: 29. 37. 41.
    42. 61. 62.
  Lewis 14.
  Maud 29.
  Nicholas 8. 33: 51:
  Petherick 3.
  Rachel 37.
  Richard 55: 85.
  Richoe 43. 43:
  Sackfeild 13: 57.
  Susan 11; 57.
  Stephen 44:
  Thomas 2: 3. 11. 11: 12: 13:
    15: 15: 27. 27. 27. 27:
    27: 31: 32. 34: 38: 41. 54:
    57. 57. 57. 57. 60. 66; 73:
  Thomasine 27.
  William 43. 43. 43. 43.
ROCH 1. ROCHE 3.
  Ann 36.
  Catherine 3.
  Elizabeth 8:
  Ellen 34.
  Grace 4.
  Honor 4. 48:
  Margaret 1.
  Mary 6. 50.
  Morishe 1. 2. 3. 4. 4. 6. 36.

48: 50.
Nicholas 2. 8: 34. 52:
Rodd 80.
  Edward Hearle 80.
RODDA 2. RODA 34. *Roddah* 70:
  Agnes 15.
  Alice 16: 23: 36: 39: 66.
  Ann 15. 22. 23. 38. 38:
  Catherine 21.
  Cyprian 18: 23. 23: 23: 23: 24:
  Dinah 63:
  Edward 2.
  Elizabeth 23: 34: 43: 48: 64:
    70:
  Emmet 2: 46. 46:
  Fortune 44:
  Grace 18. 18: 24: 37: 61:
  James 5:
  Jane 17: 32: 38: 46: 47. 64.
  Joan 2: 30. 73:
  John 2. 2. 4: 5: 6. 13. 18.
    22. 22. 23: 24: 30. 32: 43.
    43: 43: 44: 45: 47.
  Margaret 23.
  Martin 12: 12: 14. 15. 16. 16.
    19. 19: 20. 21: 36: 38: 65:
    66. 70: 73:
  Mary 13. 19: 19: 65:
  Methuselah 6. 15. 16: 37:
  Nicholas 22. 23. 39:
  Ralph 4: 21.
  Richard 14. 18. 19: 20.
  Robert 10: 34. 38:
  Sampson 13. 18. 18: 21. 63:
    67:
  Thomas 17: 18. 19: 21: 23.
  Ursula 43.
  Walter 18: 19: 38. 64.
  William 10: 13. 18. 19. 19.
    19. 21. 23. 24: 34: 38: 61.
    61: 62.
  .... 38:
  ——— 34. 67:
ROGERS 27: ROGARS 66: ROGER 18:
  Arthur 27: 27:
  Elizabeth 18:
  James 18: 67:
  John 27: 45. 45. 64. 66: 72.
  Margaret 72.
  Mary 72.
  Redigon 30:
  Richard 66:
  Robert 27:
  William 30: 64.
ROPER 43: Roper, The, 2.
  John 2. 43: 93.
  Margery 49.
  Richard 43:
  Robert 2.

INDEX.

ROSEMORAN 8; ROSEMORRAN 13.
    alias JAMES 63.
  Ann 8:
  Elizabeth 13:
  Grace 8:
  Henry 51:
  John 13; 56. 63.
  Nicholl 14:
  Richard 8: 13. 13. 13: 14:
    15: 51: 56.
  Thomas 15:
Rosetor 97.
  Christian 97.
  Robert 97.
ROSEWARNE 36; ROSEWAREN 46.
  Ann 36:
  John 46.
  Ursula 46.
Roskastel 84.
  Ralph 84.
ROSKYMMER 11. RESKYMMER 54.
  Francis 11.
  William 11. 54.
ROSVENE 5:
  Leonard 5:
  Richo 5:
ROWAN 7. ROOAN 54: *alias* DAVYE 7.
  Henry 7.
  Jane 54:
  John 7. 54:
  Philippa 30.
    ——— 30.
ROWE 13. RAW 1. RAWE 2. ROE 13:
  Row 23: *alias* STEPHENS 13.
    alias Chepy 97.
  Absalom 23:
  Alice 13:
  Ann 8:
  Elizabeth 28. 31: 34. 45: 55:
    58. 72. 78.
  Faith 86.
  Henry 28. 54.
  Honor 27:
  James 8: 28:
  Jane 59.
  Joan 1.
  John 1. 2. 9. 9. 13 13: 34.
    43. 45; 50. 51: 53; 55; 65. 66:
  Leonard 59. 60:
  Margery 52: 65:
  Mary 59.
  Paskos 45:
  Peter 27.
  Ralph 16:
  Richard 11. 11. 65. 66:
  Richard Bonnett 43.
  Susanna 13.
  Thomas 2. 16: 31: 43. 65:
    67: 72. 78. 81. 86. 86.

William 27. 27: 28: 97.
    ——— 23:
ROWLANDE 4. ROWLAND 52.
  Ann 52.
  · Catherine 56.
  Richard 4.
  Stephen 4.
ROWSE 33.
  Joan 33.
  John 33. 51:
RUNDELL 18: RUNDLE 60:
  Elizabeth 18: 60:
  John 18: 19: 60:
  Marret 19:
RUSSELL 4:
  Honor 71:
  John 4; 71:
  Margery 32.
  Mary 45.
  Patience 54.
  Peter 4: 4: 4; 32. 47. 48:
  Thomas 45.
Rutland 88.
  Henry, Lord, 88.
RYDEN 45:
  Blanch 50;
  Catherine 45:

SACARYA 2: SACARIA 4. SAKARLA 50:
    alias COTILA 50:
  Jenny 5:
  John 4. 4. 5: 50:
  Margaret 5.
  William 2: 5.
    ——— 2: 50:
Suffin 77.
  Dorothy 77.
  John 77.
SAFGARD 66.
  George 66.
Saint *Aubyn* 94. *Sentaubyn* 71: See
    DAWBYN.
  Ann 71:
  Francis 71:
Saint Madernus 83. 84.
SAINT PATERNUS 29. 97.
Salisbury 89.
  Robert, Earl of, 89. 90.
SALOMA 41. SOLOMA 41. See SOLOMAN
  Amy 41.
  Elizabeth 41.
  Mullior 41.
SAMPSON 2: SAMPSONN 4.
  Ann 9: 36. 37.
  Blanch 59:
  Catherine 2: 13: 23. 50: 51.
  Earth 16. 62.
  Elizabeth 17: 18: 24: 21: 67:
  George 21: 21: 23. 66: 66:

Grace 5:
Honor 27.
Hugh 21: 22.
Jane 13: 16. 28; 33. 36: 39:
Joan 18:
John 5: 6: 7. 8: 9. 9: 11:
    13: 15. 15: 16. 16: 16: 17:
    18: 19: 22. 23. 23: 37. 43:
    50. 50: 51. 53: 53: 53: 55:
    58: 58: 64:
Joseph 2:
Margaret 21:
Martin 11: 15: 16. 22. 35. 59.
    59: 59: 64:
Mathias 18.
Mary 23: 23: 35. 65. 66:
Nicholas 21. 22. 39:
Pascha 31.
Philip 2: 2: 4. 5. 23. 28: 31.
    47: 50.
Richard 9. 43: 57: 57:
Robert 8: 17: 18. 18: 18:
    19: 33.
Roger 15: 21.
Tammeris 23:
Thomas 13: 13: 15: 17: 23:
    23: 27. 36: 59.
Thomasine 7. 14: 57:
Ursula 20: 24. 53:
William 4. 6: 14: 18: 20: 24.
    24. 24. 24: 24: 36. 64:
    .... 15.
    ——— 5. 47? 47:
SANDERS 36; SANDARS 22.
  · Ann 67.
  Jane 36;
  Reuben 22.
  Richard 22. 67. 67.
  Susanna 67.
  Walter 36:
SATCHELL 55: See SAVHELL.
  Edward 55:
SAUNDRY 14: SAWNDRYE 6. SANDRY
    9. SAWNDRIE 7; SANDRYE 8.
  SAUNDRYE 8. *Sandro* 85.
  Anne 6. 27.
  Arthur 15.
  Christian 38. 59:
  Edmund 59.
  Edward 8. 52:
  Elizabeth 16: 60. 71:
  Hannibal 26: 27. 27. 27:
  Henry 16: 16: 17. 17: 19. 20.
    20: 26: 38. 52: 60: 63:
  Hugh 26:
  Jane 8. 19. 31; 53: 61:
  John 6. 7: 8. 9. 14: 42: 43:
    43: 56. 56: 60. 60: 60: 85.
  Mary 9. 17. 56. 64. 64:

INDEX.   131

Maud 7 :
Mellioner 43.
Redigon 8. 60 :
Richard 14 : 17 : 18 : 31 : 51 :
  64.
Sarah 27.
Susan 18 :
Thomas 20. 26 :
Walter 15. 16 : 61 :
William 20 : 60 ; 60 :
—— 63 :
SAVHELL 32 ; See SATCHELL.
  Edward 32 :
  Elizabeth 32 :
SCADDAN 20 : SKADDAN 44. SKADON 30.
  Christian 31.
  Elizabeth 30. 46 :
  Joan 71.
  John 31.
  Julian 38 :
  Michael 30. 44.
  Richard 38 : 71.
  Robert 20 : 20 :
SCISCELL, See SISSELL.
Scobell 86.
  George Richard 86.
SCOTT, See SKOTT.
Seamen 50 : 54. 55 :
SEARLE 52. SERELL 30.
  Ann 52.
  Margaret 30.
  Richard 44.
  William 30. 44. 47.
SEDGAR 45.
  Henry 45.
  Thomas 45.
SEESE 6 : SYSE 32. SISE 36. *Size* 70 :
  Catherine 7 :
  Edward 6 : 7 : 33. 36. 58 :
  Eleanor 70 :
  Elizabeth 38 : 42 :
  Jane 33. 58.
  Joan 32. 36.
  John 6 : 15 : 15 : 70 :
  Richard 42 :
  Thomas 32. 38 :
  William 44.
SELLOWE 43.
  Elizabeth 43.
  John 43. 43. 43.
SENNEN 58 : *alias* JAMES 58 :
  John 58 ; 58 :
  Margery 58 :
SEYMER 41.
  Nicholas 41.
SHACKERLY 15. SACKARLEY 63 :
  SAKERLEY 14.
  Arundell 14. 15. 37. 63 :

Bennet 14.
Bridget 37. 63 :
Margaret 15. 61 :
SHANE 47.
  Jane 47.
SHEARME 56 :
  Stephen 56 :
SHEPARD 46.
  Simon 46.
  Thomas 46.
SHEVANNE 43.
  Richard 43.
SHILLINGE 2. SHILLINGES 47.
  John 2. 47. 47.
  Mary 54.
  Sampson 47.
  William 58.
  .... 2.
Shipwrecked men 47 :
  John 47 : 47 :
  Peter 47 : 47 : 47 :
SHOALE 63.
  Ralph 63.
  —— 63.
SHOH 30 : SHOGH 51.
  Cheston 30 :
  John 30 ; 51.
SICKLEMORE 50 :
  Alice 50 :
SILVESTER 34.
  Mary 34.
  Robert 34.
SINCOCK 54. SYNKOW 58 : SYNKOE 4.
  SINKOE 4 : SINCKOWE 11.
  SYNCKOWE 10 ; SYNCKBOCK 31 ;
  alias BOND 58 :
  Catherine 4 : 31 :
  John 4. 4 : 11. 31 : 58 :
  Richard 54.
  Simon 10 : 11. 54.
  William 4. 10 :
SISE, See SEESE.
SISSELL 10 : SISCELL 18 : SCYSELL
  19 : SYCSELL 35. SCISCELL 60 ;
  SCISSELL 66 :
  Ann 12 :
  Henry 11 : 18 : 18 : 19 : 20 ; 66 :
  Jane 13 :
  John 10 : 60 :
  Margaret 12. 13 : 35.
  Martha 20 :
  Mary 19 :
  Samuel 10 : 11. 12. 12 : 13 ; 35.
SKINNER 18. SKYNNER 11 : *alias*
  GOVER 55 :
  Ann 11 : 34 : 60.
  Christian 18.

Elizabeth 19. 63.
Mary 55 : 64 :
Mathew 19. 25. 25. 38 : 63. 64 :
Michael 11 : 34 ; 57 : 57 :
Nicholas 18. 62 :
Philippa 38 :
Skewes 72 :
  Ann 72 :
SKOTT 41. SKOTTE 41.
  Christian 41.
  John 41. 41. 41. 41. 41.
  Richard 41.
  William 41·
SLADE 3 :
  Ann 3 : 47 ;
  John 3 : 47 :
SLADER 4.
  Frances 5.
  Joan 7 :
  John 4. 5. 7 : 32.
  Richoe 32.
  William 4.
SLEEP 20. SLEEPE 20 :
  Jane 36.
  Thomas 20. 36.
  Tristram 20 :
  William 20. 20 :
Smith 86. SMYTH 31 : SMYTHE 42.
  Smith, The, 5 : 8 :
  Christopher 89.
  Emanuel 43 :
  Henry 31 : 47 :
  John 8 ; 43 : 43 : 53. 64. 86.
  John Sampson 5 : 53 :
  Margaret 31 : 47 :
  Martin 42.
  Richard 8 : 9. 42.
  Roger 42.
  Thomas 43 :
  William 9.
SOLLOMAN 42 : SALOMA 41. SOLOMA 41.
  Amy 41.
  Elizabeth 41.
  Maryan 42 :
  Mollior 41.
SOMERY 34 :
  Ann 34 : 62 :
  Tristram 34 :
SOMMER 5. SOMER 10. SUMMER 13.
  SOMMAR 66. SOMMARS 67 :
  Alice 47 :
  Elizabeth 57 : 58.
  Gabriel 10 : 11. 11. 11 : 13. 34 : 53. 58. 58. 66.
  John 5. 10 : 43 : 49. 58.
  Margaret 34 : 58.
  Mary 11. 53.
  Thomas 11 : 57 : 63 :

INDEX.

Tobias 13.
William 5. 11. 43; 47; 49. 53.
54. 67;
——— 53.
SPARNAN 12;
Alice 54.
George 12;
Michael 12; 53; 54. 54. 54.
SPRIDDLE 20. SPREDLES 66;
Ann 20.
Edward 20.
Isaac 66;
STADEN 21;
Alexander 21; 21;
Stafford, Bishop, 84.
STEPHENS 2. STEPHEN 4; STEPIIINS
7. STEVENS 12. STEVEN 36.
SEEVINS 36. STEEVINS 36. *alias*
STINION 13. *alias* ROWE 13.
alias ROE 13; *alias* THEVAWIN
57.
Alice 13.
Amy 7.
Ann 15; 23. 36. 39. 57. 58.
Avis 20;
Blanch 12; 55.
Catherine 57.
Clarence 49;
Cyprian 65;
Eleanor 37; 70;
Elizabeth 4; 15; 31. 36.
English 56;
George 21; 22; 23; 39; 67.
Grace 58;
Halenight 12; 36. 55. 64.
Henry 2. 23; 31. 49;
Honor 39;
Jane 36.
Joan 31;
John 7. 10; 12; 12; 13. 13. 13;
14. 15. 15. 15; 15; 20. 20;
22; 22; 23. 23; 36. 36;
39; 57.
Justinian 4; 5; 7. 32;
Lucy 14. 36;
Luke 21; 37; 58. 58; 64.
Margaret 36.
Mary 2. 22; 23; 39; 67.
Richard 4; 5. 7. 13. 14. 36.
38; 56; 58.
Scipio 39.
Susan 37. 61;
Susanna 13.
Thomas 5; 12. 12. 20. 31; 36.
37. 38; 57. 57. 57. 61; 64;
Thomasine 5. 38; 38; 64;
Ursula 32;
William 4; 10;
——— 36.

STINIAN 12. STINION 13. *alias*
STEPHENS 13.
Henry 12.
John 12. 13. 13; 13;
Richard 13.
Thomas 67;
STONE 6. STOANE 5.
Alice 6. 26. 32; 63. 72;
Andrew 8;
Annis 51.
Catherine 64.
Cicely 18. 62.
Elizabeth 7. 31; 36. 47. 61;
Eunice 16. 16.
Grace 56; 61.
Humphry 17. 61;
Jane 5.
Joan 9; 62;
John 5. 5; 6. 7. 8; 9. 9; 9;
16; 26. 31; 32; 36. 47. 52.
54; 59. 59; 59; 74.
Mary 13;
Richard 9; 16. 16. 16; 17;
18. 59; 63.
Sarah 9;
Thomas 9; 13; 17. 17; 74.
Walter 5; 49; 54; 56; 61. 62.
William 9. 52.
SUDGIOW 3; SUGIOW 3; SUDGEO 10.
SUDGEOW 12; SUDGIOWE 29.
SUDGYOW 54. SUDGOW 66.
alias GENE 44;
Agnes 29.
Ann 30; 33; 46;
Blanch 30.
Catherine 10;
Chesten 3; 48.
Charles 3; 4. 5. 31; 56.
Christian 55.
Elizabeth 29. 31; 34; 46; 50;
59; 59;
Grace 12;
Jeffrey 29.
Joan 48. 62;
John 3; 30; 33; 39. 43. 44;
46; 46; 52; 62; 66.
Margaret 4. 5. 34;
Nathaniel 47.
Richard 37.
Sibella 39.
Thomas 3; 10. 10; 29. 34;
43. 47. 50. 52; 54. 55. 59;
60.
William 10. 12; 34; 54.
SUGER 60;
Agnes 62.
Hugh 60;
SUTTONN 43;
Amy 43;

John 43;
SWAFFEN 3. SWAFFIN 49;
Joan 49;
John 3. 3. 4; 48; 49; 49;
Thomas 4; 48;
SWAFFIELD 2;
Florence 2;
John 2;
SWAYER 30.
Joan 30.
John 30.
SYER 10;
Elizabeth 10;
——— 10;
SYMONS 14; SEMONS 65; SYMON 8.
SEMMENS 20; SIMONS 23. *alias*
CRANKAN 31;
Alexander 18;
Ann 18. 24. 24; 61;
Catherine 8. 55;
Christian 25.
Honor 33. 57;
James 20; 24. 24; 46; 65;
Jane 14; 20;
Joan 30; 31; 46.
John 30; 31; 46. 46; 58.
John Richard 46. 46; 46; 46;
Mary 24;
Nicholas 23. 23. 24; 25. 72;
Philippa 19.
Richard 18. 18; 19. 61;
Sampson 46.
Thomas 14; 65; 72;
William 8. 33.
SYMPSON 30.
Elizabeth 30.
Peter 30.
SYNKOW, See SINCOCK.
SYNNER 44;
John 44;
SYSE, See SEESE.

TABER 42;
Henry 42;
William 42;
TALMENITH 6;
Agnes 6;
John 6;
TALSKUS 44;
Edward 44; 45. 46.
Hugh 44;
John 45.
TANGIE 48;
John 48;
TANNAR 24; Tanner, The, 34;
Anthony 24;
Arthur 24;
Ellen 34;
Thomas 34;

INDEX. 133

Thomas Bennet 55:
Thomas James 96.
TAYLOR 8: TAYLER 30. TAILOR 58:
  TELLER 42: Tailor, The, 51.
  Agnes 47:
  Dionice 42:
  Elizabeth 13.
  Francis 51.
  Joan 30. 34. 42: 47: 59:
  John 8: 8: 9. 9. 30. 30. 34.
    34. 45. 47: 58:
  Maddern 45.
  Mary 9.
  Nowell 9.
TEAGE 11: TYAG 18: *alias* LAUDY
  58: See TYACK.
  Agnes 45.
  Catherine 35.
  Frances 47.
  James 59:
  John 11:
  Kay 58:
  Marret 18:
  Morish 58:
  The blind man 44:
  Thomas 18:
  William 11: 35. 58:
TELLER 42: See TAYLOR.
  Dionice 42:
  Joan 42:
TEMPIE 49.
  Jane 49.
TERRENACKE 42: TERRYNNACK 42:
  TERRYNNACKE 42:
  Alice 42:
  Catherine 42:
  Frances 42:
  John 42: 42: 42:
Thame 84. *Tame* 83.
  Philip de 83. 84.
THICK 16: FICKS 15: FIX 37:
  THICKE 61.
  Catherine 37: 61:
  Gilbert 15: 16: 17. 37: 61.
    61: 61: 95.
  Honor 16:
  Margaret 61:
  Mary 15:
  William 17. 61.
THOMAS 2: *alias* ROBERTS 7. *alias*
  ANGOVE 7: *alias* POLOGONE
  48. *alias Daddow* 70:
  Agnes 29. 31. 42.
  Amy 33.
  Ann 34: 36: 73.
  Black 50:
  Bridget 33:
  Charity 30.
  Christopher 3. 70:

David 30.
Earth 37.
Edward 42.
Eleanor 45:
Elizabeth 5: 21: 36. 39.
English 4.
Enoch 64.
Frances 42.
Francis 45: 45:
Giles 16.
Grace 35. 37.
Henry 7. 30. 30: 50: 54.
Honor 60:
James 19. 19. 39. 54: 64. 65.
Jicholas 11:
Joan 30: 30: 31. 36. 42: 45:
  62.
John 2: 3. 5. 5. 5: 7. 10: 11:
  18. 18: 21. 21: 23. 29. 30:
  33. 34: 35. 36. 41. 42. 42.
  42. 42. 42: 43: 43: 43: 43:
  44. 44. 46. 48. 48. 49. 50:
  51. 53: 55. 58. 60: 61: 61: 63.
Margaret 30.
Mark 61:
Martin 10: 18: 59.
Mary 22: 39. 55.
Mathew 18: 63.
Michael 47:
Melchisedec 64:
Nicholas 7: 18. 42.
Peter 26.
Philip 6. 71:
Philippa 71:
Ralph 31.
Rawe 2:
Richard 17. 31. 31. 33: 54.
Robert 4. 5: 39. 42. 64.
Sampson 17. 18: 21: 23. 60.
  63.
Stephen 25. 30: 72:
Sybil 31.
Thomas 2: 15. 15. 21: 26. 37.
  37. 45: 46. 70:
Ursula 60:
Wilmot 30:
William 2: 5: 6. 16. 21. 22:
  25. 28. 28. 41. 49: 49: 50.
  50. 56. 60: 72: 72: 73.
——— 7:
THOMPSON 14.
  Mary 14.
  Ralph 14.
TINCOMBE 15. TYNCOMBE 35. TINCOM
  66.
  Margaret 58.
  Margery 35. 37.
  Pascoe 15. 15. 35. 37. 58. 66.
TIPPET 31.

Robert 31.
Temperance 31.
TIRROLL 14:
  Ann 38:
  Anthony 14:
  John 14:
  William 14:
TOBMA 48.
  Thomas 48.
TOLL, See TULL.
TOLLAR 12:
  Grace 12:
  Luke 12:
TOLLVAN 44: TOLVAN 52.
  Eleanor 52.
  Elizabeth 45.
  John 44: 45.
  Peter 55.
  ——— 44:
TOMAN 23.
  John 23. 26:
  Mary 26:
  William 23.
TOMME 3: TOM 10: TOMM 34. TOME
  52.
  Agnes 3:
  Elizabeth 52.
  Margaret 34. 54: 60.
  Nicholas 10: 53: 70:
  Peter 70:
  Richard 10: 34. 52. 53: 60.
    64.
  Robert 3:
TOMPKYN 10. TAMPKYN 35: TOMCKYN
  52: TOMPCKYN 53. TOMPKIN 49:
  Catherine 35:
  Jane 35: 53.
  John 10. 54. 54.
  Robert 35:
  Roger 10.
  William 35: 49: 52:
TONKING 32. TONKYNG 2. TONKYN 4.
  TONCKYN 4: TONCKYNGE 30.
  TONKEN 6. TONCKING 30.
  TONCKEN 12: TONKYNN 48.
  TONKINGE 43: *Tonkin* 71:
  Agnes 43.
  Alice 35. 57.
  Andrew 70.
  Ann 2. 8. 14. 33: 57: 57: 70.
  Arthur 17. 21: 22: 23: 39: 67.
  Blanch 6.
  Catherine 32.
  Charles 55:
  Edward 98.
  Eleanor 30.
  Ellen 21:
  Elizabeth 5: 26. 30. 39. 42:
    71.

Grace 14. 37: 59. 64:
Jane 58.
Joan 37:
John 2. 8. 15. 15. 16: 16: 17.
  18. 22: 23: 30. 33: 35. 37:
  37: 43: 43: 45: 48. 55:
  55: 55: 56. 56. 57. 57. 57.
  57. 59. 59: 59: 62.
John Thomas 46:
Joseph 19: 92.
Lydia 71:
Margaret 39. 71. 71.
Mary 57. 57: 57:
Nell 21:
Nicholas 43.
Nuall 71:
Richard 4. 42: 48. 71. 73.
Robert 12: 12: 18. 19. 19:
  39. 57: 58. 60. 71.
Susan 19.
Thomas 20: 20:
Uriah 26: 39. 80.
Ursula 71:
William 4. 4: 4: 5: 6. 14.
  14. 26. 26: 32. 45. 48. 49.
  50: 57: 57: 60. 74.
  (Thomas Loppier, his servant
  49.)
Wilmot 45.
—— 39: 67.
TOOKER 23: TOOCKER 21.
Jane 52.
Joan 23:
John 23:
William 21. 21. 23:
Tottchale 83.
  William de 83.
TRACY 31: TRASYE 50.
Jane 63.
Joan 50.
John 31:
—— 31:
TRANNACK 49:
  Elizabeth 49:
TRATT, See TROTT.
TREBEHAR 14:
  Giles 14:
  Mary 14:
TREBIVER 36.
  Joan 36.
  John 36.
TREDENNECK 38: TREDENNACK 59.
  TREDYNNECK 42: TREDENNICK
  62:
  Alice 60:
  Elizabeth 38: 42:
  Henry 38:
  James 59.
  John 42:

Margaret 38: 63.
Michael 38: 60: 62:
TREGANHOE 44: TREGENHOE 2:
  TREGUNNOW 15: TREGONOW
  21:
Ann 21: 37.
Constance 61:
Elizabeth 44: 56:
John 2: 15: 15: 21: 37. 44:
  56: 61. 61:
Sampson 2:
TREGANHORNE 10: TREGENHORNE 60.
  Annis 10: 53:
  John 60.
  Thomas 10: 53:
  William 60.
TREGEEO 36: TREGEOW 60.
  Francis 60.
  Susan 36:
  William 36: 60.
TREGELLAS 54:
  William 54:
TREGERTHEN 13. TREGIRTHEN 2:
  Alexander 60.
  Ann 56: 59: 64:
  Christian 33.
  Clarence 5.
  Elizabeth 30. 30: 58.
  Henry 13. 14: 66:
  James 14. 56: 57.
  Joan 2:
  John 2: 4: 5. 30. 49.
  Margery 14: 59:
  Mary 19: 66:
  Nicholas 13. 19: 64:
  Thomas 14 14 30: 33, 57.
Tregose 84. *Tregoos* 81.
  Benedict 84.
TREGUNNOW, See TREGANHOE.
TRELEVAR 39: TRELYVER 44:
  Elizabeth 39:
  Honor 44:
  John 39: 44: 66:
TRELILL 3. TRELYLL 45.
  Agnes 45:
  Charity 5:
  Clarence 66.
  Elizabeth 54.
  Henry 45.
  Jane 31:
  John 3. 4. 7. 31: 45: 48: 56.
  100.
  Margaret 12.
  Pascoe 65:
  Paskas 45.
  Peter 3. 66. 66.
  Richard 65.
  Thomas 4. 12. 62.
  William 5: 7. 51.

TRELOWETH 11.
  Grace 19: 35. 66:
  James 11. 35.
  Thomas 11. 19:
TREMBAH 3. TREMBAHE 4: *Tremba*
  70. *alias* HOSKYN 6. See
  TREMBATH.
  Catherine 4.
  Christian 70.
  Elizabeth 3. 45.
  James 3. 45. 47. 48:
  Joan 3:
  John 3: 4. 4: 4: 6.
  Mary 45.
  Silvester 6.
  Thomas 70.
  Ursula 47.
TREMBATH 41. TREMBATHE 43: *alias*
  HOSKYN 51: See TREMBAH.
  James 41.
  John 41. 51:
  Margaret 66:
  Margery 43:
  Thomas 43:
TREMEARNE 62. TREMERNE 35.
  Tremearn 71:
  Henry 35. 62.
  Jane 71:
  Joan 72:
  John 99.
  Philippa 35.
  Richard 98.
  Susan 72.
TREMELLYN 11.
  Honor 11.
  John 11. 34.
  Mary 34. 58: 58:
  Richard 58:
TREMENHEERE 10: TREMENHEAR 65:
  TREMYNHEERE 12: *Treminheer*
  72. TREMENHEARE 14:
  Ann 33: 62: 63: 72.
  Blanch 12:
  Catherine 82.
  Eleanor 58.
  Francis 37. 73:
  Henry 10: 12: 13: 15: 33:
  54. 56: 65: 72.
  James 72. 73:
  Joan 58.
  John 10: 14: 15: 58. 63: 65:
  73: 74. 82. 82.
  Mary 37. 71:
  Rebecca 14: 58.
  Sybella 82.
  Wearne 61.
  William 13: 37. 37. 46. 80.
  82. 86. 94. 96. 97.
  —— 54.

INDEX. 135

TREMESACKE 41.
James 41.
TREMETHACK 2. TREMATHACKE 47:
  TREMETHACKE 2: *alias* JAMES 2.
  Ann 2. 3.
  Bennet 2: 3:
  Elizabeth 4. 4: 5. 30. 31: 46.
  James 31. 43. 43. 45.
  Jane 2. 34.
  Joan 32. 33: 45. 51:
  John 2. 3. 4. 4: 30. 31: 34.
    43: 43: 44: 46. 51: 93.
  John James 2. 33: 51: 54. 93.
  Maddern 29.
  Margaret 45.
  Margery 31.
  Mary 44:
  Maud 29.
  Richard 3: 5. 32. 43. 49.
  Susan 3.
  Thomas 3. 43. 45. 47:
  —— 2:
TRENEERE 8. TRENEYRE 3; TRENERRE
  66. TREANERE 43. TRENEARE
  43. TRENEYR 31. TRENERE
  48: See TRENERRY.
  Alice 31.
  Ascott 16:
  Elizabeth 34: 69.
  Frances 36.
  Joan 14:
  John 8. 14: 15: 16: 37. 43.
    43. 56: 60: 60: 66.
  Mary 11: 15: 31. 31: 55. 55.
    58: 61. 61:
  Priscilla 37.
  Richard 12. 31. 31. 31: 36. 43.
    43. 43. 48; 56; 56: 56: 69.
  Robert 3: 8. 11. 31.
  Roger 47:
  Ruth 12:
  Sarah 66.
  Thomas 62.
  William 3: 11. 11: 12. 12:
    34: 55. 55. 58: 58:
TRENEGLOS 57: DRANEGLOS 66:
  DREANEGLES 13. *alias* JAMES
  13.
  Dorothy 55:
  Honor 13.
  James 57:
  John 13. 55: 57: 57: 66:
  —— 66:
TRENERRY 15: TRENERREY 64.
  TRENERY 65. See TRENEERE.
  Elizabeth 15;
  Grace 37:
  John 71.
  Margery 61:

Nathaniel 15: 37: 61: 64. 65.
  Sarah 71.
  Thomas 64.
TRENGOTHELL 51:
  Nowell 51:
TRENGOVE 49: *Trengrove* 91.
  Catherine 49:
  Ezekiel 91.
TRENHAILE 5: TRENHAYLE 22:
  Ann 21.
  Catherine 5:
  George 66.
  James 22:
  Jane 57:
  Joan 53.
  John 5: 7. 53. 57:
  Peter 7.
  Reginald 20: 21. 22: 66. 74.
    85. 100.
  William 20:
TRENWITH 13:
  Constance 39:
  Elizabeth 35.
  Henry 39:
  James 13: 14. 35. 56. 56.
  Jane 14.
  John 13: 56.
  Robert 56.
TREREIFE 6. TREVE 2. TEREIFE 2:
  TEREVE 3: TREF 4: TREFFE
  33: TEREYVE 44. TREIFE 47.
  alias NICHOLLS 31.
  Agnes 48.
  Elizabeth 6. 31. 49: 50.
    (Mistris Elizabeth Toreifo's
    man 50.)
  Honor 2.
  Margaret 33:
  Mary 4: 50.
  Raw 44.
  Robert 2: 47. 47. 48. 49:
  Thomas 44. 44: 47.
  Walter 33:
  William 2. 2: 3: 3: 4: 6. 31.
    49: 49: 49: 50.
TRESIES 7: TRESYSE 8. TREZIES 33:
  TRESYES 52.
  Anthony 8. 33:
  Elizabeth 33:
  John 7:
  Mary 52.
  Tirhum 33:
  Walter 7: 8. 8. 52. 52.
  William 8. 33:
TRESTEANE 22: TRESTEAN 39:
  Dorothy 39: 67:
  John 22:
  Oliver 22: 39: 67:
  Mr. 67.

—— 67.
TRESVENACK 11:
  Joan 35:
  William 11: 11: 35:
TREVAILER 63: TREVILER 20.
  TREVILOR 34. *Trevilour* 71.
  Catherine 71.
  Eleanor 34.
  John 34.
  Richard 20. 20. 63: 63: 63: 71.
  William 63:
TREVALLES 2: TREVALLIS 3.
  Clarence 3.
  Edward 2: 46:
  Elizabeth 31. 31:
  James 2: 3. 31. 31: 46: 48.
TREVANYON 33. TREVANNYON 30.
  Trevanion 76.
  Ann 30.
  Blanch 33. 76.
  Hugh 33. 76. 98.
  Richard 30.
TREVAWIN 57. *alias* STEPHENS 57.
  Ann 57.
  John 57.
  Thomas 57. 57.
TREVEEAN 50.
  Richard 50.
Trevello 72: *alias Nicholls* 72:
  John 72:
TREVETHAN 18: TREVITHAN 19.
  Daniel 19.
  Elizabeth 20:
  John 18: 19. 19. 19. 20: 23.
  Mary 23.
  William 18:
TREWEEK 66. *Treweeke* 80.
  George 66. 80. 86.
  John 66.
TREWHEELA 36.
  Catherine 36.
TREWREN 9: TREWRYN 2.
  Alice 9:
  Avis 10:
  Catherine 39.
  Elizabeth 32: 38. 38: 62:
  Francis 38:
  Joan 19. 52:
  John 34. 55.
  Margaret 19. 34.
  Mary 34: 64.
  Nathaniel 19.
  Robert 9; 10. 10: 10: 21. 34:
    53. 54. 55. 61.
  Stephen 2.
  William 2. 10. 10: 17. 17. 19.
    20. 20. 21. 23. 32: 38. 39.
    41. 52: 53. 54. 54. 60: 60: 62:
  —— 23. 65.

INDEX.

Trewythgy 84.
  Lawrence 84.
TRICKE 6: TRICK 7.
  Agnes 13.
  Alice 9.
  Andrew 71.
  Ann 67.
  Bonnet 15:
  Elizabeth 7. 12: 71.
  English 13: 17: 35:
  George 17.
  Grace 16: 23:
  James 23: 67. 67:
  John 6: 7. 8. 8: 9. 9. 13: 33.
    50. 51. 51. 54:
  Julian 33. 56:
  Margaret 9.
  Mary 8: 54:
  Nicholas 14: 59.
  Richard 8. 12: 13. 13: 14:
    15: 16. 16: 17. 17: 35:
  Robert 6: 50.
  Sechem 67:
  Thomas 16.
TRISTRAM 8.
  William 8. 8.
TROTT 5: TRATT 6.
  Ann 5:
  Blanch 6. 7:
  Jane 7. 36.
  Mary 72:
  Peter 8. 51.
  Richard 5: 6. 7. 7: 8. 36. 51.
    52.
TRYTHALL 2. TRITHALL 5.
  Edward 5. 5: 32: 50. 50:
  Henry 2.
  Honor 5: 36:
  John 2. 3. 43: 44. 44.
  Margaret 31: 32:
  Margery 43:
  Mary 50:
  Richard 2. 3. 31:
  Robert 2.
  Thomas 5.
TUCKYE 43.
  James 43.
  Thomas 43.
TULL 58: TULE 41. TOLL 56.
  John 56.
  Margerie 41.
  Roger 41. 42:
    (John Vian, his servant, 42:)
  Temperance 58:
TUTTLIE 33.
  Edmund 33.
  Joan 33.
TYACK 60: TYAG 18: TYAGG 65:
  See TEAGE.

  Andrew 60:
  Murret 18:
  Thomas 18: 60: 65:
TYDWELL 49. TYDWALE 47:
  Elizabeth 47:
  John 47: 49.
TYER 45:
  Agnes 45:
  Richard 45:
Tyes 83.
  Henry Le 83. 84.
TYLLAM 42:
  Jane 42:
  Walter 42:
Tyntagel 83.
  Nicholas Arthur de 83. 84.

UDYE 14.
  Avis 14.
  John 14.
  Nicholas 48.
  Ralph 14.
UNDERSONNE 49.
  Richard 49.
UPRIGHTE 6: UPRIGHT 33.
  Elizabeth 33.
  George 6:
  John 6: 33.
USTICK 21: USTICKE 25.
  Ann 22. 25. 66.
  Bernard 21: 22.
  Charles 26.
  Henry 25. 25. 25. 25. 25: 26.
    27.
  Jane 27.
  John 25: 68.
  Margaret 38.
  Margery 21: 72:
  Mary 26.
  Richard 26.
  Sybolla 25.

Vade 86.
  V. R. 86.
VALENTYNE 6. VALLENTINE 32:
  VALENTINE 52.
  John 6. 32: 49. 52.
  Margaret 32:
  Rebecca 49.
  William 6.
VANSON 64:
  Catherine 64:
VARWELL 30.
  James 30. 48.
  Jenny 30.
  Joan 48.
VATER 36.
  Ann 36.
VEALE 22.

  Christopher 24.
  Constance 72:
  Elizabeth 24. 38. 71.
  George 38. 73. 73:
  Honor 22. 39: 66: 73.
  Joan 25:
  John 22. 22: 25: 39: 66: 74.
  Margaret 22:
  Margery 73:
  Nicholas 41.
  Richard 73.
  William 41.
VEAN 47. VEEAN 50. VYAN 41.
  VIAN 42:
  Ann 52:
  Bennet 41.
  Edward 52:
  Elizabeth 47.
  John 42:
  Margaret 50.
  Rawe 47. 50.
  William 41.
VELLYE 5. VELLY 30: *alias* WEBBER
    7.
  Alice 7.
  Cicely 48.
  Elizabeth 33.
  Henry 6. 50.
  Jane 7. 30:
  John 7.
  Thomas 5. 6. 30: 32. 33. 45.
    48. 49: 50.
  Ursula 32.
  William 5. 45.
  —— 49:
VIAN, See VEAN.
VIBART 35: *Vibert* 71:
  Christian 35:
  Martin 35:
  Ursula 71:
VICKER 30: VYCKER 47.
  Jermyn 47.
  Joan 30:
  Richard 43: 44.
  Richo 43:
  William 30: 47.
VICTOR 61.
  Joan 61.
Figures 74.
  Thomas 74.
VINICOMBE, See FINNICOMB.
VYAN, See VEAN.
VYVIAN 45:
  Catherine 45:

WALKE 25:
  Elizabeth 26:
  Jane 39:
  Richard 25: 25: 26. 26: 39:

INDEX.

William 26.
WALKER 54:
 Grace 54:
WALL 58. WALE 13:
 Catherine 58.
 Grace 63.
 John 13:
 Othniel 13: 59. 59.
WALLISH 28:
 Ann 28:
 Richard 28:
 Robert 66:
WALLTER 43. WATERS 7: WATER 44:
 Agnes 43. 44:
 Blanch 7:
 John 43. 43. 44:
 Thomas 43.
 William 7:
Walrond 73:
 Beaumont, Capt., 73:
WALSH 38:
 Joan 38:
 William 38:
WANNELL 9.
 Elizabeth 36. 62.
 Ellen 34.
 Henry 14: 58:
 Jane 58:
 James 9. 34. 36. 36.
 Joan 36.
 Joseph 9. 14: 58: 58:
WARREN 57: WERREN 36: WEARREN
 Alice 62. [62.
 Dorothy 70:
 Elizabeth 36: 57:
 Thomas 70:
 William 36: 57:
Warwickshire man, a, 47:
WATERS, See WALLTER.
WATKINS 4: WATKYNS 5. WATCHINS
 Alice 55: [59:
 David 11:
 Henry 7.
 Joan 60.
 Mary 5. 54.
 Richard 6. 49:
 Robert 11: 59: 59: 59: 60.
 William 4: 4: 5. 6. 7. 49: 54.
WATTYE 45: WATTIE 48:
 Agnes 45:
 Jane 48:
 Richard 45: 45:
WAVERS 45:
 Alice 45:
 Henry 45: 45:
WAYMOTH, See WEYMOUTH.
WEARE 38.
 Robert 38.
 Zenobia 38.

WEARNE 34.
 Elizabeth 57:
 Henry 34.
 ———— 34.
WEARREN, See WARREN.
WEARY 9:
 John 9:
 Mathew 9:
WEBBER 7. *alias* VELLYE 7.
 Alice 7. 50:
 Eleanor 44.
 June 7. 32: 51. [53.
 John 7. 32: 42: 44. 50: 51. 51.
 Richard 42: 45: 45:
WELMENTON 62:
 Robert 62:
WERREN, See WARREN.
WEST 9:
 Bridget 10.
 Clarence 10.
 Richard 9: 10. 10. 10.
 William 9: 10. 10.
WEYMOND 30:
 Agnes 30:
 George 30:
WEYMOUTH 33: WEYMUOWTHE 29.
 WEMUOTH 31. WAYMOTH 53.
 Waymouth 69:
 Dorothy 70:
 Elizabeth 69.
 Ephraim 69: 70:
 George 53.
 Joan 29. 33: 41.
 John 33:
 Sybil 31.
 Valentine 29. 41. 46.
 William 69:
WHITE 20: WHITTE 26: WHITT 65.
 Ann 26:
 Catherine 39.
 Gabriel 60. 67.
 James 60.
 Jane 26: 65:
 Mary 20: 65.
 Robert 20: 39. 46. 65.
 Sarah 67.
 William 26: 26: 55:
WHITEFEILD 60:
 Elizabeth 60:
Whiterowe 85.
 Anthony 85.
Whitmore 83.
WHITWELL 6. WHITEWELL 4: *alias*
 RICHARD 4:
 Henry 6.
 John 4: 6.
 Sarah 4:
WILLIAMS 5. WILLIAM 1.
 Abraham 25.

Agnes 45.
Alice 6. 12: 64.
Ann 23:
Baldwyn 5. 48:
Bennet 18.
Catherine 8: 12. 17: 31: 38.
 61:
Charles 22. 22 23: 25.
Christopher 19: 28. 96.
Edward 7. 51.
Eleanor 6. 65.
Elizabeth 1. 2. 17: 28. 30: 32.
 47: 52:
Ezekiel 57.
George 86.
Grace 17: 18. 19. 61. 66:
Henry 37: 50:
Honor 3:
James 14: 17: 61.
Jane 30: 35. 37: 46: 59. 61.
Joan 5. 30: 44: 46. 47: 60:
 62.
John 1. 3: 6. 14: 16: 17: 17:
 18. 18: 19: 30: 30: 32. 37.
 38. 44: 44: 47: 60: 61. 61:
 62. 64. 66. 66:
Margaret 35:
Martin 44.
Mary 3: 18: 66:
Peter 16: 17: 17: 30: 61.
Priscilla 55:
Prudence 35: 57.
Ralph 2. 4: 12: 47: 55:
Rawe 46.
Richard 66:
Robert 31:
Samuel 74.
Silvester 44: 46. 46: 52.
Susan 37. 57. 60:
Susannah 67.
Thomas 3: 4. 4: 5. 6. 7. 8:
 12. 35: 47: 50: 51. 57. 57. 57.
Walter 46.
William 4. 5. 11: 11: 14: 18.
 19. 35. 35: 48: 55: 60: 62.
 62. 65.
WILLOE 6. WILLOW 54: WILLOWE
 51:
Eppow 54:
Grace 6.
Lawrence 6.
Margery 51:
WILLS 5. WYLLS 32: WILL 33:
 Catherine 5.
 Chesten 32:
 Christopher 52. 52.
 Elizabeth 33:
 Henry 52.
 Margaret 71:

H

138   INDEX.

Mary 52.
Roger 5. 32:
Thomas 33; 71:
WILLY 5: WILLYE 7:
  Grace 32:
  Hercules 7:
  John 5: 7; 32:
  Samuel 5:
WOLCOCK 15. WOLLCOKE 42:
    WOLCOKE 42: *Woolcock* 70:
  Agnes 42:
  Alice 38.
  Ann 69.
  Arthur 36: 57. 69.
  Elizabeth 35. 36; 42: 60. 61.
  George 35.
  James 22: 70:
  Jane 57:
  Jennet 53.
  John 61.
  Maderne 42: 42: 42: 42:
  Margaret 70;
  Oliver 15. 60. 71:
  Richard 38.
  Ursula 71:
  Walter 15. 22;
  William 36: 42; 42; 42; 42; 49;
WOLCOTTE 44.
  John 44.
  Maderne 44.

Wood 86.
  J. A. 86.
  William 86.
  Woolton, Bishop, 85.
  Worth 82.
  Sybella 82.
  Thomas 82.
WRITE 28.
  John 47.
  Martin 28.
  Sarah 28.
WYNSELET 49.
  Elizabeth 49.

York 84.
  William of, 84.
YOUNG 60. YOUNGE 7: *Yonge* 97.
  Catherine 33.
  Joan 35: 61:
  Mary 61:
  Redigon 12: 55:
  Thomas 61.
  Tompkin 50:
  Tonkin 7;
  William 7: 12: 33. 35: 50:
    55: 60. 61:
Miss 97.

Zackrey 85.
  John 85.

Agnes 36:
Alexander 50:
Ann 2. 3: 15: 36: 39.
Blauch 53.
Catherine 3: 13: 65.
Elizabeth 2. 2; 3: 14: 21. 30.
George 4:   [41. 44:
Hanniball 45.
Henry 21.
Hugh 3:
Joane 14:
John 2. 2: 14: 14: 14: 14:
  15: 30. 38. 38;
Margaret 32:
Margerie 3: 3:
Mary 14: 37.
Nicholas 4:
Patience 2.
Phillippa 30.
Ralph 2. 3: 32;
Rawe 3: 93.
Richard 2. 2: 45:
Robert 65.
Roger 44:
Rowan 30. 93.
Thomas 3: 13: 57;
Tobias 46;
Walter 3;
William 3. 3: 1: 36: 4

Names of Places, &c.

Only names here printed in SMALL CAPITALS appear in the Register; the remainder will be found in the Notes and Appendix, with regard to which but one reference is given, though the name may occur more than once in the page.

Alverton 80. 83. 91.
  Manor of, 83. 84. 88. 90.
AMSTERDAM 48:
Arms—
  Blunt 98.
  Borlase 78. 79.
  Cock 75. 76.
  Daniel 79.
  De Hemenhale 75.
  Fleming 76.
  Harris 78.
  Honychurch 80.
  Nicholls 77.
  Pendarves 79.
  Rawles 80.
  Tremenheere 81.
  Trevanion 75. 98.
  Worth 81. 81.

Australia 93.
Avranches 83.

Belgium 79.
Bendigo 93.
Bideford 72.
BODMIN 48. 75.
Bosavern 93.
Boskenna 74.
Boskenning 93.
BOSOLLOW 28:
BREAGE 50: 72. 73. 86.
Britain 79.
Brittany 94.
Bucks 85.
Buriton 82. 91. 92.
BURYAN 54. 69: 70. 70: 71. 72.
  72: 84. 95.

BUSWARVA 50.

Castle Horneck 78. 82. 95.
CHIRICK 62:
Cirencester 88. 89.
CLOVELLY 67.
Constantine 85. 97.
Cornwall 74. 79. 83. 87. 88. 89. 90
  91. 93.
  Herald's Visitation 97. 98. 100
  Survey of 77. 85. 95.
CREWKERNE 62:
Crowan 71:

DEVON 67. 71. 77.
DOVER 53:

Exeter 83. 85. 86. 91. 100.

INDEX.

Falmouth 91. 92.

Germany 93.
Gloucester 89.
Greenwich (East) 91.
GULVAL 15. 15. 15: 16. 16. 20: 24.
  39: 61. 63: 69. 69: 70. 70:
  71. 71: 72. 72: 73. 73: 85.,
  94. 96.
GWENNAP 29.

HAMPTON 64.
Hampton Court 90.
HELSTON 30; 71. 72: 73. 73:
HERTFORDSHIRE 47:

ISLE OF WIGHT 65.
Italy 77.

Jerusalem, Priory of St. John of,
  83. 87. 89. 90.

KENEGIE 38;
Kent 91.
Kenwyn 86.
Kerris 93.
KIRKCUDBRIGHT 64.

LANDITHY 19. 38: 75. 80. 81. 86.
  94.
LANION 27. 94.
Lan John 94.
LANSALLOS 63:
Lariggan 79. 80. 95. 98. 100.
Lelant 83.
Lincolnshire 85.
Liskeard 87.
LITTLE COLAN 29.
LONDON 27. 77. 85.
  Cheapside 84.
  Friday Street 84.
  Middle Temple 77.
  St Mathias Church 84.
  Tower 84.
LUDOVAN 38: 70. 70: 71. 71: 72.
  85.

Mabe 81.
MADRON (CHURCHTOWN) 27. 29. 37.
  48. 50: 53. 69: 70. 70: 71.
  71: 72. 72: 73. 73: 74. 75.
  79. 81. 82. 83. 84. 85. 86. 87.
  88. 89. 90. 93. 95. 96. 97. 98.
  99. 100.
  Church 74. 75. 77. 80. 83. 84.
    95. 98. 100.
  Churchyard 77. 80. 81.
  Communion Plate 85. 100.
  Communion Rails 78. 86.

Curates 85. 86.
  Dedication 84.
  Free School 79. 80. 95.
    Trustees 80.
  Glebe 83.
  Incumbents 83.
  Lych Gate 80.
  Monumental Inscriptions 75.
  Parish Chest 74.
  Parish Registers 46. 74. 75.
    85. 97. 98. 99.
  Plague 85. 99.
  Pulpit 86.
  Puritanical times 99.
  Tithes 87.
  Well 100.
Middlesex 90.
Morvah 70: 71: 72. 72: 73: 85.
  95. 100.
  Chapel (St. Morwetha) 84. 85.
    86.
  Mousehole 84. 88. 99.
  Chapel of St. Bridget 84. 88.

Nanceglos 85.
NEWLAN (Walos) 54:
Newlyn (East) 85.
Newlyn (West) 95. 99.

Oxford 85.

Park-an-grouse 91.
Park-an-vounder 91.
PAUL 29. 39: 39: 43. 65. 69: 70.
  70: 71. 71: 72. 72: 73. 73:
  79. 93. 98. 99.
Pondeen 79. 86.
Penryn 71: 81. 82.
Penwith 84.
PENZANCE 2: 5. 5: 7. 20: 25. 25.
  27: 27: 27: 28. 28: 28:
  48: 49. 49. 49. 49. 49. 49:
  49: 49: 49: 49: 50. 50: 50: 50;
  50: 52. 53. 54: 54: 69. 69:
  70. 70: 71. 71: 72. 72: 73.
  73: 74. 76. 77. 80. 81. 82. 83.
  84. 85. 86. 87. 88. 89. 90. 91.
  92. 94. 95. 96. 98. 99. 100.
  Cattle-pound 88.
  Chapel of St. Clare 87. 99.
  Chapel of St. Gabriel and St.
    Raphael 84.
  Chapel of St. Mary 74. 77. 81.
    82. 84. 91. 92. 100.
    Demolished 81.
  Chapelwardens 74.
  Charter 98. 100.
  Churchyard 82.
  Communion Plate 100.

Constables 74.
Corporation 74. 100.
Curacy, Augmentation of, 91.
Curate 74. 77. 85. 86.
Glebe 91.
Hemp Garden 88.
Incumbent 74. 83.
Justice 74.
Magistrates 74.
Mayor 74. 76. 81. 94. 95. 100.
Monumental Inscriptions 81.
Officers 74.
Overseers of the Poor 74.
Quay 94.
Recorder 74.
Registers 74. 85.
Ropers' Place 88.
Sergeants at Mace 74.
Spaniards' attack 99.
Tithes 87.
Tokens 95. 98.
Vicar 74.
Penzour 77.
Pinfold 88.
POLTEGAN 62.

Redruth 84. 98.
Rosecadgwell 78.
Rosckestul 81.
Runeri 83.

St. Bridget, Chapel of, 84. 88.
ST. CHRISTOPHER'S 55:
St. Clare 87. 88. 89. 99.
St. Erth 85.
St. Gabriel and St. Raphael, Chapel
  of. 84.
St. Hilary 72. 96.
St. Ive 87.
ST. IVES 66. 78. 83.
ST. JUST 7. 50: 71. 72. 79. 84. 93.
St. Levan 84. 91.
ST. MARTINS 29.
St. Michael's Mount 83. 90.
St. Morwetha, Chapel of, 84.
SANCREED 64. 65. 71. 72:
SANCTI PATERNUS 29.
Scilly 96
SCOTLAND 64.
Sennen 71. 73:
SOMERSETSHIRE 62:
Southampton 89.
Stowford 71.
Sutton 77.
Swansea 37.

Tintagel 84.
Titles, Trades, &c.—
  Blacksmith 74.

INDEX.

Butcher 74.
Chapelwardens 74.
CLERK 7: 9: 12. 48. 51. 56;
Constables 74.
Cooper 74.
"COYN" MAKER 23.
Curate 74.
CUTLER 50:
DRYWOMAN 50.
ESQUIRE 7. 30. 38: 45. 50:
  51. 56.
Fellmonger 74. 74.
GLOVER 30.
GOLDSMITH 27.
Haberdasher 74.
JOINER 43;
Justice 74.
MARINER 20: 27. 27: 65. 67.
Mayor 74.
Mercer 74.
MERCHANT 18: 19. 20. 20: 20;
  20: 23. 24: 24: 27. 27: 36:

38: 46. 56. 62: 63: 64. 65.
  67. 74. 74. 74.
MERETRIX 41. 42:
Overseers of the Poor 74.
Recorder 74.
SEAMAN 50:
Sergeants at Mace 74.
Shipwright 74.
SHOEMAKER 47. 48; 74.
Shopkeeper 74.
SIR 37. 56:
SMITH 5: 6: 7. 8: 9. 22. 43:
  43: 53. 53:
SOLDIER 47: 47:
Stannaries, Vicewarden, 79. 86.
STRANGER 50:
TANNER 34: 55: 96.
Town Clerk 74.
VICAR 20: 21. 22: 27. 29. 48.
  58. 66.
Yeoman 74.
TOLCARN 55:

Tonkin's Weith or Land 91.
Trebigh 87.
Tremethack 93.
Tremough 81.
TRENGWAINTON 38: 77. 85. 94. 97.
TREREIFE 31. 70: 72: 77. 93. 94. 95.
Trerice 84.
Trevaylor 83.
Trewarveneth 70:
Trewidden 83.
Trewoof 95.
Truro 83.
WALES 54:
WARWICKSHIRE 47:
Westminster 88. 89. 90. 91.
  Abbey 100.
WEYMOUTH 11:
York 84.
Zennor 71. 86. 97.

Directions for finding the Irregular Entries in the Original Manuscript.
See pages 24 to 28, and note.

Entries numbered 1 to a18 will be found, in the order indicated, on the first of such pages of Irregular Entries at page 68 red numbering, 100 old numbering.

,,	19 ,, b29	,,	73	,,	107 [1]	,,
,,	30 ,, c67	,,	74	,,	[108][2]	,,
,,	68 ,, d89	,,	75	,,	109 [3]	,,
,,	90 ,, e108	,,	76	,,	[110][4]	,,
,,	109 ,, f132	,,	77	,,	111 [5]	,,
,,	133 ,, g169	,,	78	,,	[112][6]	,,
,,	170 ,, h177	,,	79	,,	103	,,
,,	178 ,, i179	,,	80	,,	[104]	,,
,,	j180 (one entry),,		81	,,	—	,,
,,	181 ,, k184	,,	83*	,,	113	,,
,,	185 ,, l193	,,	84	,,	[114][8]	,,
,,	194 ,, m200	,,	85	,,	115 [9]	,,
,,	201 ,, n212	,,	86	,,	[116][10]	,,
,,	213 ,, o225	,,	87	,,	117	,,
,,	226 ,, p236	,,	88	,,	[118]	,,
,,	237 ,, q244	,,	89	,,	119	,,

*Page 82 blank.

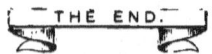

THE END.

PENZANCE: PRINTED BY BEARE AND SON, MARKET PLACE.

www.ingramcontent.com/pod-product-compliance
Lightning Source LLC
Chambersburg PA
CBHW030334170426
43202CB00010B/1127